Public Relations Inquiry as Rhetorical Criticism

Public Relations Inquiry as Rhetorical Criticism

Case Studies of Corporate Discourse and Social Influence

Edited by William N. Elwood

Praeger Series in Political Communication

Westport, Connecticut
London

HM
263
.P76568

1995

Copyright Acknowledgment

Chapter 3, "Mobil's Epideictic Advocacy: 'Observations' of Prometheus Bound," originally appeared in *Communications Monographs*, 380–394 (December 1983). Copyright by the Speech Communication Association, 1983. Reproduced by permission of the publisher.

Library of Congress Cataloging-in-Publication Data

Public relations inquiry as rhetorical criticism : case studies of
  corporate discourse and social influence / edited by William N.
  Elwood.
      p.   cm—(Praeger series in political communication, ISSN
      1062-5623)
    Includes bibliographical references and index.
    ISBN 0-275-94971-0 (hc : alk. paper). — ISBN 0-275-95150-2 (pbk :
    alk. paper)
    1. Public relations—United States—Case studies.   I. Elwood, William N.
  II. Series
  HM263.P76568   1995
  659.2—dc20   94-42837

British Library Cataloguing in Publication Data is available.

Library of Congress Catalog Card Number: 94–42837
ISBN: 0-275-94971-0
      0-275-95150-2 (pbk.)
ISSN: 1062–5623

First published in 1995

Praeger Publishers, 88 Post Road West, Westport, CT 06881
An imprint of Greenwood Publishing Group, Inc.

Printed in the United States of America

The paper used in this book complies with the
Permanent Paper Standard issued by the
National Information Standards Organization (Z39.48-1984).

10 9 8 7 6 5 4 3 2 1

To Michael, the truest believer;

To Fifi, for love, laughter, and surprise;

To the contributors whose intellect and talents made
editing an enjoyable, heuristic, and challenging task;

To the organizations, profit and nonprofit, whose discourse
and products we experience regularly and whose campaigns
provided the data for analysis in this book; and,

To you, the individual citizens, in the hope
that you will remain informed and critical consumers
of corporate communication in a time when free speech
has become increasingly expensive.

Contents

Series Foreword

Those of us from the discipline of communication studies have long believed that communication is prior to all other fields of inquiry. In several other forums I have argued that the essence of politics is "talk" or human interaction.[1] Such interaction may be formal or informal, verbal or nonverbal, public or private but it is always persuasive, forcing us consciously or subconsciously to interpret, to evaluate, and to act. Communication is the vehicle for human action.

From this perspective, it is not surprising that Aristotle recognized the natural kinship of politics and communication in his writings *Politics* and *Rhetoric*. In the former, he establishes that humans are "political beings [who] alone of the animals [are] furnished with the faculty of language."[2] And in the latter, he begins his systematic analysis of discourse by proclaiming that "rhetorical study, in its strict sense, is concerned with the modes of persuasion."[3] Thus, it was recognized over 2,300 years ago that politics and communication go hand in hand because they are essential parts of human nature.

Back in 1981, Dan Nimmo and Keith Sanders proclaimed that political communication was an emerging field.[4] Although its origin, as noted, dates back centuries, a "self-consciously cross-disciplinary" focus began in the late 1950s. Thousands of books and articles later, colleges and universities offer a variety of graduate and undergraduate coursework in the area in such diverse departments as communication,

mass communication, journalism, political science, and sociology.[5] In
Nimmo and Sanders' early assessment, the "key areas of inquiry"
included rhetorical analysis, propaganda analysis, attitude change
studies, voting studies, government and the news media, functional and
systems analyses, technological changes, media technologies, campaign techniques, and research techniques.[6] In a survey of the state of
the field in 1983, the same authors and Lynda Kaid found additional,
more specific areas of concerns such as the presidency, political polls,
public opinion, debates, and advertising to name a few.[7] Since the first
study, they also noted a shift away from the rather strict behavioral
approach.

A decade later, Dan Nimmo and David Swanson argued that "political communication has developed some identity as a more or less
distinct domain of scholarly work."[8] The scope and concerns of the
area have further expanded to include critical theories and cultural
studies. While there is no precise definition, method, or disciplinary
home of the area of inquiry, its primary domain is the role, processes,
and effects of communication within the context of politics broadly
defined.

In 1985, the editors of *Political Communication Yearbook: 1984*
noted that "more things are happening in the study, teaching, and
practice of political communication than can be captured within the
space limitations of the relatively few publications available."[9] In
addition, they argued that the backgrounds of "those involved in the
field [are] so varied and pluralist in outlook and approach. . . . it [is] a
mistake to adhere slavisly to any set format in shaping the content."[10]
And more recently, Nimmo and Swanson called for "ways of overcom-
ing the unhappy consequences of fragmentation within a framework
that respects, encourages, and benefits from diverse scholarly commit-
ments, agendas, and approaches."[11]

In agreement with these assessments of the area and with gentle
encouragement, Praeger established the Praeger Series in Political
Communication. The series is open to all qualitative and quantitative
methodologies as well as contemporary and historical studies. The key
to characterizing the studies in the series is the focus on communication
variables or activities within a political context or dimension. As of
this writing, nearly forty volumes have been published and there are
numerous impressive works forthcoming. Scholars from the disciplines of communication, history, journalism, political science, and
sociology have participated in the series.

I am, without shame or modesty, a fan of the series. The joy of serving as its editor is in participating in the dialogue of the field of political communication and in reading the contributors' works. I invite you to join me.

Robert E. Denton, Jr.

NOTES

1. See Robert E. Denton, Jr., *The Symbolic Dimensions of the American Presidency* (Prospect Heights, Ill.: Waveland Press, 1982); Robert E. Denton, Jr., and Gary Woodward, *Political Communication in America* (New York: Praeger, 1985; 2nd ed., 1990); Robert E. Denton, Jr., and Dan Han, *Presidential Communication* (New York: Praeger, 1986); and Robert E. Denton, Jr., *The Primetime Presidency of Ronald Reagan* (New York: Praeger, 1988).

2. Aristotle, *The Politics of Aristotle*, trans. Ernest Barker (New York: Oxford University Press, 1970), p. 5.

3. Aristotle, *Rhetoric*, trans. Rhys Roberts (New York: The Modern Library, 1954), p. 22.

4. Dan Nimmo and Keith Sanders, "Introduction: The Emergence of Political Communication as a Field," in *Handbook of Political Communication,* ed. Dan Nimmo and Keith Sanders (Beverly Hills, Calif.: Sage, 1981), pp. 11–36.

5. Ibid., p. 15.

6. Ibid., pp. 17–27.

7. Keith Sanders, Lynda Kaid, and Dan Nimmo, eds., *Political Communication Yearbook: 1984* (Carbondale: Southern Illinois University, 1985), pp. 283–308.

8. Dan Nimmo and David Swanson, "The Field of Political Communication: Beyond the Voter Persuasion Paradigm," in *New Directions in Political Communication*, ed. David Swanson and Dan Nimmo (Beverly Hills, Calif.: Sage, 1990), p. 8.

9. Sanders, Kaid, and Nimmo, *Political Communication Yearbook: 1984*, p. xiv.

10. Ibid.

11. Nimmo and Swanson, "The Field of Political Communication," p. 11.

PART I
Orientation

1

Public Relations Is a Rhetorical Experience

The Integral Principle in Case Study Analysis

William N. Elwood

People do not experience organizations;[1] they experience the communication organizations issue and the communication about organizations. This statement may seem self-evident. We have become accustomed to corporate entities "speaking" in the public realm. Mobil often voices its opinions in the opening pages of *Time* magazine. Newsletters frequently contain stories or statements that have no byline; thus, we assume the institution is speaking. We also are familiar with references to organizations' rhetoric, to news reports that begin, "IBM announced today" or "Sears said that it was selling its Discover card division and would concentrate on its retail core," as if IBM or Sears could speak and write for themselves. As public relations writing books inform present and future PR practitioners, "Public relations is, after all, communication, and the basic form of communication is still the written word" (Bivins, 1991, p. 1; see also Newsom and Carrell, 1991; Tucker et al., 1994).

Perhaps because organizational discourse has become commonplace, books often examine public relations case studies in abstract terms, recounting that certain organizations communicate to particular publics to achieve certain objectives. Such recountals often follow with assessments of relative effectiveness. While certainly informative and pedagogical, these campaign descriptions do not provide readers with samples of this communication, nor do they inform readers as to *how* a campaign's communication influenced anyone. Public opinion polls implemented before and after a PR campaign can be used to judge a campaign's impact; a rhetorical perspective explains *why* a campaign's communication was effective or how it could have been improved. In other words, many case studies talk *about* organizational rhetoric, but they neither present it nor analyze it to explain how such rhetoric functions. Institutions attempt to influence their environments; this influence occurs through rhetoric in the practice of public relations. The chapters in this book examine this process of influence.

In this chapter, I first discuss the two operational terms of this work, *public relations* and *rhetoric*. Second, I discuss two subjects of particular import to the rhetorical study of public relations practice, *issue management* and *ethics*. Finally, I discuss *situation,* an idea that emerged serendipitously from the chapters as they were assembled.

COMING TO TERMS WITH PUBLIC RELATIONS AND RHETORIC

The discussion regarding public relations theory remains in flux.[2] Hence, one must argue for a rhetorical approach to analyzing public relations cases. The rationale for this approach lies in the writings of a man considered to be a founding father of contemporary public relations. He demonstrates that public relations, rhetoric, and politics are inextricably intertwined.

Public relations as we know it emerged in the early twentieth century through the practices of Edward L. Bernays and Ivy Ledbetter Lee.[3] Bernays (1952) maintains, "Many people believe that public relations has no past, that it grew overnight. But public relations does have a history which, like that of other professions, follows a line of logical development" (p. 12). He traces "attempts to influence or control opinion," from the dawn of humanity to contemporary practices (pp. 12-154). Intriguingly, the man we recognize as a PR pioneer argues that public relations emerged concurrently with human society because "people soon recognized the necessity for planned interrelationship" and that "leaders even then had an awareness of their public relationships" (p. 12). For example, Bernays asserts, "Most of what we know about the rulers of ancient Egypt, Sumeria, Babylonia, Assyria, and Persia comes to us from what is left of their own . . . personal and political publicity [that] is still extant after five thousand years" (p. 13).

Not surprisingly, the "public" in public relations began to emerge in the cultures that inform our own—the societies of ancient Greece and

Rome. In ancient Greece, Bernays maintains, "The big propaganda theme was Greek solidarity" to "foster a national spirit and national unity . . . against the barbarians" (p. 14). Likewise, "Romans, too, had their concepts of public opinion and public relations and coined words which indicate their understanding of general subjects. *Rumores* ('rumors'), *vox populi* ('voice of the people'), and *res publicae* ('public affairs'), from which we get our term 'republic,' are such words" (p. 15). Bernays acknowledges art, statuary, public buildings and monuments, oratory, and writings, including the *Iliad,* the *Odyssey,* and Julius Caesar's commentaries on the conquest of Gaul, as early PR efforts. In fact, "Quintus, brother of Cicero, wrote a treatise on propaganda" (p. 15). Bernays cites Aristotle's *Politics* and *Rhetoric* to inform his discussion of the Greeks' "great civic consciousness. Every art they developed was used at one time or another as a medium of persuasion toward political and social goals" (p. 15). In fact, Aristotle's (1991) most recent translation includes "a theory of civic discourse" as a subtitle to *Rhetoric.*

Bernays views Aristotle as a public relations forebear who synthesizes rhetoric, public relations, and politics. Although Aristotle's writings speak for themselves, the ancient Hellene's most recent translator clearly states, "Aristotle thinks of rhetoric as an aspect of politics" (Aristotle, 1991, p. 312). Aristotle defines rhetoric as "an ability, in each particular case, to see the available means of persuasion" (p. 36) and accordingly devotes one of his three rhetorical forms to deliberative discourse, the rhetorical instances that address public and private policy resolutions. Aristotle maintains, "For the deliberative speaker the end is the advantageous and the harmful, for someone urging something advises it as the better course and one dissuading dissuades on the ground that it is worse" (p. 49). For example, advertisements for Cascade automatic dishwashing detergent promise "virtually spotless dishes," career advancement, and domestic bliss through its exclusive sheeting action (Procter & Gamble, 1990). Such an advertisement is, of course, not public relations rhetoric, but the familiar commercial does demonstrate the ubiquity of deliberative address that enters our homes and influences our private policy resolutions. Examples of public relations advocacy advertisements include the Philip Morris Companies' bicentennial salutes to the Bill of Rights that feature accomplished Americans and the infamous "Harry and Louise" commercials that lambasted President Clinton's health care reform proposals, which the President and Mrs. Clinton parodied in their own video.

The seemingly incongruous leap from the rhetorical theory of ancient Athens to a rhetorical practice of the late twentieth century illustrates an enduring human phenomenon: the everyday reality we take for granted is created, changed, and maintained through rhetoric. During the Enlightenment, Giambattista Vico posited that our knowledge of reality is a product of symbols; thus, rhetoric influences our realities by presenting perspectives by which to view the world in a particular way. For Vico, rhetoric is the means by which we think about probabilities and make decisions regarding competing perspectives on issues.[4] In their heuristic treatise, Berger and Luckmann (1966) state, "Everyday life presents itself as a reality interpreted by [people] and subjectively meaningful to them as a coherent world" (p. 19). The authors argue that our reality is constructed and maintained through language—in other words, rhetoric (see, e.g., pp. 58-62, 92-104). The perpetuation of culture through discourse has been a given since humans began an oral tradition; however, this tenet takes greater significance given the mass media that apparently reduce our world to a global village and the institutions that have resources disseminate their rhetoric to influence village residents. Regardless, rhetoric constructs reality because it endows reality with meaning. Our species "is, among other things, a persuading and persuaded animal" (Johnstone, 1981, p. 306).

Barry Brummett (1994) states, *"Choices and actions* that the public might adopt *depend on meaning"* (p. 69). That choice might be to write your representatives in favor of universal health insurance coverage or to believe that Exxon is a socially responsible, international corporation. That choice also might be more mundane, as in Brummett's example: "So if you pick Quaker State over Pennzoil, it is because advertisers have succeeded in causing Quaker State to mean something to you that you prefer over whatever Pennzoil has come to mean" (p. 69).

Choices and examples aside, one idea endures: rhetoric is a political practice. In this case, *politics* does not refer to election campaigns or legislative practices, but to a "strategy in obtaining any position of power or control" (*The Random House,* 1982, p. 1027). Poet and philosopher Adrienne Rich maintains that all rhetoric is "in some way political." According to Rich, "There are words that uphold the status quo either by what they don't say, or by what they do say, what they affirm. And any status quo is political" (in Trinidad, 1991, p. 83). Moreover, former Speaker of the House of Representatives Tip O'Neill

(1987) always maintained that all politics is local—whether a topic is related to international trade or school districts, it affects people at home. Human beings most often experience politics through rhetoric. According to political scientist Murray Edelman, "It is the language about political events, not the events in any other sense, that people experience; even developments that are close by take their meaning from the language that depicts them. So political language *is* political reality; there is no other so far as the meaning of events to actors and spectators are concerned" (1988, p. 104).

Aristotle's rhetorical theory focused on citizenly use of discourse. During the classic Hellenistic period, the right to participate in the governmental process was limited to a select group of free, native-born, property-holding men. Our idea of democratic citizenship has evolved; suffrage is extended to all U.S. citizens. Moreover, citizenship is granted to incorporated institutions, which have a right to freedom of expression similar to the right extended to human citizens. Corporations and individuals are entitled to participate in the public conversation regarding the course of policies that may affect them. Moreover, there are more citizens making more rhetoric through more media than ever before. Sometimes it seems as if the amount of information and perspectives regarding a subject is so overwhelming that it almost renders us immobile, rather than empowered to make a decision (see, e.g., Brummett, 1976, 1994, next chapter; Meyrowitz, 1985; Nothstine et al., 1994; Postman, 1985).

This information explosion makes it increasingly important and difficult to offer a perspective on a subject that members of a target audience will accept as their own. Media consultant Mandy Grunwald states that if you "define the dialogue" you disseminate a perspective that a public will accept (in Smith, 1992, p. 53). The ability to define the parameters of any discussion is a powerful asset, because a definition limits what can and cannot be said about a subject. The challenge is to offer a definition that people use without necessarily realizing that the words they utter and that influence their thoughts are anyone else's but their own.

Such factors influence my definition of *rhetoric:* the communicative means that citizens use to lend significance to themselves and to extend that significance to others. *Rhetors*, or creators of rhetoric, include human and corporate citizens. These definitions also assume that rhetoric is more than the spoken or printed word and includes broadcast media and nonverbal symbols. In turn, *public relations* is the strategic use of rhetoric to influence specified groups of citizens. *Rhetorical criticism* is an appropriate means of public relations inquiry because rhetorical criticism is a method that analyzes discourse, explains how specific groups responded to this discourse, and illuminates the process by which such discourse influenced the targeted publics.[5] Two areas of public relations inquiry, issue management and public relations ethics, are particularly rhetorical in nature.

Issue Management: A Particularly Rhetorical Approach to Public Relations Inquiry

Public relations professionals Jones and Chase (1979) assert, "The corporation, as an institution, has every moral and legal right to participate in the *formation* of public policy" (p. 7). The authors introduced a systems perspective to the theoretical discussion of public relations and discussed the stages of an issue and how institutions might respond and formulate public policy. Richard E. Crable and Steven L. Vibbert (1985) countermand Jones and Chase's assertion, contending, "The task of citizens and business is not to 'make' the policies, but to influence them" (p. 4). Obviously, neither corporations nor individuals can formulate public policy; we vest such power in the individuals elected to the U.S. Congress, state legislatures, and local governments. Consistent with our governmental structure, Crable and Vibbert maintain that organizations cannot create policy, but can engage in *rhetorical* efforts to "generate and nurture issues until they result in favorable public policy" for corporate entities (p. 3; see also Culbertson et al., 1993, pp. 12-31; Heath and Nelson, 1986). They also argue that issues progress through a life cycle. An *issue* is a question of fact, value, or policy that has significance among individuals. Issues emerge, and rhetoric propels them through stages until they become dormant. Although it is not the only approach, issue management is a public relations domain dedicated to the examination of rhetoric and its influence in public relations. Many of the chapters in this book use issue management in their analyses; each chapter explains how the approach informs the case study.

Public Relations Ethics: A Rhetorical Continuum

Public relations is a field of multiple debates, including definitions of the profession and a theoretical base; no subject seems more fiercely debated than ethics. This is hardly surprising. Public relations is a rhetorical practice; public relations people use rhetoric to argue for a definitive ethical perspective that, of course, will be encoded in rhetoric. Richard M. Weaver's later ideas regarding rhetoric are particularly appropriate for framing one's understanding of this discussion. Weaver (1970) believed that "language is sermonic" because all human beings are rhetors, "preachers in private or public capacities" (p. 200). He asserts, "Rhetoric impinges on morality and politics. . . . We have to think of its methods and sources in relation to a scheme of values" (pp. 211–212). In a sense, public relations is civic preaching, exhorting others to behave or to believe in a certain way (see Burke, 1937/1984 for his idea of rhetoric as "secular prayer"). Any discussion regarding PR ethics places the field's basic practices in question; a discussion on public relations ethics is preaching about preaching. The following section offers a homily on the subject, a way to make sense of the many sermons on public relations ethics.

The word *continuum* evokes an image of a horizontal line, intended to illustrate a dichotomous topic and the range of commitment on either side of the topic. When I was formulating the curriculum for a course on public relations ethics at Auburn University, communication professor Mary Helen Brown said, "That's easy. Tell 'em there aren't any. Class over." That's one end of the continuum. At the other end stand "professional standards for behavior and codes of ethics that call for individual responsibility and accountability" (Bovet, 1993, p. 29). With such disparate perspectives delineating the continuum, it hardly seems surprising that *Public Relations Journal* editor Susan Fry Bovet comments, "Public relations thus serves both as an ethical battleground and a barometer for proper business conduct" (p. 29).

According to *The Random House College Dictionary* (1982), a *continuum* is "a continuous extent, series, or whole" (p. 291). This definition seems particularly appropriate for the discussion regarding public relations ethics. Rhetoric constitutes the continuum, or battleground. Whether one subscribes to the perspectives related by Brown or Bovet or whether one has another perspective to add, one does so through discourse. Rhetoric and ethics have a synthetic relationship. Rhetoric is the means by which we construct an ethical code; it is also a human practice that can be judged by the ethical codes we create through rhetoric (see, e.g., Aristotle, 1953; *Communication,* 1981; Weaver, 1953, 1970). Henry Johnstone (1981) describes the unique relationship between rhetoric and ethics:

Ethical problems about programs and policies [are] in fact rhetorical problems. If I am worried about the course of action I do not first determine the rightness and then argue for taking the action; for the rightness resides in the argument itself, in the way the argument enhances or impedes the capacity of its audience to make up their own minds. I believe that deliberation about acts does in fact take place at this single level, and cannot be broken down into ethical deliberation and rhetorical deliberation. (pp. 312–313)

In short, rhetoric and ethics are dynamic because they constitute our culture. Just as our culture changes, so does our perspective on politics, rhetoric, and ethics. To expect to arrive at a monolithic ethics that will endure into the distant future is unrealistic. Some truths may endure, but today's ethical code may not reflect the culture that will exist in the middle of the twenty-first century.

Weatherly's (1971) statement reflects the issue on the battleground. He argues that public relations is "not inherently unethical, but can be an acceptable way of modifying attitudes. The methods employed and the motives of the speaker determine the ethics of its use in a particular situation" (p. 362). Some discussions regarding public relations ethics are based on the tradition of oratory, a tradition that hardly applies, given that most public relations rhetoric is issued by institutions and broadcast through the air for mass consumption. However, we can examine the rhetorical methods employed. And we can continue the discussion regarding ethics, rhetoric, and public relations.

This book does not offer the new *sine qua non* for ethics in public relations. Some case studies provide subjects for ethical discussions. For example, is it ethical to buy advertising time to tell Americans that plastics can be recycled into carpets and plastic lumber while plastics manufacturers lobby legislators *not* to pass mandatory recycling legislation? What ethical standards apply when a cigarette manufacturer frames cigarette smoking as a freedom of choice issue in magazines mailed to millions of smokers? The case study in chapter 14 is premised on Jacques Ellul's idea (1981) that a traditional notion of ethics does not apply to public relations practices. What does this mean for future practices and case studies?

THE RHETORICAL SITUATION REDUX: CONTEXTS
FOR PUBLIC RELATIONS CASE STUDIES

In an often cited quotation, Bitzer (1968) defines the rhetorical situation "as a natural context of persons, events, objects, relations, and an exigence which strongly invites utterance" (p. 5). According to Bitzer, this situation calls discourse into existence. This extant discourse is a fitting response to the situation, which in turn prescribes the fitting response. Moreover, he writes, "The exigence and the complex of persons, objects, events, and relations which generate rhetorical discourse are located in reality, are objective and publicly observable historic facts in the world we experience, are therefore available for scrutiny by an observer or critic who attends to them" (p. 11). The idea of rhetoric constructing and maintaining our perceptions of reality conflicts with the idea of an objective reality that Bitzer seemed to advocate (Orr, 1978; Vatz, 1973). Hence, people avoided *situation* in favor of ideas such as context and situatedness. Yet the idea of the rhetorical situation has undergone a redux, or renaissance. Providing a perspective for the criticism of organizational rhetoric, Cheney and McMillan (1990) write, "The individual and the organization both play important roles in the network of symbolic activity that is social life. The 'individual,' by participating in or associating with a variety of organizations, is party to many kinds of 'rhetorical situations' (Bitzer, 1972; Burke, 1973b) in which he or she must solve specific (and often multiple) exigencies through the use of persuasion" (p. 100; see also Pearson, 1989a). Thus, the rhetorical situation apparently applies to public relations inquiry. Sometimes situations require rhetoric: container cars involved in a train crash are leaking toxic fumes and nearby residents must evacuate; unknown persons tamper with Tylenol capsules and people die; a plane bound for the United States crashes in Scotland. These situations require responses: people near the railroad tracks must be told to move; Tylenol purchasers must be warned not to consume the capsule version of the product; friends and families want to know if their loved ones have survived. These situations are often called *crises*. However, some crises are not self-evident. For example, does "the lawsuit crisis" consist of a set of "objective and publicly observable historic facts in the world we experience," and are therefore "available for scrutiny by an observer or critic who attends to them"? (Bitzer, 1968, p. 11). Vibbert and Bostdorff (1992) contend that this rhetorical situation consisted of increased payments by insurance companies for clients who lost court cases. Briefly stated, the rhetoric involved in "the lawsuit crisis" is an attempt to shape public opinion and to create the *perception* of a lawsuit crisis, rather than the perception of negligent institutions and victims who were entitled to payments or the perception of greedy insurance companies that would rather invest their money in shopping malls than make payments to claimants.

In other words, the rhetorical situation is an issue that has emerged from dormancy. It is similar to its last incarnation, but it has emerged as particularly useful for public relations inquiry. For these purposes, a *rhetorical situation* is a configuration of physical circumstances and earlier rhetorical attempts to shape perceptions. The case studies in the following chapters illustrate this definition.

Rhetoric constitutes the core component to public relations. According to Bernays, public relations began with humans' first utterances to influence other people. The reputations of rhetoric and public relations last reached their zenith in ancient Greece and Rome. Given the resurgence of rhetorical studies in the social sciences, it seems only appropriate to pay rhetorical attention to public relations. In fact, the following chapters demonstrate that rhetorical criticism as public relations inquiry is a beautiful choice.[6]

NOTES

1. For this study, the term *organization* refers to a legal, organized entity. Such entities can be profit, nonprofit, public, or private. Examples include Sears, Roebuck and Company, a Roman Catholic parish, and a city council. To convey an inclusive idea of organization, terms including *institution* and *corporate entity* appear as synonyms. The use of the term *organization* does not refer to the realm of study known best as organizational communication.

2. See, e.g., Botan and Hazelton, 1989; Culbertson et al., 1993; Newsom and Carrell, 1991, p. 3; Toth and Heath, 1992.

3. Many sources discuss the history of public relations. See, for example, Crable and Vibbert, 1986; Goldman, 1948; Grunig and Hunt, 1984; Newsom et al., 1989; Seitel, 1992. Likewise, Bernays' works (1923, 1928, 1952, 1965) include not only a personal history of the field's evolution, but also document his thoughts, theories, and practices as they unfolded.

4. Vico, 1968, 1990; see also Adams, 1971, pp. 294-301; Brummett, 1994, p. 49; Golden, Berquist, and Coleman, 1983, pp. 133-187.

5. For discussions of methods in rhetorical criticism, see Brummett, 1994; Campbell, 1982; Hart, 1990.

6. This sentence alludes to a public relations advocacy campaign sponsored by the Arthur S. DeMoss Foundation. Its advocacy advertisements end with the slogan, "Life. What a Beautiful Choice."

2

Scandalous Rhetorics

Barry Brummett

Medieval and renaissance humanists were given to using allegory to portray the concerns and institutions of their time. They sometimes did so for the arts and sciences. One of the seven liberal arts was *rhetoric,* the study of persuasion, which is the ancestor and umbrella term for public relations, advertising, marketing, and their suasive brethren. Rhetoric was often depicted allegorically as *Lady Rhetoric,* "a woman of loftiest stature and great assurance," wielding great power in the affairs of people (Murphy, 1974, p. 45; Clark, 1957, frontispiece). Rhetoric has been studied and valued throughout the centuries as an "architectonic" art, managing the contributions of other arts and sciences toward the resolution of important issues in human affairs (McKeon, 1987).

In this chapter, however, I will speak to another portrayal of rhetoric. The character of that good Lady has sometimes been impugned. There is a tradition that calls her the Harlot of the Arts, willing to put her skill to any purpose good or bad, as long as the price is right (Condit, 1990). Rhetoric, it has been pointed out, can be used to lie and confuse. It can be employed (for a fee) to defend rapacious businesses and tyrannical governments. Dishonest car sellers persuade poor widows to buy junkers. Unscrupulous lawyers use it to secure the release of the guilty.

Specifically in regards to the teaching and practice of public relations, there is no shortage of pundits today who bemoan the employment of PR professionals in the service of wicked politicians and corrupt business practices. Lest we think that the figure Harlot of the Arts is out of date, take note of Michael Burgoon's description of public speaking professors as "campus whores" (1989, p. 305) or Donald Ellis's characterization of communication departments that teach public relations as "social science whorehouses" (1982, p. 2).

There is, in other words, a long tradition of thought that sees rhetoric and its bastard children, such as public relations (begot during a rake's progress of carnal pursuits), as scandalous. The lawyer who speaks so persuasively that a serial rapist is released is a scandal; the public relations professional who keeps Exxon's image clean in the face of a disastrous oil spill is an embarrassment. This chapter explores the basis for that cry of scandal against rhetoric and its illegitimate progeny. The charges of scandal are philosophically consistent. They constitute a distinct vision of discourse in human affairs.

Finally, this chapter will say why the charges against rhetoric are not only true, but actually virtues to be developed. There have been theorists who have defended Lady Rhetoric, such as Cicero (1942). But the defense often takes the form of denying the charge, of claiming that it does not apply to rhetoric, or of shifting the focus of discussion. These apologists argue that the Lady is not the naughty thing she has been alleged to be. That sort of prissy moral coverup will not be found here. I will offer a different defense—indeed, a scandalous defense—of scandal, in which I celebrate the very charges made against rhetoric. Clutching shameful rhetoric in an abandoned embrace, I will argue for why the very faults ascribed to it are in fact a consummation (so to speak) devoutly to be wished.

THREE DICHOTOMIES

Arguments and disagreements over rhetoric and its place in society have been long and complex. The scheme I am about to propose is therefore not meant to present a complete picture of the history of rhetorical theory. Instead, the scheme tries to organize three dimensions of the point of view that sees rhetoric as scandalous. I want to identify just this one voice crying "shame," even if the ongoing gossip about rhetoric has other accusations and justifications to make. We will hear this voice in three texts: First, Plato's *Gorgias* (1960),[1] his longest dialogue that centers on rhetoric; second, a letter by Donald G. Ellis to the editor of *Spectra* (1982), the newsletter of the Speech Communication Association, that provoked a great deal of controversy and response; third, an article by Michael Burgoon (1989) that is representative of a stance that Burgoon has argued vigorously in other publications and in convention programs. These three representative anecdotes of scandal contain the essence of the accusations made throughout history against Dame Rhetoric's moral character.

The charges of scandal against rhetoric are structured in terms of three dichotomies (or are they *continua*?). First, a distinction is drawn between *theory* and *application,* or, one might say, between knowledge and performance. Second, a distinction is made between *community* interests and *partisan* interests. Third, a dichotomy between *expert* and *democratic* decision making is identified. In each case, rhetoric is found in bed with the second term of the dichotomy, and cries of shame ensue.

Theory and Application

What is rhetoric? That question and its answers structure Plato's *Gorgias.* But question and answer is also one of its subtexts. For when we question we theorize, we pull back from the immediate problems of action and application to wonder, Why? And when we answer we empower people to apply knowledge, to confront some issue in life. We find the characters of the dialogue in these two modes. Gorgias himself has offered to *answer* any question put to him by a group of Athenians (Plato, 1960, sec. 447). Socrates, on the other hand, steps forward to *question* him. Socrates has come to wonder and query; Gorgias is here to use his skill.

Of all the questions that Socrates might ask of Gorgias, Socrates presses first and hardest with, "What is it that oratory is the knowledge of?" (sec. 449). Poor Gorgias Strawman does not refuse the question; he might, were he true to himself, insist upon saying what it is that oratory *does* and to what uses it is put. Indeed, describing how he applies his skill and what he does with it is often his "real" answer; he notes that he goes about the city with his brother, a physician, persuading patients to submit to dire and painful treatments that his brother has prescribed (sec. 456). But he has allowed that answer to be trapped within the context of theory. Plato's puppet character is trying to say what oratory theorizes about by saying what it does; playing by Socrates' rules, he is bound to fail.

Clearly, Socrates values theoretical knowledge over the application of knowledge in everyday uses. When pressed to define oratory himself, he calls it "a sort of knack gained by experience" (sec. 462), and it is clear that he despises any facility gained by doing (i.e., a "knack") rather than by philosophizing. Thus Socrates taxes Polus that "while I thought you admirably well-trained in oratory you seemed to me to have neglected the art of reasoning" (sec. 471). One can be trained in oratory, much as a dog can be trained to leap through hoops, but it is not at all the same thing as theoretical, philosophical knowledge based upon reason. Oratory, it turns out, does not require knowing anything at all. Socrates draws a distinction between knowing and believing something, and oratory is assigned to management of the latter but explicitly not the former (sec. 454).

Plato did not use terms such as *theory*. But his recent descendants do, and they prefer theory and its handmaiden, *research,* to today's applied disciplines. Ellis (1982) charges that "most programs in organizational communication, public relations, and advertising are narrow, theoretically vacuous, without a research base . . ." (p. 1). Practitioners of those arts are not grounded in "the extant scholarship and research" and thus go about "appearing to actually know something" when in fact they do not (p. 1). Notice that Ellis's complaint is not couched in terms of what they do or how their skills are applied, but rather in terms of their theoretical, abstract knowledge. He articulates Plato's dichotomy in other terms more familiar to today's academy. Schools are turning "from research and education to training," the last term echoing Socrates' belittling description of the knack that Polus had acquired. Ellis puts the pursuit of "research" on one side and satisfying "the vagaries of market needs" on the other (p. 2).

An even more explicit attack on rhetoric's applied offspring is found in Burgoon's suit "divorcing Dame Speech" (1989, p. 303). Burgoon puts teaching on the side of application, as opposed to research, as indeed it is in most universities today. He is annoyed at courses that focus on training students for practical application of principles of speaking, interacting, and writing. Theory must be primary, he argues, or else "pedagogy of performance retrodictively defin[es] the central questions of scholarly inquiry" (p. 303). "Theory and research in communication have far outstripped what is presently being taught in Speech," he complains (p. 303). Thus, departments of communication have sadly allowed themselves "to be solely identified with a pedagogy of performance (or skill development, if you prefer)" (p. 306), whereas they need to "be defined by its scholarship/research" (p. 307). He does not call, however, for a rapprochement between research and *speech,* the latter term marked by its historical grounding in applied public speaking instruction. He calls for a *divorce,* with departments concentrating on the production of theoretical knowledge, canceling wholesale high-enrollment performance courses, and teaching fewer students in favor of spending more time in laboratories.

Community Interests and Partisan Interests

A second scandal bruited against rhetoric is that it furthers the pursuit of partisan rather than community interests. That was a charge first leveled for financial reasons against the early Sophists such as Gorgias, who went about teaching the public how to speak on their own behalf at public assemblies. The Sophists, of course, served *their* own interests by charging a fee for their advice. Rhetoric, the allegation goes, by its very nature serves the selfish interests of those who prepare persuasive messages. Of course, one *could* use rhetorical skills altruistically to serve community interests. But Plato, especially in the *Phaedrus,* implies that as rhetoric moves toward community interests it moves toward becoming *dialectic.* When it is most truly itself, it is most truly partisan, which Plato calls a scandal.

Gorgias is made to explicitly articulate the personal, partisan ends of rhetoric, for he says it gives the orator "not only freedom for himself but also the power of ruling his fellow-countrymen" (Plato, 1960, sec. 452). Socrates agrees that orators serve their own interests. For that very reason they are the least powerful members of a community, since they have no wisdom for the furthering of the *common* good (sec. 466). Such wisdom would be used not to appeal to and flatter the public, but in the unpalatable service of curing the public of their excesses. That, Socrates argues, oratory will never do, and thus it is useless (sec. 478). Socrates' claim is from experience rather than principle, however: "There are two kinds of political oratory, one of them is pandering and base clap-trap; only the other is good, which aims at the edification of the souls of the citizens." But, alas! "I don't believe that you have ever experienced the second type," and Socrates is dubious that it can exist (sec. 503).

Oratory serves partisan ends beyond the purely political realm. Near the beginning of the dialogue, Socrates subtly stacks the deck against Gorgias by inquiring "what sort of man he is." He is asking for Gorgias's social identity; he wants to know what Gorgias is in terms of the role he takes in the community. Thus, Socrates suggests ways to define Gorgias based on clearly identifiable roles or professions. Perhaps he is like a doctor, or perhaps a painter (secs. 447–448). Gorgias as sheer rhetorician, as someone endowed with a skill to pursue his own partisan interests no matter what his professional identity, is a definition that is not allowed to emerge. Public relations practitioners might confront similar difficulties in defining themselves today.

Socrates' famous definition of rhetoric as "pandering" or "flattery" (sec. 463) charges rhetoric explicitly with being self-serving, for it "pays no regard to the welfare of its object" (sec. 464), being concerned instead with "producing gratification and pleasure" (sec. 462). Pleasure, not the common good, is its object (sec. 465). Plato makes Callicles take this position to its extreme, in arguing that "the man who is going to live as a man ought should encourage his appetites" (secs. 491–492). Socrates argues against this, claiming that rhetoric is incapable of even serving true partisan interests in the long run. This is because it is bound to be used by evildoers to escape punishment, whereas punishment is precisely what evildoers need to experience for their own good (secs. 472, 476–478). That position, of course, is challenged by Callicles, the ultimate partisan, who praises the use of rhetoric in the service of personal gain and scorns community interests as mere "convention": "The experience of suffering wrong does not happen to anyone who calls himself a man" (sec. 483) if he can use rhetoric to help himself.

More recent cries of scandal have alleged the same focus on partisan rather than community interests among Gorgias's latter-day heirs. Ellis (1982) identifies public relations teachers and practitioners as partisan, as "a fringe element that exploits the research of the profession and draws upon its substance for self aggrandizement" (p. 1). Public relations and organizational communication teachers are responsible for "the proliferation of a managerial class that identifies with accumulation and self-fulfillment rather than responsibility," with this last term standing in for service to the common good (p. 2). Similarly, the substance of Burgoon's article (1989) is to argue that departments of communication should serve the academic community's larger good of advancing research instead of their own partisan good of expanding majors and course enrollments.

Expert and Democratic Decisions and Leadership

The Sophists went about the Aegean world training people for participation in democratic decision making. Of course, Sophists were not all the same, nor were their curricula identical. Many of them, such as Isocrates, set up schools that followed high standards in teaching the arts and sciences of the time, providing not only a broadly based education, but also philosophical training and technical expertise in particular subject matters. It is not to those Sophists that Plato objects. He is scandalized at the primarily rhetorical Sophists, who were providing the masses of citizens with enough rhetorical training to be able to participate in public debates, but not with the technical depth of knowledge necessary to become experts in any particular subject. In other words, Plato was scandalized by Sophists such as Gorgias, who trained his students in his own likeness, as being able to speak on *any* subject; the focus of the training was on the ability to speak rather than on the substance of the subject.

As Plato makes clear throughout his works, especially in *The Republic,* decisions should be made by experts, by specialists in knowledge, rather than by ordinary citizens. When the general populace is enrolled in decision making, they will do so by arguing the issues. And since nobody is an expert on every issue, the populace will rely on rhetoric rather than on specializations of knowledge in making those decisions. In other words, rhetoric and democratic decision making go hand in hand. In the *Gorgias* (Plato, 1960), Socrates makes this point clear. "A popular audience means an ignorant audience," he opines (sec. 459). Place the orator before specialists in knowledge, and the orator's power disappears: "He won't be more convincing than the doctor before experts" (sec. 459). Because orators claim to speak on any subject, "the orator need have no knowledge of the truth about things; it is enough for him to have discovered a knack of convincing the ignorant that he knows more than the experts" (sec. 459).

Socrates contends that there are specialties of knowledge even for the moral or political issues with which public assemblies often deal. "It needs an expert" to distinguish between good and bad pleasures, he claims (sec. 500). Even in political matters, "this is a matter of expert knowledge" (sec. 503). That expertise is often more narrowly defined as *philosophy.* Callicles is made to scorn philosophy in favor of the active life of participation in politics (sec. 485).

Similarly, Ellis (1982) complains that there are no experts, no "research and scholarly tradition," in public relations and organizational communication. Instead, "departments of speech communication have turned to salesmanship" in training practitioners who will direct persuasive appeals to the general public (p. 2). Burgoon (1989) is even more explicitly Platonic. He specifically calls for a "meritocracy" in academia, based on research. In contrast, "neither can it be accepted that democracy is the panacea for what ails academia" (p. 304). He is *not* interested in equipping the general public with speaking skills: "Communication departments do not exist to provide general education courses for the masses" (p. 305). Like Plato's Republic, he would call for a "meritocracy of scholars" instead (pp. 305, 307).

The Seamless if Spotted Garment of Scandalous Rhetoric

Theory, community interests, and expertise, on the one hand, and application, partisan interests, and democracy, on the other hand, form two distinct and conceptually consistent clusters. The elements of each cluster go together, and a valorization of one element is consistent with a valorization of the other.

Plato (1960), for example, makes Callicles admit that pleasure and knowledge are different things (sec. 495).The effect of this admission is to enable Socrates to align the pleasure that comes from pursuing partisan interests against the valorized term *knowledge*. But he leaps across dichotomies here; the effect is also to assert that the accumulation of knowledge that comes with a preoccupation with theory is opposed to the pursuit of partisan, pleasurable interests, and thus it is consistent with community interests. One theorizes so as to accumulate knowledge in the service of the community's greater good. But on the other hand, true happiness comes not from pursuing partisan interests, but from pursuing enlightenment through attaining knowledge—in other words, from the theoretical side of the dichotomy (sec. 470). Expertise is included in this web of linkages as well. "The good orator," says Socrates hypothetically, "being also a man of expert knowledge, will have these ends [of righteousness and moderation] in view in any speech; . . . his attention will be wholly concentrated on bringing righteousness and moderation, and every other virtue to birth in the souls of his fellow-citizens" (sec. 504). Here Socrates makes the obvious link between theoretical knowledge and expertise and use of that expert knowledge to serve community, rather than partisan, interests. Ellis (1982) likewise asserts linkages among the Platonic side of the dichotomies. In the same sentence, he attacks public relations as "without a research base, and just as an aside, morally degenerate. . . ." (p. 1). But it is not just an aside. The linkage is intentional: public relations is degenerate *because* of the lack of a research base. The same linkage occurs in his suggested solution: "Genuine and meaningful research in these areas will only come when political and moral issues are included as considerations" (p. 2).

The scandalous side of the dichotomies, wherein reside public relations and its inbred cousins, is conceptually consistent as well. Democracy depends on the application of knowledge rather than on the hoarding and refinement of knowledge, in decisions about problems in the here and now. The sense of urgency given to rhetoric by its preoccupation with a motivating problem in the context encourages the pursuit of partisan interests. Even if one is "partisan" on behalf of a whole city or nation, it is partisan nevertheless.

What do we make of these scandalous rhetorics of public relations, advertising, and the like? One response is to teach public relations practitioners to be ethical, as Ellis proposes and as Plato hopes for in principle but despairs of in practice. I will not oppose such a plan. But in keeping with the theme of scandal, I will put forth the best argument I can for why the charge of scandal should be embraced, even flaunted. The charges alleged to be shameful are actually desirable characteristics for public communication today.

FLAUNTING IT: A SCANDALOUS DEFENSE OF SCANDALOUS RHETORICS

Should rhetors, including public relations practitioners, be well informed in their subjects before they craft messages? Should their rhetoric be grounded in reasonably complete and accurate knowledge? Should one say with Plato (1956) in the *Phaedrus* that "a man must first know the truth about every single subject on which he speaks or writes" (sec. 277), grounded in the theoretical pastime of "leisurely discussion, by stargazing, if you will, about the nature of things" (sec. 270)?

These questions are pointless. We live in an era of exploding knowledge and exponentially increasing databases, in which nobody can have any real knowledge of any depth on the range of important issues confronted each day. Read all the books, newspapers, and magazines you like; listen to the highest quality public radio and television shows you can find; expose yourself to information outlets from a wide variety of political perspectives. To become "well informed" can only mean becoming aware of the deep seas of unfathomable knowledge upon which you merely bob about, scooping up half-measures-full as fast as you can. Today, nobody can be well informed about the broad range of issues that affect people.

On this fact of late twentieth-century life may be built an indictment of the whole complex of charges against rhetoric, as well as an urgent revaluation of its scandalous shortcomings. True expertise under conditions of exploding knowledge becomes narrower and narrower. One can scarcely be a physician today, for instance, nor even more narrowly a specialist in internal medicine. Even keeping up with the research in endocrinology or gastroenterology will overwhelm the most industrious reader of medical journals. The same is true for every other specialty of knowledge. Therefore, the ability of specialists to make decisions for the public, even to advise the public meaningfully, becomes increasingly questionable. Plunging deeper and deeper into the black hole of a given specialty becomes a trained incapacity when it comes to synthesizing knowledge in the service of public decisions, for synthesizing requires a broad viewpoint, a grasp of many different issues impinging upon a given decision. How can medical expertise alone, for instance, help the public decide what to do about surrogate motherhood? It is an issue that calls for the advice of the ethicist, the psychologist, the sociologist, and more, each specialty likewise drowning in its own glut of information. When Plato (and his heirs) call for knowledge grounded in expertise, they are calling for conceptually connected expertise. Yet as expertise narrows and deepens, connections to cognate disciplines weaken.

The cry of scandal against rhetoric's preference for application over theory is actually an indictment of application that is underinformed by theory. Even Ellis and Burgoon could scarcely object to a pedagogy that knows what the latest research findings are and imparts them to students. But the knowledge explosion turns the indictment and creates a theoretical body of knowledge that is underinformed by application. The pursuit of knowledge for its own sake is a fine academic shibboleth, but, as specialties of knowledge deepen, theory turns in upon itself. Nowhere is this more clearly seen than in the rage of fashionable humanities today, critical studies. Here, theory is pursued with a fine disdain for the empirical. One need only read Jean Baudrillard or Frederic Jameson to see theory gnawing upon itself, tuned to its own self-monitoring and self-connection, a servomechanism keyed to itself, a vast thermostat connected to no actual furnace. What real student can learn from these writings? What actual experience of injustice or oppression can be resisted with that mangled prose? The deepening research bases of the science, although often less arrogant, are no more accessible to real people confronted with everyday problems. The truly bottomless pits of all research bases are becoming less and less usable for buttering the actual parsnips of real life.

When the available research base of knowledge becomes so complex and so deep that its relevance to one's everyday situation becomes unclear, the issue of partisan versus community interests also comes to the fore. "Community interests" sounds like a fine thing. But the question, *"Whose* community?" could legitimately have been raised in Plato's time as well as today. *Community* means *hegemony,* the dominance of established power interests. In our society today, there are many competing interests based on divisions of class, race, gender, sexual preference, and so forth. To pretend that there is a community interest to be served is actually to hide the interests of empowered groups behind the facade of "the community." Those privileged interests are presented as community interests. The "citizens" of Athens in Plato's time, even if they served "community interests," were in fact only about 15 percent of the population. Their community interests were highly partisan. In such a situation, the moral imperative actually lies with those who would speak for the partisan interests of the factions comprising the other 85 percent of the population: women, foreigners, children, slaves, and so forth. So it is for us today, as well. In the unmelted pot of fragmented and diverse American culture, using rhetoric in the service of "community interests" lends itself more to using rhetoric in the service of entrenched powers and principalities.

For each of the scandalous accusations against rhetoric, then, I would embrace the scandal and flaunt it. What kind of rhetoric does this shameless exhibition of scandal call for? What model of public discourse or what public relations practices are implied by this headlong rush toward rhetorical abandon?

A rhetoric, a public relations practice, that has given up on conventional respectability will feature *narrative* (Fisher, 1984, 1989). Careful argument, lengthy exposition, logical appeals, all the panoply of respectable rhetoric that Plato loved so much depend upon the manageability of information. They depend upon speaker and audience sharing a base of knowledge. Thus, they depend on the hegemonic sharing of the same knowledge. But when knowledge has grown so vast, unwieldy, and fragmented that it can neither be managed nor predictably shared, rhetoric must pursue *strategies of reduction.* That is, it must develop ways to reduce complexity to manageable proportions and to simplify confusion and fragmentation and encode issues in forms that people will share and understand.The principal strategy of reduction in use today is narrative. Rhetoricians, from political speakers to public relations practitioners, must cast their appeals in terms of stories if they expect to be heard and understood. Complex social and political issues are cast into the forms of half-hour sitcoms. Political speakers embody ideals of civic virtue in particular heroes and heroines and then tell stories about them. Public relations becomes the practice of telling and managing stories that are told about people, institutions, and groups.

A narrative simplification of complexity also serves partisan interests. Part of the hegemony of empowered "community interests" is a monopoly over the means of "respectable" rhetoric. If your group is disempowered and marginalized, one sure way to keep you there is to insist that you register your complaint using the means of logical argument and polite debate that prop up the established power interests in the first place. A shift to a rhetoric structured around narrative is a move around the flank of the discursive roadblock of respectable rhetoric. Every group has a story to tell, even if every group cannot, does not, or will not use expositional argument or statistical proofs. Empowered groups already have access to as much information as can be handled; insisting on a rhetoric that is based in theory and expertise is an insistence on a rhetoric that already privileges power. Narrative levels the playing field.

In conclusion, to embrace scandalous rhetorics is to embrace a metaphor of piracy, privateering, and free-for-all swashbuckling on the high seas. Plato's rhetorical vision is one of a stern and oppressive Britannia ruling every wave of a dead sea. Some will prefer the latter. But since public relations and its brethren will never be recruited into that starchy fleet, let them raise the Jolly Roger and accept the charges made against them with wicked willingness.

NOTE

1. Classical text references will be to section rather than page numbers so that the passage may be easily found in other translations.

PART II
Case Studies with National Purviews

Mobil's Epideictic Advocacy
"Observations" of Prometheus Bound

Richard E. Crable and Steven L. Vibbert

By the end of 1975, the cliché "business as usual" had acquired a whole new meaning for American industry. The American Machine moved no longer through an environment of laissez-faire government and complacent public sentiment. Such a setting, if it had ever existed to the extent imagined by the Machine, had been replaced by a pressure cooker environment heated by the accusations and demands of both government and the public. "Business as usual" had acquired the implications of defense and, perhaps, even defensiveness. As early as 1970, the American Industrial Machine had been charged with despoiling the American Garden of Eden, with polluting and deflowering the pastoral setting that had served as ground for the Machine itself (Brown and Crable, 1973).

Industry's protest that it either had been helping retain the Garden or was involved in regaining it began to fade with the advent of the oil crisis and the OPEC oil embargo of 1973. One distinguished economist concludes, "With only the treacherous exceptions of political assassinations and international terrorism, no single issue has so shaken America's balance in this turbulent epoch than the amalgam of superevents clumped together in the household headline: 'Oil Crisis'" (Hazlett, 1982, p. 1). Short on oil and long on lines at service stations, Americans were rudely awaken from their dream that they would always have cheap and plentiful petroleum. In response, the question became not "How may the American Garden be restored?" but rather, "How is what *is left* of the Garden to be maintained?"

In a culture that was not American, the answer might have lain in autonomous government response: a strong national policy affecting national energy production. But this was America; problems as complex as the need for energy would involve the President, the Congress, the energy industry, and the individual American citizen. The President and the Congress were engaged in analyses of the problem and the creation of alternative solutions. Meanwhile, the energy industry concentrated on the pragmatics of production and the garnering of support for those enterprises.

In this chapter, we examine "Observations" as a specific set of support-seeking communication strategies used by one of the major suppliers of American energy, the Mobil Oil Corporation. To that end, the chapter focuses on the period from 1976 to 1980 and examines four ideas: "Observations" as a rhetorical response to a complex public relations problem, the argumentative approach of "Observations," the cultural foundations of those arguments, and a summary assessment of "Observations."

"OBSERVATIONS" AS RHETORICAL RESPONSE

What *were* "Observations"? *Fortune* magazine identified "Observations" as "a potpourri of odd and interesting items of news, illustrated with a cartoon and woodcuts, with the Mobil message delivered in an offhand, breezy fashion" (Ross, 1976). To analyze "odd and interesting" comments presented in paid advertising space in Sunday newspapers requires explanation. That explanation emerges with an understanding of Mobil's public relations situation circa the end of 1975 and with an appreciation of "Observations" as a response to that situation.

Mobil's Public Relations Situation

The years following the oil embargo and the unparalleled concerns for energy shortages altered American priorities. The need for environmental improvement began to be balanced against the need for increased production of energy. But the needs were not in balance for long: environmental concern was upstaged by the need for power. Public opinion embraced the idea that, if America was to survive, the country would have to rely still more heavily on its own industrial machine.

The energy sector of the American Machine was willing to play the role of Prometheus, the Greek mythological character who defied the preeminent god Zeus when he introduced fire to human beings. In 1975, foreign energy sources were suspect; however, the American public also distrusted American energy giants. Americans wondered if the energy crisis was artificial, or at least was created artificially, in hopes of higher corporate profits. The complexity and uncertainty of this situation created a context for interesting and significant public relations responses by representatives of the American energy-producing machine, including the Mobil Oil Corporation.

To understand those responses, however, one must understand the specific situation that Mobil faced in 1975. Mid-1975, for example, brought a proposal to decontrol oil prices, an event long awaited by almost all members of the industry. Yet Mobil emerged as the maverick among major oil producers in arguing that precipitous decontrol would bring skyrocketing oil prices. The negative impact of this seemingly positive policy, Mobil warned, would be unprecedented profits and uncontrollable demands for windfall profits taxes (Mahdenberg, 1975; "What made Mobil," 1979). In Mobil's opinion, deregulation was not in the energy producers' long-term interests. Moreover, Mobil was confronted with three other critical situational factors.

First, Mobil was faced with a world that did not seem to appreciate its efforts to bring the sources of power to the people. Industry third-quarter profits were down, despite higher oil product prices, and few commentators envisioned a rebound in either the fourth quarter or in 1976. This first factor of low profits might have been overcome either with help from the federal government or, at least, with lack of interference that would have allowed the free enterprise system to function. Instead, Mobil perceived a second problem: the energy giant was victimized by federal regulations discouraging higher production and profits. Mobil's director and vice president for public affairs, Herbert Schmertz, said in retrospect, "We felt that litigation, legislation, and regulation were creating problems for our nation by impeding energy production and by raising energy costs" (in "Industry fights," 1978). These victimizing regulations included low wellhead oil prices that depressed the incentive for exploration and production[1] and the lack of enabling legislation and support for ventures in shale oil and coal development (FW, March 27, 1977, p. 25). The situation worsened with yet another regulatory policy: the Energy Policy and Conservation Act, while not favorable toward decontrol of the industry, actually would have "rolled-back" prices and provided for widespread auditing of industry books.[2]

As if the profit and regulatory problems were not troublesome enough, the third quarter of 1975 also witnessed events that might have led to the divestiture of certain aspects of the oil industry's energy operation. In July 1973, antitrust action had been initiated against eight major oil producers, including Mobil. On October 21, these energy giants breathed a sigh of relief as administrative judge Alvin L. Berman unexpectedly recommended that the Federal Trade Commission (FTC) withdraw its complaint (Cowan, 1975a). The third quarter of 1975 ended that sense of relief and continued to produce discomfort: by a three to one vote, the FTC rejected Berman's opinion (Cowan, 1975b). The steps toward ultimate divestiture were to proceed; an antitrust trial was to begin on February 23, 1976 (Cowan, 1975b).

In short, Mobil faced many problems at the end of 1975. It differed from other major oil producers on the issue of precipitous decontrol of prices. Simultaneously, it confronted a dim profit picture, regulations it viewed as detrimental, and the threat of corporate divestiture. To Mobil, the situation demanded federal action and corporate creativity; it also demanded various rhetorical responses.

"Observations" as Epideictic   As Mobil surveyed its situation, its public relations responses might have been aimed exclusively at America's power brokers of public policy. It might have chosen to exert all its influence through lobbying, through personal contacts with governmental leaders, or even through its by-now-established editorializing in such formats as *The New York Times* Op-Ed page.[3] In fact, it continued all these efforts, but it also began a different campaign. According to Schmertz, "Advocacy advertising is aimed at opinion makers who are well informed and well educated." Mobil also responded to its feeling that "the oil industry and big business were losing public esteem and understanding" (in "Industry fights"). Thus, Mobil initiated "Observations" to attract the attention of and to affect the publics of citizens and oil and gasoline consumers.

"Observations" were half-page olios in Sunday newspaper magazine sections, composed of cartoons, line art, chatty news items, wide-ranging editorial commentary, letters from readers, and a sprinkling of quotations from such diverse sources as John Locke, Robert Frost, Samuel Gompers, and Will Rogers. The special office of "Observations" was the appeal to populist sentiments within the popular audience through a popular medium over which Mobil had editorial control. Mobil used "Observations" to get its "side of the issues" to the public with the apparent belief that popular sentiment could be useful in affecting the situation in a way that Mobil could not or had not. Mobil's dedication to such tenets led to the continued and refined use of the "Observations" format. By June 1980, "Observations" was carried in 503 newspapers and reached, according to Mobil, over half the American homes (FW, June 22, 1980, p. 20).

In a general way, "Observations" was a series of communications aimed at enlisting and re-enlisting the esteem and understanding of the average American. While expecting to influence policymakers by lobbying, political action committees, and Op-Eds, Mobil also expected them to be affected by pressure from the public who comprised the readership for "Observations." More specifically, "Observations" functioned as vastly more sophisticated rhetoric that clearly melded the ancient concern for *epideictic* (rhetoric that praises commonly held values and beliefs) with Stephen Toulmin's emphasis on "warrant-establishing," or premise-building, arguments (1969).

Whether by accident or intent, "Observations" presented Mobil with a superb rhetorical vehicle for building premises. A first glance at "Observations" might result in the conclusion that these were no more than noncontroversial messages delivered on Sunday morning to people who already believe them. The importance of such messages is as easily overlooked as the role of Independence Day speeches delivered by politicians and civic leaders in countless American communities. These messages, both on Sunday morning and in early July, function as epideictic. Claiming that the ancients did not appreciate the function of the epideictic, Perelman and Olbrechts-Tyteca (1969) argue, "The purpose of the epideictic speech is to increase the intensity of adherence to values held in common by the audience and speaker" (p. 52). This increased adherence is important because it "strengthens the disposition toward action" (p. 50). Even people who disagree with a message can be motivated to act on agreed-upon beliefs.

In another sense, the value reinforcement that is at the heart of the epideictic "has an important part to play, for without such common values upon what foundation could deliberative and legal speeches rest?" (p. 52). The epideictic "forms a central part of the art of persuasion" (p. 49), including those efforts presented through lobbying efforts and Op-Ed messages. The study of "Observations," then, allows the critic to observe Mobil's building of premises for later use. That some arguments build premises while others use them has been noted by Toulmin (1969) in his discussions of the difference between "warrant-establishing" arguments and "warrant-using" arguments. A warrant-establishing argument hinges on the acceptability between claim and data. In such arguments, the novel warrant is applied to a number of cases in which the claim and data are *not* the source of argument; instead, the warrant, the "bridge" between them, is "on trial." In contrast, the warrant-using argument relies on an already established bridge between claim and data (something commonly accepted and usually unchallenged), so that the focus is not on the link between claim and data, but instead is on either claim *or* data. In its "Observations," Mobil even asked its readers to contribute materials that actually help establish warrants. As basic, generalized, and normative beliefs, these warrants could then be used later to link evidence to the claims that Mobil wanted its publics to accept.

In sum, "Observations" are interesting because they were messages aimed at correcting what Mobil feared was a problem of public acceptance and sympathy. They are important also because they provide a rare opportunity for studying a campaign heavily engaged in premise building for use in later advocacy efforts. How "Observations" can be appreciated in these ways requires a closer scrutiny of the messages themselves.

THE ARGUMENTATIVE APPROACH IN MOBIL'S "OBSERVATIONS"

An analysis of the arguments presented in "Observations" can proceed by studying examples of the messages and then summarizing the major issues developed. This study reflects the analysis of 149 "Observations" columns appearing from 1976 through 1980.[4] While there is no way to include all of these, it is possible to provide examples from the several years that reveal the diversity of message topic, the general approach of the columns, and the Mobil style in this format.

On January 18, 1976, for instance, "Observations" was, not atypically, divided into four segments (FW, p. 19). The first was labeled "Salute to News Hounds" and was an attempt at balancing an earlier comment about "sharks" in the news business who "shot from the lip" in articles criticizing the oil industry. Said Mobil, "We know that for every shark-toothed lipshooter, there are scores of conscientious news hounds who dig carefully for facts and think twice about gnawing on skeletons that aren't really there. . . . The truth *does* eventually win out, even the truth about America's complex energy problems, which are still far from solved." This section, appropriately, was bordered by a cartoon dog in glasses and press-card-carrying hat, sitting at a typewriter.

Item two turned to press coverage of the proposal to "break up the larger integrated oil companies." Mobil printed as "typical" a lengthy quotation arguing against divestiture in Alabama's *Birmingham News.* Mobil "observed" that "we couldn't have said it better, except maybe to remind our readers of the old cries to break up baseball's New York Yankees. Now that the Gehrigs and Babe Ruths are no longer there, wouldn't it be nice to see some of their home-run efficiency again?"

The need to balance environmental concerns with the need for energy production was the topic of the third item. In summarizing quoted remarks from the Wilmington, Delaware, *Evening Journal,* Mobil said, "In other words: the environment counts but so do new jobs and the health of the economy. " This edition of "Observations" concluded with an attack on the "politicians' low-gear crawl toward an equitable energy policy." In underscoring a *Washington Post* "kudo" about the average American helping the energy problem by buying more efficient cars, Mobil added, "Grassroots movements work faster when they've got the help and coordination of the men and women running the country. Maybe Washington will finally get the message and provide the sound energy policy the country needs."

Just as there is no obvious pattern to the topics within a single "Observations," there is no discernable pattern between and among installments. Another "Observations" on June 5, 1977 (FW, p. 19), began with a section on "Better Buying." It promoted the government's publication called "Your Money's Worth in Foods," which would answer such questions as "What's the better buy: boneless round steak at $1.80 a pound, bone-in loin roast at $1.50, or spare ribs at $1.39?" Mobil called the publication "a wealth of information." Without transition, the next item dealt with the relative merits of energy conservation and energy production. Mobil's position was that "both conservation and increased production are 'musts' for the U.S. But with today's emphasis on the former, let's not forget about the latter."

Item three involved government paperwork. Taking the idea that government agencies print enough forms—which Americans have to use, by the way—to fill 4 million cubic feet of space each year, a Mobil "research scientist" translated that into energy potential. Burning this (valuable? frustrating?) paper would be equivalent to the energy in 12 million gallons of gasoline. Quipped Mobil, "If all the cars in Washington ran on red tape, we know where a 20-day supply could be found." The final item again presented a typical contrast: "Inspired (and otherwise) names for businesses." Readers sending "winning names" of actual businesses would be mailed a $25 savings bond. Among the winners in this column was "I Scream Koner" located in Cocoa Beach, Florida.

A third example of "Observations" was published in newspapers on February 19, 1978 (FW, p. 6). Under the heading "How High Is Up?" Mobil took the opportunity to salute Washington and Lincoln on their birthdays and to criticize the federal budget for 1979, which was to be just under one-half trillion dollars. Observed Mobil, "That's more money than the nation spent during its first 160 years of existence!"

The second item concerned "Phantom Oratory," speeches by members of Congress that appeared in the *Congressional Record,* but were never actually presented. Mobil argued that phantom oratory represented 70 percent of the record's 51,000 pages, "printed at a cost of some $10 million. Ghost writing has received a degree of respectability in Washington. But ghost *speaking?*"

Item three cited *U.S. News and World Report*'s study of "bureaucratic babble." One of Mobil's favorites was the Food and Drug Administration's admonition that "innovative processes should be considered to better integrate informed societal judgements and values into the regulatory mechanism." Mobil decided that the FDA was urging employees to "think." Headlined with "Bobbing Along," Mobil also used this edition of "Observations" to point out a certain discrepancy in government regulations. While the Federal Endangered Species Scientific Authority was trying to protect the dwindling number of bobcats, government trappers were killing bobcats for the Interior Department. In addition to being "Endangered," Mobil pointed out, bobcats were also "unwanted predators."

This installment of "Observations" ended with "a quote we like." This quotation was from former President Ford, who cited the creation of 45,000 pages of "very small type" in the *Federal Register* to report rules and regulations passed in 1977 alone. Mobil cited Ford: "I mourn for the trees that were felled in America's forests to make this exercise in governmental nagging possible."

In the final example of "Observations," we turn to the publication of November 11, 1979 (AJCM, p. 8). The first item explained what was then America's number one problem. Mobil tells the story: "Picture two kids. Out playing on the beach, they spot an unusual seashell. Both want it, so one offers a dime to buy out the other. The second produces three nickels. The first, clever kid, writes an IOU for next week's allowance. Pretty soon, they're talking about IOUs for a zillion dollars." Says Mobil, "They have just invented inflation."

Item two concerns the rate of inflation and argues that (at 1979 rates) "today's $50 basket of food will cost $129.69 in 10 years." The third item extols the importance of personal savings to the health of the economy. Mobil points out that both German and Japanese citizens save at a higher rate than Americans. Because "*savings are critical to investment,* it's not surprising that those two nations outpace the U.S. in new factories and equipment to produce more goods more efficiently, and help create *jobs.*"

Mobil concluded its observations by warning of even higher inflation ahead. "Washington must cut back" regulations that "encourage shortages and make goods more costly to produce," and "we must avoid . . . stagnation." All this and more, says Mobil, is "something to bear in mind as we move into another election year."

The preceding four examples of "Observations" reflect the consistent style and flavor of this Mobil medium. That the columns differed in topic among one another and that items within any one column differed among themselves is also typical of the approach. Still, despite the seeming lack of topic pattern, a summary analysis of 149 columns indicates that the "potpourri" of "Observations" is actually a fairly tightly disciplined campaign revolving around a small number of premises-in-the-making.

Issue Positions as Premises

Mobil used "Observations" as a forum for "discussing" and "sharing views" on six major issues: regulation, the Congress, the media, technology, conservation, and the "common sense" of the American people. Each of these issues contributed in an important way to Mobil's role as a corporate rhetor and thus made possible an identification and argumentative alliance between Mobil and the readers of "Observations."

Regulation was a recurring theme in "Observations" and was characterized variously as stifling, costly, inefficient, and, perhaps most importantly, often ludicrous (FW, December 5, 1976, p. 6; FW, January 23,

1977, p. 10; FW, February 6, 1977, p. 16; FW, October 29, 1978, p. 10; FW, July 6, 1980, p. 11). "Observations" frequently pointed out the absurdity and proliferation of regulations related to corporate activity. For instance, Mobil noted that dump trucks are required to have alarms that sound whenever they are placed in reverse gear, even though all workers wear ear plugs (FW, August 8, 1976, p. 7). Equally important are examples of "silly" regulations that apply to (and limit) individual conduct: in some places, one may not carry bees in one's hat; in other places horses are required to wear pants when they are ridden in public; in California, noted "Observations," the sale of olives is governed by an 11,400-word document (FW, August 8, 1976, p. 6; FW, June 26, 1977, p. 14). Regulation, both corporate and individual, is typified as a "maze," a "muddle," and a "morass" of red tape (AW, September 14, 1980, p. 57; AJCM, August 31, 1980, p. 10; AJCM, May 27, 1979, p. 6). Also, Mobil observed, "nothing cripples innovation and enterprise like heavy-handed regulation" (FW, October 1, 1978, p. 10). In short, regulation was depicted as a problem not only for corporate America, but also for all America and all Americans: regulation constrains both corporate and individual activity.

Turning to a second major issue, Mobil used "Observations" to observe that Congress is possessed of a powerful, unwieldy, and vindictive character. Congress frequently creates unnecessary regulations, but paradoxically it also is paralyzed by inactivity, moving at a "low gear crawl," and holding up energy policy measures to "bamboozle" politically (AJCM, May 27, 1979, p. 6; AJCM, January 18, 1976, p. 19; AJCM, May 9, 1976, p. 17). Indeed, the Congress was seen as having treated the oil companies as a "scapegoat" in the interests of preserving its own powers.

Mobil also found ongoing problems with the individuals and organizations that theoretically are supposed to report the news fairly and objectively. As the focus of a third issue, the media were described as "anti-business," selectively "irresponsible," and decidedly self-interested (AJCM, May 13, 1979, p. 6; FW, January 30, 1977, p. 8; AJCM, February 1, 1976, p. 21). Some news reporters were described as "sharks who move constantly in search of bloody prey" (FW, January 30, 1977, p. 8). And the media, particularly the television networks, have their daily opportunity to attack indiscriminately.

As an energy producer, Mobil also used "Observations" to discuss a fourth issue: technology. The treatment here stressed the positive benefits of nuclear development, coal resources, petroleum recovery techniques, and solar power (AJCM, April 1, 1979, p. 8; FW, February 6, 1977, p. 16; AJCM, February 8, 1976, p. 11). Technology is not some alien force to be understood and used only by the gods; technology can lead to the practical benefits of increased gas mileage and greater crop yields (FW, June 25, 1978, p. 20; FW, October 9, 1977, p. 22).

The fifth major issue, conservation, requires careful forethought and judicious actions. Pragmatically, this means that carpools, public transportation, home insulation, and vacation planning to avoid excessive use of fuel are valued (AJCM, March 18, 1979, p. 8; FW, September 25, 1977, p. 10; AJCM, September 30, 1979, p. 8; FW, May 25, 1980, p. 7). Corporately, this means that oil producers should not rush quickly, and perhaps unwisely, to embrace proposals such as the precipitous decontrol of prices.[5]

A sixth, and final, issue that emerges from the analysis of "Observations" is the common sense of the common people. Mobil used public opinion polls as evidence of the polity's right thinking, even in the midst of Congressional and regulatory chaos. Polls show, noted Mobil, that Americans support the development of alternative sources of energy, that an energy policy is a national priority, that conservation and development of resources are essential, that the bureaucracy is getting worse, and that energy is a top national need (FW, August 1, 1976, p. 5; FW, March 6, 1977, p. 16; FW, October 16, 1977, p. 8; FW, January 25, 1976, p. 21; FW, July 18, 1976, p. 9). When Americans vote, observed Mobil, they vote "good sense" (FW, August 1, 1976, p. 5): the "grassroots" are the locus of "good sense" in the American system, and when people have the chance to speak their mind, they do so sensibly (FW, January 18, 1976, p. 19). Mobil argued that the best solution to most problems is to leave them to "common sense" (AJCM, December 9, 1979, p. 10). The "can do" spirit of the American people can aid in the solution of all the other issues addressed, just as it had done so historically.

A summary analysis of "Observations," then, reveals that the seeming collage of "offhand and breezy" items focused on a limited set of issues. Moreover, as we shall see in the next section, Mobil treated these issues in ways that created a particular corporate ethos and a specific reality for the reader.

THE STRATEGIC AND CULTURAL FOUNDATIONS OF "OBSERVATIONS"

The regular reader of "Observations" was confronted with a constant flow of seemingly noncontroversial ideas. Interestingly, those ideas were used by Mobil both to create certain strategic identifications and to make even more universal persuasive appeals. As Kenneth Burke has noted and as others have developed more fully, identification occurs at three different levels: explicitly, by scapegoating, and implicitly (see Burke, 1969; Cheney, 1983; Crable, 1977; Holland, 1955; Nichols, 1952). Mobil used each of these levels in its "Observations" to define itself and to align itself with its audience. Implicitly, Mobil was identified with "windfall profits," "gas shortages," "pollution," and certainly a host of other issues. To counter the possible (and likely) negative force of these implicit identifications, Mobil identified explicitly with the conservation of resources and the promise of technology. Further, in its explicit identification with these issues, Mobil stressed the practical worth of each for a public conditioned historically to the value of both thrift and scientific "progress." Alternatively, as common enemies of both itself and the common person, Mobil treated federal regulation, the Congress, and the media with scapegoat identifications. Individuals face, with increasing disgust, regulatory intrusion into their lives; confidence in government remains at an all-time low; and the media are a growing source of consternation for their perceived bias and sensationalism. Mobil identified itself with the interests of the people by offering a common scapegoat for ridicule. Mobil's motives, thus, reflected the motives of the American people. Mobil opposed the caprice of the federal government because the common sense of the common people demanded it. In its "Observations," Mobil structured a series of identificational strategies that encourage individuals to identify their interests with those of the energy giant.

In the role of epideictic rhetor, Mobil used apparently noncontroversial messages to define a reality of identifications, a foundation of premises for use in more blatant advocacy efforts. The rhetorical force of this Mobil-created reality is explained partly by identificational strategies, but there is an even deeper appeal to values and premises that is the stuff of myth.

The Archetypal Appeal of "Observations"

Understanding Mobil, its situation, and its "Observations" rhetoric can be enhanced by archetypal, or mythic, interpretation. Between 1975 and 1980, Mobil played the role of Prometheus.

Of course, all energy producers can be generally categorized as Promethean. All have provided sources for power and light for the human race, just as the mythical Prometheus gave the stolen gift of fire to humans (see Gayley, 1894; Hamilton, 1942; Pinsent, 1969; Reinhold, 1972). That prize, designated as the distinguishing gift of humans, was the first major step in civilization. As Gayley (1894) has noted, "With fire in his possession man would be able, when necessary, to win her secrets and treasures from earth, to develop commerce, science, and the arts" (p. 43). In this sense, Mobil stands as merely equal to other energy producers. However, there is more to the Promethean myth and more to Mobil Oil that isolates Mobil as the American Prometheus.

First, Prometheus symbolizes rebellion against superior and controlling power. This mythic character presented the gift of fire to human beings in direct defiance of Zeus, who was determined to deprive humans of its potential. According to legend, Prometheus himself was responsible for humans being shaped in a god-like manner, for them walking upright and looking audaciously toward the heavens instead of toward the earth, as did lower animals. Mobil captured this spirit of irreverence for tradition and of rebellion, created as part of a business sector that carried a low profile, Mobil was one of the first major companies to voice its opinion on public policy in public forums. Mobil came to be considered not only the most sophisticated voice of corporate dissent, but the loudest and most aggressive voice raised often in defiance of a federal Zeus (see "The corporate image," 1979). Embodying the Promethean spirit of rebellion, Mobil stands apart from the other energy Titans as the legitimate American Prometheus, as a unique corporate rhetor.

Such a view is furthered, both critically and mythologically, by the relationship between Mobil and the other giants of the oil industry. For example, on the mid-1975 proposal of precipitous decontrol of oil prices, Mobil played Prometheus to the other giants' enactment of Epimetheus. In Greek myth, Epimetheus, or "Afterthought," was one of the brothers of Prometheus, "Forethought." Epimetheus always acted quickly but unwisely, as in the story misnamed "Pandora's Box." Pandora, the first woman, was created by all the gods; her name translates as "gift of all" or "all gifts." The gods gave Pandora an ordinary jar, but forbade her to open it because it contained uncommon things (Hamilton, 1942, p. 88). In turn, the gods gave both Pandora and the jar to Epimetheus. Prometheus warned his brother not to accept gifts from Zeus, but Epimetheus acted characteristically: immediately, unthinkingly, and unwisely. He accepted the gifts just as Mobil's oil-producing brethren embraced the proposal to decontrol oil prices immediately. As Prometheus warned Epimetheus, so Mobil warned its brothers of the industry about the gift of decontrol and its probable consequences. Mobil stood apart from its after-thinking brothers and cautioned against a Pandora's jar of decontrolled prices. In contrast to the other oil companies, Mobil played the archetypal role of Prometheus.

The myth of Prometheus signifies more than kindliness toward human beings, rebellion in the face of power, and action based on forethought. The tale also deals with divine anger, the suppression of rebellion, and anticipatory reaction by superior forces. It is a tale both of what Prometheus did and what was done to him. In late 1975, Mobil-as-Prometheus existed in a situation that echoed the power of a federal Zeus. The perceived governmental constraints on this American "bringer of fire" completes the identification of Mobil as the contemporary Prometheus.

Low profits, government regulation, and the threat of oil company divestiture were all part of Mobil's world in 1975. In mythology, Zeus punished Prometheus for giving fire to humans by having him bound on craggy Mount Caucasus. For Mobil, iron chains were regulations forged by Congress rather than by Hephaestus, the divine and lame smith and architect. Mobil's ability to continue the Promethean role suffered anew with Congress's forging of yet another regulatory chain, the previously described Energy Policy and Conservation Act of December 1975. Finally, the threat of dismemberment, or divestiture, released new echoes of the original Prometheus. In mythology, Zeus knew that Prometheus was eternal. Immortality, though, did not preclude the suffering of torment. So the mighty Zeus sent a bloody eagle who fed as a vulture on Prometheus's liver. Because the liver renewed itself every day, there was always a ready piece of Prometheus to mutilate. In 1975, Mobil perceived media criticism as the attacks of a scavenger upon a bound, helpless oil industry. These attacks proved the industry's vulnerability and, according to the modern Prometheus, set a precedent for even more serious mutilation, this time by Zeus himself.

At the end of 1975, then, Mobil as the energy titan Prometheus surveyed its situation. Standing in defiance of the federal Zeus and apart from its oil-producing brethren, Mobil faced a dim profit picture, the continual chains of regulation, and the threat of dismemberment. In character as Prometheus, 1976 was a time for deliberate and thoughtful action. It was a time for a rhetorically oriented response to a mythological-like situation. It was a time for carefully calculated "Observations" that were as contemporary as the cartoon and as timeless as mythical appeal.

OBSERVATIONS ON THE SOCIAL INFLUENCE OF "OBSERVATIONS"

A complete and fair assessment of Mobil's "Observations" requires views through several different lenses, including those of effectiveness, ethics, and rhetorical art. Arguments about the effectiveness of even so seemingly simple, public rhetorical acts become the immediate charges of the *post hoc* fallacy. More difficult still is any proposed assessment of the effectiveness of one set of mass media messages that function as an integral part of a mass-mediated rhetorical campaign. In fact, there is no way to distill the impact of "Observations" from concomitant Mobil efforts, the efforts of other oil producers, and the socio-economic-political events that served as a frame for all of them. Yet, although it would be unjustified to argue the pure effect of Mobil's "Observations," it likewise would be irresponsible to ignore the evidence of Mobil's improved situation following four years of rhetorical efforts through the newspaper magazine. Three *signs of correspondence* are particularly significant.

First, the Promethean Mobil faced a very different situation by the early part of 1981 from that previously described. Christmas of 1975 had brought visions far removed from sugar plums: low profits, restraining legislation, and the threat of divestiture. New Year 1981 ushered in a much more pleasant and different scenario. The oil titans experienced a fourth quarter in 1980 that saw "a brisk improvement in earnings from last year. Or any other year, for that matter" ("Progress report," 1981). In fact, the earnings were about the same as the fourth quarter of 1979, but the 1980 figures included the moderating effects of the "windfall profits" tax ("Progress report," 1981). As positive as this aspect of the situation appeared, the general outlook was even more sanguine. The new year brought a new president, a man who completely ended what was left of the Nixon-imposed wage and price freeze on the energy industry. Within days of his inaugural, Ronald Reagan ended all remaining controls on the production and distribution of crude oil, gasoline, and propane and obliterated the program that subsidized small, independent producers. In 1981 and beyond, market prices would prevail (Hershey, 1981).

Second, 1981 brought record profits and the end of federal chains. In addition, the Reagan transition team was studying government regulations on the day that decontrol was announced; it also merited news coverage. Their 300-page report criticized "impediments to capital formation" (Gerth, 1981). Interestingly, five days later the FTC staff "backed away from the proposals" to break up the energy titans. This particular focus for the Securities and Exchange Commission's (SEC) enforcement power suddenly disappeared (Cowan, 1981). With it, the threat of corporate dismemberment no longer existed. The third of three major problems that faced Mobil in 1975 had ended. Prometheus was bound no longer.

While 1976 through 1980 brought changes in Mobil's scene, the period, happily for Mobil, was a time of somewhat wide public acceptance. The American Prometheus traditionally had wanted special acceptance by "the people." One of their chief spokespeople, Vice-President Schmertz, boasted in 1978 that an April 1976 Harris poll "Showed that Mobil, among the seven oil companies included in the survey, ranked highest in public perception as a company that had consumer interests in mind, is helping to improve the quality of life, is seriously concerned about the energy problem, is committed to free enterprise, is working for good government, and is honest and direct in talking to consumers" ("Industry fights back," p. 20). Later polls reveal that Mobil's enviable position vis-à-vis its oil-producing brethren remained (see discussion in Ross, 1976, p. 202). The issue here is not whether any of the oil companies' evaluations were terribly high; instead, the point is that given identical socio-economic-political stages, one corporate actor's role was comparatively more applauded or, at least, less the subject of attack. Ignoring absolute judgments, Mobil succeeded well in relation to other players.

A third and final corresponding sign of effectiveness is that through this period Mobil rose to unrivaled heights in its attempt to attract attention to itself and the issues in which it was interested. The agenda-setting power of the media is well documented (e.g., Donohue et al., 1972). Not so well documented, but firmly believed, is the public relations axiom that advantages accrue to a company that differentiates itself from "big business" generally and others in its industry specifically. Mobil's high-profile approach clearly seems related to concomitant forces pushing the energy issue to the fore; in addition, it succeeded in establishing Mobil as the principal voice of big oil. Other companies had seemed more content to remain in the background. All the while, the American Prometheus was able to solidify its identification with the role of leading advocate.

In sum, no grand claims can be made about the effectiveness of "Observations." What can be said is that, between the years of 1976 and 1980, profits rose to unparalleled levels, prices were decontrolled, and the threat of divestiture was quieted at least for a time; Mobil remained unchallenged as the predominant voice of the oil titans. Although these changed situations do not necessarily constitute proof of effectiveness, Mobil continues to spend millions of dollars on "Observations" and yet exhibits no obvious desire to announce the effectiveness of its advocacy efforts. Mobil is a rhetor not prone to boast effect. The best rationale for the situation seems to be that Mobil can do nothing but lose by heralding the effectiveness of its advocacy. Dramatic successes, if clearly documentable, almost certainly would bring cries of undue influence on the policy process and attempts for limiting opportunities for corporate advocacy. What exists is a situation in which a demonstration of effectiveness would be counterproductive.

Observations on Ethics and "Observations"

If the critical standard of "effect" prompts complex assessments, an ethical evaluation is even more complex. Analysis indicates only two cases of clear misstatement, both of which were corrected. "Observations" claimed that the sale of cabbage was governed by a 26,911-word regulation. Mobil later corrected this misstatement by acknowledging its error, but by adding that olive growth *was* governed by an 11,400-word regulation. While wrong in the specific instance, "Observations" asserted that it was correct in principle—that needless regulations were proliferating—and it gained the additional advantage of showing that it would admit error when presented with common sense reasons why it should. In the second case, Mobil claimed to have spent $1.19 for exploration and development for every dollar it earned. A concerned reader sent them a check for 19 cents to cover part of the loss. Because the statistics "confused several readers," "Observations" admitted that its apparent loss was offset by depreciation allowances that it used for investments (see FW, April 10, 1977, p. 8; FW, June 26, 1977, p. 14; FW, June 22, 1980, p. 6).

On the other hand, "Observations" never acknowledged the oil producers' abuse of regulation or social responsibility. It did not discuss Mobil's use of its earnings to purchase Montgomery Ward as well as to explore for and develop more energy. It reported that major oil producers were threatened with divestiture, but it neglected to note that these threats were based on alleged antitrust activity. In not one of its statements did Mobil acknowledge its *own* reliance on government regulations, regulations it wanted kept while the regulations controlling price and profits were labeled contrary to common sense. In essence, Mobil can be accused of telling only a carefully selected side of the story of oil, oil companies, and government. In addition, Mobil is open to charges of the deceitful use of statistics. For the middle American reader of "Observations," percentages, profit figures, and earning ratios became misted in an economic fog. Mobil showed the public a path through the fog, but the light was deceiving; there was more rhetorical intensity than light. Mobil's goal is obviously more profit-making than humanitarian in nature; the gift of fire to the people was not without its price.

Mobil's selection of what to say about what it chose to highlight, however, seems no more one-sided than similar selections by rhetoricians through the centuries. By historical standards, then, Mobil was simply a wise rhetor reacting to a particular sort of business situation. But Mobil did not claim to be "just another voice"; it claimed to be a true Promethean character, a rebel against unfair practices and an ennobler of the people. Mobil forced the application of a uniquely demanding ethical standard, one far above the standard of prevailing practice. And by its own choice of standards, the American Prometheus seems rather ungodly and typically susceptible to the profit-making motive.

"Observations" as Rhetorical Artistry

Not all judgments about the "art" of Mobil's "Observations" are as simple and straightforward as the judgments about effect and ethics are complex and involved. The Mobil Oil Corporation's choice of media and message for "Observations" shows it to be a rhetorical artist. Current students of corporate advocacy seem impelled to concentrate on the explicit messages of corporate advocacy: messages supplied by Mobil and others in the Op-Ed pages of large newspapers, full page newspaper ads, or paid ads in mass magazines. Yet in 1975 Mobil already had launched attacks against the media. Why was "Observations" begun? Why would a "down to earth" set of messages be aimed at Middle American readers of Sunday newspaper magazines? Though the creators of "Observations" may not have been conscious of the wisdom of their action, the wisdom existed, even if accidentally. The Sunday newspaper is part of the American way of life. The Sunday magazine section, whether *Parade, Family Weekly,* or local variations in larger newspapers, synthesizes the American consciousness: self-helps, travel features, cartoons, recipes, behind-the-scenes stories of the famous, and the exaltation of the (specially selected) "common person." In one sense, the Sunday magazine section is a directionless collage; in another sense, it is one of the best encapsulations of the American character and experience. Categories of traditional American values can be used as research categories for the analysis of the Sunday magazine section.

What then are "Observations" but an orchestrated set of appeals to the American value system? They are that, certainly; but these messages are also an important form of epideictic address. For other forms of corporate advocacy to function, they must be based upon strongly held values; the intensification of value acceptance is accomplished, not while the public is at work, but while the public relaxes on the sofa on a Sunday afternoon reading "the papers." Policymakers are addressed in suitably more sophisticated media, but they are placed in office by those on the sofa. Knowingly or unknowingly, "Observations" establishes the epideictic that allows the deliberative discourse of corporate advocacy to flourish.

Though Perelman's position on the epideictic provides a clue to the rhetorical artistry of "Observations," Toulmin's explication of warrant-establishing and warrant-using arguments rounds out the explanatory equation. Argumentatively, the direct corporate advocacy efforts by Mobil are warrant-using arguments. In order to function, these arguments require antecedent warrant-establishing arguments; many of these were provided by "Observations."

In sum, Mobil's "Observations" were the viewpoints of a self-proclaimed American hero, clad in the surprisingly appropriate garments of ancient myth. "Observations" were not polemical treatises artfully crafted for the discriminating reader of *The New York Times* editorial page. In a sense, the "appeal to common sense" may be an appeal to the mightiest American of all: the common person. The messages were short, casual, almost offhand, and yet they merged with the American value system. They seemed to provide ground for advocacy efforts that appear more lofty. So "Observations" should not be ignored. The universal appeal of the cartoon format, the identification with the famous people who are quoted (even if out of context), the "public interest" messages, the published views and suggestions of readers, the reports of favorable public opinion polls: indeed, all the available means of influence are used. More importantly, they are used in a medium uniquely suited to this collage of strategies. The newspaper magazine section surrounds the argumentation with a blanket of recipes, helpful hints, human interest stories, and special features. The magazine section, like Mobil Oil, is a part of America's Sunday afternoon.

NOTES

1. "Observations," "Family Weekly" (1976, July 11). Lafayette, Indiana *Journal and Courier*, p. 8. "Family Weekly" is a Sunday newspaper magazine that is purchased by various newspapers and newspaper chains across the country. "Observations" also appeared in the Sunday magazine sections of larger metropolitan newspapers. Materials for this study were drawn from the *Journal and Courier*'s "Family Weekly," from the *Atlanta Journal and Constitution*'s "Atlanta Journal and Constitution Magazine," and from "Atlanta Weekly," that magazine's successor. They will be abbreviated as FW, AJCM, and AW, respectively, in the remainder of the citations.

2. For a discussion, see *The New York Times*, August 26, 1975, editorial opinion, p. 30. Ultimately, the bill was passed by the House of Representatives on December 15, 1975, and by the Senate on December 17, 1975.

3. Mobil acknowledges that its Op-Ed and related corporate advocacy were designed to reach "opinion leaders," while "Observations" was intended to serve a less elite audience (see "Industry fights back," 1978).

4. The sample includes 43 columns from 1976, 35 columns from 1977, 26 columns from 1978, 26 columns from 1979, and 19 columns from 1980. The samples vary primarily because the appearance of "Observations" was irregular through these years.

5. Recall that Mobil was opposed to the precipitous decontrol of oil prices when its fellow titans quickly embraced this gift. Mobil's use of conservation as an argumentative topic reflects a conservative corporate policy that is premised on Promethean forethought.

4

The Engineering of Outrage

Mediated Constructions of Risk in the Alar Controversy

Jamie Press Lacey and John T. Llewellyn

For most of the American public, the Alar controversy began on February 26, 1989, when "60 Minutes" reporter Ed Bradley identified "a silent killer in their midst, perhaps right at their dinner table" (Smith, 1990, n.p.). Bradley's report contained testimony from scientific experts who warned that eating apples sprayed with daminozide, the chemical name for Uniroyal Chemical Company's Alar apple growth regulator, could lead to a heightened risk of cancer, especially in children. Smith, editorial writer for *The Washington Times,* described public reaction: "Washington's regulatory apparatus cranked up to prevent the looming baby slaughter. The apple industry turned to apple sauce as apple prices plummeted and sales fell off. Hysterical parents fretted over lunch box contents. . . . School administrators expelled the apple summarily. Taxpayers got stuck with the bill for apple leftovers" (p. 1).

In the wake of the broadcast, there were strong and informed dissents from the "60 Minutes" position. However, due to their timing and lack of dramatic elements, these pro-Alar views were either ignored or minimized. Messages from scientific experts who disputed the Alar-condemning study were lost "amid the talk shows and headlines trumpeting news about poisons in the vegetable patch" as the media urged parents to stop feeding produce to their children (Smith, 1990, p. 1).

This chapter examines how and why the Alar controversy unfolded as it did. The key elements in the outcome were an advocacy group's carefully crafted public relations campaign, the news media's patterns of attribution in covering stories of risk, and government agency and industry ineptitude in responding to public concerns.

THE ENGINEERING OF CONSENT: PUBLIC RELATONS AS ISSUE MANAGEMENT

Edward Bernays, the father of public relations, used the phrase, "the engineering of consent," to define the field. Bernays (1952) understood public relations as a vehicle for reconciling popular government and private economic interests. He saw that the profession was forever and essentially linked to public sentiment: "Any person or organization depends ultimately on public approval and is therefore faced with the problem of engineering the public's consent to a program or goal" (p. 159).

The imprint of Bernays's reasoning is clear in the Alar controversy. In this case, as in so many others, a public relations firm set out to engender public consent for its client's goals. The novelty here is that the firm took a very aggressive stance against the usual allies of public relations firms: established interests, including government agencies and private industry.

In October 1988, the Natural Resources Defense Council (NRDC), an environmental advocacy group, hired Fenton Communications to orchestrate a media campaign for its "Intolerable Risk: Pesticides in Our Children's Food" report. According to David Fenton (1989), his firm made arrangements for "60 Minutes" to break the story in late February. The segment on the NRDC Alar-condemning report aired before an audience of 40 million viewers.

One exposure of a favorable message, however successful, does not constitute a public relations campaign. Between February and September 1989, Fenton and the NRDC released numerous messages that identified Alar as a cancer-causing agent. Fenton (1989) explained, "Our goal was to create so many repetitions of NRDC's message that average American consumers . . . could not avoid hearing it—from many different media outlets within a short period of time" (p. A22).

Such a sustained public relations campaign is in actuality an attempt at issue management. Institutions or insurgent groups are constantly working to enflame or mollify public sentiment about some conditions in society. For example, Mothers Against Drunk Driving (MADD) campaigns to reduce public tolerance for drunken driving. In other words, MADD seeks to make an issue of or get the public to attach significance to long-standing patterns of behavior in the society (Crable and Vibbert, 1986, p. 64). In response to shifts in public sentiment, brewers begin advertising with a public service tone that emphasizes responsible drinking. MADD and the brewers are both attempting to manage the issue of drunk driving; MADD wants reduced public tolerance, increased enforcement, and stiffer penalties, while brewers want members of the public to reduce or eliminate their concerns about the use of alcoholic beverages or, failing that, to see problems as the result of the abuse of a legal product by a deviant individual.

Approaches to issue management vary in their aggressiveness. Crable and Vibbert (1985) have identified the most aggressive form of issue management as the catalytic approach. In this method, in contrast to more laissez-faire stances that advocate reactive, adaptive, or dynamic strategies, the organization actively "aims at prompting or making things happen" (p. 9). The NRDC/Fenton strategy is clearly catalytic; what is particularly unusual is that this public relations initiative was designed to have its effect not through conventional argument or persuasion, but through the inspiration of public outrage.

THE JOURNALISM OF OUTRAGE:
ENGINEERING VOX POPULI

The tradition of American journalism as a source for information and motivation for civic betterment is one of long standing. Coverage of the workings of government at all levels is undertaken for the avowed purpose of educating the electorate. Beyond this routine coverage, the press and its electronic compatriots have also as a prime motive the unmasking of corruption and ineptitude in government. The standard reasoning has held that these revelations catalyze citizen electoral action to restore the polity through what is known as the mobilization model (Protess et al., 1991, p. 15). This understanding of journalism and its impact undergirds the conventional explanations and justifications for many of the roles and behaviors undertaken by the media in contemporary America.

Protess and colleagues (1991) have challenged many of the assumptions of the mobilization model by carefully examining the connections between investigative reporting and agenda building. These authors borrow the phrase "the journalism of outrage" from Ettema and Glasser (p. 250) and then scrutinize its implications. In brief, these authors review six investigative probes and find that outrage as generated by investigative reporting is not always catalytic. Mobilization is most likely to happen, the investigators note, when journalists and policymakers have entered into an effective coalition early in the process (p. 250). Their studies seem to question the power of outrage as a product of journalistic investigation and a pathway to civic reform. They propose instead a coalition model in which journalist and policymaker are influential, especially when they cooperate and play to a receptive public audience (p. 251). These conclusions should temper but not dilute our examination of the Alar case—a case that brings together journalists, policymakers, and an intensely concerned public as they all examine some of the most volatile elements in American life and values, including children, cancer, investigative media, diet and health, pesticides and chemicals, big business, and government regulation.

THE ALAR CONTROVERSY
AND THE FAILURE TO RESPOND

The industry and government agencies accused in the "60 Minutes" broadcast were neither weak nor inexperienced in the ways of the news media and interest group campaigns. Nevertheless, these groups were clobbered in what was essentially a public relations battle for credibility. For all of their scientists and epidemiologists, these interests never mounted a successful response to the NRDC's charges. There seem to be several reasons for this failure: the groups lost control of defining the terms very early in the life of the controversy; that loss was compounded as they failed to grasp the role that public outrage was playing in the evolution of this issue; and, finally, growing public outrage put them in a double bind by requiring them to act against Alar (and thereby contradict earlier statements concerning its safety) or to refuse to act and seem doubly insensitive to public concern (the charge that the NRDC had leveled at them from the outset).

Question for Study

The question under study is, "How do competing rhetorical strategies presented by organizations and represented by the media shape public perceptions of risk during a major risk controversy?" We seek to answer this question by inspecting and assessing theories of organizational rhetoric (including those specific to a risk communication situation), analyzing the rhetorical thrusts and parries of multiple institutions (i.e., the EPA, a government representative, and the NRDC, an environmental activist group), and considering the media's role in a risk communication situation.

According to Llewellyn (1990), communication scholars need to establish how organizational rhetoric fits into a society. Rowan (1990) identifies a similar need for a sociological perspective in risk communication research. She calls for a rhetoric of risk communication in which emphasis is placed on the goals of risk communicators (e.g., establishing trust and motivating action).

Many previous studies concentrate on one corporate rhetor responding to a crisis (e.g., Benson, 1988; Foss, 1984; Seeger, 1986). The multiple-source approach used here is more appropriate to risk communication, however, because messages from several organizations compete to frame public perceptions of risk. For example, Gwin (1990) found that three parties—scientists, the federal government, and industry—engage in joint efforts to foster a set of values surrounding nuclear power that are known as "the nuclear ethic" (p. 73). An example of a multiple-source approach to the study of risk communication is found in Farrell and Goodnight's (1981) study of accidental rhetoric after the Three Mile Island incident. They believe that the only way to find answers to questions concerning risk exigencies is to examine the discourse of *all* involved actors. Our study observes the media's role in defining the Alar controversy. Smith (1990) described public reactions to media coverage of Alar, including school boards stopping the distribution of apples and parents pouring apple juice down drains. Due to its magnitude, the Alar case is prime ground on which to investigate the rhetorical processes entailed in the clash of powerful societal forces: the media, big business, government regulatory agencies, and activist groups.

Although Alar remained in the headlines for many months, the key issues surrounding the controversy were defined within the first few months after the "60 Minutes" episode. Therefore, in seeking answers to our research questions, we will analyze eleven newspaper articles that featured Alar as a risk issue and that appeared in *The Wall Street Journal* and *The New York Times* between February and September 1989.

The New York Times was selected for two reasons: it represents "the nearest thing the United States has to a 'national' newspaper in news orientation" (Balutis, 1976, p. 510), and it is the newspaper of choice in many academic studies (e.g., Balutis, 1976; Beniger and Westney,

1981; Charles, Shore, and Todd, 1979). *The Wall Street Journal* was also a natural selection for this study of business institutions' rhetoric because it is the leading U.S. business newspaper.

NEWS MEDIA COVERAGE OF RISK CONTROVERSIES: PROFOUNDLY INFLUENCING DEFINITIONS OF RISK

Criteria for valuable news include timeliness, consequence, prominence, rarity, proximity, conflict, change, action, concreteness, and personality (Wilkins and Patterson, 1987). In the quest for valuable news, reporters usually focus on discrete events rather than on underlying issues. This phenomenon, which Iyengar (1991) dubs "episodic news reporting," leads viewers and readers to make issue-specific attributions that "tend to shield society and government from responsibility" (p. 137).

For example, Wilkins and Patterson (1987) found three influential attribution patterns in media coverage of nuclear disasters:

1. *pseudo-novelty,* or presentation of the risk as being event-centered so that each risk episode seems new and independent;
2. *withheld linkages,* or failure to examine the social and technological systems surrounding the events; and
3. *incendiary language,* or reliance on provocative images in describing the situation so that the variety of interpretations is limited.

As the media cover risk controversies, they create a debate regarding whose perception of risk is "correct": the public's or the scientific experts' (Moore, 1989; Wilkins and Patterson, 1987). Moore points out that the standards of evidence for scientists are very different from the rules of publication for journalists. Consequently, the public often responds preemptively to mass fear elicited by news media accounts, without having the opportunity to understand the scientific aspects of the risk issue.

Looking specifically at the Alar case, Friedman and associates (1991) concluded that coverage of the controversy relied on event-oriented reporting, few sources, government and establishment views, wire service sources, and short articles with little depth: "Reporters appear to have chosen to cover the conflict itself instead of the science behind the conflict. This does nothing to help readers get a rational and objective view of an important health and political story" (p. 40).

So, while news reports framed Alar in the public mind as a stand-alone problem, the parties in the Alar controversy worked to provide the media and the public with persuasive definitions of both "risk" in general and the nature of the problem at hand. Defining the concept of "risk" is a complex issue for researchers of risk communication because, as Sandman (1987) explains, scientists see risk as hazard or "expected annual mortality," while the public's definition of risk includes additional factors, such as control, voluntariness, and familiarity. Sandman offers a complete definition of risk that is a combination of hazard plus factors contributing to public outrage. At its heart, the Alar dispute is a disagreement about which definition of risk should dominate.

With regard to Alar, the Environmental Protection Agency (EPA, the Agency) equated risk solely with the concept of "hazard" (e.g., carcinogenicity or exposure levels). This definition lacked a key ingredient: audience sentiment. Once the NRDC succeeded in getting its definition of risk in place, the EPA was required to work within that meaning. The EPA never grasped this reality or overcame its implications.

Redefinition, a strategy that often accompanies definition, is the use of symbolic transformation or transcendence to alter perception of a situation and its key terms (Olson, 1989). In the Alar controversy, actors attempted to redefine "risk," the nature of the problem, and other concepts whose meanings were vital to the situation.

Because the NRDC laid the groundwork for this controversy and reinforced its views through multiple and dramatic media appearances, its definitions tended to have more staying power in the minds of the American public. If one group accuses another of negligent behavior with potentially deadly consequences for children, those accused appear indecisive and coldhearted when they respond by attempting to reframe the situation. Such emotional charges must be answered at the same level of emotional intensity. Thus, by attempting redefinition and ignoring public outrage, the defendant institutions decreased their legitimacy and credibility with the public.

Media Coverage: Insurgency Strategies

To build intensity and legitimize its assertions, the NRDC used strategies previously identified by scholars of rhetoric and social movements. The NRDC's press releases included examples of Stewart's (1988) positive legitimation strategies, Alinsky's (1971) tactics for powerless groups to use against those with power, Murphy and Dee's (1991) zero-sum model, and Berg's (1972) prediction of outgroup reliance on emotion-evoking actions.

Stewart (1988) distinguishes between positive legitimation strategies (e.g., aligning with traditions, establishing actions as those of a legitimate organization, and appealing to the common good) and negative legitimation strategies (e.g., nonviolent protesting and militant confronting). The NRDC artifacts that we examined contained both types of strategies.

Finally, Berg (1972) claims that groups challenging societal norms must often rely on emotion-evoking actions to gain the attention of the media. First, to evoke the emotions of the American public, the NRDC alleged that defenseless children were endangered by pesticide residues in foods. Second, to appeal to parents and capture media recognition, the group used vivid language and accused government and business of neglecting the safety of children: "America's preschoolers are being exposed to dangerous levels of toxic pesticides in fruits and vegetables which can cause cancer, neurological damage, and other health problems" (Allen, 1989b, p. 1). Third, the NRDC designed the titles of its press releases to invoke media attention. The headline "NRDC Report Showing Children at Risk from Pesticides: Massive Public Health Problem Ignored by Federal Agencies" (Allen, 1989a, p. 1), for example, incorporates each element of the media's crisis attribution pattern: pseudo-novelty, withheld linkages, and incendiary language.

Public risk perceptions were also framed by the NRDC's use of the "ist"-like accusation that the institutions knew that certain chemicals caused cancer yet refused to remove them from the market. According to Wood and Pearce (1980), "-ist" accusations (e.g., "racist") are particularly difficult to deny because they create a self-reflexive paradox. The opponent is accused of both membership in one disparaged subgroup and also of thinking and/or acting in terms of the "-ist" class of subgroups. Thus, when the NRDC identified the EPA as negligent, the Agency became at the most a contributor to the spread of disease (perhaps a "cancerist," although no such term was ever used). At the least, the EPA appeared to be a regulatory body that knew children were being endangered, but failed to do anything about it. Furthermore, in an effort to deny both levels of the NRDC's charges, the EPA had to defend both Alar and the universe of chemical regulations. In other words, the EPA had to claim that Alar did not harm children and that no other chemicals harmed children either.

"60 Minutes": A Special Forum. The news of "60 Minutes" is cultural performance, similar to storytelling or mythology. According to Campbell (1991), "'60 Minutes' has redirected the structure of television news programs away from the appearance of facticity—describing and listing information in neutral reports—and toward the narrative intrigues of character, setting, plot, and conflict" (p. 29). He describes the show's mystery formula in which reporters identify a crime and distinguish among victims, villains, and bystanders. Campbell notes that the "60 Minutes" reporter is more concerned with assignment of guilt (a novel, nonsystemic, and intense guilt) than with punishment of the criminal or even solution of the problem identified.

The "60 Minutes" reporter mediates conflicts by either siding with one party or interposing a third party that places the viewers between the victim (e.g., an individual) and the villain (e.g., an institution). According to Campbell, "'60 Minutes' constructs a largely Middle-American mythology . . . that celebrates the dignity of the *self* in the face of bullying bureaucracy and sinister *others*" (p. 137).

Analysis of the "60 Minutes" segment "A is for Apple" confirmed the program's use of the mystery formula. The victims were obviously young children, while the villains were personified organizations (e.g., Uniroyal and the EPA) and chemicals (specifically, Alar and its breakdown product, UDMH). The heroes within this narrative were the NRDC's senior attorney, Janet Hathaway, and Congressman Jerry Sikorsky. The plot centered around the NRDC's accusations that the EPA knew that certain chemicals caused cancer yet failed to remove them from the market. Additionally, the plot contained two conflicts: (1) Uniroyal versus the EPA (industry versus government), and (2) the NRDC versus Uniroyal and the EPA (activist group versus institutions).

A major function of "60 Minutes'" mystery formula is to display "heroic reporters straddling tensions between individual and institution, safety and danger, honesty and injustice" (Campbell, 1991, p. 63). Analysis of each speaker in the segment showed that reporter Ed Bradley made the most references to risk and served as the anchor for reality and morality as he challenged institutional actions.

Interestingly, the EPA referred to risk with the second greatest frequency, but most often in the context of refutations. The necessity of denial made the EPA participate on the NRDC's terms, even while seeking to refute the charges. Consider an example of this convoluted risk talk. During the segment, Bradley asked the EPA's acting deputy administrator, Dr. John Moore, if the agency had authority under law to remove unacceptable risks from the marketplace. Moore replied, "In rare instances you might have a risk that is so provocative that you do not want to allow this chemical to stay on—in use during the period of the cancellation process" (CBS News, 1989, p. 13). Bradley stepped outside of his "objective" role to identify the potential cancer risk to children, and Moore was forced to defend his agency by denying Bradley's claims in Bradley's terms. For the American public and the institutions involved in the controversy, the narrative context catalyzed by the NRDC and articulated by "60 Minutes" and Bradley defined the terms and actors for a sophisticated media campaign that would redefine public risk perception with regard to food safety.

INSTITUTIONAL DEFENSE: REFUTING
CLAIMS IN A RISK CONTROVERSY

To explain organizational response to a risk controversy, we examined the rhetorical actions of the EPA as a representative institution involved in the Alar food scare. One perspective is particularly helpful in explaining institutional actions—Kenneth Burke's notion of *occupational psychosis.*

According to Foss, Foss, and Trapp (1985, p. 176), occupational psychosis is a state of mind caused by one's occupation or a certain way of living. When we develop a particular perspective on life, it creates a framework for seeing, which Burke calls a "terministic screen" (Burke, 1966, pp. 44–55). The language we employ, according to Burke, directs our attention to certain aspects of reality rather than others. For example, as a government agency charged with using scientific data to compute risk factors, the EPA's highly trained experts practice a profession that leads them to define risk as high or low based on purely scientific standards. In contrast, members of the public think as ordinary citizens rather than as scientists and have adopted perspectives that lead them to consider risk in terms of the capacity for harm to themselves and their families. Therefore, a procedure that seems rational to EPA representatives in the business of risk assessment can easily appear uncaring and thoughtless to individual citizens who fear for the safety of their children.

Organizations that face challenges to their legitimacy (such as the EPA in the Alar case) can adapt to the prevailing definition of legitimacy, use communication to change the prevailing definition of legitimacy, or attempt to align with legitimate symbols or persons (Dowling and Pfeffer, 1975). The EPA aligned itself with legitimate symbols, individuals, and institutions, but also adhered to Dowling and Pfeffer's first strategy by adapting its practices to conform to prevailing definitions of legitimacy. For example, under mounting public pressure the Agency canceled food uses of Alar and, eventually, worked to remove the product from the market. As a result of the Agency's reversal, the public, while pleased at this action, could still infer that some of the EPA's earlier practices might have been illegitimate. This inference is one costly result of adapting to public sentiment after a crisis has begun.

Because the NRDC accused the EPA of failing to act in a socially responsible manner, the Agency attempted to establish counterarguments in support of its safeguarding of the public. The EPA followed four of the commandments of corporate social responsibility:

I.   Thou shall take corrective action before it is required.
II. Thou shall work with affected constituents to resolve mutual problems.
III. Thou shall work to establish industrywide standards and self-regulation.
IV. Thou shall publicly admit your mistakes (Alexander and Matthews, 1984, pp. 63–64).

By announcing its intent to proceed with canceling Alar on February 1, three weeks before the NRDC released its report, the Agency took corrective action before it was required. It worked with Uniroyal, the alleged carcinogen's producer and a mutually affected constituent, to cancel food uses of Alar. The Agency also advocated improvements in food safety. For example, it offered more accurate monitoring data on pesticide residues in foods that would help improve industry standards and promote self-regulation. Finally, the EPA admitted that its Scientific Advisory Panel had failed to conclude in 1984 that regulatory action against daminozide was necessary, although later EPA studies had deemed Alar as potentially cancer causing. Although the EPA followed to the letter these four commandments of social responsibility, these actions or admissions were not sufficient to stem the tide of public outrage engineered by the NRDC.

The EPA and other accused institutions were also obliged to respond to the NRDC's "ist"-like accusation that they were "producers of cancer in children" because of faulty regulations. In response to the accusation, the EPA identified itself as a scientific authority. From this vantage point, the EPA both condemned the NRDC's scientific report and explained its own scientific policies. In a criticism of the NRDC report, for example, Moore said, "[the NRDC's] practice of using data rejected by scientific peer review, coupled with food consumption data of unproven validity to calculate 'risk estimates,' is misleading," (CBS News, 1989).

Furthermore, Moore explains that the EPA's stated policy regarding cancer is that lifetime dietary risks should be no greater than one cancer per million persons exposed. The Agency's messages implied, "Although Alar may lead to some incidence of cancer, the NRDC's estimations of its degree of risk are based on faulty science. And science is the transcendent principle upon which we base our role as protector of the public's health" (CBS News, 1989).

MEDIA BEHAVIOR AND LANGUAGE USE: NURTURING OUTRAGE IN THE NEWS

More than half of the newspaper articles analyzed contained all three attribution patterns—pseudo-novelty, withheld linkages, and incendiary language—identified by Wilkins and Patterson (1987). Only one article out of eleven was free of the patterns. The media displayed these patterns in its coverage of the controversy, allowing the public to (1) perceive Alar as a chemical that was uniquely risky (pseudo-novelty), (2) fail to understand the complexities of the regulatory system in which the use of Alar was embedded (withheld linkages), and (3) perceive Alar as a cancer-causing agent for children (incendiary language). Through reliance on these attribution patterns, the media actually reported the negative *potentialities* of risk rather than the risk itself, but the distinction was lost in the public furor over Alar.

A *New York Times* article that appeared on February 25, 1989, provides a sense of the role of attribution patterns in the Alar controversy. Entitled "Pesticides Termed High Cancer Risk for Children," the article contained pseudo-novelty, withheld linkages, and incendiary

language. First, the article disregarded previous authoritative information about chemicals and food safety as it played on the pseudo-novelty
of the NRDC's claims that Alar and other chemicals were dangerous to
young children. Second, the article contained no explanation of the
U.S. pesticide regulatory system or its manner of evaluating risk, thus
providing no links between this story and broader food safety issues.
Finally, the article contained incendiary language, as in the following
excerpt: "An environmental group contends in a news report that
preschool children are *consuming chemicals* in fruits and vegetables at
levels that expose them to *a risk of cancer many times greater than the
Government considers safe*" ("Pesticides termed," 1989, p. 130, emphasis added).

We also found evidence of misleading attribution patterns in *The
Wall Street Journal*'s coverage of the Alar controversy. In one article,
for instance, Rosewicz (1989a) reported that the notion of risk had
developed out of the first study to focus on pesticide residues in the
foods children eat (pseudo-novelty), failed to provide an analysis of
the social system in which the chemical was used and produced (withheld linkages), and relied on the information that "children can face
cancer risks hundreds of times greater than the EPA considers safe"
(incendiary language) (p. B3).

The predominant provocative image throughout media reports is one
of preschool children being exposed to enormous cancer risk. Thus, the
"unnecessary threat" to children became the central message about
Alar. Although journalists espouse objective standards (Condit and
Selzer, 1985), attribution patterns employed in the coverage of risk
controversies nullify media claims of objectivity.

Headlines and Beyond

In the seven-month period between February and September 1989,
the headlines and the type and amount of coverage that The New York
Times and *The Wall Street Journal* gave to the controversy combined
with attribution patterns to create a context for the public's perceptions
of risk. When the headlines from each newspaper are arranged in
chronological order, they reveal two divergent narratives about this
risk incident. Headlines in *The New York Times* feature neutral language used to describe the events as they occurred, while the headlines
in *The Wall Street Journal* report and evaluate the actions of the
involved organizations.

On February 25, 1989, *The New York Times* announced, "Pesticides Termed High Risk for Children" (1989, p. I30). From March until mid-May, *The New York Times* featured the governmental agencies' and apple growers' indignant responses in headlines: "3 U.S. Agencies, to Allay Public's Fears, Declare Apples Safe" (Shabecoff, 1989a, p. A16), and "Fruit Growers Pull Commercials to Protest Report by CBS on Alar" (1989, p. I36). In contrast, the two stories that appeared in mid-May reported acts of institutional compliance as the government began its ban on Alar and growers agreed to stop using the chemical: "Steps to Ban Alar Announced" (1989, p. I24), and "Apple Industry Says It Will End Use of Chemical" (Shabecoff, 1989b, p. A1).

The five *New York Times* headlines traced major events in the controversy. *The Wall Street Journal,* meanwhile, printed articles that evaluated the controversy as well as articles that focused on action. First, on February 27, the paper announced, "Group Maintains Rules on Pesticides Endanger Children" (Rosewicz, 1989a, p. B3). Throughout March, *Journal* reporters evaluated NRDC's charges and the public panic that ensued with headlines such as "Killer Apples" (p. A16), "Pesticide Risk from Apples: Who's Right?" (Rosewicz, 1989b, p. B1), and "Fruit Frights" (1989, p. A14). In May, the *Journal* resumed straight coverage of action with a front-page blurb indicating that apple growers would stop using Alar by September 1989 ("Apple growers asserted," 1989). Finally, in September, the newspaper reported, "EPA Moving to Phase Out Sales of Alar-Treated Food" (1989, p. C9).

Coverage and headlines in *The New York Times* and *The Wall Street Journal* indicate consistent behavior on the part of each newspaper. *The New York Times* objectively labeled the actions within the controversy in its headlines and gave all actors balanced coverage by including an average of five agency, five industry, and four activist quotations and/or references per article. In contrast, *The Wall Street Journal* provided no such balance in either its headlines or its use of sources. For example, the paper provided an average of 3 agency, 2.7 activist, and only 1 industry quotation and/or reference per article. The *Journal,* then, identified the conflict as one between environmentalists and the federal government, downplaying industry's involvement. These actions confirm Deetz's (1992) findings that the news media monitor government actions more closely than they do business actions. Deetz claims that when either social irresponsibility or illegal conduct is identified, "the government is faulted for insufficient surveillance or action" (p. 35). Thus, the *Journal's* reports may be part of a larger world view in which the media and its consumers hold the government and corporations to different sets of standards.

Word Choice By charting the presence of metaphors, ultimate terms, and code words used by the NRDC, the EPA, *The New York Times,* and *The Wall Street Journal,* we also analyzed the role of language use in a risk controversy. While both the NRDC and the EPA were heavy users of metaphor (the NRDC averaged 7 and the EPA averaged 5), an average *New York Times* article on Alar contained only 2 metaphors and an average *Wall Street Journal* article contained 4.5. The metaphors used by the institution, the activist group, and the newspapers reveal how these players viewed this risk issue and how they attempted to frame public risk perceptions.

First, the EPA relied on metaphors related to above/below, theater, and growth. In a joint release issued by the USDA, the EPA, and the FDA (Young, Moore, and Bode, 1989), for example, the controversy was depicted in theatrical terms. The agencies claimed that the use of Alar "has decreased *dramatically,*" that they have "*acted* in the past" to ensure food safety, and that they will continue to expose "pesticide uses which *pose* a cancer risk" (pp. 2–3, emphasis added). Theatrical images imply a view of the controversy as a drama in which each actor plays a part. The agencies, evidently, saw themselves fulfilling the roles of protector and regulator.

As the heaviest user of metaphors, the NRDC filled its messages with images of death, above/below, protection, structure, mechanics, and the human body. By using mechanistic images, the NRDC sought to create enthusiasm for its Mothers and Others For Pesticide Limits Committee in the release "NRDC *Launches* a National Campaign to Protect Children" (Allen, 1989c, emphasis added). The activist group reflected its view of the Committee as an alchemist. The release explained that the Committee would be "*working* to call attention to the problem" of pesticides, would serve as a "*catalyst*" for important societal changes, and would enable concerned citizens to "turn . . . *anger* into action" (pp. 1, 3, emphasis added).

Finally, based on claims of objectivity in news reporting, one would expect little use of metaphor by either of the major newspapers. Therefore, it is not surprising that *The New York Times* articles contained an average of only two metaphoric images. However, just as *The Wall Street Journal* went beyond the boundaries of objective standards in its coverage and headlines, its articles contained an average of 4.5

metaphoric images per story, metaphors created most often by its reporters. The most interesting metaphors appeared in the articles that evaluated the controversy, as opposed to those that reported action. For example, "Fruit Frights" (1989) contained at least 10 metaphors likening the controversy to a medieval horror story. The following editorial excerpt is particularly illustrative: "The witchcraft tales have been drummed into the American psyche these last 20 years, principally by environmental groups *flogging* issue after issue as *threatening* America with an *apocalypse* of cancer and disease" ("Fruit frights," 1989, p. A14, emphasis added). The author goes on to say that "public officials, forced to live in the *werewolf world* of health risks" must stand up to the "*howling* of activist groups, politicians, and melodramatic TV reporters" (p. A14, emphasis added). Readers of the *Journal* editorial may have envisioned the controversy as a modern-day thriller with activist monsters and institutional victims.

To further investigate language styles, we used Hart's (1990) treatments of ultimate terms and code words. In this study, "ultimate terms" were those words with intensified meaning in a risk controversy (e.g., cancer, preschoolers). "Code words," on the other hand, referred to jargon and euphemisms used by the actors (e.g., carcinogenicity, exposure levels, surplus agricultural commodities). Not surprisingly, the NRDC used the most ultimate terms (averaging nineteen per artifact) and the fewest code words (averaging four per artifact) as it sought to attract media and public interest.

Ultimate terms used by the NRDC centered on patriotism, evil, and family. In the category of patriotism, the NRDC used words like "national," "American," "government," and "citizens" to appeal to American traditions of protest and unity against the enemy. These terms reflected a view of the controversy as a battle without using specific war-related terms. Through fear appeals, the NRDC's adjectives connoted evil or wrongdoing—e.g., "dangerous," "toxic," "cancer-causing," "carcinogenic," "life-threatening," and "hazardous." Family words included "parents," "children," "toddlers," "preschoolers," and "infants." These terms played on parental fear and evoked images of helpless young victims.

Comparatively, the EPA and other institutions involved in the controversy relied on ultimate terms much less often than did the activists. The categories of terms they used included patriotism, institutional responsibility, and safety. Patriotic terms, including "Americans," "the nation," and "American farmers" were coupled with terms that evoked institutional responsibility, including "vigilance," "truth/trust," "government regulations," "authority," and "faith," to represent the role of institutions as protectors of public welfare. Safety terms—"safe," "tolerable," "allowable," and "negligible"—functioned to negate accusations of risk.

The words that each spokesperson employed to describe the controversy reflected underlying world views and, ultimately, affected coverage and public perception. Both newspapers used many ultimate terms and few code words; their word choice was more similar to the NRDC's than to the EPA's. *The New York Times* articles contained an average of ten ultimate terms and two code words, while *The Wall Street Journal* articles contained eight ultimate terms and one code word. Because EPA spokespersons saw the dispute through the lens of occupational psychosis, they relied on a bland, scientific language style unlikely to appeal to readers. Average readers could relate more easily to terms the NRDC used, such as "risk," "cancers," and "disease," than to institutional terms, such as "carcinogenicity," "consumption figures," and "exposure levels." As a result, the activist group may have established a degree of perceived similarity between itself and readers, while the institutions probably created a gap that intensified public distrust.

PUBLIC REACTION: OPINION AND ACTION

According to Buxton (1989), a United States Department of Agriculture (USDA) economist, media coverage about Alar and apples initially affected sales of the fruit. Apple shipments dropped 16 percent below those of the previous year following the first wave of reports. However, two years after the crisis, Buxton asserted that sales had revived. He claimed that, although shipments dropped from March until June 1989, they resumed normal pace and continue to improve (Marshall, 1991).

Nevertheless, two consumer surveys conducted after the controversy found that the Alar crisis affected public opinion of the broader issue of food safety and pesticide use. First, in a Michigan food-safety study conducted in March 1990, when 600 consumers were asked if they thought Alar had weakened confidence in Michigan apples or other food products, approximately 30 percent answered, "Yes" (Lawler, 1990). Because another 66 percent said, "No," however, we conclude that the long-term effects of the Alar controversy have softened, at least with regard to food safety. Second, a 1991 study conducted by the

Center for Produce Quality polled 1,029 adults to learn how public attitudes have changed since the Alar crisis. The Center's survey showed that 92 percent of the public believes that health benefits of fresh produce far outweigh the risks from possible pesticide residues. Nevertheless, 70 percent of those polled want farmers to further limit use of pesticides and agree that current pesticide regulations "do not sufficiently take into account the risk that pesticides may pose to children," an argument reminiscent of the Alar controversy (Means and McClung, 1991, pp. 2–3).

OBSERVATIONS ON THE ENGINEERING OF OUTRAGE: CONCLUSIONS AND RECOMMENDATIONS

Five years after the initial "60 Minutes" segment on Alar, media reports continue to focus on the potential dangers of pesticide residues in the foods children eat. For example, on March 30, 1993, PBS aired an hour-long "Frontline" episode that criticized the government's pesticide regulatory system. The program concluded that Americans are still unsure of the potential consequences of pesticide residues in the foods they eat. The Alar controversy did not resolve the dispute about what are acceptable levels of exposure for children and may have only added to public distrust of institutional claims.

After examining news releases, press accounts, and the "60 Minutes" transcript, we have identified two stages in framing public perception of risk. These stages represent critical junctures for influence in a public controversy. The outcome of the dispute may well hinge on which party—the insurgent, change-oriented group or the institutional defender of the status quo—succeeds in defining the roles for characters in the risk controversy (step one) and developing standards for judging the risk event (step two).

Defining Roles for the Controversy's Characters

When an insurgent group seeks to create a risk controversy, its first goal is to define roles for the controversy's leading characters. Institutional groups rarely use this technique because they are already favored in the reigning definitions. The critical skill for defenders of the status quo is to take seriously the early rumblings from insurgent groups. Groups that cannot imagine that they can be overthrown are on the road to just that result. The best response that late-starting institutional forces can muster is often an attempt at redefinition, but this is more difficult when the opponent has the momentum.

An efficient way for the insurgent group to identify victims, villains, and heroes to a national audience is to "sell" its story to a television news/entertainment show. Programs like "60 Minutes" are ideal vehicles for "breaking" risk stories because they contain narrative elements, including conflict and characters, and because they reach mass audiences. In one broadcast, news magazine programs can define the roles of all major players for a large portion of the American public. Additionally, their story lines frequently feature ritual scapegoating of institutions, and their viewers readily accept the anti-institutional "facts" that reporters provide.

As "60 Minutes" and similar programs define guilty parties, attribution patterns come into play. When reporters present each risk as novel, fail to make systemic links, and use incendiary language, audience members often become more concerned with specifying perpetrators than with eliminating the identified risk. Thus, by choosing a television news magazine as a vehicle, activist groups place institutions on the defensive—the accused organizations must attempt to remove the label of villain and reestablish their legitimacy.

Developing Standards for Judging the Risk Event

The second goal for an activist group interested in creating a risk controversy is to develop a set of standards for judging the risk; these standards are integral to the narrative and will be publicized by the media in hopes that they will be accepted by the public. To accomplish this goal, the group must expand the argumentative realm from purely rational to a rational-emotive argument. An activist group can be successful in using emotive arguments to promote its standards for judging risk; institutions often fail to get their views accepted because they remain loyal to their rational scientific standards.

Because media reports of risk controversies tend to contain attribution patterns favorable to activist interests, arguments based on pathos (emotion) are more compelling than institutional arguments grounded in logos (reason). The NRDC relied on fear appeals and dramatic celebrity quotations to capture media attention and to convince the public that each individual should fear risks associated with Alar. The quantity of coverage the NRDC received from multiple sources over a long duration (e.g., appearances on "Donahue," "The

Today Show," and "Crossfire"; seven months of newspaper coverage) indicates that the Council effectively called media attention to its cause and that the EPA and others were ineffective in defending their position.

With the aid of attribution patterns, the NRDC successfully developed emotively grounded standards for judging risk. We found that the public perceived Alar as a uniquely risky chemical that caused cancer in children and viewed government and industry as negligent. The unnecessary threat to children, clearly an emotive image, was the central message in media reports about the chemical and its risk throughout the controversy's duration. The NRDC's emotive arguments triggered a decline in apple sales and an increase in demands for organic produce (Hathaway, 1990).

When institutions attempt to counter pathos-based reports of unnecessary risks, they are hindered by the attribution patterns of incendiary language and withheld linkages. First, the scientistic, code word–ridden language of institutions fails to capture media attention because it cannot match the dramatic power of the prevalence of ultimate terms and incendiary language in media coverage. Additionally, as individuals make judgments about risks, Douglas (1985) claims that they ask two questions of the institutions involved: Do promises match performance, and is there logic behind institutional decision making? To answer the second question, individuals search for either rules that contradict each other or a coherent rule system. Because the media attribution patterns do not present the systemic links used in regulating chemicals, however, the public cannot evaluate the rule system in which the alleged risk is imbedded. Thus, institutions must defend themselves against *each* unnecessary risk accusation *separately* and without a systemic context.

In contrast, emotive arguments from insurgent groups and media attribution patterns allow activists to create a favorable rhetorical superstructure for judging risk. This superstructure shapes the "court of public opinion" so that any inconsistency in institutional actions is taken as negligence or proof of guilt. In this court, the definition of "risk" becomes the core issue. Once that battle is won, guilt allocation can proceed. For instance, in the Alar controversy, the EPA equated risk with hazard (e.g., cancer rates) and *failed to include any measure of public outrage in its definition.* By omitting any sensitivity to public outrage from its understanding of the issues, the Agency was unable to successfully manage the controversy—for one cannot hope to control a factor that one fails to take into account, especially an emotive, nonrational one. When turbulence exists or insurgents foment it, pathos and public outrage must always be factored into institutional attempts to reestablish legitimacy and gain control of controversies.

The Aftermath

On September 5, 1989, *The Wall Street Journal* reported that the EPA would phase out sales of Alar-treated food by 1991 ("EPA moving," 1989, p. C9). Uniroyal had halted sales of the product in June 1989. From a short-term perspective, it would appear that the NRDC had won the battle over public perception of Alar-related risk. However, the incident left unanswered the question: "Were foods any safer for children?"

Our study asked the question, "How do competing rhetorical strategies presented by organizations and represented by the media frame the public's perception of risk during a major risk controversy?" Institutions have inherent advantages in the realms of power and influence, but those assets can be made liabilities when opponents charge that those advantages were used against the public interest.

When activists seek to create risk controversies, they maintain advantages in the struggle for shaping the public perception of risk. First, activist groups may launch the controversy as the NRDC did here and, therefore, have a head start in defining character roles and in setting standards for judging both the risk and its actors. Furthermore, activist groups use emotive rhetorical tactics that mesh with the media's attribution patterns and effectively capture public interest in their cause.

If future risk controversies are to be resolved on a more balanced field, institutions must recognize the need to consider public outrage in their definitions of risk and go beyond logical, scientific language use and arguments in their efforts to minimize the effects of emotion-laden descriptions of risk events. Data suggest that the Alar controversy did no harm to apple sales in the long run; however, what is endangered every time such a controversy arises is the process of communal sense making that is essential to society.

For now, risk controversies seem like baseball games in which activists capture the adoration of the fans and establish their credibility. Institutions, meanwhile, remain in the outfield logically calculating the distance of each hit while the activists are rounding the bases. Until institutions grasp the necessity of speaking to the public's heart as well as its head, when risk controversies arise, the public will remain poised to readily believe that its safety has been jeopardized by institutional negligence.

5

"I Am a Scientologist"

The Image Management of Identity

Jeffrey L. Courtright

The business world has recently devoted much attention to the importance of a good public relations "image." Business and trade periodicals
recommend changes in logo or corporate name, office appearance, and
clearer communication of organizational goals and objectives to handle
image problems (e.g., Burns, 1992; Cobb, 1990; Croft, 1989; Franzoni,
1991; Marken, 1990; Napoles, 1988). A closer look at the concept of
"image" indicates that such recommendations treat the symptoms of
image problems with a public relations bandage. True, images may be
related to these observable features of business operations (and many
others—see Marken, 1990; Sobol, Farrelly, and Taper, 1992), but the
presentation of image must focus also on the intangible aspects of
images, fleeting and ephemeral perceptions of publics. Thus, image is
a projection of corporate identity and a reflection of public opinion, a
complex of cognitive interpretations that members of key publics hold
of an organization (Alvesson, 1990; Cheney and Vibbert, 1987; Dutton
and Dukerich, 1991; Grunig, 1993; Treadwell and Harrison, 1994).

The difficult duality of organizational image may be more critical
for nonprofit organizations (NPOs). Social agencies sell "intangibles"
(Cutlip, Center, and Broom, 1985); therefore consumer response to
their "products" is as hard to measure as their images. Indeed, the
organization and the service it offers become fused in the minds of
publics: "Churches and other religious and charitable organizations
depend on positive public images for their very lives" (Baskin and

Aronoff, 1992, p. 386). The study of religious organizations and their rhetoric therefore may provide an ideal entrée to the study of how organizations manage public image.

The purpose of this chapter, then, is to employ a rhetorical approach as a method to understand organizational image management. In particular, this chapter analyzes an image campaign that the Church of Scientology International (CSI) presented in full-page advertisements in *USA Today* during the summer of 1991. The analysis illustrates the value of Kenneth Burke's "cluster-agon" methodology to the study of organizational images. The analysis of CSI's advertisements yields what Burke calls an epic "frame of acceptance." The chapter concludes with a discussion of advantages and disadvantages of CSI's rhetorical choices with respect to various publics, as well as implications this study holds for the study of organizational images in general.

The Advertisements: Response to a Public Relations Situation

On May 6, 1991, *Time* magazine printed Richard Behar's "The Thriving Cult of Greed and Power," an eight-page exposé of the CSI (Behar, 1991). CSI responded with a counterattack on *Time's* credibility as a news source. Quickly, CSI contracted with *USA Today* to place advertisements to tell its side of the story. Full-page ads began May 28. Two weeks of attack culminated in a twenty-eight–page glossy insert, "The Story *Time* Couldn't Tell" (Buckley, 1991; Church of Scientology International [CSI], 1991a, 1991b).

CSI had stumbled onto the ideal vehicle to purify its image. From mid-June to early August, CSI would present its corporate image through advertisements devoted to Scientology's founder, L. Ron Hubbard, its literature, its doctrines, and its followers. The last of these concluded the series with nine advertisements of testimonials from believers, entitled, "I Am a Scientologist."

BURKE'S "CLUSTER-AGON" METHOD AND THE ANALYSIS OF IMAGE

According to Crable (1986, 1990), contemporary rhetoric has returned to a focus on the speaker. The focus is not on the classical "good man speaking well," but on organizations and their corporate representatives (see also Cheney, 1991). Briefly stated, Crable (1986) argues that organizations employ multiple messages and media to address multiple publics. Organizational rhetors "represent a constituency" (p. 62) and address publics with the goal of securing support for products and issue positions (see also Gregory, 1991; Sobol et al., 1992).

Any study of contemporary organizational rhetoric therefore transforms Aristotelian concerns for a speaker's ethos, pathos, and logos into a concentration on image and the emotional and discursive appeals used to present it. Such an approach evades the difficulties in the determination of organizational intent and the measurement of public perceptions of image. Ideally, as Alvesson (1990) notes, "It can of course also be argued that the image exists somewhere 'in between' the communicator and the audience" (p. 376). But this complex process by which an organization's image is formed poses some difficulties for the rhetorical critic. An organizational image is the result of a process in which an organization's identity is projected through a variety of messages and media, with the hope that external and internal audiences may interpret such messages in ways similar to the intent of those who created the messages. Not all such attempts are successful, since other voices within an organization's "public sphere" contribute often conflicting information, and publics are free to filter any or all of what they have seen and heard about an organization to form an image of it in their minds. For the critic of organizational rhetoric, it becomes virtually impossible to analyze the development of an organization's *images* (multiple publics produce multiple interpretations of an organization) with any degree of depth and rigor.

In the absence of data regarding public opinion of an organization and/or audience reaction to a set of particular media strategies (e.g., image advertising), a post hoc rhetorical analysis of organizational efforts to project an image can yield insights as to how an organization views itself and how various constituencies might perceive that organization.[1] How such messages portray organizations and invite support from publics is one of the many subjects found within the work of Kenneth Burke.

For anyone interested in the concepts of "image" and "publics" as they apply to religious organizations such as CSI, the introduction of Burke's *Attitudes toward History* (1937/1984) should intrigue. The book, according to Burke, "deals with characteristic responses of people in their forming and reforming of congregations. You might call it . . . 'Manual of Terms for a Public Relations Counsel with a Heart'" (n.p.). Within the book's pages, Burke points out the rhetorical uses of the poetic in the inculcation of attitudes through "frames of acceptance"—"the more or less organized system of meanings by which a thinking [person] gauges the historical situation and adopts a role with relation to it" (p. 5).

Central to Burke's discussion of these "frames" is the idea that any message acts as a "prayer" that the rhetor hopes others will accept. "Secular prayer" petitions no heavenly deity, but significant others in society—for present purposes, an organization's publics. Thus, in "'secular prayer' there is character-building, the shaping of one's individual character and role with respect to a theory of collective, historic purpose" (p. 159). "Secular prayer" is thus an "interpretation of events" (pp. 322–323) and is used to combat the alternative prayers proposed by others through propaganda and exhortation. Secular prayer is the act of *naming one's self.* In the case of contemporary organizations, image advertising serves an "identity-management" function (Cheney and Vibbert, 1987; see also Samra, 1993).[2]

Thus any image advertisement, such as those CSI presented in the pages of *USA Today,* invites publics to accept the image presented. The proper method to analyze such "secular prayers" is Burke's (1941/1973a) "cluster-agon" approach. This process charts the relationships between symbols to derive the pattern of experience the rhetor asks the audience to accept:

> [T]he work of every writer contains a set of explicit equations. He [*sic*] uses "associational clusters." And you may, by examining his work, find "what goes with what" in these clusters—what kinds of acts and images and personalities and situations go with his notions of heroism, villainy, consolation, despair, etc. And though he be perfectly conscious of the act of writing, conscious of selecting a certain kind of imagery to reinforce a certain kind of mood, etc., he cannot possibly be conscious of the interrelationships among all these equations. Afterwards, by inspecting his work "statistically," we or he may disclose by objective citation the structure of motivation operating there. (p. 20)

The analysis should result in three types of "statistical equations," to borrow Burke's metaphor. First, the critic looks for "what equals what," which terms are aligned together (p. 30). Second, the critic examines these clusters for which terms are opposed to one another. The clusters in opposition serve as agons in the text. Finally, the critic gauges which terms follow others. These are indications of transformations in the text. Burke (1942) further suggests, "A work of art is a *development* or *transformation* that proceeds *from* something, *through* something, *to* something" (p. 15). The result of the analysis indicates its poetic form, and the character of the rhetor that the rhetor wishes the audience to accept.

From a public relations perspective, the organizational image revealed through a cluster-agon analysis of advertisements should reveal more than the observable or quantifiable aspects, the "substance" (Alvesson, 1990) of image (see, e.g., Chajet and Shachtman, 1991, Ch. 3; Gray, 1986; Olins, 1989/1990; Sobol et al., 1992, Ch. 2). To borrow a few ideas from Olins' (1978) earlier writing on the subject, an image should be based on an organization's "soul" and "style." While concrete features contribute to image management, the creation and perception of images also occur on a cognitive level. Image advertising attempts to tap cognitions in such a way to influence positive associations in the public mind. In short, attempts to improve public opinion of an organization appeal to schemata, attitudes, values, and group identifications (Price, 1992).

I Am a Scientologist: Cluster-Agon Analysis of the CSI Campaign

To reveal the discursive associations CSI offered *USA Today* readers through its image campaign, this section follows the three steps of Burke's cluster-agon approach. First, I examine clusters of terms linked to CSI. Second, I trace the clusters of terms opposed to CSI (the "agons"). Third, and finally, I locate the associations developed over the course of the campaign as clusters are linked one to another.

Since "secular prayer" focuses on the character of the rhetor, I begin with the clusters associated with CSI. These clusters center around its founder, L. Ron Hubbard, the philosophy he developed, and Scientology's causes that result from its philosophy. As the "developer of the philosophy" (CSI, 1991c), Hubbard is the key identity from which CSI's image emanates (CSI, 1991m): "L. Ron Hubbard's research has generated tens of millions of words on the subject of the human spirit which comprise *Dianetics* and *Scientology* philosophy. His works cover subjects as diverse as drug rehabilitation, education, marriage and family, success at work, statistical analysis, public relations, art, marketing and much, much more" (p. 46). Several advertisements highlight one or more of Hubbard's vocations, often related to a particular book (e.g., *Problems of Work, The Basic Study Manual, Clear Body, Clear Mind;* see CSI, 1991j, 1991k, 1991l).

Each of these vocations and Hubbard's achievements are described dramatically in the insert, "L. Ron Hubbard: The Man and His Work." Hubbard's philosophy allegedly stems from an altruistic motive derived from his own struggles from injuries in World War II (CSI, 1991m). This autobiographical account of how Hubbard used his mind to heal himself has been questioned (Corydon and Hubbard, 1987; Miller, 1987/1988), but it is central to the character of CSI's founding principles. As a result, CSI serves mankind. Hubbard's own words express the importance of life:

> Common man likes to be happy and well. He likes to be able to understand things, and he knows his route to freedom lies through knowledge. Therefore, for 15 years I have had mankind knocking on my door. It has not mattered where I have lived or how remote, since I first published a book on the subject my life has no longer been my own. I like to help others and count it my greatest pleasure in life to see a person free himself of the shadows which darken his days. (CSI, 1991g)

The terms associated with Hubbard's philosophy are dramatic as well: "truth" that "goes forward" (CSI, 1991c); "a route to knowledge" (CSI, 1991g); it has no political aspiration and does not teach dialectical materialism (CSI, 1991g); it is "a precise and exact science" (CSI, 1991d), based on humanistic values (CSI, 1991e), and concerned with "how to show man how he can set himself free" (CSI, 1991g). Additionally, Scientology is a "simple story," open to almost anyone (CSI, 1991c, 1991g), a moral code, based on common sense (CSI, 1991f), and a workable technology based on natural laws (CSI, 1991m, p. 5). It is a philosophy that "calms the environment" (CSI, 1991g). The causes such a philosophy might influence thus become numerous as well: freedom from drugs, study skills, human rights, voluntarism, social concerns, freedom of religion, children, and political and tax freedom (CSI, 1991n, 1991o, 1991p, 1991q, 1991s, 1991z).

However, if an organization is known by its enemies, the terms opposed to CSI, its founder, and its philosophy create the impression of an organization ready to do battle with any of the foes who cause the problems of the world. According to the June 17 advertisement, "These disturbing elements are the Merchants of Chaos. They deal in confusion and upset. Their daily bread is made by creating chaos. If chaos were to lessen, so would their incomes" (CSI, 1991c). The politician, the reporter, the medico, the drug manufacturer (see also CSI, 1991l), the militarist and arms manufacturer, the police (see also

CSI, 1991p), and the undertaker, to name the leaders of the list, fatten only upon "the dangerous environment." Even individuals and family members can be "Merchants of Chaos."

In other ads, CSI singles out "Marxist psychologists" who believe that "man could not be bettered" and perpetuate mental illness (1991d); intellectuals who hide the wisdom of the East and West (1991g); job stress and insecurity in the workplace (1991i); illiteracy (1991k); and the Internal Revenue Service (CSI's representative of the corrupt police state [1991o, 1991p, 1991kk]). More broadly, CSI's enemy to conquer is the "anti-social personality" (1991q, 1991v, 1991w). This persona is linked to other individual problems: the "angry man," the failure to communicate with the "third party" who really causes disputes, self-ishness, people's attitudes, savage instincts, hatred, dishonesty, and the "reactive mind" (1991h, 1991r, 1991t, 1991u, 1991x, 1991y, 1991z, 1991aa).

The means CSI uses to achieve its ends may be traced through the clusters related to the implementation of its philosophy. CSI's training techniques, of course, are based on L. Ron Hubbard's discoveries. According to the advertisements, Hubbard "developed the technology to handle life" (1991i), "isolated the basic causes of job stress and dissatisfaction, and found *the* answers which can be used by anyone to be happier in the work place" (1991j). In addition, Hubbard "clearly laid out the basic principles of the first truly workable technology on *how* to study" (1991k) and "was the first to uncover that not only drugs, but also toxins, poisons, and pollutants remain lodged in the fatty tissues of the body and cause a wide variety of harmful mental and physical side effects" (1991l). Naturally, these problems can be solved through reading Hubbard's books on each particular subject, or can be alleviated through "auditing" and courses from CSI. Scientology's basic principles of human relations are also displayed in advertise-ments from July 8–19.

What, then, are the results? The clusters surrounding the benefits of Scientology's philosophies, writings, and training center on how wide-spread the movement has become, particular successful programs CSI has sponsored, and testimonies from eighty members of CSI.

According to the June 21 ad, Scientology has grown because it is "very popular with people" (1991g). The philosophy has helped mil-lions around the world, and individual books have helped hundreds of thousands. In particular, programs sponsored by CSI or using its principles have received accolades from academe and endorsements from legislators (albeit not many well-known ones). Programs include schools in Soweto, teacher training programs in China, and, most notably, Narcanon, the drug rehabilitation program founded by CSI. Additionally, Hubbard's *Organizational Executive Course* has been used by two Fortune 500 companies and around the world.

Testimonials from Scientology's members focus primarily on freedom from drugs and turning careers around. One example combines both:

> I figured I was doing about average for my peer group: my second marriage was in trouble; my business was heading out of control; I was drinking heavily and taking cocaine two to three nights a week on a gradually increasing basis. Now, nine years later, my marriage is happily intact, my business is stably expanding. I take no drugs. . . . Only one thing altered that course for me: the truth and wisdom contained in the teachings of L. Ron Hubbard. (CSI 1991ee)

This testimony was from a farmer. Testimonials are from people of all walks of life, and also illustrate the solutions to the concerns stated earlier, as well as others related to Scientology's principles: communication, self-esteem and depression, family, education, and quality of life (see, e.g., CSI, 1991bb, 1991cc, 1991dd, 1991ee, 1991ff, 1991gg, 1991hh, 1991ii, 1991jj).

Taken together, the clusters of terms form a cohesive whole: Hubbard's autobiography, his principles, and Scientology's concerns overlap to create a world view in which human beings are unlimited in potential. It requires Scientology's principles, literature, and training to overcome physical and psychological problems. Moreover, the very concerns Scientology attempts to answer have enemies in every aspect of society. Hubbard and CSI stand against these with books, programs, and various activities. Based on the testimonial advertisements, Scientology becomes a philosophy that solves problems and vanquishes enemies in the lives of everyday people. The themes of Hubbard's life, CSI's enemies, and the improvements made in CSI members' lives become roughly isomorphic.

Scientology and the "Epic Frame"   At the beginning of the June 17 ad, "The True Story of Scientology," CSI presents its story as a "simple, concise, and direct" five-part narrative: "(1) A philosopher develops a philosophy about life and death; (2) People find it interesting; (3) People find it works; (4) People pass it along to others; (5) It grows" (1991c). However, the story as revealed through the preceding cluster-agon analysis is not that simple. CSI's "secular prayer" presents a "frame of acceptance" that includes intermediate steps between the founding philosopher, L. Ron Hubbard, and publics finding the philosophy interesting and workable. The potential for publics to take an interest in Scientology's books, principles, and training may be facilitated by the appeal of the "epic" frame displayed in the seven weeks of advertisements CSI placed in *USA Today*.

According to Burke (1937/1984), there are two key characteristics of the epic frame. First, it is "designed . . . under primitive conditions, to make men 'at home in' those conditions." Second, it "'accepts' the rigors of war (the basis of the tribe's success) by magnifying the role of the warlike hero" (p. 35). The magnification of the epic hero serves two purposes: it "lends dignity to the necessities of existence, 'advertising' courage and individual sacrifice for group advantage— and it enables the humble man to share the worth of the hero by the process of 'identification'" (pp. 35–36).

The clusters of Hubbard, Scientology, its believers, and its opponents fulfill the major requirements of the epic form, but in reverse order of Burke's comments. First, Hubbard's achievements as described in the campaign portray a larger-than-life individual. This magnified hero then serves as an example for others, as the ads describe Hubbard's achievements and his service to mankind. The epic hero is altruistic. Although larger than life, he gives his life for others. Northrop Frye (1957) notes that the classic epic form can be found in the messianic narrative of the New Testament. A supernatural hero gives his life that his followers might have "life more abundantly" in a world condemned by sin.

Similarly, Hubbard's writings purportedly serve Burke's first characteristic of epic form: to improve the lot of mankind, despite a world filled with hatred, dishonesty, and the other generalized evils associated with the "antisocial personality." We should not be surprised that various elements of Hubbard's philosophies are antithetical to Scientology's enemies and directly correspond to the benefits Scientology members report as improvements in their lives (all as a result of Hubbard's teachings and books). In Burke's terminology, Scientology's philosophies become a "salvation device" (1937/1984), "taking up the slack between what is wanted and what is got" (1941/1973a, p. 54). Hubbard's principles supply what is needed for Scientologists to cope with situations.

What should be emphasized here is that this is a secular form of epic, since, in the traditional epic, gods affect the action (Frye, 1957). The appeal of the CSI ads is vicarious identification with Hubbard through his principles and his followers. As Burke (1937/1984) puts it:

> When heroes have been shaped by legend, with irrelevant or incongruous details of their lives obliterated, and only the most "divine" attributes stressed, the individual's "covert boasting" (by identification with the hero) . . . should tend rather to make for humility. . . . He [the legendary hero] possesses characteristics which his followers can possess only in attenuated form: Heroism loses this property of humility as soon as the "divine" emphasis gives way to a secular emphasis. . . . The individual hero is replaced by a collective body (and one has property in this body insofar as he participates in the use and strengthening of its traditions). (pp. 267–268)

In short, the advertising campaign presents the image of CSI in many of its facets. We begin with the "founder of the line," the epic hero, who has fought the "Merchants of Chaos" so that others may enjoy the fruits of Scientology unhindered. The propagation of the philosophy leads to a transmission of Hubbard's heroic qualities to his followers. The strength of its appeal lies in the ability to communicate the heroic qualities of Hubbard, the provision of a scapegoat for humanity's ills in the form of the chaos merchants, and the humility of the testimonials from CSI believers who demonstrate the effectiveness of the Church's philosophies. As Burke (1937/1984) observes, humility and self-glorification work together within the epic frame.

Implications

Whether the CSI ads actually obtained new converts for CSI can only be a matter of speculation. Preliminarily, I suggest that the advertising campaign attempted to fulfill two primary purposes: an extended public response to the *Time* exposé, and an opportunity to present the fundamentals of Scientology in an extensive fashion, thereby creating a widely read, mediated forum for proselytization. The choice of an extended image advertising campaign generates both risks and benefits to CSI's image, depending on how its publics are defined.

First, readers of the two periodicals in which the attack and defense of CSI's image appeared, *Time* and *USA Today,* may be termed primary publics as witnesses to CSI's public "identity crisis."[3] Typically, organizations have responded to crises with two "change strategies" (see Crable and Vibbert, 1985). According to Jones and Chase (1979), the "reactive" stance occurs when the organization does nothing in the face of public criticism. The "adaptive" stance occurs when publicity is used to cope with crisis in some symbolic way. What CSI did in 1991 was to respond to the *Time* exposé *dynamically*. There is evidence that CSI had been in similar situations on a localized basis (see Hinsberg, 1990), and knew of Richard Behar's (1986) investigations into CSI activities as a fraudulent religion, exhibiting cult-like qualities. From the standpoint of an issue's status, CSI recognized its image as the issue, and kept the matter before the public for two months, maintaining its level of "currency" (Crable and Vibbert, 1985) in order to obtain a public hearing. *Time*'s article attacked CSI's image; CSI purchased a sustained rebuttal to counter the exposé. The exposure of *USA Today*'s readers to advertisements over several weeks certainly created more impressions than the single article that catalyzed the issue. This is similar to the recent trend of organizations responding to attack with "in your face" types of publicity (e.g., PepsiCo's handling of syringes allegedly found in pop cans; General Motors's rebuttal to NBC News's "crash test"). Perhaps the best defense is a good offense.

Second, CSI used the advertisements as a dramatic way of presenting its doctrines and principles to an important public to any religious sect—potential believers. For years, Scientology has limited its advertising to the marketing of Hubbard's books, notably *Dianetics*. The *USA Today* image campaign offered a rhetorical appeal to CSI philosophy in a narrative form. Very few religions can provide an extensive discussion of their tenets in a coherent fashion. The simplicity that CSI claims for Scientology is revealed through the epic frame. And the ads provide various aspects of the epic as appeals to different publics. If you don't have problems with drugs, don't you have problems at work? Or, if you don't have problems in study skills, wouldn't you just like your life to be happy? Publics who respond to epic heroes as heroes might find identification with Hubbard's difficulties from World War II. As Frye (1957) writes, "an epic poet normally completes only one epic picture, the moment when he decides on his theme being the crisis of his life" (p. 318). Hubbard's story invites participation in others' life crises, and presents Scientology as the panacea. If, however, you are looking for others just like you, the final two weeks of advertisements portray Scientologists from all walks of life with whom to identify.

The advertisements may indeed provide a suitable response to purify CSI's image with publics who read the *Time* exposé and to present the desired image to readers of *USA Today* who eventually may seek help from and become Scientologists. Certainly some advantages of the print medium accrue. Abstract philosophy and ideology are made accessible and concrete through simple narratives and descriptions of L. Ron Hubbard's many books. Other message strategies invite identification through helpful personifications. Even though he is no longer alive, Hubbard becomes the ideal hero with whom to identify; CSI's enemies, the "Merchants of Chaos" and other human ills, are easily conquered through Scientology's teachings; and testimonials from current believers imply the value of Scientology, no matter the problem, to people from all walks of life. Although perhaps not as compelling as television images, similar results may yield from print advertising of organizational image, through a process that Goethals (1990) calls "persuasive imaging": modern image making builds charismatic leadership, communicates issues in easily understood dichotomies of right and wrong, and provides "some tangible form of contact with authority and power" (p. 175; see generally pp. 170–176).

What these print advertisements may lack is the fourth advantage that Goethals maintains is endemic to broadcast media: the spectacle of the medium, as an almost sacred place, to persuade viewers. The sheer length and fragmentation of the print message over time may militate against the strengths of reduction noted previously. People who read USA Today every day from June until August, and took the time to read each advertisement, received a complete catechism in Scientology. The likelihood of publics doing this is slim. Instead, readers may get only fragments of the projected image, perhaps subconsciously at best. The series of advertisements depends on progressive, discursive form (Burke, 1932/1968; Langer, 1942/1957). In contrast, CSI's USA Today advertisements, in September/October 1991, created an organizational persona and a corresponding enemy, the Internal Revenue Service, in each full-page ad. Each message capitalized on the energy of "presentational form," from which could be inferred that a hero, CSI, was prepared to act on behalf of helpless tax victims (Courtright, 1992). The epic hero is present no matter the reading habits of the target public. The image advertisements used earlier that summer, although they simplify CSI's message into manageable chunks, run the risk of fragmenting the image and the potential for proselytization. The presentation of Scientology's founder, enemies, doctrines, and "everyday" believers over an eight-week time frame may be a questionable persuasive choice.

What, then, might we conclude regarding the epic, and other, frames of acceptance as a rhetorical choice in public relations, specifically, the management of images? Goethals' (1990) work outlines the potential advantages of the organizational image as epic hero, especially in mediated contexts. But what are the risks of the epic hero as an organizational image? At least one problem lies in its image as a "100% solution" (Arnett, 1992). An epic hero, like many organizations in today's business, promises the public perfect performance. Instead, Arnett maintains that organizational rhetors should be more modest in their claims so that, when difficulties or crises arise, they retain a more positive public image. Religious organizations may well be the paradigm case of the "100% solution." The televangelist scandals of the late 1980s and early 1990s support Arnett's point. Yet many of them have survived and continued to broadcast and generate needed "love offerings."

Publics who read the CSI image advertisements may have responded positively, negatively, or indifferently to the image presented. Indeed, the presentation of Hubbard the epic hero and his followers may appeal especially to Scientology's internal publics and potential converts who subscribe readily to an authoritarian mindset and are looking for the same answers proclaimed in the advertisements. In ways similar to Stewart, Smith, and Denton's (1984) analysis of the John Birch Society, the cluster analysis of Scientology's image suggests that the world is a dangerous place, a "jungle" in which only acceptance of the hero's principles as a way of life make sense. This image is consistent with first- and second-hand accounts of CSI's organizational culture, in which a strict hierarchy of spiritual achievement is maintained by belief in a strong, dominant leadership and a submissive attitude toward authority (Corydon and Hubbard, 1987; Miller, 1987; Wallis, 1975, 1977). These responses and the dangerous world to which they respond are characteristic of authoritarianism.

This case study thus provides one of the few examples in which an organization's projected image approximates the way its members view and live it; that is, the internal image and its actual identity (Cheney and Vibbert, 1985).[4] This suggests that the advertisements themselves may have limited appeal to publics outside the organization. As such, the advertisements may function as self-persuasion (Burks, 1970). The public relations effort reinforces the organization's identity and culture, probably more so than to persuade other audiences of Scientology's high moral character and resulting social responsibility.

More likely, external publics may view the Church's image advertisements as public relations puffery. The difficulty with the epic
frame's perfect hero is that he/she can easily become humorous (Burke,
1937/1984; Frye, 1957). If members of the public interpret the frame
differently, less desirable images form. If the organization/hero is
viewed not as noble but as merely mistaken, a comic frame dwarfs CSI.
If the charge against the "Merchants of Chaos" is perceived to be
exaggerated, a confusing image of satire ensues. The Church of
Scientology has attacked weaknesses in others that it, too, in reality
shares (Burke, 1937/1984). In short, not all publics may respond the
same way to the epic frame. While CSI hopes that its sustained efforts
to purify its image were successful, the epic frame may easily become
ironic or grotesque (Burke, 1937/1984) if the reader has also read the
Time article and given it credence (or, for that matter, the reader may
be familiar, as some are, with the criticisms of Hubbard and Scientology found in books, articles, and numerous appellate court cases).[5]
This is a simple principle, but it should be emphasized: just because
the epic frame invites identification does not mean that publics will not
be suspicious of a founder who has been miraculously healed from
wounds by putting his mind to it (CSI, 1991g).[6]

Clearly, further exploration of the form and content of organizational
images in general is in order. First, what effect does choice of medium
play in the presentation and perception of image? The Church of
Scientology's image (and, I suspect, those of others) depends on the
"energy" of form (Blankenship and Sweeney, 1980) and/or the successful inculcation of premises for persuasion (see, for example, Crable
and Vibbert, this volume) in order to influence publics. At the very
least, can minimal exposure to image advertising provide a "foot-in-
the-door" to create awareness and interest, and thereby facilitate an
impetus toward public support for an organization and eventual adoption of its goods and services (Baskin and Aronoff, 1992)?

Second, how compelling are epic heros and other archetypal images,
implicitly or intentionally adopted by organizations and their internal
publics? The critical assertion of an archetype presumes that audiences
find universal appeal in common "cognitive units," "schemata," and
"patterns of experience" (Burke, 1931/1968; Grunig, 1993; Price,
1992). How do publics perceive, interpret, and respond to such images,
and do these images, whether positive or negative, persist? Moreover,
how consistent is such imagery with perceptions of an organization's

primary external publics? To what extent does consistency enhance the relationship of these publics with the organization?

To answer these questions of both form and content, academics and practitioners must engage rhetorical and other methods to determine the various contributors to an image's formation. In this essay, I have offered several possible audience interpretations of CSI's image advertising. This critical stance was taken to promote the notion that CSI's efforts were an example of image *management,* for "[w]hen symbolic relationships are divorced from behavioral relationship, public relations practitioners reduce public relations to the simplistic notion of image building" (Grunig, 1993, p. 136). Speculations such as those I have offered are but foundations for further study.

Other questions arise, applicable to the present case and other organizations' efforts. How do publics perceive CSI's trustworthiness, expertise, and goodwill (Samra, 1993)? What are the sources of these perceptions? These question's components, along with other measures of public opinion, could be surveyed both qualitatively and quantitatively. Differences and similarities between publics also could be determined. Various evaluation methods could be used to gauge audience information sources and media impressions. With multiple sources of data, a more complete picture of an organization's image and how it is created and maintained could be derived. Only with multiple methods and perspectives applied to the same organizations over time, can critical scholars and public relations practitioners begin to understand the confluence of organizational efforts, competing voices, and public opinion formation that generate the abstract, complex images that subtly affect an organization's ability to function within the public sphere.

NOTES

1. For the foundation to the critical principles on which I base the contention that an organization's desired image may be inferred from organizational discourse, see Black (1970) and McMillan (1987).

2. This notion of "prayer" as "character-building" has its roots in Burke's earliest work. According to Burke (1931/1968), any artist (that is, any symbol user) engages in a conflict between self-expression and a "desire to produce effects upon an audience" (p. 54). This conflict can be difficult to resolve due to the nature of the rhetorical situation. As Burke (1973b) describes it, human beings are unique individuals yet members of groups with aspects in common. "Perfection could exist only if the entire range of the reader's and the writer's experience were identical down to the last detail" (1931/1968, p. 179). Therefore

the *form* that the writer gives a message is only an approximation of what the writer intends or what the audience can appreciate. An image advertisement, for example, does more rhetorical "work" than reveal an organizational logo, name change, or statement of corporate goals and objectives.

The form that a rhetor gives a message is what Burke (1931/1968) calls a "pattern of experience," converted into a symbol. Most importantly, the strength of the relationship of the Symbol to the rhetor's pattern of experience can produce an effect in the audience, for "[t]he Symbol is perhaps overwhelming in its effect when the artist's and reader's patterns of experience closely coincide" (p. 153). Terms and imagery as "Symbols" are important to the artist and his or her efforts to induce effects in an audience, for the "[s]ymbol is the verbal parallel to a pattern of experience" (p. 152)—a formula. Symbols in various patterns may suggest the epic or tragic hero, irony or satire, or the rhetor's comic or grotesque persona (Burke, 1937/1984).

3. From the standpoint of traditional rhetoric, the *Time* exposé functioned as a *kategoria* that elicited the CSI's *apologia*. For an extended discussion of organizational *apologia*, see Hearit (this volume).

4. For more extensive discussion of the relationship between an organization's identity and its image, see Alvesson (1990) and Grunig (1993).

5. For a brief description of CSI's genesis and its tumultuous history, see Moore (1994). For extended critiques of Hubbard's and CSI's practices, see Behar (1991), Corydon and Hubbard (1987), Miller (1988), and Wallis (1977).

6. It may be that the epic frame differs in character when it moves from the poetic (traditional fiction) to rhetoric (the realm of the contingent, in which public relations may communicate both truth and, lamentably, some convenient fiction). Burke's (1937/1984) and Frye's (1957) comments on the epic frame merely indicate the possibility for readers to participate in the narrative and identify with the hero in some way, not always desired by the organization. Does a rhetorical extension of the epic frame such as CSI's require explicit examples of publics who have, to borrow Burke's phrase, "cashed in on" the heroic qualities of the epic (e.g., the testimonial advertisements)?

6

Plastic as Planet-Saving "Natural Resource"

Advertising to Recycle an Industry's Reality

Patricia Paystrup

In an Environmental Challenge Fund print ad, a photograph frames the ocher-colored angles of two pyramids against the contrasting background of a deep blue Egyptian sky as it juxtaposes the pyramids, a striking image of timelessness and human ingenuity, with what some see as the modern world's symbol of engineered durability, the polystyrene "clamshell." The headline claims, "Your cheeseburger box will be around even longer." The copy block continues, "Most things made on this planet last a few centuries. But styrofoam is forever. It will never decompose. Never disintegrate. Never go away. And neither will the garbage problems it creates, unless we find solutions."

The pyramid/cheeseburger box ad began running in *Time* in November 1990, about the same time McDonald's USA President Edward A. Rensi announced the company's response to boycotts by environmentally concerned consumers: "Although some scientific studies indicate that foam packaging is environmentally sound, our customers just don't feel good about it. So we're changing" (Hume, 1991). The fast-food chain's change spelled victory for grade-schoolers in the 800 chapters of Kids Against Pollution. In addition to a standard letter-writing campaign, these young activists also mounted a Send-It-Back effort; they mailed greasy polystyrene containers to local McDonald's stores or to the company's headquarters in Illinois (Castro, 1990). Kids Against Pollution celebrated, but overall reaction to the announcement was mixed.

The announcement surprised members of the National Polystyrene Recycling Corporation (NPRC) as they prepared for a joint news conference on plans to expand the NPRC-McDonald's polystyrene recycling program from its pilot stage to a nationwide effort involving 8,500 restaurants (Leaversuch, 1990). One advertising executive working with the NPRC accused McDonald's of "getting out for the wrong reason" because "they made a business decision, not an environmental one" and "just didn't want to fight the battle anymore" (Colford, 1991).

The plastics industry was not the only sector to criticize the move. Nancy Wolf and Ellen Feldman (1991) of the Environmental Action Coalition wrote, "Ironically, McDonald's decision to switch to bleached paper/polyethylene wrappers led the company to abandon a recyclable package in favor of one that is neither recyclable nor compostable" (p. xii). The irony deepened: The switch reversed what McDonald's founder Ray Kroc believed was the environmentally sound choice based on the Stanford Research Institute's environmental impact study, which concluded that when all stages of production were considered, from manufacturing through disposal, polystyrene was superior to paper. The 1976 study told Kroc: "Polystyrene uses less energy than paper in its production, conserves natural resources, represents less weight and volume in landfills, and is recyclable" (Hume, 1991).

Kroc's 1976 decision to change to polystyrene was based on scientific studies; the company's 1990 decision to return to paper packaging was admittedly based on perceptions: "The bottom line was that there were people who still didn't understand that plastic is recyclable. And that drove our switch back to paper," said Michael Roberts, McDonald's vice president for environmental affairs (in Hume, 1990). A Dow Chemical executive saw the McDonald's action as caving into customer pressures based "on perceptions and without understanding the myths and realities involved" (Sternberg, 1990). A spokesman for Huntsman Chemical, the company headed by the man who pioneered the "clamshell" in the early 1970s, noted that McDonald's "responded to the *perception* of polystyrene foam rather than to the *reality*" (Leaversuch, 1990). But there was more to the McDonald's polystyrene phaseout than bowing to public perceptions: McDonald's Senior Vice President Shelby Yarrow claimed the company was disappointed with the polystyrene industry's slowness in building a viable recycling infrastructure and felt the time and money invested with the NPRC "had created a financial drain on the company" (Wolf and Feldman, 1991, p. xii; Sternberg, 1990; Leaversuch, 1990).

McDonald's rationale to eliminate polystyrene illustrates how the plastics industry's recycling advocacy advertisements and supporting public relations campaigns are sabotaged by the harsh reality of an unstable and inadequate plastics recycling infrastructure further weakened by market forces that make virgin plastic resin much cheaper to use than recycled resins. By 1993, after some five years of pushing public awareness of plastics recycling, only 2.2 percent of the plastics packaging produced made it to recycling facilities, compared to aluminum's 70 percent rate. With current market forces, "of all the junk that constitutes America's household wastes, plastics are the most recycling resistant. The material comes in so many varieties, produced from such different polymers, that just separating it in the recycling process is cumbersome and expensive" (Van Voorst, 1993, p. 17).

This chapter examines the communication strategies used in advocacy advertisements developed by the plastics industry to address its "image" and "public opinion" problems during two waves—the first in the late 1980s and the second in the early 1990s. This chapter also examines the public policy issue-management ironies surrounding the industry's efforts to push plastics recycling as a way to combat anti-plastics legislation in the first wave and to defeat measures that would create market forces needed to support plastics recycling in the second phase of the industry's advocacy efforts.

For an industry in crisis, advocacy advertising as rhetorical activity is "a mode of altering reality, not by direct application of energy to objects, but by the creation of discourse which changes reality through the mediation of thought and action" (Bitzer, 1968, p. 3). These two very different campaigns both set out to alter what the plastics industry sees as harsh legislation and widespread public misperceptions of plastics.

The first wave of advocacy advertisements in this analysis ran in major magazines during 1989 and 1990 and was launched in an attempt to defeat plastic bans and to change what the industry called misunderstandings and inaccurate perceptions of the "myths" and "realities" of plastics' contribution to the solid waste crisis. A number of these advertisements employ a rhetorical device Kenneth Burke calls (1984a, p. 308) "perspective by incongruity," to place two previously unconnected things together in ways that transfer meanings and revise perceptions; in this case, to recategorize plastics as both a recyclable material and the new "natural resource." These advertisements mimic the closed system found in nature; post-consumer plastics become symbolically connected to natural lifecycles, they are "born again" with a "second life" and then finally sluff off their negative synthetic identity as they are positively transformed into the new "natural resource."

The second wave of advocacy messages, the initial "Take Another Look at Plastic" campaign, began running in late 1992 with media buys scheduled through May 1993. While the first series was primarily a defensive or reactive response formulated to fight legislative plastics bans, the second campaign was launched as a proactive or positive attempt to improve plastics' overall poor image by showing how high-technology plastics contribute to modern living and, incidently, help "save the planet."

When these two campaigns are compared and contrasted, they contradict the accepted wisdom in public relations and issue-management circles that says proactive communication programs are inherently better than reactive responses. In this case, the reactive campaign has a focus and clarity that is missing in the proactive campaign. The first campaign powerfully challenges readers to radically revisualize and revise their perception of plastics. In contrast, the positive "Take Another Look at Plastic" campaign presents a superficial glance at a glossy surface. The reactive campaign tells a fascinating, almost archetypal, story of transformation and rebirth as it reclassifies plastic as recyclable. The proactive campaign borrows the patter of a bad stand-up comic and throws out nonsensical one-liners in an attempt to appeal to everyone with an upbeat "plastic is your friend" message.

The major differences between the two campaigns are grounded in an understanding of the larger "rhetorical situation." The first campaign responds to the pressing "exigence" of plastics bans; it addresses one set of "constraints," the belief that plastics cannot be recycled. The "Take Another Look at Plastic" ads do not answer any specific exigence-generated questions. Nor do they demonstrate an understanding of a target audience's primary concerns or the broader cultural constraints operating in the situation. Such constraints include what one anthropologist describes as the schizophrenic love/hate relationship we have with plastic as the basic substance of our modern material culture (Gutin, 1992).

Understanding how advocacy advertising campaigns, when used to manage issues or reshape images, need to respond to the demands of a rhetorical situation points to the importance of answering a concerned audience's questions. To examine how these two major advertising campaigns address the components of the rhetorical situation, this chapter first explores how the plastics and solid waste disposal issues developed in the late 1980s by placing them into an issue-management context. Second, it discusses the industry's decision to use advocacy advertising as an issue-management strategy. Third, it analyzes how the first recycling advocacy campaign employed "perspective by incongruity" to show an industry "transforming used plastics into a 'natural resource.'" Fourth, it discusses how changing public policy issues in the early 1990s met with contradictory issue-management tactics. The fifth section shows how the "Take Another Look at Plastic" campaign fits into the industry's advocacy efforts. Sixth, and finally, this chapter analyzes and speculates how this latter campaign may actually further damage the industry's image by failing to address the real issue on consumers' minds: a still woefully inadequate plastics recycling infrastructure.

TURNING UP THE HEAT ON PLASTICS: ACTIVISTS SET THE AGENDA

In 1959, Procter and Gamble's new packaging for Ivory Liquid placed the first plastic bottles on supermarket shelves. Thirty years later, the offspring of those original shatterproof bottles faced some tough legislation that threatened to break the plastics industry. By the end of 1989, at least 800 solid waste bills involving plastics were on the docket of state and local policy-making bodies in at least thirty-five states. A few years earlier there might have been ten at the very most (Stuller, 1990). With environmental activists pressing for outright bans on plastics, the industry was forced to enter into a high-stakes game to influence policy makers and the public on solid waste disposal issues.

Issue Management: Influencing Public Discourse and Public Policy

Faced with increasing public policy pressures in recent decades, business and industry turned to a more powerful form of public relations, *issue management,* a strategic planning approach aimed at combating activist groups' public policy agendas. An *issue* is a contestable question of fact, value, or policy. Originally designed by American Can executive Howard Chase to defend the business sector in a hostile "court of public opinion," issue management would become the way industry could exercise "every moral and legal right to participate in *formation* of public policy—not merely to react, or be responsive, to policies designed by government" (Jones and Chase, 1979, p. 7).

The Chase and Jones process model gave industry a systems-theory based tool for monitoring issues. Crable and Vibbert (1985) added a cyclical perspective to the growing field of issue management literature. The Chase and Jones model neglects issue development. Crable and Vibbert, and subsequently Hainsworth (1990), address the need to understand issue lifecycles. According to Crable and Vibbert, issues go through five basic stages: "potential," or latent interest; "imminent," in which interest builds and legitimation occurs as people begin to see linkages; "current," during which people participate in discussions of the issue and the media cover it; "critical," when the issue demands a decision; and "dormant," when the issue is resolved or forgotten. Often a "trigger event," like the Summer 1987 media coverage of the Islip, N.Y., garbage barge that sailed up and down the east coasts of North and South America looking for a willing dumping ground, will project an issue into the current or critical stage.

When Jones and Chase (1979) identified an issue management model of the public policy process, they defined three basic issue change-strategy options: reactive, adaptive, and dynamic. Crable and Vibbert (1985) added a fourth issue change-strategy option, the catalytic. The type of change-strategy option an organization may decide to use to respond to challenges or opportunities is also related to the issue's place in the issue status lifecycle.

The four change option strategies suggest a sort of hierarchy of time and effort: long-term, mindful "management" versus short-term, defensive "fire-fighting." The catalytic strategy begins as early as the potential stage in the form of "agenda stimulation." The other strategies primarily respond to agendas set by others. The dynamic stance anticipates action and may initiate projects and policies as early as the imminent stage, but, as explained by Chase and Jones and critiqued by Crable and Vibbert, it usually waits until the issue is current before acting. The adaptive strategy adjusts to change through compromise or proposed alternatives. Adaptive strategies often begin in the current stage, but are also adopted after the issue has reached the critical stage. When organizations employ reactive strategies, they usually face issues in the critical stage, when a "crisis" demands policy decisions

(Crable and Vibbert, 1985; see also Heath and Nelson, 1986). Catalytic and dynamic strategies involve increased effort in the early stages to favorably manage the issue's status. Adaptive and reactive strategies are mainly defensive tactics that demand attention at the current or critical stage in which others have set the agenda and have defined the issues.

At first, no single group or sector seemed to be actively "issue managing" the solid waste problem. By the late 1980s, proposed plastics bans multiplied as one reaction to larger concerns over solid waste disposal. Nationwide, the number of available landfill sites declined from 18,000 in 1985 to 9,000 in 1989 (Wood, 1990). Experts estimated that more than half the landfills serving the East Coast would close by 1990 (Earthworks, 1989). The developing solid waste disposal issue riveted the public's attention and entered the "current" stage in the summer of 1987 "when the sorry image of the wandering garbage barge towed by the tug *Break of Dawn* was seared onto the collective retina" through ongoing news coverage (Gutin, 1992).

That ill-fated barge made trash the new cause célèbre as Americans began to take a closer look at what went into the "waste stream" (Gutin, 1992; Callari, 1989). As a result of the renewed scrutiny, plastics, the fastest growing segment of the packaging industry, received critical reviews in just about every popular discussion of environmental and solid waste issues (Lawren, 1990). The public's growing anti-plastics sentiments fed on statistics found in environmental best-sellers like *50 Simple Things You Can Do to Save the Earth*: "Each American uses about 190 pounds of plastic per year—and about 60 pounds of it is packaging which we discard as soon as the package is opened"; and "Americans go through 2.5 million plastic bottles every hour" (Earthworks, 1989, p. 66).

With the public's eye now on solid waste disposal, plastics' original virtues, high-performance qualities like strength, durability, and light weight, became their new vices. Another irony emerged: The new definition of plastics as a major part of the pressing national environmental crisis also symbolized how successful the plastics industry had been in developing new product applications. The plastics industry saw itself as the most direct expression of ultimate product utility and convenience in packaging; environmentalists saw the plastics industry as the foremost expression of product wastefulness and social and economic dysfunction (Blumberg and Gottlieb, 1981). As the proposed plastics packaging bans added up, a plastics industry journalist wrote,

"Obviously, this entire controversy amounts to more than a hill of garbage. The future of an entire industry, or a least certain key components of it, is at stake" (Callari, 1989).

The plastics industry first adopted a reactive stance when the solid waste issue was catapulted into the critical stage because the industry just was not ready: Not ready, that is, to be labeled a "villain," "scapegoat," or "target" as the industry lamented in its own publications (Callari, 1989). With its advantages having become disadvantages, plastic is caught in an ironic cosmic joke as the versatility that enabled it to fill so many packaging niches also made it difficult to recycle (Gutin, 1992). Since plastic comes in so many varieties, separating it is so cumbersome and expensive that "of all the junk that constitutes America's household wastes, plastics are the most recycling resistant" (Van Voorst, 1993, p. 79).

With the issue already at the "critical" stage, the plastics industry's automatic fight response guided its initial reactions to the individual bans. The plastics industry's test case, in the legal system and in the court of public opinion, may have been the Suffolk County, N.Y., 1988 ban of all nondegradable packaging materials. The Society of the Plastics Industry (SPI), especially society members Dow and Mobil, the Flexible Packaging Association, and the Polystyrene Packaging Coalition, lobbied heavily against the ban. Saying the ban was arbitrary, capricious, and that it violated environmental impact regulations, the industry battled the ban all the way to the New York Supreme Court. The court agreed with the industry in 1989, and decreed that the ban could not be implemented until there was conclusive proof that plastics do indeed pose an environmental threat (Wolf and Feldman, 1991).

The New York Supreme Court may have agreed with the plastics industry's arguments, but the American public did not. Opinion poll after opinion poll indicated the public believed the environmentalists' side of the plastics story. A Gallup poll commissioned by Dow Chemical in the fall of 1989 showed 72 percent of the public viewed plastics as the *most harmful* material to the environment. An industry-sponsored poll in 1988 showed a 56 percent response to a similar question. The Gallup poll also showed that 60 percent of those responding were *not* aware that plastics are recyclable ("Dow calls," 1990). A Cambridge Reports Survey taken in the summer of 1989 showed 48 percent favored bans on plastics to solve solid waste problems; 26 percent favored bans when asked the same question in 1988 (Toensmeirer, 1990; see also Silas, 1990).

For American businesses, this threshold also marked the point between two very different worlds: the old one in which business was to
push for growth, market expansion, and a healthy profit, and the new
one in which business would be expected to put environmental impacts
before bottom-line considerations. As businesses began to operate in
this new environmentally conscious world, one advertising executive
observed in response to the McDonald's polystyrene decision, "What
is environmentally the right thing to do is becoming increasingly more
the economically right thing to do" (Levin, 1990). With this in mind,
an executive with Dow Chemical was concerned the McDonald's move
might have a ripple effect with more plastics defections as
"environmentalists' attacks (however uninformed or ill conceived)
may cause other large users of plastics to rethink their options because
they fear the results of being considered 'environmentally incorrect'"
(Leaversuch, 1990).

FIRING BACK: THE INDUSTRY'S ATTEMPT AT ISSUE MANAGEMENT

By 1989 the plastics industry was at a crossroads. Would it "reactively" continue to battle legislation piece by piece, as it did with the
Suffolk ban? Or would it commit to an "adaptive" issue-management
strategy more consistent with the environmental concerns of a changed
business and political climate? Experts like Susan Selke, a professor
at Michigan State University's School of Packaging, advised, "The
plastics packaging industry can no longer proceed with business as
usual because legislators will no longer allow it. Through the use of
taxes, bans, deposits, and other tools, restrictions will be placed on the
ability of businesses to use plastics packaging. The most effective way
to combat restrictions is for the industry to promote recycling, because
recycling is politically popular" (Stuller, 1990). Or, as Ralph Nader
warned, "While what's happening at the state and local level is important, the federal government is the one holding the big ticket" (in
Callari, 1989). With the issue at the critical stage, one industry journalist wrote, "For the plastics business the challenge can probably be
reduced to this: Come up with some answers and demonstrate that they
work, or have the government impose their own brand of solution on
you" (Callari, 1989).

From the plastics industry's perspective, the decision to push recycling as the "way out" of the solid waste crisis signaled a shift from a

predominantly reactive issue-management style to more adaptive strategies. An article in *Modern Plastics* indicates a change in the industry's issue-management stances: "By late 1989 the PS industry was no longer reacting defensively to badmouthing, boycotts and bans. What is emerging is a multifaceted action program that meets criticism head-on by tackling the very problems detractors say the industry cannot solve" ("PS," 1990).

But there were two serious problems associated with pushing recycling as the new "adaptive" strategy. First, a post-consumer plastics recycling infrastructure was not yet in place; and second, consumers retained the widely and deeply held belief that plastics are *not* recyclable. Ironically, the first problem, the fact that virtually no plastics were being collected for recycling, was probably the biggest factor in the public's perception of plastics as the nonrecyclable "villain" in the waste stream.

Industry groups scrambled to begin building a post-use recycling system. Resin producers and soft drink bottle manufacturers formed the National Association for Plastic Container Recovery (NAPCOR) and set the goal that by 1992, 50 percent of the polyethylene terephthalate (PET) produced would be recycled. In June 1989, the seven polystyrene (PS) giants, Amoco, ARCO, Dow, Fina, Huntsman, Mobil, and Polysar, chipped in $2 million apiece to start the NPRC. The group announced immediate plans to build five regional recycling centers and set a goal of recycling 25 percent of the post-consumer PS by 1995 ("Companies combat," 1989). Seven major resin suppliers formed a new division of the SPI in June 1988. Called the Council for Solid Waste Solutions (CSWS), the group planned "to put money, brain power, and political clout behind a push into plastics' waste reuse" ("Resin suppliers," 1988, p. 14). In June 1989, *Time* magazine reported, "About 130 companies ranging from bluechip behemoths like DuPont and Dow to small firms like Wisconsin's Midwest Plastics Materials and Iowa-based Hammer's Plastic Recycling are reincarnating used plastics." The article also points out, only 1 percent of the plastics produced in 1989 were recycled, compared with 25 percent of the aluminum, although mandatory curbside collection systems in states like New Jersey, Florida, and Rhode Island would begin to increase the percentages ("Second life," 1989).

With a recycling infrastructure slowly taking shape, the plastics industry was finally ready to begin its national recycling advocacy campaign by late 1989, some two years after the Islip garbage barge sailed the solid waste issue into the current-critical stage of the policy agenda. But getting the campaign together was no easy task, due in part to the industry's conservative nature. The plastics industry is an extension of the petrochemical and chemical industries. The structure of plastics production further breaks it into two separate industries, resin production and product processing. The resin producers are dominated by a handful of large petrochemical and chemical corporations, including Dow, Mobil, Amoco, DuPont, and Monsanto. The processors who turn the resins into secondary products and manufacture the final product are a more diverse group (Blumberg and Gottlieb, 1989, p. 265). The two major divisions of the industry unite in associations like SPI.

When SPI members deliberated over how to meet the anti-plastics furor, some, including Dow, Mobil, and DuPont, were accustomed to high-profile image and issue advertising, while others, usually the smaller companies, did not use national institutional or advocacy campaigns. SPI's overall cautiousness was reflected in the announcement of its plans for a new image campaign in the spring of 1989: "SPI has chosen this moment to start what it calls a 'special communications program' that 'seeks to educate external audiences.'" SPI's communications vice president said that current-wave anti-plastics sentiment and legislation warranted spending on "proactive" as well as "defensive" actions: "We've reached a point where a positive image program is no longer a luxury" ("SPI creates," 1989). SPI's moment of decision on an image campaign did not come in 1987 or 1988, but in 1989, after some 1,000 pieces of proposed anti-plastics legislation. SPI's seeming reluctance to enter the fray may have come from three decades of self-imposed silence. The last time the plastics industry carried its case on a controversial issue directly to the U.S. public was in 1959 when it refuted claims that polyethylene bags were to blame in infant suffocation deaths ("Resin companies," 1989).

Some members of the SPI's new CSWS, created to bring "money, brain power, and political clout" to the issue, were more comfortable speaking out, however, and their push for a higher profile, more aggressive issue and image campaign split the association into opposing camps and torpedoed plans for more CSWS advertisements like the 12-page insert that kicked off the plastics-are-the-most-recyclable-of-recyclables drive. An article in the November 1989 issue of *Modern Plastics* discussed advertising campaigns planned by individual resin producers Amoco, Mobil, and Huntsman, and suggested developing tensions between CSWS members. All twenty-one members of the CSWS had to reach unanimous agreement before actions could be taken. Huntsman Chemical Vice President Don Olsen was quoted saying, "It is difficult to get a resin company consensus on the issues at stake in planning an advertising campaign." Amoco's director of marketing communication noted that the company's commitment of $1 million for their campaign was based on the feeling that the company could act quicker to "meet a need it defines as urgent" by acting alone ("Resin companies," 1989).

Once again the plastics industry's inability to agree on a centralized issue-management strategy disrupted its advocacy, and any spirit of unity-in-adversity disappeared by the year's end as SPI and CSWS members turned from battling plastics bans to fighting one another. In the CSWS December 1989 meeting, Dow's call for the SPI to mount a "media blitz" and a three-year, $150 million campaign to improve plastics' image, "ignited a fierce debate within the industry." Some voiced a desire to see that kind of money spent on developing new technologies and building more recycling programs—not on advertising. SPI president Larry L. Thomas agreed with Dow. In a confidential letter to members about the proposal's discussion in the coming January 15, 1990, meeting, he cited opinion poll experts' advice that the public's view of plastics as an environmental issue had plummeted so fast that it approached "the point of no return." These opinion experts predicted the industry would be swamped by "a fast-moving tidal wave of growing negative public perception." An opponent of Dow's proposal leaked Thomas' letter to columnist Jack Anderson, who ridiculed it as a "propaganda drive" in a January column. The head of a public relations firm representing one of the major resin producers suggested that Dow's proposal would be like waving a flag under the nose of environmentalists: "It would be pure Hollywood and it will provoke a huge backlash" ("Dow calls," 1990).

NATURAL PLASTICS: PERSPECTIVE BY INCONGRUITY

The plastics industry's inability to choose between the more conservative, reactionary change-strategy options and more aggressive, adaptive change-strategies or -styles is apparent in an analysis of the series of advertisements produced by the CSWS and the individual resin companies. The same pattern of tensions between more reactive strategy messages versus messages with a more adaptive stance continues throughout the series of ads. In fact, the copy for many ads mixes elements of both. The "reactive" elements are pretty mundane arguments over the "facts" of the solid waste issue. The better executed "adaptive" messages, however, transcend the mundane to change post-consumer plastics packaging from "trash" to a new "natural resource." This transcendence is explained best through Kenneth Burke's notion of "perspective by incongruity" or the "comic corrective."

Perspective by incongruity gives the plastics industry a way to attempt to redefine and recategorize a product the public sees as inherently *unnatural* and environmentally antagonistic in three major ways: it is a nonrenewable petroleum product; it is nonbiodegradable; it is not recyclable. In this case, perspective by incongruity becomes a method for gauging situations and changing meanings through verbal "atom cracking": "That is, a word belongs by custom to a certain category—and by rational planning you wrench it loose and metaphorically apply it to a different category" (Burke, 1984a, p. 308). By linking previously unlinked words, concepts, and categories, perspective by incongruity's comic frame impiously challenges our established sense of what properly goes with what and transfers meaning from one setting to another (Burke, 1984a, p. 309; 1984b, p. 90).

Burke (1984a) sees perspective by incongruity as a serious method for holding up traditional views to their opposites to overcome the limitations a classification places on us: "The metaphorical extension of perspective by incongruity involves casuistic stretching since it interprets new situations by removing words from their 'constitutional' setting. It is not 'demoralizing,' however, since it is done by the 'transcendence' of a new start. It is not negative smuggling, but positive cards-face-up-on-the-table. It is designed to 'remoralize' by accurately naming a situation already demoralized by inaccuracy" (p. 309). The "transcendence" used in perspective by incongruity turns "problems" into "assets": "Thus we 'win' by subtly changing the rules of the game—and by a mere trick of bookkeeping, like the accountants of big utility corporations, we make 'assets' out of liabilities" (p. 308). Acceptance of the new perspective or categorization completes the translation or revision of the situation (p. 173).

The conceptual revisions offered by the comic frame occur when the *material* aspect or "essence" combines with the *transcendent* as "A" and "B" cease to be opposites and a new categorical identity forms. As Burke (1984a) explains, "Viewing the matter in terms of ecological balance, one might say of the comic frame: It also makes us sensitive to the point at which one of these ingredients becomes hypertrophied, with the corresponding atrophy of the other. A well-balanced ecology requires the symbiosis of the two" (p. 166).

The *material,* used plastic packaging, and *transcendent,* useful, new, durable products, join in the comic frame in Amoco's two-page spread headlined, "We'd like to recycle the thinking that plastics can't be recycled." The left page of the spread shows typical plastic containers, including a PET two-liter pop bottle, a milk jug, PS clamshell and cup, and has "Before" as a subhead. The right page's artwork includes a parka, a park bench, a roll of carpet, a paintbrush, tulips growing in flower pots, and an ultramodern house. The subhead reads "After." The copy further juxtaposes the material with the transcendent: "Contrary to public opinion, plastics are among the easiest materials to recycle. In South Carolina, one company is recycling 100 million pounds of used plastic soft drink bottles a year into carpet yarn, flower pots, and fiberfill for ski parkas. In Chicago, another company is recycling 2 million plastic milk jugs a year into 'plastic lumber' for decks. In Tennessee, another company is recycling plastic beverage containers into bathtubs and shower stalls." After this recountal of recycled plastics' new second lives, the copy builds to a final transcendent leap: "The recycling of plastics is rapidly catching on. Recycling is transforming used plastics into a 'natural resource' that can be used to produce many new products." Juxtaposed on two pages, the plastics pictured on the left side of the spread are no longer garbage; on the right side, they become "a 'natural resource' that can be used to produce many new products." Through visual and verbal "atom cracking," the advertisement attempts to reclassify plastics as "among the easiest materials to recycle," to "'remoralize' by accurately naming a situation already demoralized by inaccuracy" (Burke, 1984a, p. 308).

Huntsman Chemical provides readers with perspective by incongruity to help them look at a photograph of a PS "clamshell" and cup, in order to "Think of them as your new home. Think *recycle.* " The copy begins, "Look closely. What do you see? We see a convenient and economical means of packaging—a resilient resource that can be brought back to life in any number of forms. Like insulation board in the walls of your home. Or products for your office. Or playground equipment. That's because polystyrene is recyclable." The Huntsman ad gives more examples of how this "recyclable" and "resilient resource" becomes "a variety of durable consumer products, from videocassette boxes to cafeteria trays to trash cans." Perspective by incongruity turns liabilities into assets through transcendent renaming. Thus, these "convenient and economical means of packaging" are no longer part of the solid waste disposal crisis, but are instead "a resilient resource that can be brought back to life in any number of forms." The comic frame is at work when Dow Plastics shows a strikingly designed chair and tells readers, "You're looking at 64 milk bottles and 2 shampoo containers." The material and the transcendent join again in Fina's rebus-styled ad, with a whimsical headline and artwork combination that simply juxtaposes, "How to recycle" with a picture of a PS clamshell and cup and then shows a series of pictures with commas between them: a tape dispenser, a plastic spray bottle, a brush and dustpan, a watering can, and poker chips. These two simple ads exemplify how the comic frame "also makes us sensitive to the point at which one of these ingredients becomes hypertrophied, with the corresponding atrophy of the other" (Burke, 1984a, p. 166). When the emphasis is on the wide range of new products made from recycled plastics, the transcendent hypertrophies while the material, post-consumer waste atrophies. Plastics are no longer trash, they are chairs and office supplies.

Perspective by incongruity also makes it possible for the plastics industry to redefine and recategorize their products through advertisements and arguments that merge the technological and the natural. In *A Grammar of Motives* (1974), Burke advises merging what seems to be divided and then dividing what seems to be merged by lumping and splitting until you see the "essence" of something by then seeing its opposite. The Amoco headline, "We'd like to uncover a hidden natural resource," merges nature with technology as synthetic plastics become a part of the natural world through technological transformations. The full-page art on the left page is a drawing of a plastic trash can next to a white picket fence. A man dressed in a Hawaiian-style shirt with parrots printed on it is either putting a plastic garbage bag into the can or taking it out. Although houses and well groomed lawns are in the background, the foreground area surrounding the trash can suggests the Garden of Eden: lush foliage with twining morning glories and columbines; a dragonfly darts to the left; a bright yellow and blue bird perches on a branch; a hummingbird sucks nectar from a flower. Idyllic nature peacefully coexists with suburban America while this man rummages through the trash. But that trash is, after all, "a hidden natural resource." The copy begins, "Did you know that the empty plastic drink bottles you throw away everyday can be transformed into carpet yarn or automotive parts or fiberfill for ski parkas? . . . It all happens because of recycling. The simple trash we throw away is a 'natural resource' that, with recycling, can be used to produce a multitude of new products." The copy recounts additional ways plastics are transformed: "Right now, almost 200 companies are recycling millions of used plastic containers into paint brush bristles, traffic signs, toys, floor tiles, wastebaskets and 'plastic lumber' for decks and park benches." The metamorphosis images continue at the end of the ad as recycling "transforms things that would ordinarily be thrown away into useful new products."

The copy for this "hidden natural resource" ad also explains overall recycling efforts: "Used glass bottles and aluminum cans can be transformed into new ones" and "yesterday's newspaper can be transformed into tomorrow's." In short, other recycled materials remain glass bottles, aluminum cans and newsprint. But plastics, with an implied inherently superior technology, undergo exotic transformations to become "a multitude of new products," the greater "natural resource" and the more *truly* recyclable material. This theme, because-of-their-technology-plastics-are-better, reoccurs in additional advertisements.

A GE Plastics ad ranks the substance above metal in a recycling hierarchy. The two-page spread features a dramatic photo of four half-buried sculptured copies of a late '50s-styled car—tail fins in the air—juxtaposed with a new BMW Z-1 and the headline, "Life After Death—A Recycling Strategy to Stop Burying Technology Alive." The copy begins: "With exterior body panels of high-performance GE plastics, the BMW Z-1 epitomizes industry's sweeping move to advanced materials. In the next decade, the automotive industry alone will use over 30,000,000 tons of engineering plastics eventually destined for landfills. We can no longer afford to simply trash reusable technology." The next paragraph touts plastics' technological superiority: "Pound for pound, engineering plastics are many times more valuable than metal. They are far less costly to reclaim and maintain their superior performance in successive generations of products." The comic frame's recycling narrative casts technology as the hero as it changes plastics from garbage, to flowerpots, to snazzy BMW Z-1s.

The ultimate expression of technologically recycled plastics as the new *supra* "natural resource" might be the entire twelve-page special advertising insert produced by the CSWS. Titled "The Urgent Need to Recycle," the copy on page one begins: "Imagine this. A child is running down the dock at a marina to join his father for a summer sail in the family boat. Suddenly, his foot slips out of its sandal, and his bare foot scrapes across the wide planks. There are no screams of pain, no frenzied dash for the first-aid kit." And why not? "Because in addition to being impervious to water and insects and weather, the dock is splinterless. It's not made of wood, it's made from recycled plastics." According to this introductory copy block, "plastic lumber" is *better* than wood: It is impervious to water, insects, or weather—*and* it is splinterless so it inflicts no harm on running children whose feet slip out of their sandals. The copy draws on another face of perspective by incongruity—caricature. "In caricature, certain aspects of the object are deliberately omitted while certain other aspects are over-stressed." As a result, "Caricature usually reclassifies in accordance with clearly indicated interests" (Burke, 1984b, p. 115). Using caricature, "plastic lumber" has all of natural wood's good qualities, but none of wood's drawbacks. As the insert's copy notes: "The plastic wood can be drilled, planed, sawed and nailed in much the same way as real wood. Yet, unlike real wood, it is impervious to weather, insects, and the decaying effects of time."

When the plastics industry's advocacy ads do not focus on transforming recycled plastics into the new *supra* "natural resource," they refute "the facts" about plastics packaging and solid waste disposal. Because these ads do not employ perspective by incongruity to correct or rename the situation, they contrast sharply with those ads that do use the comic frame to invite reclassifications and transcendent translations.

One example of the ads designed to present the industry's side of "the facts" is an Amoco ad with a left-page art piece suggesting a shower in progress as a glass shampoo bottle shatters on the floor—female toes perilously close to the shards—and the right-page headline, "Do we really want to return to those good, old-fashioned days before plastics?" The copy reads, "Some people believe that banning plastics and substituting other materials will solve the problem. We don't think they have all the facts. If plastics were banned, we'd lose safety and convenience features such as closures for foods and medicines, shatter-resistant bottles, freezer-to-microwave packages, and wrappers that preserve food freshness."

The ad's straight talk continues with "the facts" to refute charges that plastics' volume takes up one-third of the space in a landfill: "According to a recent study, plastics make up about 18% of the volume of solid waste in our landfills; paper and paperboard about 38%; metals, 14%;

glass, 2%; and other wastes, 28%." In another Amoco ad headlined, "Let's dig a little deeper into the notion that much of our garbage is made up of plastics," the solid waste issue is framed by weight, not volume: "A lot of well-intentioned solutions are being offered. One is that foam plastics, plastic bottles and plastic packaging should be banned. The fact is that plastics make up less than 8%, by weight, of our nation's waste. Paper and paperboard make up about 36%, glass and metal about 9% each, all by weight. The rest is anything from yard wastes to lumber to rubber tires." Either way, according to the solid waste studies the plastics industry chooses to quote, plastics are not that large, or heavy, a problem. After citing what the company is doing to make plastics recycling a reality, the ad closes with, "At Amoco Chemical, we believe we're only beginning to see the benefits of recycling. In the not-too-distant future, it can turn solid waste from a national problem into a national resource."

Although the copy mentions how recycling "can turn solid waste from a national problem into a national resource," these ads don't recycle our thinking about plastics. The plastics in these ads remain throw-away packaging and trash and part of the solid waste problem. When refuting the solid waste "facts" by weight or volume, the issue focuses again on plastics as garbage. Without the powerful transformations offered by perspective by incongruity, plastics still are headed for the landfill. But with the "atom cracking" reorientations offered by the comic frame, our perceptions of post-consumer plastics change from the *material*—nonrecyclable, nonbiodegradable garbage—to the *transcendent*—a recyclable resource that becomes neat, new, durable products like sleek new BMWs.

SHIFTING FROM BANS TO RECYCLED-CONTENT LAWS: ROUND TWO

The advocacy advertisements the individual resin companies ran in 1989 and 1990 explaining how recycling technologies could turn "solid waste from a national problem into a national resource," increased awareness of plastics' recyclability, and created new criticisms and expectations. Now that state and local decision makers and the consumer public knew that plastics are recyclable, they began demanding plastics recycling in their communities. While the plastics industry had been working to build recycling plants, the recycling infrastructure was still so inadequate that Minnesota State Attorney General Hubert H.

Humphrey III asked a poignant question: "Is it really fair to tell Minnesota consumers that plastic foam cups are 'recyclable' when there isn't a single recycling plant between Minneapolis and Brooklyn, NY?" (Humphrey, 1990).

With the undeveloped recycling infrastructure in mind, environmentalist John Javna (1991) took the industry to task for confusing consumers with "misleading public relations campaigns" that are "more likely to trumpet information about limited recycling programs than to discuss how widespread plastics recycling really is. As a result, consumers think that plastics recycling is imminently available at local recycling centers, when in fact it may be a long way off." But Javna found one positive aspect: "The good news it that, having given us the impression that their products are recyclable, plastics manufacturers now have to meet our expectations. So they're working hard to create the infrastructure that will make more plastics recycling practical."

Meanwhile, leading members of the plastics industry worked to sabotage plastics recycling. As shifting pressures in the public policy arena added to the plastics industry's need to clarify issue management strategies, the industry instead turned to confusingly mixed and contradictory tactics that obfuscated the issues. On the policy front, the industry publicly touted its recyclability while at the same time reactively fought to defeat the types of recycled-content packaging laws that would have made plastics recycling a practical reality—not just a promise. In the "public relations" area, the industry's willingness to create new organizations with large budgets and an "outreach" mandate suggested that the industry recognized the importance of communicating with its various publics and pursuing adaptive strategies. The programs launched by these new groups, on the other hand, reveal that the industry's definition of "communication" was stuck in the old, linear, one-way, "tell our side of the story" model. The advocacy messages demonstrated no clear understanding of the relevant audiences' interests or concerns. In an attempt to point out the "positive" points about plastics, the industry's advocacy program sidestepped the real issues on the public agenda.

The best examples of how the industry's recycling policy efforts worked at cross-purposes is found in its reactions as recycled-content packaging bills replaced the earlier outright plastics bans. With recycled-content packaging laws, lawmakers seemed to be saying: "OK, if you are so recyclable, let's see you recycle." The industry, led by Dow and Mobil, fought the laws on the national, state, and local levels by manufacturing arguments that recycled-content packaging laws would increase consumer costs and ultimately limit consumer choices because smaller companies would be unable to compete if forced to use recycled-content packages.

The Dow-Mobil–led industry coalition defeated a 1992 Massachusetts recycled-content ballot initiative, the most far-reaching to date, by using these arguments to cast the law as essentially antibusiness and anticompetition. The irony of the industry adopting this reactive and defensive public policy stance is that plastics recycling has been hampered by market forces that make virgin resin cheaper than recycled resin. Recycled-content laws would create the needed market demand for recycled resin, and the accompanying higher prices needed to make recycling cost-effective. With the industry trumpeting its self-proclaimed recycling successes and at the same time maneuvering to defeat measures that would make recycling a solid reality, one scientist working for an environmental interest group accused "Dow and other plastics producers of lacking sincerity" when they oppose legislation mandating recycled material in packaging (Reisch, 1992).

While the industry fought measures that would make recycling economically feasible, consumers became increasingly frustrated with the fact that they could not recycle their supposedly recyclable plastic trash. One representative of the recycling industry remarked, "Most plastics are not recyclable today, and yet, if you turn over any plastic container, you see the recycling symbol with the familiar chasing arrows with a number inside of it." This is misleading and confuses consumers, the recycling executive claimed, as he called for "the plastics industry to remove the recycling symbol until a national system for recycling those plastics has been established" (La Rue, 1993).

With a growing segment of the public aware that plastics are recyclable, especially with the chasing-arrow recycling logo and resin code number firmly stamped onto plastic containers, managers of civic and private recycling programs around the country reported that piles of plastic bottles sprouted up overnight like mushrooms around recycling drop-off bins (Gutlin, 1992). Without a market for recycled resins, recyclers continue to drop their plastics collections while "tons and tons of reprocessed plastics lie unsold in the New York region alone" (Van Voorst, 1993, p. 80). Industry critics charged that, at the same time the plastics industry praises one pilot recycling success, even more recycling ventures falter and fail (Reisch, 1992).

The difficult realities of plastics recycling may explain some of the contradictions in the industry's own efforts to address the problem itself and its accompanying public policy and public relations headaches. While a number of industry spokespersons became early recycling cheerleaders, others expressed doubts and "called for greater realism in appraising the proper role and extent of recycling" as they discussed recycling "myths" and realities—for example, that recycling costs far more than any other current disposal method. Industry leaders claimed, "Pragmatism must prevail over ideology in order for plastics and the environment to be reconciled"; "economics, not idealism, will dictate the progress of the recycling movement"; and "public enthusiasm for plastics recycling presently outpaces the reality of high costs." Industry publications frequently referred to the CSWS-set recycling goals as "controversial" ("Industry leaders," 1991; "What's the future," 1992; "Recession brings," 1992). Industry publications reveal more than ambivalence over recycling during the early 1990s. While outright plastic bans were no longer a pressing issue, the industry still felt threatened. From the industry's point of view, plastics manufacturers and companies like McDonald's were victims of "senseless attacks by environmental groups," which the editor of *Modern Plastics* wrote, "have almost taken on a McCarthy-like tone in their use of nasty public relations tactics and refusal to acknowledge facts." In order to win "the public relations war with the environmental action groups," the industry needed "a united effort to get the facts across before it's too late." In this sense, "The McDonald's clamshell bombshell must have the same effect on the plastics industry that the Russians' Sputnik had on American education in the late 1950s" (Smock, 1991).

Feeling victimized, the industry continued its efforts to defend itself by telling the recycling story. Dow's 1990 television spots—one with an earnest backpacker telling his hiking companions about recycled plastics and the other set at a Dow company picnic with a plastics recycling engineer's young son pitching the plastics recycling story against the backdrop of a softball game—were designed as "an attempt to bring plastics up to parity in the public's perception with other well-known recyclable products" ("Dow ads," 1990). But these ads apparently had little impact on the public's overall assessment of plastics' environmental friendliness.

Opinion polls showed that the public's perceptions of plastics further deteriorated despite the industry's advocacy efforts. By late 1990, 51 percent rated plastics "unfavorable," up from 34 percent in 1989.

Sixty-one percent believed the risks associated with plastics out-weighed plastics' benefits, up from 57 percent in 1988 ("Education on," 1991).

Attacked by environmentalists and misunderstood by the public, the industry considered turning to advocacy advertising to defend itself and restore its reputation. By mid-1991, industry publications reported, "A massive public outreach campaign is being quietly revived by top leaders of the U.S. plastics industry." Unlike the earlier divisive Dow proposal, this "new effort is being planned with care" through "low-key deliberations" at "high decision-making levels." According to a spokesperson, "The idea is to avoid a Band-Aid approach" by address-ing both plastics' role in solid waste issues and plastics' *positive* contributions to modern life ("Education on," 1991).

Tensions continued between those in the industry who favored agressive campaigns to confront plastics foes and correct "misconcep-tions" and those who more cautiously advocated changing the situation before advertising about recycling successes. The industry disbanded the CSWS and replaced it with the new Partnership for Plastics Prog-ress (PPP). In announcing the new group, the emphasis was on one industry problem, the perceived failure to communicate with the gen-eral consumer public. One industry executive claimed, "We have done too little too late to communicate the facts and to correct misinforma-tion so that practical and lasting solutions can be implemented" ("Ed-ucation on," 1991). The president of Union Carbide stated,

> The mandate of the partnership is to coordinate and improve existing recycling, conservation, and resource recovery programs; to develop new initiatives when required; and to do a better job of communicating with the public about our commitment and efforts. . . . It is very clear that our ability to continue providing for the needs of society depends upon our successfully responding to public concerns about plastics and the environment. (Thayer, 1991)

Reports mentioned that the PPP's proposed strategy is "far broader, more agressive (and much better funded) than the one it inherits from the CSWS" and that "in contrast with other industry initiatives aimed at individual problems involving plastics, the partnership expects to address broader issues and to attract a wider range of member compa-nies" ("Powerful new group," 1991; Thayer, 1991).

With annual funding of around $60 million, more than three times greater than CSWS ever enjoyed, plastics industry insiders believed that the PPP would "give our industry direction and momentum" and "change the ways in which it responds to its environmental critics"

("Industry group," 1992; "Powerful new group," 1991). The PPP strategy involved programs coordinated through three task forces: outreach, advocacy, and product stewardship. The outreach segment was designed to "forge a nationwide network of 'activists' drawn from a cross-section of the industry" and "awaken a sleeping giant." The advocacy program would rely heavily on an advertising program that "communicates what this industry has long taken for granted, that plastics contribute to our personal and environmental well-being" ("Industry group," 1992).

The PPP's major mission, taking the industry's story to the consumer public, took shape in its first major advertising and public relations campaign launched under the slogan, "Take Another Look at Plastic." Some industry members feared that it might backfire. As one environmental officer at a major resin company argued, "The industry can't talk its way out of the solid waste crisis." Others agreed and claimed, "A publicity campaign should await more substantive industry solutions and implementation of practical (albeit often painful and slow) achievements" ("Industry group," 1992). As one industry consultant noted earlier, "The public is more likely to believe plastics are recyclable when they themselves are involved in a curbside program" ("Education on," 1991).

Disagreements over executing an advertising campaign constituted some of the "travails and doubts" that went into forming the PPP coalition ("Industry group," 1992). The PPP was renamed the American Plastics Council right before the initial $18 million campaign kicked off in late 1992. Timed to lead into the new 1993 Congress and state legislative sessions, the campaign included four television spots, supporting radio spots, and print advertisements that "seek to restore plastics' image before a skeptical public" (Gardner, 1992).

TAKE ANOTHER LOOK: ADVOCACY
IN THE BLINK OF AN EYE

The "Take Another Look at Plastic" campaign's broad, basic purpose statement, to polish plastics' tarnished image, suggests why these ads, when compared to the earlier ads using the powerful reframing device of planned perspective by incongruity, present a fuzzily myopic and confusing, unplanned or unconsciously incongruous view of plastic. The earlier ads respond to public concerns and powerfully reframe the issue. In contrast, the second campaign addresses vague, self-centered industry concerns about an overall negative image and appears to be nothing more than vacuous, self-congratulatory nonsense. In the "Take Another Look at Plastic" campaign, there is no compelling exigence, no clear response—and no need for readers to accept the plastics industry's invitation to do even a cursory double take. One rhetorical public relations idea accounts for the disparity between the two campaigns.

Bitzer's (1968) definition of the "rhetorical situation," as adapted by public relations theorist Ron Pearson (1987), illuminates how the first campaign's compelling "exigence" or question led to a clear response: "Yes, plastics are recyclable." While there are often a number of exigencies or problems that may need to be addressed in a rhetorical situation, a controlling exigence becomes the organizing principle. Bitzer argues that the controlling exigence specifies the audience, those who can act as "mediators of change," and the change to be effected. As Pearson (1987) applies Bitzer's rhetorical situation to public relations writing, the controlling exigence also dictates an advocacy campaign's message and its central theme or thesis. Bitzer (1968) warns about the trickiness of clearly perceiving the essential exigence, especially as it relates to the audience's interests.

These two plastics industry advocacy campaigns serve as prime examples of Bitzer's description of key factors a rhetor must understand when faced with the challenge of clearly perceiving the factors in a rhetorical situation. In the first series, the controlling exigence, its accompanying audience interests, and important operating cultural constraints are addressed and used to the industry's advantage. In the "Take Another Look at Plastic" campaign, the industry misreads the audience's interests and overlooks cultural constraints. The campaign's fuzzy view of plastics' environmental attributes (saving water, energy, and topsoil) misses what the public sees as the issue: a still woefully inadequate recycling infrastructure. While the industry may have set a new environmental issue agenda in the attempt to polish the plastics industry's image, the public holds tight to its own perceptions of what is at stake. Ironically, the solid waste crisis seemed to have eased as more landfill space became available and more waste incineration plants began operating, "But Americans don't want to send their garbage into the earth or into the air. They want to recycle" (Van Vorst, 1993). While the industry fought recycled-content laws that would create a market for recycled resins, the public pushed for more plastics recycling in their communities as fewer and fewer programs collected plastics.

With Pearson's Bitzer-based guidelines for gauging campaign acuity, it is easy to see how this effort misreads its target audience's interests and concerns: solid waste reduction, not energy savings. The industry and the ads' creators also fail to see how certain audience-centered cultural "constraints," like our ambivalence toward plastic, are not addressed. Actually, the attempt to present plastics' positive contributions to modern living faces several cultural constraints that work against the industry.

Bitzer (1968) identifies the constraints operating in a rhetorical situation as the audience-centered attitudes, beliefs, images, interests, facts, and traditions that have the power to constrain decision and action needed to modify the exigence. But the savvy rhetor can make positive use of constraints, as illustrated in the ads using perspective by incongruity to reclassify plastics as the "new 'natural resource.'" By working within the constraints of current cultural beliefs that state "natural" is good, the plastics industry co-opted the natural lifecycle; "natural resource" plastics are good. While this did not necessarily become the new widespread definition of plastics, it did tap into positive current beliefs and images.

There are more deeply embedded cultural definitions of "plastic" than a campaign focused on the ways plastic permeates our lives verbalizes and visualizes. Unfortunately for the plastics industry, these associative meanings speak to truths about our culture that we might be reluctant to admit. As one anthropologist notes, "The fact is that plastic will soon be to modern Americans what the walrus was to the Aleut or the buffalo was to the Sioux: nothing less than the basis of an entire material culture." As such, "In some form or other, we wear it, eat with it, write with it, cover our floors with it, insulate our houses with it, the list is practically endless." But we are ambivalent about the substance of our material culture: "We loath plastic instead of respect it; we're addicted to it, but make fun of it." In this sense, "Plastic is not just a substance, but a code word for a way of life that all right-thinking people despise." As a code word, "Plastic has gone in thirty years from a symbol for high technology and inventiveness to a symbol of rampant consumerism, from the space program to Cup O'Noodles." For an anthropologist, "It is this schizophrenic attitude that makes the current struggle over what to do with plastic trash so interesting to watch" (Gutin, 1992).

The major problem with the "Take Another Look at Plastic" campaign is that, in attempting to appeal to both aspects of our love-hate relationship with plastic, it addresses neither. Instead of showing high-tech problem-solving inventiveness, it pictures plastic-encased hot dogs and styrofoam egg cartons. While it could show plastic "lumber" or a vast array of durable products made with post-consumer recycled plastics, it pictures a section of plastic-wrapped watermelon. By trying to combine the two levels of the meaning of "plastic" as code word without using a powerful device like perspective by incongruity to place the two side-by-side and then transform them, little happens to plastic packaging's "image" problem. Ironically, there is an unconscious, unplanned, even natural, incongruity to the very concept of "plastic" as code word for both the best and the worst high-technology offers.

Without a clear understanding of the plastic-as-code-word cultural constraints, "Take Another Look at Plastic" ignores its intended audience's persistent issue concern, uncollected "recyclable" plastic containers filling their trash cans. Before the campaign even began, critics pointed out that these ads sidestep real consumer concerns in their attempt to tell the industry's positive story. After viewing the campaign's four television spots, Bob Garfield (1992), resident television spot critic and columnist at *Advertising Age,* opines,

> It all seems so Pollyanna, so obvious, so . . . plastic. D'Arcy Masius Benton & Bowles, which also gave us the unbelievably insipid "Dow lets you do great things," tells the plastics story as if in a vacuum, as if there were scant consumer suspicion to overcome, as if viewers were just salivating to hear *more great news about polymers!!!* They aren't. We're talking about a hostile audience here, many of whom think foam coffee cups will destroy the earth, possibly by Thursday. How do you suppose they regard the motives of those who tell us to "Take another look at plastic"? Answer: dismissively.

Several scientists working with environmental groups reviewed the campaign and noted that consumers already know the advantages of plastics packaging and products. Recycling is their major concern: "People don't dislike plastics; they just don't like the fact that they don't know what to do with them when they're done. An advertising campaign that focuses on perceptions, on plastics' advantages, is not going to work. You've got to change the underlying reality" (Gardner, 1992).

While the television spots may not be able to "change the underlying reality," there is an air of magic tricks, a sleight of hand, as plastic products become illusory shape shifters. Two of the four television spots emphasize that plastics are recyclable with special effects designed to create metamorphosing visual images. With this technique the spots employ a visual application of perspective by incongruity as one object transmutes into another. In one spot, the spokesperson tosses plastic detergent bottles that transform into plastic trash cans that seem to descend from the sky. But the wonder of this magic act is interrupted by a disclaimer at the bottom of the screen telling viewers to check to see if plastics recycling is available in their communities. Of the two ads illustrating plastics' recycling metamorphosis into new forms, *Advertising Age*'s Garfield prefers the spot that opens with small boys playing with toy cars on a carpeted floor. One toy car turns into a real car. The voice-over says the car's lightweight plastic side panels save energy and resist denting, as a runaway shopping cart filled with plastic two-liter pop bottles slams into the car's door. One bottle tumbles out of the cart and onto the ground as the voice-over says, "You probably don't think plastic can be recycled but it can," and the bottle turns into the toy car being pushed on the carpet. Both the toy car and the carpet are now revealed as products made from recycled plastics. With this spot, Garfield (1992) writes, "We see how plastics fits into the full circle of our lives."

The other two television spots also use visual shifts as they address plastics' safety and energy-saving features. In these commercials the background and foreground vantage point change as the spokespersons tout plastics' advantages. Garfield (1992) recreates the spot that opens at a grocery checkout stand as the clerk/spokesperson spies a host of plastic containers and says,

> "When you look at plastic, you know how it helps things stay fresh and safe and unbreakable and strong and easy to carry. But take another look. [The whole checkout is passed by a moving car, and then itself seems to pass in front of a suburban home.] Plastic also saves energy, because it helps make cars lighter and saves gas. And plastic insulation helps save energy at home. [Now the checkout stand moves off-camera, and the clerk grabs two plastic bags full of groceries.] Even these strong plastic bags, because they take less energy to make than other grocery bags." [And so on, sponsored by the American Plastics Council, urging you to] "Take another look at plastic."

The other plastics' safety-and-energy advantages spot features a father and his young son, plastic safety helmets in place, bicycling through the story-telling backgrounds/foregrounds.

While the television spots use special effects for swiftly changing images to expand on the notion of taking another look at plastics, the print ads are visually static and conceptually confusing. Three ads appear in both two-page spreads and full-page versions. The spreads' left-hand page is devoted to a photograph. The headline and the copy are on the right-hand page. The single-page ads use the same photograph and headline with shortened copy. These ads must operate on the assumption that the reader already knows certain things since the most important connecting information, relating the headline to the picture, is often delayed or suppressed. If informing the assumedly unaware public is the major purpose of the "Take Another Look at Plastic" campaign, it is curious that the two print ads dealing with recycling and environmental issues require the readers to contribute information they may not have. Even if they stick with the ad copy, which makes little sense, and read all the way to the end of a copy block, the connecting information is only alluded to, not presented. While the print ads' headlines make provocative claims, the photographic art shows mundane plastic packaging, and the copy block falls short of that transcendent leap that would take pictured packaging to the heroic planet-saving heights, or floor-covering plains, hinted at in the headlines.

The best example of how these print ads can be more confusing than clarifying to all but the careful or patient reader is found in the ad that features a photograph of the inside of a refrigerator, with several two-liter pop bottles, two egg cartons, a one-gallon plastic milk jug, a maple syrup bottle, and more. The headline reads, "Your new carpeting may already be in your refrigerator." If readers do not already know that the PETE (polyethylene terephthalate) plastic in two-liter pop bottles is commonly recycled into carpeting fibers, the headline, photograph, and copy block will not make much sense unless they endure until the final paragraph that merely hints at the connection between the contents of the refrigerator and the future new carpet. The longer version of the copy begins, "If you're looking for ways to help make the earth a better place to live, one solution is in your refrigerator right now. Next to the pillow. Behind the picnic table. It's called recycling. And when you look at plastic and recycling, you'll see it's turning into some pretty remarkable things." After listing the myriad products that can emanate from recycled plastics, the copy continues, "If you think recyclability is the only earth-friendly benefit of plastic, take another look. Plastic saves energy by insulating homes to save fuel. And helps reduce pollution by making cars lighter to save gas. Plastic even helps save the earth, literally. Plastic geotextile fabrics protect beachfront land from erosion and encourage plant growth." After urging readers to call a toll-free number for a free booklet, the ad copy ends, "And just think. Someday that soda bottle in your fridge may be a beautiful addition to your living room floor." But the copy fails to mention that carpeting is one of the major products using recycled plastics. That's a huge gap the reader has to fill, especially if the original assumption of the campaign is that consumers are not aware of all the everyday products using recycled plastics.

Another confusing print ad, "How to save the planet and the picnic at the same time," pictures a red-checkered tablecloth, picnic basket, plastic dishes, plastic-wrapped hot dogs, a plastic-encased hunk of watermelon, and potato salad in a plastic container. The copy block begins, "It's simple. Just look for something that helps your picnic while it helps your favorite planet. In other words, take a look at plastic. Surprised? You shouldn't be. You know how plastic keeps food fresh and locks in flavor. Your refrigerator is probably full of plastic right now. But what does plastic do for the earth? A whole lot of good." The copy recounts the plastic products that prevent erosion, help converve water, and reduce "spoilage" of "fruits and vegetables . . . in transportation and storage." But if these miracles of modern science were not enough to make readers forget about recycling, "Take another look. Over 650 *million* pounds of plastic packaging was recycled last year, and that number will keep growing. To make everything from new plastic bottles to plastic 'lumber' for picnic tables." The ad closes, "The next time you use plastic packaging for a picnic, just think. You're helping to save something a whole lot more important than just your lunch."

The headline and the final paragraph of the copy might make more sense if the copy made connections between exactly what is currently recycled or whether any of those earth-saving products, "plastic geotextile fabrics," plastic liners to repair leaky water mains, and "plastic mulch," are made by recycling the plastic packaging shown in the photo. Even at the end of this ad, the reader might still wonder how using plastic wrap or plastic plates saves the planet. Once again readers are expected to build the missing logical bridges, without any solid information, as the ad copy recycles the same glossed-over vague generalities found in the other print ads and the television and radio spots.

CONCLUSIONS: CHANGING THE
SUBJECT TO SIDESTEP THE ISSUES

The "Take Another Look at Plastic" campaign's attempt to remind the American consumer how plastics make life safer and better rightfully boasts about one plastics application. The print ad headlined "Some benefits of plastic last for only half a second" pictures both driver- and passenger-side airbags inflated to protect a mother and son in a collision. The ad's copy also points out other "lifesaving benefits": "Look at the protective clothing firemen wear. The bullet-resistant vests policemen wear. And the bicycle helmets you and your family wear. They are all made from plastic."

If we accept the American Plastics Council's invitation to look at the industry and its products through its eyes, we might admit that we appreciate plastic, even in its mundane applications. With safety and convenience in mind, we reach for the shatterproof plastic juice bottles instead of the glass. We tell the checker "plastic" when asked which type of bag we want to safely and conveniently tote our groceries home. As dissenting voices within the industry who argued against the $18 million image campaign feared, deep-down we already know that we love plastic, and that we hate it. An "image" campaign is not going to do much to change the intensity of either emotion in our culture-induced schizophrenic relationship with plastic.

When it comes to plastics, it is not automobile airbags, protective clothing for public safety personnel, or safety helmets that Americans want to talk about. Many Americans still hang on to the solid waste issue and want to know why the only thing they can do to lessen the plastics load at the local landfill is to stomp on those two-liter PETE soda bottles and HDPE (high-density polethylene) milk jugs and detergent containers to compress their volume before consigning them to garbage cans and landfills. Americans want to know when plastics recycling will reach their community. Rather than answer those concerns, the industry would rather change the subject by talking about the "positive" aspects of plastics safety or its energy-saving features.

Just as the "Take Another Look at Plastic" campaign tries to tout plastics' advantages without clearly showing them, it also attempts to allay our solid waste anxieties without fully addressing plastics recycling issues. It reassures us that used gallon milk jugs and two-liter pop bottles will find new life as pillows, toys, or even garbage cans. But it does not depict or explain the transformations.

While both print ads aimed at environmental concerns brag that "650 *million* pounds of plastic packaging was recycled last year," environmentalists counter that this campaign "is putting a happy face on plastics recycling." The 650 million pounds may sound impressive; but compared to other materials recycled in 1990, only 2.2 percent of plastics, mainly PETE soda bottles, were "reborn." Although the industry celebrates significant progress in increased recycling programs, the amount of plastics used increases each year as more manufacturers adopt plastic packaging because of its advantages. A 52 percent increase from 4.4 million tons of plastic packaging discarded in 1985 to 6.7 million tons discarded in 1990 indicates the growing plastics solid waste problem that recycling "650 million pounds" barely begins to reduce (Stipp, 1992). Recycling rates for plastic held steady at a mere 2.2 percent in 1993 while the rates for aluminum reached nearly 70 percent, paper hovered at 50 percent, and glass rose to 33 percent (Van Voorst, 1993). It may be that the plastics industry's "Take Another Look at Plastic" advocacy campaign hopes that the public will overlook the way it slights solid waste and recycling issues.

To answer consumer concerns, the industry might have to admit that it is not really serious about plastics recycling. This would contradict the image of the good, environmentally conscientious corporate citizen the industry seeks by spending more money on advertising and public relations than on research or pilot projects to address the plastic waste problem (Gutin, 1992). Plastics industry members who thought that $18 million designated to change the reality should be spent *not* on the image advertising campaign but instead on further developing the recycling infrastructure must also face the dark reality of ironies that make successful plastics recycling programs scarce. The first set of ironies are found in the marketplace and within the industry's attempts to defeat legislation that would change market forces to favor recycled resins. As petroleum refining byproducts, virgin resins will be cheap and abundant so long as the oil supply lasts. In contrast, recycled resins are scarce and expensive. Plastics' advantages of safety and convenience are a result of a wide range of resins and resin mixes that fill a limitless number of packaging niches. These advantages are the very reason why, from a cost perspective, plastics recycling is "difficult and nearly pointless" (Gutin, 1992). When the plastics industry marshalls its forces to fight recycled-content packaging legislation that would create a demand for recycled resins, it defeats market forces that would make recycled resins more valuable.

While the advertisements in the "Take Another Look at Plastic" campaign are upbeat about the wonders of plastics recycling, industry publications find plastics executives sounding themes that counter the industry's pro-recycling messages. The spokesperson for the industry's "product stewardship" task force advances the need to push for plastics' new, environmentally friendly "transformation": incineration or the more euphemistic "waste-to-energy recovery" or "waste-to-energy conversion." At the same time, the "advocacy" task force creates a network of industry-employed "activists" to fight against recycled-content legislation. Industry members point to the realities of the marketplace to explain why plastics recycling is not cost-effective and in the same breath decry any type of government intervention, claiming that the industry must retain control so that the recycled resins market will develop freely (Carbone, 1992; "Education on," 1991; "Industry group," 1992).

While two of the industry's three task forces are basically undermining plastics recycling, the plastics industry's third task force, "outreach," put together the $18 million "Take Another Look at Plastic" campaign as a public education effort to "correct misconceptions" and "make the case that plastics have benefited consumers and are recyclable" (Gardner, 1992). While the campaign's two major message objectives seem to address the two sides of our love-hate relationship with what is indeed the basis of our entire material culture, these advertisements are so lacking in informative "substance" that we have little to either intensify our infatuation or to soften our disdain. Little happens to "plastic" as code word for features of our culture, hollow or phony consumerism, that we often despise.

Throughout time, cultural artifacts endure and speak of the material basis of a way of life. Anthropologist Gutin (1992) points to the connections among the Sioux and the buffalo and the Aleut and the walrus. For an issue so fraught with policy and product paradoxes, the final plastics recycling irony may be predicted in the last paragraph of the Environmental Defense Fund advertisement that juxtaposed the polystyrene clamshell "cheeseburger box" with the pyramids of ancient Egypt. The ad observes that, if we do not pursue answers to the solid waste problem with the same vigor that we pursue new packaging applications, "The most enduring monument left on earth by our civilization may be a mountain of trash."

7

From "We Didn't Do It"
to "It's Not Our Fault"

The Use of Apologia in Public Relations Crises

Keith Michael Hearit

In a June 2, 1988, press conference, *Consumer Reports* charged that the Suzuki Samurai was an unstable vehicle prone to roll over if maneuvered quickly (Levin, 1988a). Consequently, the magazine demanded that Suzuki immediately remove the Samurai from the market and buy back the 150,000 vehicles currently on the road. Suzuki responded to this public relations onslaught as vigorously as it was initiated. To the charges that the Samurai is an unsafe vehicle, Vice President and General Manager of American Suzuki Doug Mazza answered, "The Samurai was thoroughly tested for safety, including stability and handling, prior to its introduction into the United States. We have absolute confidence that we are selling a safe and stable vehicle" (Levin, 1988a, p. D4). Additionally, Mazza questioned the motives behind the accusations leveled by *Consumer Reports*; he claimed that the charges were part of a political campaign by *Consumer Reports* to increase the safety standards of vehicles across the industry, and the Samurai, because it is a Japanese import, is a convenient scapegoat (Levin, 1988a).

The Suzuki Corporation responded to charges of wrongdoing with a form of communication commonly recognized as an *apologia,* a discourse of defense. An apologia is not an apology, though it may contain one; rather, it is a justificatory form of address in which an organization seeks to provide a compelling explanation of its behavior. Apologiae offer counter-interpretations of the "facts" that surround charges of corporate malfeasance.

The need to deliver an apologia is as old as human history. Whether the defense is the archetypal Adam, who insisted to God that "it was the woman You gave me that made me eat," Socrates, who denied that he had corrupted the youth of Athens, or Ronald Reagan, who insisted that he knew of no diversion of arms sales funds to the Nicaraguan *Contras*, the speech of defense has regularly been a part of human history. Rooted in Burke's (1984) notions of hierarchy, guilt, and the negative, the phenomenon appears to be a peculiarity of the human condition. Yet with the advent of the modern organization, apologetic discourse has evolved into a new form: corporate apologia (Dionisopoulos and Vibbert, 1983; 1988).

Historically, the research on apologia has formed a rich and varied tradition. Of all the different types of generic analyses available to critics, apologia is the most developed (Campbell and Jamieson, 1976). Research in this area traditionally has taken one of three approaches: first, the neo-Aristotelian approach (Linkugel and Razak, 1969; Rosenfield, 1968; Butler, 1972); second, the generic approaches, including the factoral approach[1] and the speech-set approach (Ryan, 1982; 1984; 1988); and third, the nongeneric, terministic-based approaches (Ling, 1972; King, 1985).

Taken as a body of research, three conclusions can be drawn concerning understanding of apologia. First, apologiae are a situationally controlled form of address. As Ryan (1982) has shown, apologia are responses to accusations, or *kategoria;* consequently, their substance bears considerable resemblance to the charges at hand. Second, since policies are but reflections of character, corporate apologiae are defined as defenses of either policy or character (Ryan, 1982). Finally, apologiae constructed to defend policy and character state the accusations and then attempt to refute them using well documented rhetorical strategies (Ware and Linkugel, 1973); it is the charge of wrongdoing that coalesces these elements into a form of discourse recognized as an apologia.

While the genus apologia is well developed, two significant weaknesses exist. First, recent applications of the Ware and Linkugel factoral approach have stifled development of inquiry in apologia; additionally, the criticisms offered by Conley (1986) raise serious challenges to the factoral approach.

Second, scholars have considerable knowledge of the apologetic efforts of individuals but know comparatively little about those delivered by corporations. Of the extant research on the subject of apologia, almost all are analyses of individuals; only Dionisopoulos and Vibbert (1988) and Benoit and Brinson (1994) have examined the apologetic discourse of corporations. If corporate discourse represents a paradigmatic shift to a new "managerial" rhetoric, as a number of critics argue (Crable, 1986; Sproule, 1988; Cheney and Dionisopoulos, 1989; and Cheney, 1992), a subsequent shift needs to be made from an individualist perspective to analyses of corporate discourse.

Therefore, this chapter analyzes the rhetoric of corporations charged with wrongdoing that consequently face public relations crises. Using a generic method (Campbell and Jamieson, 1976), I examine as paradigmatic cases the rhetoric of three organizations charged with wrongdoing: the aforementioned case of the Suzuki Samurai after *Consumer Reports* charged that the vehicle was likely to roll over; American Airlines after it canceled a large number of flights due to an employee "sick-out"; and the Volvo Corporation after the attorney general of Texas charged the company with "deceptive advertising" in its promotion of the strength and durability of Volvo automobiles.

In explaining how corporations attempt to propitiate their alleged guilt for committing indiscriminate or illegal acts, I argue that there are three prototypical dissociational stances corporate rhetors take to distance themselves from wrongdoing: stances of denial, differentiation, and explanation. The ultimate goal of all three stances is to diffuse hostility—to make those who judge unable to condemn. However, these stances diffuse hostility by using three different and ultimately less efficacious strategies. Denial disputes the validity of the charges; in effect, it seeks to render the charges groundless. Differentiation, on the other hand, argues that individuals who acted without organizational sanction are responsible for the wrongdoing; it seeks to transfer guilt to another by separating one idea into two rival ideas. Finally, explanation admits responsibility but adopts a posture that explains the rationale behind organizational actions. Consequently, an explanative stance argues that the corporation should be judged on its long-term record rather than a single act of wrongdoing. These stances are rooted in the three primary dissociations used by corporate rhetors charged with wrongdoing: denial uses an opinion/knowledge dissociation, differentiation uses an individual/group dissociation, and explanation uses an act/essence dissociation. All three dissociations argue, in different ways, that current understanding of organizational malfeasance is but an appearance of the actual reality of the situation.

This study extends understanding of apologia, for case studies frequently reflect the lesson from the story of the proverbial blind men who describe an elephant; each describes one aspect without understanding how it fits into the larger whole. Apologiae are issued because of a wide variety of exigencies: some are the result of environmental damage that carries with it horrific long-term consequences, while others are the result of a test program that suffers some well publicized abuses. Hence, this study uses a generic perspective to refine understanding of apologia, concluding that there are three paradigmatic forms of corporate apologia: denial, differentiation, and explanation. To accomplish this purpose, I first survey the nature of an accusation of wrongdoing; second, I note the three substantive stances available to the corporate apologist; third, I address stylistic concerns in the presentation of an apologia; and fourth, I draw a number of conclusions about the nature of corporate apologiae as responses to public relations crises.

THE SITUATION OF CORPORATE APOLOGIAE: LEGITIMATION CRISES

Apologiae are the result of charges of wrongdoing. The nature of the charge is such that the emphasis is placed on the misguided policies of the corporation. In such instances, key publics as well as media and public advocacy groups that purport to represent the public interest demand an explanation from the corporation. For example, *Consumer Reports*, the magazine of Consumer's Union, a well-known consumer group, charged Suzuki to have sold vehicles prone to overturn easily; American Airlines failed to dependably deliver passengers to their destinations; and finally, Volvo "rigged" an advertisement. Consequently, the charges thrust such companies into social legitimacy crises: organizational stakeholders perceive an incongruity between corporate values and those of a larger social system in which the organization operates (Mitroff, 1984). Dowling and Pfeffer (1975) succinctly state the relationship between values and wrongdoing involved in apologia: "When actual or potential disparity exists between the two value systems, there will exist a threat to organizational legitimacy" (p. 122). The fact that challenges to social legitimacy can be brought through actual or potential disparities highlights the rhetorical nature of both the maintenance and loss of legitimacy. While a crisis of social legitimacy does not necessarily mean that a corporation will be forced to close, it typically results in constraints on how it conducts its business. Consequently, corporations use rhetoric to reestablish their social legitimacy.

Corporations continually confront challenges to their social legitimacy, yet not all corporations respond to charges with apologiae. Indeed, corporate history is filled with examples of corporations that have acted unethically, but faced no legal or social sanction. Only when there is an intersection between corporate interest in the preservation of the status quo and their recognition that key publics perceive charges to be valid is there likely to be a public response (Post, 1978). If one of these two conditions is not met, a corporate response is improbable.

When corporations face legitimation crises and determine their best interest is to deliver apologia, they do so primarily for one of two reasons: incompetence or indifference to community. Corporations and maintain corporate social legitimacy by demonstrating their competence and concern for community (Hearit, 1992); conversely, corporations use apologia when publics perceive corporations to be incompetent in fulfilling their mission, or when they have acted in a manner that exhibits little concern for their community by being irresponsible, dishonest, or having broken the law. In situations such as these, corporations are inclined to adopt one of the following stances in their defense.

THE STANCES OF CORPORATE SELF-DEFENSE

While persuasion generally is viewed as an attempt to create identification (Burke, 1984), there are certain times in which rhetors use persuasion in an effort to sever identifications. Such is the case with dissociation. Dissociation is the rhetorical process whereby a unitary idea is bifurcated into two rival ideas.[2] The prototypical way rhetors use dissociation is through an appearance/reality division; as it concerns apologia, for example, rhetors claim that the alleged wrongdoing is but an "appearance" of the "true reality" of the situation. Dissociations are valuable because they offer methods for apologists to separate the juxtaposition of the organization with wrongdoing and thus diffuse the degree of guilt and reduce organizational culpability.

Depending upon the particulars of the kategoria, corporations accused of wrongdoing use three different forms of the prototypical appearance/reality dissociation: first, to deny guilt, they use an opinion/knowledge dissociation; second, to differentiate their guilt by scapegoating another, they rely upon an individual/group dissociation; and, third, to distance themselves from their guilt and to salvage their reputation, they use an act/essence dissociation. Each dissociational form represents a different apologetic stance. Consequently, the substantive choice of strategy (i.e., denial, differentiation, and explanation) informs the stylistic tone apologists enact. A corporation that denies wrongdoing can claim the moral high ground and attack the credibility of its accuser. Conversely, a corporation that scapegoats another must accept some responsibility due to its formal association, and hence takes a more conciliatory tone. A corporation that faces little choice but to admit some guilt responds in a more explanative tone.

Opinion/Knowledge

When the "facts" that precipitate apologiae are arguable, corporate rhetors use an opinion/knowledge dissociation to deny charges of wrongdoing. They assert that critics' claims are groundless and do not represent "actual knowledge" of the "facts" at hand (Perelman and Olbrechts-Tyteca, 1969, p. 421). Apologists can choose this dissociational strategy only when the "facts" are contested; in so doing, they assert that those who level the kategoria do not have "all the facts."

Suzuki used this strategy when *Consumer Reports* charged that the Samurai was unsafe due to its propensity to overturn when maneuvered quickly. Robert Knoll, the head of testing at *Consumer Reports,* leveled the charge: "The problem [with the Samurai] is inherent in its design. The only way to fix it is to make the vehicle longer, wider, and heavier" (Levin, 1988a, p. A1). Concomitantly, the Center for Auto Safety, a Washington, D.C.–based consumer advocacy organization, claimed that the Samurai was responsible for thirty-two rollover accidents that resulted in eight deaths and numerous injuries (Levin, 1988a). Such a charge violates the community dimension of legitimacy, for Suzuki manufactures a vehicle that puts consumers in harm's way.

In its initial response on June 3, 1988, Suzuki uses a denial stance to disavow any wrongdoing (Levin, 1988a). The company responds to the charges by labeling them "defamatory" (Suzuki, 1988a, p. 1). Such a strategy contests the validity of the charges; it challenges the interpretation of the act. In so doing, Suzuki uses an opinion/knowledge dissociation to attempt to redefine the charges. In asserting that the charges are "defamatory," Suzuki claims the allegations that its vehicle is likely to roll over are opinions and not reflective of the actual knowledge of the situation. Suzuki vice president Doug Mazza claims that the Samurai is "a safe and stable vehicle" and that the magazine's tests were "not representative of actual driving conditions" (Levin, 1988a, p. A1).

While it is standard for corporations to express concern for any harm done to people, companies such as Suzuki that utilize opinion/knowledge dissociations to refute the legitimacy of the charges do not respond with any statement of regret. To do so would admit a degree of validity to the charges and imply that the company is at fault.

Ultimately, the charge that the Samurai is unsafe is a charge against the integrity of the Suzuki Corporation, for critics alleged that the company is irresponsible for selling an unsafe vehicle. At a press conference one week later, Mazza further develops the opinion/knowledge dissociation. He begins by defining the charges as false: "We will not allow the magazine's biased and untrue statements that impact our company and our product to go unchallenged" (Suzuki, 1988b, p. 2). Mazza later reveals Suzuki's evidence that contends the allegations: "When questions about the Samurai's stability were first raised, we thoroughly reviewed the testing conducted prior to the Samurai's U.S. introduction, to ensure that our aggressive support of the vehicle's safety was well founded. And it was" (Suzuki, 1988b, p. 4). Mazza further buttresses the opinion/knowledge dissociation claiming that Suzuki had commissioned independent engineering tests of the Samurai that were stricter than those of *Consumer Reports,* tests which the vehicle passed. He intones: "We have had independent testing done, to subject the Samurai to severe handling tests. These tests . . . go even further than *Consumer Reports'* test, and were conducted within the standards set by the I.S.O., the International Standards Organization" (Suzuki, 1988b, p. 4). In sum, Suzuki asserts that the charges that the Samurai has a propensity to roll over are false; in reality, the vehicle is quite safe as evidenced by the successful completion of rigorous tests.

Suzuki uses a second opinion/knowledge dissociation when it levels a counter-charge at *Consumer Reports.* The "opinion," of course, is that *Consumer Reports* is a trustworthy source of consumer information; the reality is that the magazine is biased. Mazza charges, "The magazine changed its test for the first time in history. It appears as though the magazine wants the Samurai to fail" (Levin, 1988b, p. D1). Here Mazza refers to the fact that the Samurai had passed *Consumer Reports'* first maneuverability test, the standard test used on hundreds of vehicles. However, the magazine then gave the Samurai a stricter test, which it subsequently failed. The implication that Mazza raises is that *Consumer Reports* is a less than objective source of information. The opinion/knowledge dissociational pair has positive implications for Suzuki: the automaker portrays its accusers as less than knowledgeable about the Samurai's safety record; this undermines its critics' credibility. In so doing, the company presents itself as a socially responsible corporate actor; for by its revelation of the "true knowledge" of the situation, Suzuki asserts that it is trustworthy and its critics are not.

Suzuki, then, dissociates itself from the charges at hand to reassert its social legitimacy and simultaneously attacks *Consumer Reports'* legitimacy. This apologetic interchange demonstrates that legitimacy is not only a constraint on corporate behavior but also a resource that corporations employ against each other (Dowling and Pfeffer, 1975).

Individual/Group

Corporate apologists offer an individual/group dissociation when they find it in their interest to scapegoat a particular part of the organization, whether it be a union, a rogue subsidiary, or a group of disgruntled employees (Perelman and Olbrechts-Tyteca, 1969). The use of this strategy reveals an attempt to redefine the identity of who the corporation is and who acts for it. In situations like the one American Airlines faced, a corporation that cannot deny committing an act attempts to deny that the corporation qua corporation is responsible; in so doing, it seeks to scapegoat members of the organization by drawing a distinction where none previously existed.

American Airlines faced a problematic situation during the Christmas holiday season of 1990 when an average of over 500 pilots called in sick daily, a figure twice the usual number; such action by the pilots forced American to cancel about 11 percent of its flights (Solomon, 1990; "American Airlines says," 1990; "Even captains," 1991). The cancellation of flights is a problem rooted in the competence dimension of corporate social legitimacy, for American Airlines was unable to accomplish its primary mission: the transport of passengers from one point of the country to another.

In its apologia, titled, "AApology," issued on January 3, 1991, and again on January 8, 1991, American uses a differentiation stance to define its inability to deliver customers to their desired destination as a "disruption." In so doing, American Airlines uses an individual/group dissociation to scapegoat the Allied Pilots Association by claiming that the failure was the result of an "an illegal 'sick-out'" (AApology, 1991, p. A5). By defining the disarray to be the result of an "illegal sick-out," the company chooses a term that transfers blame and guilt for the "disruption" from American Airlines to the pilots union. Such a strategic choice portrays American Airlines not as a guilty corporate actor, but as a victim of the malicious actions of another.

In scapegoating the Allied Pilots Association, American Airlines uses an individual/group dissociation to divorce itself from the perception that it is unable to deliver its passengers to their destinations. To bifurcate the prevalent notion of incompetence, the apologia argues that in reality American Airlines is both a capable and a responsible company. American does so by scapegoating the Allied Pilots Association; it claims that the company's inability to do its job was not caused by the management team or the rank-and-file employee, the "group" that makes up the organization as a whole, but by an "individual" disgruntled union. In so doing, the company describes its inability to transport passengers as the result of an identifiable group within the organization that does not represent the interests of the organization as a whole. The company asserts, "During the holidays, some American Airlines pilots and their Union, the Allied Pilots Association, disrupted our operation and inconvenienced our passengers by means of an illegal 'sick-out'" (AApology, p. A5). Such actions by individuals do not reflect the group as a whole. The company writes: "American Airlines has built its reputation by providing superior service for its customers. Most of our 100,000 employees are dedicated to that goal and are embarrassed by our temporary inability to serve you properly during the holidays" (AApology, p. A5). The temporary inability to deliver passengers, according to this dissociation, was the result of an act by a few.

Typically, corporations that use a differentiation posture express surprise or outrage by the act; nevertheless, because the corporation is in some way involved, it suffers guilt by association. Consequently, American's apologia contains the following statements of regret to diffuse hostility directed toward the company: "We want to offer our sincere apologies to everyone who was delayed or inconvenienced.... We apologize for any inconvenience you may have experienced. We're doing what needs to be done to fix the problem and we look forward to serving you soon" (AApology, p. A5).

Here the company offers an apology that expresses sorrow, but does not accept responsibility for what has happened. While the organization does apologize for the disruption of airline schedules, it makes it very clear where the guilt for its inability to deliver services ultimately lies; American scapegoats the Allied Pilots Association.

The choice of the individual/group dissociation defines the pilots union as having an identifiable status whose interests are other than those of the organization; such a choice of scapegoat reifies the distinctions between the union and the organization, and suggests the probability that the air carrier will have long-term labor problems. Anticipating such a possibility, American Airlines goes to great lengths to explain what it is doing to alleviate its problems. The company writes, "American and the APA have been negotiating for well over a year, and we have offered our pilots a new contract that provides large wage and benefit increases" (AApology, p. A5). The company also claims, "We will continue to negotiate with the APA. However, we cannot and will not accede to demands that will create unacceptably high costs" (AApology, p. A5). American's discourse presents the organization as a company that makes a good faith effort to deal with legitimate contractual issues, while at the same time the apologia makes it clear that the pilots union violated such a spirit in its actions.To ensure that there is no future need for an individual/group dissociation again, the company asserts,

> Here's what we are doing to make things right: We have obtained a Temporary Restraining Order from a federal court forbidding this and other illegal job actions. We are reducing our flight schedule substantially, which means we'll keep more pilots in reserve than normal. Even if an assigned pilot decides to call in "sick" we'll get you where you want to go, when you want to get there. And we'll keep the reduced schedule in place until the dispute with our pilots is resolved. (AApology, p. A5)

In sum, in an effort to reassert its corporate social legitimacy, American Airlines attempts to dissociate itself from its "illegal" employees, though arguably their interests are consubstantial. In attempting to demonstrate its adherence to the important values of competence and responsibility, the corporation redefines its identity as an organization.

Act/Essence

Corporations that find they have no other option but to acknowledge some guilt use an act/essence bifurcation; they admit that while the wrongdoing occurred, it does not represent the "true nature" of the organization. In the final case study, Volvo employs an act/essence dissociation to address the perceived incongruity of its actions with the public value of honesty.

On October 24, 1990, Texas attorney general Jim Mattox sued the Volvo Corporation, charging that the company had violated the Deceptive Trade Practices Act by engaging in "deceptive advertising" (Meier, 1990, p. D1). In the lawsuit, Mattox charged that "[t]he car-crushing competition was a hoax and a sham" (Meier, 1990, p. D17). The allegation that Volvo had violated the community dimension of social legitimacy was based upon a series of allegations made by individuals who participated in the filming of the advertisements. The advertisements, which showed a Volvo 240 station wagon as the only vehicle in a long line of cars that was not crushed under the weight of a "monster truck," were based upon an actual "monster truck" rally (Volvo, 1990). Mattox charged Volvo with deception because Volvo's advertising agency, Scali, McCabe, and Sloves, structurally reinforced the Volvo wagon in order to ensure the safety of the crew as well as have the Volvo withstand the requirements of filming, which necessitated numerous takes. According to the Attorney General, the campaign violated the Deceptive Trade Practices because the Swedish automaker failed to portray the advertisement as a "dramatization" (Meier, 1990, A1).

To reestablish its adherence to the value of honesty, Volvo uses an explanative stance to admit that changes were made to the automobiles, but the changes were not done to mislead. Volvo (1990), in the person of president and CEO Joseph L. Nicolato, writes,

> Volvo management learned for the first time [on October 30] that the film production team had apparently made modifications to two of the vehicles. There were two reasons for the modifications: first, to enable the filming to be done without threatening the safety of the production crew, and second, to allow the demonstration Volvo to withstand the number of runs by the "Monster Truck" required for filming. We are proud of the strength of our Volvos, but even they cannot withstand being run over so many times by a "Monster Truck." (p. 2B)

By using a technical justification for a production decision, Volvo seeks to redefine the degree of offense from a serious act of deceptive advertising to a less offensive act of simply adapting to the constraints necessary to film a television and print advertising campaign.

Because the company indeed admitted to wrongdoing, it issued an apologia that uses an act/essence dissociation. Though it does not issue a statement of regret, Volvo does strike an explanatory tone to admit responsibility for the act. The company writes, "It was never the intention of Volvo to produce an advertisement which deceived or misled" (Volvo, 1990, p. 2B). Corporations like Volvo, which find they have no other choice but to rely on an act/essence dissociation, frequently deny intent because a denial of intent reduces the level of guilt. In addition, Volvo (1990) assures its key publics that it has taken "corrective action" to "insure that this does not happen again" (p. 2B). While there was a scapegoat available—Volvo's advertising agency, Scali, McCabe, and Sloves—Volvo (1990) chooses not to blame the agency in its apologia; instead it simply refers to the firm as "advertising agency management" (p. 2B).

To distance itself from the wrongdoing, Volvo uses an act/essence dissociation. The act, of course, was the deceptive advertisement. Volvo (1990) writes, "The advertisement which was produced inaccurately characterized the event as a car crushing exhibition when in fact is was a dramatization of the actual event in Vermont" (p. 2B). The deceptive advertisement, in this case, however, in no way reflects the essence of the automaker's public communication. Nicolato argues, "For nearly 35 years Volvo has earned an outstanding reputation not only for high quality products but for high quality advertising as well. . . . Volvo has built its reputation on honesty and candor" (Volvo, 1990, p. 2B).

The company argues that the failure to label the advertisement a "dramatization" leaves the appearance that the organization is less then veracious. In reality, Volvo asserts that the one-time failure to label the advertisement a "dramatization" is a deviation from the essence of the Swedish automaker. In effect, Volvo argues that the deceptive advertisement is really an aberration and not indicative of the long-term record of the Volvo Corporation, which has an outstanding advertising reputation. To support the dissociation, Volvo cites its thirty-five-year history of high-quality advertising as evidence that the deceptive advertisement is not representative of the true nature of the company.

Act/essence dissociations are useful because they offer a differentiation strategy; they allow a corporation to claim that, while it may have committed the act, it was not representative of the company's true nature. In other words, the company appeals to be judged based on its lifetime reputation, not on a solitary, isolated incident. Such a strategy is useful to a corporation that cannot deny committing the act, but can deny that the act is representative of the totality of its reputation.

These dissociational stances, denial, differentiation, and explanation, should be understood as clusters of forms rather than as fixed types. Indeed, while these stances are useful because they provide prototypical ways to understand how corporations posture themselves based on their understanding of the validity of the charges against them, it should be noted that corporations sometimes use multiple dissociations within a given stance. For example, within the differentiation stance, corporations primarily rely upon individual/group dissociations, yet they also use act/essence dissociations to deal with the bothersome implication that organizational members nonetheless were guilty of the wrongdoing.

THE STYLE OF CORPORATE SELF- DEFENSE

When charged with wrongdoing, corporations respond in one of two ways: they speak in a corporate "we" (Cheney, 1983), or they respond in the persona of the chief executive officer (Thompson, 1981; Dionisopoulos and Vibbert, 1983). This study suggests that the current trend within corporate apologia is for corporations to deliver apologia in the persona of the chief executive officer (Fox, 1982a; 1982b); both Suzuki and Volvo used the persona of high-level executives to personally respond to the charges. American Airlines, on the other hand, employed a corporate persona. Indeed, the legitimation of the organization to society is one of the primary tasks of those at the strategic apex of the organization (Dowling and Pfeffer, 1975). Such legitimation activity accrues rhetorical benefits for the organization: it personifies an otherwise faceless corporation; it provides an image of a leader in control of an otherwise uncontrollable situation; and, if the apologia eventually shows itself to have been ineffectual, it furnishes a potential scapegoat who publicly has claimed responsibility for what has happened.

The public relations decision to respond in the persona of the chief executive is rhetorically sagacious. Apologiae are forensic, or law-based, situations in which rhetors respond in a nonforensic manner; they are driven primarily by personal character justifications (Campbell and Jamieson, 1976). Rhetorically, an individual in charge of a corporation can accomplish an ethos-based defense more readily than can a corporation. A person speaking for a corporation offers an identifiable source by which the public can more readily gauge the veracity of their justifications and control over the situation.

Since these apologetic responses by CEOs use character defenses, they do not respond to the "factual" questions with "factual" answers. Apologists seldom cite evidence in a traditional sense (Crable, 1976); no apologist in this study offers a means for independent confirmation of its actions. Rather, corporations attest to their integrity while often calling into question the virtue of those who level charges against them.

CONCLUSION: APOLOGIA AND PUBLIC RELATIONS CRISES

At root within any kategoria/apologia exchange is the attempt to assert definitional hegemony, or terminological control, over the interpretation of the act (Dionisopoulos, 1986; Dionisopoulos and Crable, 1988). Obviously, the charge of wrongdoing carries considerable effect, and, in the sense that the apologist has to respond to those charges, the accuser has control of the terms used to define the situation. The corporate apologist seeks to wrest the definitional hegemony from the accuser and, in the process, propose a persuasive description that suggests an alternative framing of the act.

It is paramount for the corporate rhetor to redefine its behavior from being incompetent or immoral to a rival and preferable behavior. In giving such an account, the corporation attempts, in the words of Giacalone and Payne (1987), to "provide the public with a reasonable explanation for the event, carefully posturing the explanation to minimize the company's blameworthiness" (p. 24). This explains the rhetorical benefit of dissociational stances; they redefine understanding of the "facts" that surround the allegations of wrongdoing.

Corporations face considerable public hostility when they are accused of wrongdoing. At such times, the use of dissociations functions to dissipate public animosity. The diffusion of public hostility appears to be one of the primary motivations for corporations to issue apologia: the belief that a public apology will help counteract ill will toward the company, or will at least give resolution to the public ritual of wrongdoing, guilt, and absolution, and consequently deprive journalists of a continuing story.

Burke (1984) wisely recognizes that not enough is known concerning the role of rhetoric in legitimating capitalism. Accordingly, in this analysis, I have presented three dissociational stances that corporations facing public relations crises seek to enact: denial, differentiation, and explanation. These stances are driven by the substantive choices made by rhetors when they address kategoria of wrongdoing. The choice of the stance is dependent on the validity of the charges as well as the availability of a scapegoat. In so doing, not only has this analysis attempted to further understand the sub-genres of apologia, but it also has provided strategies and examples for corporate communicators to follow.

NOTES

1. Notes removed for reader clarity. In order, Ware and Linkugel, 1973; Harrell, Ware, & Linkugel, 1975; Kruse, 1977; 1981; Gold, 1978; Hoover, 1989.

2. Perelman and Olbrechts-Tyteca, 1969; Schiappa, 1985; Zarefsky, 1980; Zarefsky, Miller-Tutzauer, and Tutzauer, 1984.

PART III
Case Studies of Targeted Influence

8

Philip Morris Magazine
An Innovation in Grass Roots Issue Management

Rachel L. Holloway

When an organization faces potential regulation detrimental to its objectives, issue management is in order. Issue management, according to Chase (1982), is "the capacity to understand, mobilize, coordinate, and direct all strategic and policy planning functions, and all public affairs/public relations skills, toward achievement of one objective: Meaningful participation in creation of public policy that affects personal and institutional destiny" (pp. 1–2). Communication with key publics is essential to any issue-management strategy. An issue manager chooses, legitimizes, and promotes issue definitions to support the organization's desired policy outcome (Crable and Vibbert, 1985; Hainsworth, 1990). Ongoing issue communication is "designed to prevent an issue from becoming engrained in the public mentality to the extent that it begins to demand legislative remedy. This phase is preventative, trying to help the public understand a company or industry, demonstrating corporate responsibility and countering false information and charges" (Heath and Nelson, 1986, p. 170).

No public is more important to this "preventative" process than "organizational stakeholders," those publics invested in a company's or industry's success, either financially or symbolically or both. Heath and Nelson (1986) note that an issue manager needs to galvanize the support of those publics already favorable to the desired issue resolution (pp. 172–179). In many cases, the stakeholders already accept the company's or industry's position and therefore do not require "persuasion" per se; they do need updated strategic information, reassurance and support, ongoing indoctrination, and specific action recommendations if they are to serve as effective organizational advocates. As they adopt the company's issue definitions and proposed policies, they are prepared to be source of grass roots supporters for later issue-management campaigns.

Unfortunately, on highly controversial issues, a message designed for stakeholders may generate intense criticism if received by other, less sympathetic publics. Rather than galvanizing support as intended, the issue communication may fuel the opposition's fire and heighten a public call for a response counter to the organization's desires. Sometimes a message is best heard only by a select few.

Philip Morris, U.S.A. provides an excellent case study to explore the challenges of reaching stakeholders with controversial message. In 1991, a survey of corporate and agency public relations professionals ranked Philip Morris Companies Inc. ninth overall and first for the tobacco industry for its issue communication ("The secrets of success," 1991). The professional journal *inside PR* singled out Philip Morris from other tobacco companies because of its success in "turning what had previously been a health issue into a first amendment issue also."

Philip Morris developed a distinctive "offense through defense." Guy Smith, former vice president of corporate communications at Philip Morris, reported that the company "made a strategic decision several years ago that it was going to be proactive in defending the rights of smokers to enjoy its products" ("The secrets," 1991, p. 14). While the company could not prevent smoking issues from reaching the public agenda, they could create and legitimize issue definitions of a force equal to or greater than those of their opponents and build an active and vocal grass roots constituency. The company's hope was to build a public well versed in the company's political positions, ready to delay, derail, or defeat antismoking policies at the local, state, and national levels. A central component of their overall strategy, and the object of this analysis, was the company's innovative "stakeholder strategy," *Philip Morris Magazine (PMM)*.

The country's first magazine dedicated to the interests of smokers, during its seven-year publication, *PMM*'s circulation peaked at nearly 13 million readers, greater than *Time, Newsweek, U.S. News and World Report,* and *The Wall Street Journal* combined. Winner of the Society of Publication Designer's 25th Anniversary Competition, *PMM* looks like a typical high-quality corporate magazine or periodical that markets Philip Morris products and promotes a positive image through stories about the company's many good works (Riley, 1992; Ford, 1969). Closer scrutiny shows *PMM* to be much more. Through production and distribution of a free, forty-eight-page, quarterly magazine, Philip Morris was able to reach organizational stakeholders with highly strategic and otherwise controversial messages central to the company's political objectives, all without significant risk of open opposition. Through *PMM,* the company met three interrelated issue management objectives: first, the magazine defined smoking issues in favorable and strategic terms; second, the magazine built a context of values, endorsements, and issue linkages that legitimize Philip Morris's position; third, the magazine reinforced a positive political identity and proposed action to smokers. The purpose of this chapter is to describe, analyze, and evaluate these strategies. In order to do so, a first step is to place *PMM* in the context of relevant public opinion and public policy.

THE PUBLIC CONTEXT:
INFLUENCE, OPINION, AND POLICY

Since its earliest days, the tobacco industry has met public challenges with public relations expertise. Pollay (1990) reports that as early as 1920, Chesterfield hired Edward Bernays and Ivy Lee to counter competitors' advertising claims. Lucky Strike hired Bernays to break the taboo against women smoking in public. Throughout the 1950s and beyond, tobacco companies fought the connection between smoking and negative health consequences (Miller, 1992). In 1971, cigarette advertising was banned from the airwaves. The late 1980s and 1990s presented new challenges.

The Surgeon General, members of Congress, and public health organizations frequently remind the public that cigarettes contribute to the premature death of 300,000 Americans every year ("Tobacco's toll," 1992; "Tobacco issues," 1990). Ongoing research links second-hand smoke to poor health, especially among children (Tilsner, 1993; Janofsky, 1993). Tobacco dollars that support women's sports are labeled "blood money" (Gladwell, 1990). Tobacco marketing practices are attacked from many quarters. Some accuse tobacco companies of "luring kids to light up" (Green, 1990; Mintz, 1992). Others report company attempts to subvert the ban on cigarette advertising (Blum, 1991; Colford, 1991b; "Not out," 1989). Conservative columnist

George Will (1990) likened tobacco marketing strategies to "a sniper's rifle, drawing beads on the most vulnerable, manipulable Americans." Negative press coverage mirrors public opinion. A 1990 Gallup Poll (Gallup and Newport, 1990) identified a "growing anti-smoking sentiment in the United States." Nonsmokers generally favored smoking restrictions and used social sanctions to prevent smoking. Almost three out of ten nonsmokers reported that they would be less likely to hire someone for a job if they knew that the person smoked; almost six out of ten say they would ask a person not to smoke in their home; 51 percent favored a total ban on smoking in public places; and 49 percent of all respondents (57 percent of nonsmokers) believed that tobacco company advertising and promotion attempted to get teenagers and young people to start smoking. Of nonsmokers, 22 percent reported that they respect persons less because they smoke. Even opinion among smokers was negative: 93 percent of smokers believed that cigarette smoking is harmful to health; 61 percent claimed that they were addicted to cigarettes; and 83 percent reported that, if they had it to do all over again, they would never have started smoking.

Public opinion frequently leads to corporate and public policy: airlines banned smoking on all domestic flight; cities passed antismoking ordinances; companies became nonsmoking areas. In 1992, Secretary of Health and Human Services Louis Sullivan launched a seven-year, $135 million program to reduce smoking in seventeen states. Universities removed "tobacco stocks" from their portfolios and became nonsmoking areas ("School tied," 1993; Wiseman and Cox, 1990; Blum, 1990). In 1993, President Clinton proposed increased cigarette taxes as a funding source for health care reform (Janofsky, 1993).

Despite negative media coverage and these somewhat discouraging statistics, Philip Morris does have a loyal "smoking" public. Green and Gerkin (1989) and Dixon, Lowery, Levy and Ferraro (1991) found that smoking issues produce clear polarization between smokers and nonsmokers in terms of public policy support. Although self-interest fails to predict policy positions on many other social policy issues such as job programs, it does predict a person's stand on smoking issues. Smokers generally oppose smoking restrictions and excise taxes; nonsmokers, especially those who report they are "bothered" by smoke, favor smoking restrictions and excise taxes. Not surprisingly, Dixon et al. (1991) found that those respondents who personally profit from manufacture or sale of tobacco products are more likely to view most smoking issues from a pro-tobacco perspective.

Despite smokers' reported distaste of their own habit and their acknowledgement of negative health consequences for self and others, when it comes to public policy remedies, Philip Morris has a clearly polarized public, highly supportive stakeholders and generally negative non-stakeholders. The chances of swaying nonsmokers, especially those "bothered by smoke," is minimal. However, smokers and those who profit from tobacco sales are a loyal and large stakeholder public that should be cultivated continuously.

Theory would suggest that tobacco companies need to reinforce the positive position of their stakeholder "smoker" public. However, almost every public statement from tobacco companies generates a counterattack. Antismoking activists are vocal and well organized. Headlines tell the story: "Where there's smoke—A firestorm over a new cigarette highlights two rival marketing strategies" (Work, 1990); "Smoking under fire in Virginia" (1991); "Billboard foes put up a fight, Baltimore activists say signs glamorize alcohol, tobacco" (Valentine, 1991); "*Seattle Times* places a ban on tobacco advertising" (Galberson, 1993); "N.Y. to ban tobacco ads on transit vehicles" (1992). Even when tobacco companies create what they hope will be a positive public campaign, their opposition responds quickly and effectively. When the Tobacco Institute, the industry's lobbying organization, launched a campaign to curb youth smoking, the industry's opponents called the effort a "hypocritical public-relations move" (Suplee, 1990). The company's attempt to influence the implementation of a nonsmoking ordinance in Pittsburgh generated vocal opposition and significant negative press coverage (Samuels et al., 1992). Even Philip Morris's sponsorship of the celebration of the bicentennial of the Bill of Rights was the object of multiple congressional hearings, ongoing protests, and news scrutiny (Colford, 1989; Conroy, 1989). It even shows up as a textbook example of an unanticipated public relations crisis (Seitel, 1993).

How could a tobacco company build a base of stakeholder support when its every move is attacked in the press and countered by antismoking advocates? How could it define issues in its own terms without inviting negative media attention and further discouraging its loyal supporters? The answer was a controlled medium, *Philip Morris Magazine*.

THE RESPONSE: *PHILIP MORRIS MAGAZINE*

The first issue of *PMM* appeared in 1985. The magazine's staff compiled the initial quarterly distribution list of approximately 150,000 from consumer responses to Philip Morris product promotions. Through the purchase of "smoker" mailing lists and solicitation of referrals from readers, the magazine's totally free distribution to American homes climbed to over 8.2 million people in 1988. By 1990, nearly 12 million Americans received *PMM* and twice that number read it (Philip Morris news release, 1991).

Guy L. Smith, the magazine's first publisher, introduced *Philip Morris Magazine* as "the colorful quarterly that puts you in touch with the world of Philip Morris" (*PMM, 1*(1), inside cover). That world, he noted, was comprised of Philip Morris's extensive sponsorship program and its "commitment to the tobacco industry and to the 55 million Americans who enjoy tobacco products" (*PMM, 1*(1), inside cover). Smith's statement is intentionally disarming. Close inspection of the magazine's content shows that its much more than a simple "brag sheet."

Defining the Issues

The most fundamental step in any issue-management communication effort is to define issues strategically (Crable and Vibbert, 1985). Defining issues involves identifying a situation or act as problematic, making arguments that define the nature of the problem, and identifying actions consonant with the definition. As people recognize situations as problematic, the words they use order the jumble of unorganized experience and thereby create perspectives that promote and favor particular actions (Bennett, 1975; Dionisopoulos and Crable, 1988; Graber, 1976; Zarefsky, 1986). If abortion is defined as a "medical procedure," decisions about control of that action rest with doctor, patient, and other decision makers within the medical realm. If the same action is defined as "murder," the judicial system offers the appropriate remedy. These fundamental definitions, with their incumbent responses, provide the basis for later issue resolutions.

In the case of smoking issues, Philip Morris wishes to defeat or at least delay further government regulation of marketing, distribution, and consumption of tobacco products. The issue definitions that support that preferred issue resolution center around a legal terminology

of "rights" and "discrimination." Philip Morris asserts several definitional corrollaries, primarily in its "Forum" section: one, tobacco is a
legal product; two, smoking is a personal and private choice; three, any
restriction on smoking is an infringement of personal freedom and
therefore "discrimination"; and four, restrictions on tobacco marketing
degrade the consumer's "right to choose" and limit free speech.

An obvious definitional move for Philip Morris is simply to declare
its much maligned product "legal." In and of itself, smoking is a legally
sanctioned activity, no different than the consumption of food or drink.
Consequently, whether one smokes is a free, personal, and private
choice. As one activist argued, "Forcing smokers out of the public eye
has not made us quit; it has simply made us angry. We live in a country
that glorifies freedom—in all forms—but at the same time wants to
deny the personal choices that make that freedom complete" (*PMM,*
5(2), p. 43). To limit smoking is to limit freedom.

Any limitation of smoking is labeled "discrimination." In workplace
smoking issues, Philip Morris aligns smoking restrictions with other
"discriminatory" hiring practices and argues that "employers violate a
basic right to privacy when they reach beyond the workplace and seek
to control activities that even the law does not." The company applauds
laws that "prevent overzealous employers from firing or not hiring
qualified people solely based on whether they have engaged in legal
activities, such as smoking, outside the workplace" (*PMM, 5*(2), p. 28).
Excise taxes "discriminate" against smokers, "a hypocritical system of
behavior control for the poor and middle classes, which allows full
freedom of choice for the wealthy" (*PMM, 4*(1), p. 20). Restriction of
smoking in public places is tyranny of the majority. In a response to a
critical letter to the editor, *PMM* replied: "For over 200 years, this
country has been a haven for those seeking human rights and freedom
of choice—regardless of whether their informed choices reflect minority or majority views. *PMM* does not condone the behavior of 'militant'
smokers—or non-smokers—who try to impose their beliefs and behavioral patterns on others. We believe that all people should treat each
other with courtesy, common sense, and consideration" (*PMM, 3*(3),
p. 30).

On advertising issues, Philip Morris turns to "freedom of speech"
and the legality of its product to support their practices. Philip Morris
claims on multiple occasions that advertising does not increase cigarette consumption and reiterates compliance with the law: "Like any
other legitimate and ambitious enterprise, Philip Morris U.S.A. will

continue to make the highest-quality products we are capable of, and sell them with every appropriate marketing tool legally available to us" (*PMM, 5*(4), p. 39). Moreover, to further regulate tobacco marketing, they say, would be "censorship":

> Nothing could be more inconsistent with—and more corrosive to—this country's commitment to individual dignity and free choice than a regime of censorship that assures people that they are free to choose, while secretly stacking the information deck to manipulate their choice. Banning speech about lawful choices—whether economic or political—treats people like rats in a laboratory maze. Seeking to guide behavior patterns that seem "wiser" to the elite and rationing the flow of information, is an Orwellian process that has no place in our system of political and economic democracy." (*PMM, 5*(2), p. 43)

Guest writer Judith Christ continued the Orwellian theme, calling smoking opponents "anti-smoking Big Brothers" (*PMM, 5*(2), p. 44). Marketing regulation is defined as government interference with a corporation's freedom to speak.

Philip Morris also promotes the consumer's right to hear. Some critics of tobacco marketing argue that the companies take advantage of minority consumers in particular. Philip Morris reverses the argument and becomes a self-appointed advocate for minorities: "Self-righteous crusaders are doing the minority community a disservice by implying that minority adults are somehow less competent than others to make a decision, and by attempting to deny advertisers the opportunity to connect with a dynamic market" (*PMM, 4*(5), p. 24). To limit marketing to minorities infringes on both the consumers' and Philip Morris's freedom.

As yet another extension of this definitional turn, Philip Morris ties smoking issues to "cultural diversity." The magazine argues that "accommodation, the spirit of tolerance that enables people of different races, cultures, and lifestyles to live together, is one of America's most basic principles. . . . Because of our country's diversity, the need for accommodation comes up in situation after situation, and in issue after issue. One of those issues, these days, is smoking" (*PMM, 6*(4), p. 23). Personal accommodation, not regulation, is the appropriate response to smoking issues.

In defining its positions, Philip Morris places smoking issues firmly within American discourse about legally protected personal freedoms; the company asserts that smoking, as a legal choice, should be free from legal restriction. Any restriction attempted is labeled "discrimination" or "censorship." Not only does the discourse create a broad definitional base to approach specific policies, but also the definitions are grounded in traditional American political values.

Legitimizing Definitions

Issue definitions must be legitimized if they are to influence public policy. Legitimacy may be created through a range of rhetorical strategies: gaining endorsements of influential individuals or groups; building ties to already legitimate issue definitions; creating linkages with other groups; and linking issue definitions to the already established values of society through epideictic rhetoric (Crable and Vibbert, 1985; Vibbert and Bostdorff, 1992). Philip Morris uses the full range of legitimizing strategies, each based on the foundation created through epideictic discourse.

The purpose of epideictic discourse is to reinforce values already held by the audience. The speaker uses the audience's preexisting values to praise an esteemed object or person or to denigrate the blameworthy (Perelman and Olbrechts-Tyteca, 1969, pp. 47-54). The audience participates with the speaker as it judges the quality of the speaker's representation of the audience's values and the accuracy of the application to some person or object (Oravec, 1976). If the rhetor presents the community's values in an acceptable manner, the creator of the discourse becomes associated with the reaffirmed values and the community that upholds them. Thus, skillful epideictic rhetoric reinforces a speaker's character and credibility.

The values consensus and identification established through epideictic rhetoric may support the organization's policy discourse at a later time. Much as childhood political socialization and indoctrination shapes adult political participation, an organization's ongoing value discourse creates a context for later political positions. Vibbert (1994) highlights the long-term, strategic implications of epideictic discourse in his definition of "epideictic advocacy"—"the persuasive enactment of value premises, the present use of which is shared orientation, the future use of which is directed action" (p. 19). Crable and Vibbert (this volume) identified epideictic advocacy as central to the corporate communication of Mobil Oil. Vibbert (1984) noted a similar goal in the image ads of Philips Petroleum. In each case, seemingly inconsequential corporate discourse built a base of support for later policy argumentation.

Philip Morris offers similar value orientations in *PMM*. The first surrounds "individualism," the belief that individuals can and should make personal decisions without government interference and that individual action is effective. In epideictic rhetoric's most traditional form, *PMM* has celebrated a range of heroes from the Vietnam veteran (*PMM, 1*(2), pp. 14–17; *PMM, 3*(3), pp. 16–17) to the "everyday heroes" that make a difference in their local communities. Whether it's Bea Gaddy feeding the homeless in Philadelphia (*PMM, 2*(4), pp. 15–19), Kenny Wheeler counseling streetgang youths (*PMM, 3*(3), pp. 37–39), or James Jones walking his police beat in Milwaukee (*PMM, 5*(2), p. 9), *PMM* reminds readers that the individual still counts in America. Not surprisingly, the archetypal American individualist, the cowboy, is often featured in *PMM* (*PMM, 2*(6), pp. 10–14; *PMM, 5*(1), pp. 36–40). Beyond the obvious connection to Philip Morris's Marlboro brand, the image of the cowboy and the American frontier spirit support the company's political agenda as well.

Philip Morris also supports "community-based action." Many articles highlight Philip Morris's support of the arts, sports, and other community-centered events. The magazine's first issue set the tone. In it, Eleanor Berman gave the reader a behind-the-scenes look at the Philip Morris–sponsored Vatican exhibit at the Metropolitan Museum of Art (*PMM, 1*(1), pp. 7–10) and Mary Witherell previewed the new young stars who would appear on the Virginia Slims Women's Tennis tour (*PMM, 1*(1), pp. 25–28). While many articles highlight entertainment in which Philip Morris plays some part (for example, the Marlboro Country Music Tour), others turn to more serious efforts: for instance, a Vietnam veterans memorial in New York City (*PMM, 1*(2), pp. 14–17) or the rock concert/benefit FarmAid (*PMM, 1*(3), pp. 14–17) and the company's extensive relief effort following Armenia's devastating earthquake in 1989 (*PMM, 4*(2), pp. 14–17). These and other articles demonstrate Philip Morris's commitment to community service.

Perhaps most central to Philip Morris's goals is its celebration of "freedom" and "the American way." In one issue, award winning photographer David Hume Kennerly shared thoughts and images from the final days before the Tiananmen Square uprising to remind American's of their own freedom (*PMM, 4*(5), pp. 12–15). In 1990, an exclusive interview with Lech Walesa produced a story titled "Words of Freedom." Walesa described the outcome of years of political struggle in terms tied to American democracy: "We succeeded in fighting the cruelest system, a system that did not consider the rule of law. A system that liked to use the strength of force. But we proved the force of law is the strongest force after all" (*PMM,* 5(2), p. 12).

One article in particular combines values of American individualism, freedom, and success. Titled, "Coming to America: four international stars talk about their love affairs with the country we call home," the article sings America's praises (*PMM,* 5(5), p. 11). Novelist Jackie Collins says, "America is the most energetic, innovative country in the world. You have this feeling you can achieve anything here." Composer Lalo Schifrin and gymnastics coach Bela Karolyi add their thanks to their adopted home. Gloria Estafan, a pop music superstar, sums up "America" in one word—"freedom"—saying, "The more I travel, the more I realize how much I love this country. It really bothers me when I see that so many people who live here seem to take it for granted. We are lucky to live where we do and to have the kind of government that we have" (*PMM,* 5(5), p. 11).

Taking America for granted and the potential for losing the American way of life are common themes in *PMM.* In an article about the FarmAid benefit, one farmer expressed the concern about a dying way of life: "Farmers are the backbone of a lot of good small rural communities. Small communities are what holds the state together. It's the good, honest, American way of doing things we're talking about losing" (*PMM,* 1(3), p. 17). Even George Plimpton's apparently uncontroversial article about July 4th fireworks takes on a political tone. The title, "Light up the sky: fireworks celebrate America's freedom. But have government regulations taken the independence out of Independence Day?" reveals the article's political agenda (*PMM,* 2(1), pp. 26–29). Publisher Guy Smith previews Plimpton's article as one that "brings up an idea that will no doubt sound familiar to readers of *Philip Morris Magazine,* that of unnecessary government intervention. As Plimpton demonstrates, smoking is not the only pleasure that government has taken an active role in limiting over the years" (*PMM,* 2(1), p. 3). Even an article about telephone answering machines highlights the losses of freedom in modern society: "Answering machines restore the freedom of choice that a simple telephone takes away" (*PMM,* 3(1), p. 44).

Values of "individualism," "community action," "freedom," and "the American Way" all reinforce Philip Morris's policy agenda. Individual response and community action, as opposed to government regulation, are recommended as the answer to most problems. "Freedom" and "the American Way," democracy, and the rule of law again suggest that government's role should be minimized. The potential to "lose freedom" cautions citizens to be vigilant. This discourse, although unrelated directly to smoking, creates a context of traditional values that support and reinforce Philip Morris's issue positions. A belief in individualism, freedom, and community action makes Philip Morris's issue definitions more, rather than less, legitimate.

Philip Morris reinforces its position with contemporary endorsements of academic researchers, legislators, corporate representatives, and editorial writers. In the 1990 issues alone, Philip Morris reported the support of a professor of law at the New York University School of Law and former national legal director of the ACLU, a professor of economics at the University of Georgia, the cofounder of Smokers' Rights Alliance, a Maryland state senator, the executive vice president of corporate affairs and communications for American Express Co., an Ohio District Court of Appeals judge, and two national syndicated columnists.

The magazine's, and the company's, legitimacy is enhanced further by prestigious contributors: broadcast journalists Walter Cronkite, Eric Sevareid, and Charles Kuralt; humorists Milton Berle, Larry L. King, and Martin Mull; Pulitzer-prize winning playwright August Wilson and feature writer Alice Steinbach, novelist Elizabeth Benedict and Nobel prize laureate Isaac Bashevis Singer, among others. The high-quality writing is enhanced in every issue by award-winning photographers. Philip Morris evidently hopes that some of the credibility of these contributors will transfer to the company and its issues. Moreover, the prestige of these people suggests that Philip Morris Companies' positions are not outside the mainstream, but still are represented by those people firmly entrenched in American political, social, and cultural life.

While individual endorsements increase the company's legitimacy, linkages to constituencies within the readership also are important. Heath and Nelson (1986) remind issue managers that they are "power resource managers" (pp. 199–204). Much of that political and economic power comes from building coalitions. Philip Morris Companies, Inc., sponsorships, and the articles that draw attention to its generosity, create linkages to key political groups, not surprisingly minority groups interested in gaining and protecting "rights." While best known for the millions it gives to the arts, minorities receive significant funding from Philip Morris as well. Over 180 African-American, women's, and Hispanic groups received at least $2.4 million from Philip Morris in 1987 alone. Philip Morris contributed part of a $60,000 gift to the National Black Caucus of State Legislators and $120,000 to the United Negro College Fund in that year alone (Levin, 1988, p. 14).

The linkages, and potential dependencies, created through money are reinforced in *PMM*. Celebrations of the "working class" draw connections to organized labor and to Americans bearing the nation's tax burden. Philip Morris's extensive support of women's sports aligns the company with women's issues. The covers of *PMM* alone reinforce the groups Philip Morris wishes to draw to its side. In its seven years, over half the covers presented women, many famous athletes. While only three covers feature African-Americans, celebrity profiles and human interest stories target all Philip Morris constituencies; they range from creole zydeco music star Ida Gruillory and Cherokee Nation Chief Wilma Mankiller to Dolly Parton, Charlie Daniels, Bob Hope, Mickey Mantle, and former President Gerald Ford. Everyone can feel at home within the "world of Philip Morris."

While upholding its own legitimacy, Philip Morris attempts simultaneously to undermine the opposition's legitimacy. Not only does it describe antismoking forces as "overzealous" and "Big Brothers," Philip Morris challenges their ethics. One article accuses the American Cancer Society, the American Heart Association, and the American Lung Association of exploitation and deception. The author states that "health charities . . . like to be regarded as at the forefront of the war on various diseases, but play only a minor role in supporting the research needed to find the cures. . . . Most people are unaware that some health organizations are thinly disguised political organizations" (*PMM,* 6(1), p. 25). Philip Morris accuses federal regulators of manipulating science on the environmental tobacco smoke issue: "Sometimes the government makes policy decisions based on *selective* research results, rather than relying on an *objective* evaluation of all research. In other words, if the science doesn't fit, don't use it. . . . The EPA cannot play fast and loose with the facts and still claim a scientific basis for its actions" (*PMM,* 5(3), p. 38).

Scientific research is denigrated generally. Mike Royko added his voice to the complaints about antismoking research. He reported that University of Pennsylvania researchers found that smokers have a less acute sense of smell than nonsmokers. The researchers wrote, "Smoking creates the possibility of losing, at least in part, the ability to appreciate flowers, good food, and good wine." Royko responded vehemently:

This is the best example I've seen of how far America's nonsmokers will go with their ever-growing, nagging attack on smokers. It isn't enough that the packages have warnings; that smoking is forbidden in most buildings and workplaces; that airline passengers must now risk imprisonment if they light up. It isn't enough that many nonsmokers frantically begin gasping for breath even before a smoker 20 feet away lights up. (*PMM, 5*(3), p. 39)

Science is a means to abuse reasonable, respectful smokers. Non-smokers who wield "science" are "militant," "rude," "zealous," and "fanatical."

The issue definitions and legitimacy strategies appearing in *PMM* encourage smokers to continue to fight for their rights. Smith notes, "Any one of America's 60 million smokers who has been made to feel isolated by the anti-smoking lobby will certainly find plenty of friendly voices on the pages of *Philip Morris Magazine*" (*PMM, 2*(1), p. 3). As Elwood (1989) finds, the magazine builds the egos of readers who, "by preserving their own freedom to choose to smoke cigarettes, preserve all Americans' freedom of choice" (p. 23). Letters to the Editor published within *PMM* affirm these judgments. Some write as if the magazine is a beacon of hope in a hostile world: "Three cheers for a blow struck for freedom! Hip, hip, hooray for Philip Morris! With the increasing onslaughts by 'militant smokers' it is time we smokers had an influential spokesman!" (*PMM, 1*(2), p. 19). The discourse unifies smokers. Indeed, Philip Morris reminds smokers of their strength in numbers with articles such as "United We Stand" (*PMM, 6*(4), p. 22).

Preparing for Action

Philip Morris does not stop with creating value orientation, political legitimacy, and smoker unity for its product and its company. Philip Morris prepares and encourages its readers to act. Readers are given statistical research, key message points, argumentation strategies, and direct guidance to take political action in support of smoker's issues.

In the sections "PM Notebook" and "Forum," readers learn the ins and outs of particular issue controversies, such as workplace smoking laws, advertising and marketing issues, and excise taxes. For instance, in the January/February 1989 issue, the magazine created a special pull-out section on excise taxes. The articles report statistics to support their definition of excise taxes as "regressive" and "unfair," describe earmarking practices in legislation, and detail effects on business. Not only does *PMM* give readers all the information they need to fight excise taxes, but the magazine places protest within a laudable history, the most famous "exise tax protest in American history," the Boston Tea Party. The protest was not made by radicals or fanatics, but by "prominent business men and political leaders."

A second special section gives readers tips on how to take specific political action. "Make your voice heard: How to reach your representative," reassures readers that contacting elected representatives makes a difference. The section gives readers do's and don'ts of letterwriting and explicit instructions on what to say when calling a representative's office. They even provide a sample script (*PMM, 6*(1), pp. 20–21). *PMM* sets the agenda, defines the issues, presents potential arguments, and then promotes action.

For those who are more concerned about day-to-day interaction with nonsmokers, *PMM* provided a particularly innovative section designed to counter the American Cancer Society's "Great American Smoke-Out," a day set aside to promote smoking cessation. People are encouraged to persuade friends and coworkers to stop smoking. In response, *PMM* readers are provided with a countercampaign. They receive a doorknob hang-sign that reads "Great American Smoker at Work" and a threefold desktop display called the "Great American Smoke Screen." All materials are star-spangled, red, white, and blue. A person facing the smoker's desk sees the screen with the logo in the shape of the cigarette pack. On the back of the screen, the smoker views a three-panel "cue card." One panel shows two verbal defense strategies—one for what Philip Morris calls a benign approach and one for a belligerent approach. The second and third panels list "comebacks," such as "smoking is the leading cause of statistics," and "comforts," such as "Those who give up cigarette smoking aren't the heroes. The real heroes are the rest of us—who have to listen to them" (*PMM, 2*(3), insert, pp. 20–21). Philip Morris validates and assists smoker's self-defense at an interpersonal level.

Supporting all of these strategies is *PMM*'s reassurance that their actions do make a difference. In 1990, the magazine reported that the nation's 55 million smokers won battles in 29 states. The reason? "These victories were won because you shared your feelings with your elected representatives. . . . You argued with the knowledge that truth was on your side. And you succeeded because you were a unified force to be reckoned with. . . . As we look to the 1990s, remember that your individual acts—calling and writing to legislators, sharing information with a friend or colleague who chooses to smoke—are important. Then multiply those acts by 55 million" (PMM, 5(1), p. 42). They also periodically report the buying power of smokers, their political clout, and their professional status.

Philip Morris created symbolic and political support for its readers through its articles and its advocacy, provided them with information and arguments, told them what to do, and then reinforced the readers' positive actions. Philip Morris created well-prepared grass roots advocates.

PHILIP MORRIS MAGAZINE:
IMPLICATIONS OF MEDIUM AND MESSAGE

Analysis of *PMM* points to several principles of public relations and issue-management practice that should be included in a practitioner's body of knowledge.

Implications of the Medium

Philip Morris Magazine demonstrates the importance of strategic and innovative media choice. Given the political environment in which tobacco companies operate, publicity media offer little opportunity for Philip Morris to get its message out to its primary constituencies *without opposition*. Since smokers already are under attack, any publicity effort launched by Philip Morris potentially could discourage smoking publics further. A controlled medium allowed Philip Morris greater flexibility and latitude in its message strategies. Words Philip Morris would say cautiously in a publicity medium are spoken freely and without fear of retribution within its own magazine.

The magazine format not only provides audience selectivity but also more space in which to develop a range of ideas and stories. Its color, visual support, and divided sections all contribute to the broad range of Philip Morris's strategies. Direct political messages, subtle epideictic, and calls for action all have their place in *PMM*. Readers may choose sections according to their interests; the magazine can also reach a variety of stakeholders, targeting articles or sections to smaller subgroups: stockholders, consumers, farmers, retailers, and others. As the most permanent of print media (Russell and Verrill, 1986), a magazine creates a regular and positive presence in smokers' homes. Direct mail advocacy or other controlled strategies do not have the inherent appeal or long life of a glossy, well-written, colorful magazine.

The general lack of public comment on the magazine's content is a sign of success. Database searches on Philip Morris, the tobacco industry, *PMM* and other related topics (both subject and key-word searches), revealed very few negative articles over the magazine's life.[1] When writers did comment, their reaction was generally favorable and tended to overlook the magazine's overall content. *Jack O'Dwyer's Newsletter* described the magazine's content as "cigarette and tobacco themes . . . interspersed with articles that have nothing to do with smoking" (O'Dwyer, 1991, p. 8). *Forbes* offered a slightly more in-depth analysis, but still drew little attention to the majority of the magazine's content: "a potpourri of light, general-interest features wrapped around its sledgehammer Forum section, whose thrust is not subtle" (Levine, 1991). That the magazine was generally ignored or accepted as innocuous and unthreatening gave its editors significant latitude to promote a range of ideas.

The magazine format also allowed Philip Morris to accomplish other communication goals. While this analysis focused on issue-management strategies, the magazine simultaneously accomplished marketing and public relations goals. For instance, *PMM* functions as a market research tool. A particularly innovative strategy was *PMM*'s readership survey. This fifty-nine-item prepaid-postage questionnaire appeared as an insert in the Winter 1988 issue. Questions tapped everything from readers' leisure-time activities and media habits to their political positions and attitudes toward the future. Over 400,000 readers responded and the results, tabulated by the Roper organization, were reported in the Summer 1988 issue. The survey findings indicated that poll respondents were "better educated, more politically and socially active, and [had] higher family incomes than do American adults in general" (PMM, 3(3), p. 22). Not surprisingly, 73.2 percent of the people who responded were smokers. From this survey, *Philip Morris Magazine* developed a series of advertisements that emphasized the buying power of American smokers. By gathering information from its readership, *PMM* not only gained the ability to adapt better to its readers but also provided Philip Morris Companies, Inc., with data important to its marketing and to its advocacy for smokers' rights.

Philip Morris Magazine also demonstrated a company's innovative combination of a long-term, proactive issue-management strategy with other public affairs efforts. The company's efforts are extensive, at the local, state, and national levels (McAllister, 1990; Lee, 1991; Freedman and Cohen, 1993). Philip Morris uses a combination of lobbying, direct mail, coalition building, litigation, sponsorship, and controlled media of all sorts, including brochures, issue papers, and internal newsletters. With 24 million readers nationwide, *PMM* prepared grass roots advocates for potential local and state campaigns. Its readers knew the central questions and recommended responses from *Philip Morris Magazine*. It was integrated with all other issue communication. As higher standards of efficiency are applied to corporate communication functions, the importance of consistent messages across functions, marketing, public relations, public affairs, employee relations, will be heightened among communication professionals (Broom et al., 1991; Caywood and Ewing, 1991). Philip Morris provides an example of a unified communication strategy.

Philip Morris Magazine shows the range of message strategies available to issue managers in a controlled medium. Advertising, direct mail, and other controlled media are limited to one or two key messages. They often oversimplify issues or promote emotional images devoid of substantive argument. In either case, the public is left unable to advocate a position effectively. Through a combination of clear issue argumentation and value-laden discourse, Philip Morris provides a clear message to its stakeholder publics.

The question remains, is that message politically tenable beyond the stakeholder public? Will it hold sway and shape public policy in the way Philip Morris intends?

Implications of the Message

While the legal rhetoric proposed by Philip Morris diverts attention from health claims and unifies smokers, its fundamental premises embrace somewhat contradictory political positions and leave smokers open to attack.

Philip Morris attempts to make an argument for "smokers' rights," an argument based on the acceptance of "smokers" as a "minority" worthy of protection. Those "rights" are based on the fundamental value of "freedom," both freedom *to* act and freedom *from* undue government restraint. However, most civil rights protections arise because a group's rights are limited or restricted due to some innate characteristic, not because of individual choices those people make. Women, racial groups, ethnic minorities, and homosexuals are protected from "discrimination" on the basis of "who they are," not because of "what they choose to do." Philip Morris attempts to promote "smokers" as an analogous group. They even suggest that "diversity" is promoted through accommodation of "smokers."

To be a smoker is not quite the same as to be African-American, Jewish, or Italian. To "respect and tolerate" the differences of race is not quite the same as tolerating a smoke-filled room. One's race is neither a choice nor a potential threat to another's health. Smoking, defined as a "choice" by Philip Morris, is not analogous to innate characteristics that define most protected minorities.

Attributions of responsibility reflect the fundamental difference in definition. Brummett's (1979) analysis of a gay rights controversy highlights how differing conceptions of what it means "to be" gay and "to act" gay lead to equally divergent political responses to the issue. Those who believe homosexuality is an individual trait, similar to gender or race, afford homosexuals the same protections as other minority groups. Those who consider homosexuality a "choice" do not confer equal protections (Brummett, 1979). Similarly, "discrimination" and "diversity" promote reactions to smoking that do not stand up to scrutiny. Minority by choice and minority by nature do not receive equal political protection.

If smoking is a "choice," then tough legal battles and extensive legal restraint should be expected. Many individual "choices" are offered legal protection, but such acts are also limited and regulated according to their consequences for others. "Freedom of speech" is limited, both for corporations and individuals. As with yelling "fire" in a crowded theater, lighting a fire in a public place—even if a small one at the end of a cigarette—is a choice with potential consequences for self and others. Philip Morris promotes this definition and suggests that "accommodation," not regulation, is the appropriate response.

"Choices" need not have direct public consequences to be subject to government restraint; the "choice" to die at one's own hand or with assistance of a physician, to "choose" an abortion, or to choose to buy a gun all generate significant controversy. Advocates for most "choices" argue that government has exceeded its bounds by "legislating private behavior." Ironically, Philip Morris plays both sides. The company simultaneously uses an argument based on group politics in which the role of government is to protect minority individuals from the "tyranny of the majority" and another based on a more conservative conception of the relationship between individuals and government, in which government itself is the force that impinges on an individual freedom. In the first, government must protect people from unfair external control. In the second, government *is* the unfair external control. Philip Morris's terminology casts a wide but highly suspect political net. Its message blurs these distinctions quite seductively in an attempt to generate broad-based support.

What happens when smoking *is* defined as an uncontrollable characteristic, a response to a biological tendency toward substance abuse and addiction? If smoking is an "addiction" rather than a "free choice," responsibility and response change accordingly. An "uncontrollable predisposition" could be defined as a "genetically predetermined disability" and thereby could be protected along with other debilitating physical conditions. A full extension of the terminology, however, would be a worst case scenario for tobacco manufacturers. If smoking is an addiction, then cigarettes are an addictive drug. What was once a "legal product" might be redefined as a "controlled substance," warranting stringent government control. In a best case scenario, tobacco companies would join pharmaceutical manufacturers. In the worst case, they would be a drug cartel. The extension of the terminology certainly is not in the company's best interest.

Philip Morris's message is best conveyed in a controlled medium not only because of the circling oppponents but also because their definitions are rife with inconsistency and shifting views of government. Smokers are reassured by words such as "freedom" and "rights" and "discrimination" linked to their choices. They feel empowered and legitimate and justified. Unfortunately for smokers, the very words they enjoy in *PMM*'s safe environment do not stand up to close scrutiny and provoke powerful reaction.

PHILIP MORRIS MAGAZINE: FINAL ISSUES AND FINAL THOUGHTS ON ISSUE MANAGEMENT

Philip Morris Magazine highlights the importance of thinking of issues as communicative phenomena. Without attending to the ongoing needs of stakeholders and building a basis of definition and legitimacy on issues, companies like Philip Morris would miss valuable opportunities in issue management. At the same time, the opportunity created through an innovative medium must be exploited with a strategic and politically strong message.

In June 1992, Philip Morris folded *PMM* after seven years. Spokespersons said that the magazine became redundant as regional prosmoking groups began to publish newsletters. Cost probably played a role as well. While the advantages of magazines are many, they are extremely expensive, especially when distributed free to millions of readers. One report estimated the cost of a 32-page quarterly sent to 300,000 names at $1 million a year (Levine, 1991). *PMM* was a longer, especially sophisticated magazine with a distribution many times that of the estimate. Even with the revenue generated by advertising, *PMM* was an extremely expensive strategy.

This analysis suggests that the problems in the message, rather than the medium, might be the primary motivator behind the magazine's demise. Behind the scenes, Philip Morris drastically changed its approach to government relations in 1992, favoring more direct lobbying over its earlier, high-profile, grass roots efforts. As an American Heart Association vice president noted, "When they came out with some of the First Amendment strategies, they were easy to pick apart" (Landler and Carey, 1993). High profiles make easy targets.

Was the decision to end *PMM* a wise one, given the many opportunities offered in the controlled magazine format? Local consituencies are now united, armed with information. The company still has its massive mailing list that can be broken down easily by geographic area for special initiatives. The work of the company's high-profile lobbyist, Craig Fuller, and the Tobacco Institute continue. But the company ended an opportunity to build a base for issue management. They gave up one of very few places where they could speak to their stakeholders on a regular, uninterrupted basis, without fear of criticism. That place, if short lived, was unique among corporate communication strategies.

NOTE

1. Searches included InfoTrac and Lexis/Nexis. Only one article directly attacking the magazine appeared. See Slater, R. S. (1987). One magazine we can do without. *Business and Society Review, 60,* 45–47. The magazine was featured in at least one column on smoking generally. See Dyckman, M. (1992, June 2). A chance for redemption. *St. Petersburg Times,* p. A9.

9

Janus in the Looking Glass

The Management of Organizational Identity in Corporate Recruitment Videos

Theresa A. Russell-Loretz[1]

A young woman's voice is heard as the camera follows her to the podium during graduation ceremonies: When I was little, I never understood what mom meant when she said, "Clean your plate Cindy, there are places where kids are starving." Well, mom, now I am old enough to understand—and I love you and daddy for teaching me to care. That's why I'm eager to walk into a Dow lab . . . to work on new ways to help grow more and better grain for *all* the kids who need it so desperately. I can't wait. I'll be doing something that really matters.[2]

With this introduction to its recruitment video, Dow attempts to titillate college job seekers' aspirations for employment. Dow's video segment, which ran in part as a television commercial, might be familiar. Dow's recruitment message may be familiar as well to those who have visited their campus placement center. This familiarity stems from the rhetorical characteristics the message shares with other organizational attempts to influence the employment decisions of college graduates.

In their attempt to attract college graduates as potential employees, recruitment videos serve to "adjust people to organizations and organizations to people," the crux of what Crable and Vibbert (1986) describe as the function of public relations (p. 5). Indeed, Crable and Vibbert's description of the function of public relations is based on the function of rhetoric identified by Bryant: "adjusting people to ideas, and ideas to people" (1953, p. 413). In the case of recruitment videos, of course, the "idea" to which college job seekers are adjusted is the concept of employment with a particular company. Inherent in this adjustment is the presentation of an organizational "self," so that, in addition to adjusting the organization and the recruit to one another, recruitment videos also perform what Cheney and Vibbert (1987) call an identity management function (p.185).

Thus, as recruitment videos attempt to attract potential employees to their would-be employers, they accomplish vital public relations functions of adjustment and identity management. These public relations functions, in fact, are vital not only for future employees, but also for those whose sole contact with the company may be limited to the video. As organizations increasingly come to rely upon video to introduce a "self" to their various publics, rhetorical criticism is an invaluable means with which to analyze the communicative strategies of these public relations tools. While scholars have acknowledged the proliferation and multiple applications of corporate video, however, few have examined these phenomena as public relations tools from a rhetorical perspective.[3] This chapter conducts such an examination and answers the call by Toth and Trujillo (1987) to reveal the symbolic elements that underlie application of technology by corporate communicators. Such an examination demonstrates how video messages targeted to a specific public might further the broader public relations goals of an organization.

Whatever the technology used, an organization engaged in recruitment faces a universal rhetorical challenge: to establish itself as an employer worthy of consideration by job seekers in a claim that might be construed along the lines of "Dow is a good employer." In the process, the organization must gain acceptance of *itself* or, more specifically, its representation of self, as substantive evidence for that claim. The challenge to gain acceptance for a corporate self as one that job seekers might find to be a good or excellent employer is especially apparent during those times when the demand for college graduates outweighs the supply, such that organizations must vie for recruits with multiple employment options. This situation was, in fact, predicted as the outlook for the 1990s by human resource forecasters who expressed concern that organizations would face competition over a dearth of qualified employees based on the birthrate (Davids, 1988; Johnston and Packer, 1987; Schauer, 1990). While multiple employment options have not proliferated for college graduates in recent years due to recession and organizational downsizing (Bolles, 1994; Pomice et al., 1992), the study of how an organization strives for acceptance by its future employees is an important exercise for those who wish to understand what a corporation values. Indeed, a recent emphasis in recruitment literature is on how employers might find employees who "fit" or match the values of the organization (McDonald and Gandz, 1992; Bowen, Ledford, and Nathan, 1991; Chatman, 1989; Weiss, 1989). This implies that at least some attention is paid to the values associated with the organization in its portrait of "self" depicted in these videos. And, reflexively, job seekers should attend to the values portrayed as constitutive of the organization, because these may fore-tell whether an individual's value priorities match those of the employer (Dusky, 1990). These admonitions, emphasized by job-seeking handbooks (Bolles, 1987; 1994; Crowther and Wilson, 1990), point to the importance of investigating the communicative strategies that organizations use to project a "self" or an "identity" with which recruits may begin to identify.

One of the communicative strategies of organizational self-representation in recruitment videos seems to epitomize the inherent paradox of what Cheney and Vibbert (1987) call "identity management," wherein the organization seeks to "develop a distinct identity, while at the same time being recognized as part of the cultural crowd" (p. 185). This apparent contradiction that Cheney and Vibbert point to as a paradox of uniqueness/sameness may raise suspicions for those who question the sincerity of such a message. In fact, logicians have long questioned the strategy of paradox as cunning, deceptive, or, as Rosetti (1988) puts it, "recourse to some clever subtleties . . . something that vexingly reminds us of conjuring tricks" (p. 147). Yet poets would remind us that the world is full of paradox. Schlegel and DeQuincy (1974) consider paradox a powerful means by which the poet may reflect "the paradoxical nature of the world that poetry imitates" (cited in Wight, 1990, p. 68).

Indeed, paradox helps organizations portray how they are distinct from other employers, even as they depict themselves as not so "unique" that they might be considered out of the mainstream. In addition, a communicative strategy of paradox enables organizations to convey to potential recruits that an employer's "uniqueness" is built upon a collection of "samenesses," or identities, shared with others (Cheney, 1985; Mackenzie, 1978). The "unique/yet same" contradiction, Cheney and Mackenzie have pointed out, captures the *inherent* paradoxical nature of "identity."

Rather than a mere trick, then, paradox is a necessary means to convey organizational identity, and this paradox reveals itself in critical investigation of recruitment communication. More striking, however, is the revelation that the inherent "unique/yet same" identity paradox encompasses a number of subtle and strategic paradoxes that manifest themselves in recruitment communication. In the attempt to build identification with would-be employees, the focal paradox of identity, "We are Unique/we are the Same," subsumes four strategic paradoxes: "We are big/we are small;" "We are old/we are new;" "We are people/we are technology;" and "We are our products/we are not our products." I argue that the strength of these paradoxes lies in their resolution, which helps to build a multifaceted entity much like Janus, who is often represented with two faces, which allowed him observation of the interior and exterior of houses and the entry and exit of public buildings. Janus was the Roman god of doorways, gates, beginnings, and, significantly, communication (Aldington and Ames, 1974). In this chapter, I discuss the paradoxical nature of identity and then describe the strategic paradoxes located in twelve recruitment videos.[4] Finally, I offer an interpretive framework through which these paradoxes may be viewed.

THE PARADOX OF ORGANIZATIONAL IDENTITY: MANAGING THE CORPORATE "SELF"

To say that an "identity" is inherently paradoxical warrants discussion of the nature of paradox. A paradox invokes contradiction, or "seemingly contradictory or mutually exclusive qualities or phases" (Wight, 1990, fn. 2, p. 68). The definition of paradox in *Webster's Unabridged Dictionary* (1983) itself may seem contradictory, because, due to its contradiction, a paradox may prove to be true or false.[5] In any instance of contradiction, such as a statement presented as both "true" and "false," the audience demands resolution. The rhetorical strength of paradox lies within the resolution of the contradiction so that an idea can be understood in terms that oppose one another.

In both poetry and logic, the strategy of paradox is powerful. Wight (1990) offers the work of T. S. Eliot in "East Coker" as an exemplar of paradox in poetry. Eliot opens with, "In my beginning is my end," a reversal of Mary Queen of Scots' final words, "In my end is my beginning." As Wight points out, this and other paradoxes allow Eliot to demonstrate the supranatural transformation of despair into hope and effectively imbue the reader with Eliot's religious beliefs.

Paradox is often resolved in poetry by illustration of how a work imitates the paradoxes in nature. In contrast, the power of logical paradoxes lies in the demonstration that what at first seems "familiar and unproblematic is actually terribly paradoxical" (Rosetti, 1988, p. 146). A rhetor might demonstrate that something "logical" is instead irrational. In fact, Rosetti shows how Zeno demonstrated that the idea of things in space could be construed as absurd or contradictory: "If everything is in a place, and place is something, in what will it be?" (p. 148). A master of paradox, Zeno also showed that the laws of physics were paradoxical, such that a flying arrow could be considered motionless: "If everything when it occupies an equal space is at rest, and if that which is in locomotion is always occupying such a space at any moment, the flying arrow is therefore motionless" (Aristotle, *Physics* 239b 10–240a, cited in Rosetti, 1988, p. 145).

To note the inherent paradoxes of identity may itself seem paradoxical; a thing is, after all, what it is. But like Zeno's paradox, which demonstrated the complexity of the idea of things in space, a number of scholars have suggested that the concept of "identity," applied both to individuals and organizations, is rich in complexities and paradoxical in at least three senses. The underlying assumption, of course, is that a corporation has an identity, much like a person.

Several authors posit that "identity" can be applied analogously to corporate entities.[6] Citing Weber (1978), Cheney and Vibbert (1987) argue that such an analogy is meaningful, since people act as if such entities have identities (p. 174). Mackenzie (1978) and du Preez (1980) center their investigations around "national identity" and incorporate prior discussion of individual identity. Cheney (1985) treats identity as the representation (or "*re*-presentation") of an individual or group.

As a representation, Cheney and Vibbert (1987) assert, "An identity is developed dialectically over time, by both the focal person or group and others. Moreover, much of what one calls an identity is composed of words" (p. 176). This view, which reflects the symbolic interactionist perspective, treats organizational communication as a process in which the organization engages in its own symbolic creation. Cheney and Vibbert observe that this creation is mediated inherently through the values "revealed primarily in the ongoing discourse of that individual or collectivity" (p. 175). Blumer's discussion of the development of identity applies; the organization engages in "a process of self indication in which it makes an object of what it notes, gives it a meaning, and uses the meaning as a basis for directing its action" (1979, p. 146). These "shared meanings" form the basis of two paradoxes of identity illustrated by Mackenzie (1978, esp. chapters 13 and 14). The first paradox stems from the notion that an identity, one's *unique* self, is shared. An entity "shares" identity with others in terms of space, nation, race, religion, and class. In fact, a person often defines oneself in terms of those qualities or characteristics that are *shared with* others. For instance, a person might describe herself as an African-American Roman Catholic who plays basketball for a Big 10 university in the Midwest. Because of this unique combination of qualities, she is different from others. However, she implicitly *shares* some of her individual qualities with other women, other African-Americans, other Catholics, other student athletes, and other Midwesterners.

Mackenzie echoes Burke's observation that an individual shares membership in multiple groups that sometimes conflict (Mackenzie, 1987, p. 124; Burke, 1969, p. 23). For example, the demands of being a student and an athlete may be in conflict at times. Other individuals may also experience identity conflict based on roles. Graduate teaching assistants, for example, have affiliations with both teachers and students, and sometimes the interests aligned with these memberships conflict. Or one's religious convictions may conflict with their political party's position on some issue. The resolution of potential social friction lies in Mackenzie's reference to Goffman's (1970) concept of "face," where an entity chooses an identity that mediates those interests that conflict: one prepares a "face," much like a mask, for presentation to others and so avoids such friction. In this way one can be both student and athlete, as in the first example. Or one might explain apparently contradictory positions, since this mediation allows one to associate with a political party's philosophy and to dissociate from its position on a particular issue, perhaps expressing the belief that change can best be influenced by someone on the inside.

Though potentially in conflict, these shared meanings illustrate that identity is paradoxical because it draws on or *mirrors* others. Shared aspects of identity both emerge from and foster identification with others. McCall and Simmons (1978) propose that identity stems from "continual self appraisal, which is carried on in terms of standards internalized from significant others and individually elaborated" (1978, p. 54). Mackenzie (1978), Burke (1969), Cheney (1983) and others have posited that identity reflects those internalized standards and fosters *identification with* others. These authors observe that this reflective process becomes subtly subsumed in the personal pronoun "we." Identity and Burke's notion of identification, described below, thus become a reciprocal process: "A is not identical with B. But insofar as their interests are joined, A is *identified* with B. Or he may *identify himself* with B even when their interests are not joined, if he assumes that they are, or is persuaded to believe so" (1969, p. 22).

Burke's concept of identification provided the basis of Cheney's (1983) investigation of the identification strategies located in employee newsletters. The four strategies he found include (1) use of *common ground,* wherein an organization explicitly articulated the interests shared by the employer and its employees; (2) *identification by antithesis,* wherein the organization relied on a shared enemy (such as heavy government regulation) to build shared interests; (3) *implicit identification,* which used the personal pronoun "we" to posit shared interests; and (4) *unifying symbols,* such as corporate logos or icons, that function to build strategic identification with employee publics. Because of the reciprocity of "identity" and "identification," these four strategies also constitute the means by which an organization can manage an identity and foster adherence to organizational values and actions. Particularly in the recruitment process, employees who *identify with* the organization through a process of self-and-other persuasion come to see themselves as having a share in the values associated in portrayals of the organization's identity.

So far I have described two implications of paradox inherent in how an individual or an organization presents an identity. The first results from a multifaceted "face" that one might don to appease interests that, while important to one's identity, may be in conflict. Second, identity is paradoxical, since the "self" is not the self at all, but a reflection of those with whom the person or organization would seek to identify.

A third sense in which identity is necessarily paradoxical invokes a communicative paradox of definition and an appreciation for the term "identity" as used in logic. Such an understanding is appropriate for an organization's presentation of its identity, since in this communicative process the organization presents a definition of "self," or a claim about "Who We Are." As Perelman (1982) explains, "In the process of defining a term, the claim to identify the defining expression (the *definiens*) with the term to be defined (the *definiendum*) constitutes an argumentative, quasi-logical usage of identity (p. 60)."

To posit that Dow (the *definiendum*) is *"its people"* (the *definiens*) is to define Dow in a particular manner. Because words are used to define words, definitions themselves are arbitrary and, hence, inherently involve both circular and paradoxical reasoning to establish themselves. As Perelman shows, the definitional paradox invoked in a presentation of self can best be demonstrated with the *apparent* tautology of a definition of identity: "A is A." Though the reasoning appears circular ("Dow is its people" and "These people are Dow"), we can also show that the tautology contradicts itself. Afterall, "A is *not* A," because where A is *the thing*, A is *the word*. Likewise, our earlier discussion has shown that "a self is *not the self*" at all, since it is drawn from others. While "A is *not* A" and "a self is *not the self*" contradict at face value, Perelman illustrates that the contradiction is only apparent using a familiar tautology: "Boys will be boys." The expression loses meaning if "boys = boys." Rather, we interpret the axiom as "boys = *not* boys, but the *attributes* of boys," and this allows a particular instance to be considered as the expression of an essence (p. 136). According to Perelman and Olbrechts-Tyteca (1969), "It would be incorrect to think that the exact meaning of the terms is fixed in advance or that the relation between the terms is always the same. The formulation of an identity puts us on the track of a difference, but does not specify as to what we should set our attention" (p. 217).

In other words, the terms used to identify attributes may themselves refer to a myriad of characteristics. The phrase "Boys will be boys" may be called upon at any time to associate salient qualities, such as the purchase of a desired car, attendance/participation in a sporting event, or working late, as expected attributes of "boys."

Hence, the looking-glass paradox: a representation of self by definition invokes a tautology, yet the tautology itself is only *apparent,* and rather a contradiction. This paradox is similar to the manner in which the *apparent* image of self one sees in a mirror is in actuality the *reverse* of the image seen by others. Perelman cautions that this paradox of tautology and contradiction, "A is A/A is *not* A," warrants investigation, since both tautological and contradictory definitions use a strategy of dissociation in order to reconcile the paradox. The strategy of dissociation involves invoking pairs of antithetical terms, attributing value to one quality, and negatively valuing its antithesis. To explain this strategy, Perelman uses the example of an oar in water that looks broken, but feels straight to the touch. The incompatible "straight" and "broken" appearances of the oar demand explanation. One way to resolve the paradox is to label one description of the oar as an "illusion" or "erroneous" and one as "real." In the very act of the dissociation of "real" from "illusion," Perelman observes, the concept of "real" becomes "a criterion for judging appearances. Whatever is conformable to it is given value, whereas whatever is opposed is denied value and is considered a mere appearance" (p. 24). Consider the recent debate before a Congressional committee to investigate U.S. tobacco companies' manufacture of cigarettes. Prompted in part by charges that these manufacturers "manipulate" levels of nicotine in cigarettes, Philip Morris (1994) published a print ad that claimed, "Both smokers and non-smokers deserve to know facts, not innuendo, about cigarettes." In this case, the claims presented by Philip Morris were "facts" to be contrasted to the claims presented by the tobacco companies' opponents, which were disvalued as "innuendo."

Paradoxes inhere in recruitment videos' identity presentations, which help to convey the values to which organizations adhere and, reciprocally, the values they expect their would-be employees to espouse. An examination of the recurrent paradoxes in corporate recruitment videos and their resolution, then, provides insight into the means by which organizations reconcile such paradoxes in order to attract college job seekers. This in turn yields a snapshot of the organization's attempt to establish and span the boundary(ies) between its "self" and its environments.

THE FACES OF THE ORGANIZATIONAL JANUS: MANAGING STRATEGIC PARADOXES IN RECRUITMENT VIDEOS

For this exploratory study, twelve recruitment videos were critically analyzed to unearth the strategic paradoxes that invite recruits to identify with the organization.[7] I first located definitional statements, which attempt to define the organization, often with the linking verb "is" (e.g., "Dow is . . ."). I next located possessive statements, wherein the organization attempts to define itself through that which it "owns," as in "Our people are. . . ." Though I considered verbal statements the primary source of self-presentation, I also incorporated visual depictions in the analysis, since these served as evidence to support claims about an organizational "self." Thus, pictures of employees who receive accolades testify that the organization "cares about its employees." From these statements, I isolated four characteristic paradoxes that recurred within these videos: we are old/we are new, we are big/we are small, we are people/we are technology, and we are our products/we are *not* our products.

We Are Old/We Are New

This paradox is most readily detectable in the organizational structure of the videos. Most open with historical commentary and change direction, both visually and verbally, to "update" the company's role in contemporary society. Dow's video provides an example. After the initial cap-and-gown sequence mentioned earlier, narration over a series of aged, still photographs states that Dow first began in 1887, with "Herbert H. Dow, one of the pioneers of the American Industrial Revolution, when young men were starting the companies that have become today's giants in business and industry. In the same way that Henry Ford pulled together the skills of many people, Dow gathered probing, inquisitive minds around him . . . to transform a common substance like brine into hundreds of products we now take for granted."

Familiar, contemporary graphics eventually appear and wipe the screen to colorful, motion-filled scenes and displays of new facilities and laboratory equipment. The narrator continues, "Today, Dow's people are made up of the same kind of inquisitive minds that Herbert Dow gathered around him."

Thus, Dow indicates that while it is "new," it still holds to its "old" values of skillful, inquisitive minds. This structure is also apparent in Thiokol's video, though notably the past is given less emphasis than in Dow's. Rather, the future is emphasized heavily with prominent use of contemporary graphics. Reference to the past is limited to a brief statement; however, the "pioneer" image again appears:

> For generations, scientists, engineers, and specialists challenged the limitations of their era, building Thiokol's reputation. . . . The first generation began to establish that reputation in the 1940s. Thiokol was one of the earliest pioneers in solid propellant rocketry. [Picture tone has changed to color, implying "time change."] Future generations went on to develop much of the key technology that has made modern rocket propulsion possible. [Graphic displays of the planetary system revolve and move about the screen.] Now it's our time to begin challenging tomorrow.

Lord Corporation also begins with historical background and notes a supportive role in the U.S. "fight for freedom" in World War II: "Lord helped turn the U.S. into the arsenal of democracy." After this reference, which is visually illustrated with an aged-looking clip of a tank rolling over small moguls in battle, Lord turns attention to its role "today." The narrator remarks that Lord has "eight domestic plant locations which produce a wide variety of products. Lord's world headquarters is located overseas, which shows a commitment to command a worldwide leadership position."

The historical references ground Lord in traditions readily shared by the audience. Structurally, progression from "old" to "new," as well as the increased number of plant locations, demonstrates "progress" and allows Lord to document its role as a "leader" in contemporary society.

We Are Big/We Are Small

Lord's reference to "globalness" is not unique; others also refer to this aspect of identity. A global map pinpoints the organization's many plant locations to depict its "globalness," its "commitment to command a worldwide leadership position." But though Lord is *big*, "smallness" is also a featured benefit. One mention of Lord Corporation's globalness, "Our products are sold in over 90 different countries around the world," soon turns to employee testimony of the benefits of Lord's smallness:

Male employee #1: When I got out of college, I had all but accepted a position with a major corporation, and before I got a chance to accept that position, I got a call from a small company in Northwest Pennsylvania that I'd never heard of before.

Male employee #2: I wanted to do good scientific research and make a real impact on the corporation, and I thought that it was small enough that I could make an impact.

Size becomes paradoxical in Thiokol's video through its conception of location: Various locations or divisions represent a cross section of American culture . . . from small Southern towns to Eastern communities or rural west. . . . All offer a relaxed atmosphere. On the other hand, each is located near a bustling, progressive metropolis."

Pillsbury also uses this paradox. First, the narrator notes an intricate link to Minneapolis: "The Pillsbury presence is felt in Minneapolis. Pillsbury is a name that is respected in Minneapolis." As pictures of bustling night life are projected, the narrator intones, "Minneapolis is a sophisticated lady with a small-town heart." Such an overt paradox is reconciled, since the organization can be both big and small; this in turn appeals to audiences who value either big *or* small. The apparently schizophrenic assertion can work to demonstrate uniqueness, as does Thiokol's suggestion that big and small offer a "unique combination."

We Are People/We Are Technology

Both people and technology are valued within the examined recruitment videos. Although people and technology are often culturally juxtaposed, recruitment videos manage to feature both people and technology as being characteristically bound. Even the department store chain Mervyn's, the "people-oriented" organization, prominently features the technology link. Computers "assist the buyer" and information systems focus "on customer service." While "people make the difference," technology is their tool. Thus, both can be prominently featured.

The prominent display of people allows the organization to demonstrate (1) its own vicarious identity, (2) the role individuals are expected to assume upon job acceptance, and (3) the organization's philosophy and attitude toward employees. People are depicted as "competent," "inquisitive," "responsible," "talented," "hardworking," "leaders," and "team players." By implication, the organization is also all of these. Pillsbury, for example, notes that, in order to achieve its mission to be the best food company in the world, "We hire the most talented people. Once they are here, we give them the opportunity to develop their potential." One Pillsbury employee confirms, "It is your role to be a leader. Right away [I was] given new product responsibilities. It was assumed I knew what was important."

Individual initiative is a primary "person" value, and serves to illustrate a role for newcomers. One Eastern Chemicals employee demonstrates his own transition process and the company's reliance on individual initiative. "Obviously, Eastman's big in the fibers business. When I came out of school, I didn't know anything about fibers. . . . They assigned me to a fibers job. The only way to learn is to get in there, put something on paper, and start designing."

Individual initiative and contributions to the organization provide a reciprocal link by which the organization is collectively constituted by the contributions of its employees. In turn, contributions to the organization allow for personal "growth" and "satisfaction." This transformation of something *undesirable* (work) into something *desirable* (personal growth) is fostered by the organizations' own desires to identify themselves with their potential employees. Lord Corporation affirms the vested interest it has in employee growth: "Our future depends on the caliber of our people." Simultaneously, the organization subtly aligns "caliber" with "technological knowledge." This subtle alignment can be seen in the organization's depiction of its "state of the art" technological support systems, which allow the organization to feature its facilities, laboratories, and computers, while simultaneously reasserting its commitment to progress.

People and technology thus vie for position, and the paradox is manifest in the remarks by one Lord Corporation employee who recalls a plaque he saw that states, "'We believe in the worth and dignity of every individual'. . . that statement really impressed me. After the interview process, individuals lived up to that." But this same individual later relegates people to a secondary role, when he comments: "There is no doubt in my mind that the key to success is manufacturing."

We Are Our Products/We Are Not Our Products

As one might suppose, prominent display of products is another recurrent feature within the videos, as the organization affiliates "self" with product. Yet, at the same time, the organization often asserts, "We are *not* our product."

This dissociative "we are not our products" takes two forms. The first involves the transcendent claim "We are *more* than our product." "We" are our public service, our people, our facilities, the communities within which we are located, our technology, and our philosophy. Earlier discussions demonstrate this variety and provide classificatory subsets that the organization can point to in its description of "self."

A second manifestation of "we are not our products" is the transformation of the product into something *other* than the product. The products are not mere products; rather, they fulfill a vital function in society. This transformation allows the organization to assert its own role within society and provides the opportunity to assert attitudes toward the work environment.

Eastman Kodak's Eastern Chemicals Division video provides an example of the second claim. When asked by two college students why a photographic company "became involved in so many different products," an Eastern Chemicals representative responds, "That is a classic example of how good leadership can develop opportunities from what others may see as problems." An approach to "problems" as "opportunities" allows the organization to progress *and* play social hero as the solver of problems.

At another point in the Eastern Chemicals video, the camera follows a young employee from job site to office meeting as his voice-over articulates his thoughts: "We don't produce goods; we produce a service. That service is timely, accurate engineering of products." Thus, products are transformed into something beyond a tangible good.

Dow uses this transformation strategy prominently. As the video displays a host of Dow products, the narrator remarks, "On products like these you see the Dow Diamond. Dow materials show up in a lot of other ways. Dow is the world's major producer of plastics which end up in a wide variety of materials you touch and use every day."

The visual channel cuts to a series: two small children playing with plastic toys/a telephone/an alarm clock/a refrigerator. The implication of familiar and necessary plastic items makes the home a prominent place of sanction from charges by environmentalists that plastics are harmful. Dow uses the same strategy to describe its chemical products:

Narration: Over the years, Dow people have solved some of the biggest weed and pest problems American farmers have faced. Helping them provide more and better quality food at lower cost than most other countries in the world.

Visual: Farmer upon tractor in the field/man in lab coat with needle pointed to plant leaf/grocery store clerk near produce counter. Cut to uniformed man spraying a lawn.

Narration: And our industrial line of herbicides and pesticides meet specialized forestry needs. Keeps your lawn green and your home termite free.

The transformation of product into that which is relied upon, even needed, by others, allows Dow to demonstrate its role within society as "keeper of cherished values" such as the home, which remains safe under Dow's watchful eye.

The Illinois Department of Transportation (IDOT) uses the strategy in a more contradictory manner. It notes that its Division of Aeronautics alleviates life-or-death situations: others rely on the IDOT for transportation of drugs and patients to hospitals. The transportation system itself is relied upon: O'Hare Airport is featured as evidence of efficient transportation "while keeping adverse factors such as noise and air pollution to a minimum." Thus transportation noise, a product of IDOT's own creation, becomes a factor with which IDOT must contend and provides justification for the organization's existence. The organization is *needed* to control aspects of that which it attributes to itself.

JANUS IN THE LOOKING GLASS: CORPORATE COMMUNICATION AND IDENTIFICATION THROUGH PARADOX

The representation of the Roman mythological figure Janus presents a lens through which to view the strategic paradoxes of organizational identity located within recruitment videos. *The Larousse Encyclopedia of Mythology* notes that Janus appeared only in Roman mythology, and his functions derived from one another. He is often represented with a double face, which stems from his guardianship of all doorways, of public gates through which roads pass, and of private doors. The two faces allowed him to look over the exterior and interior of a house and the entrance and exit of public buildings. As the god of gates, one of his insignia was the key that opens and closes all doors. By extension, he also was god of departure, return, beginnings, and all communication (Aldington and Ames, 1974, pp. 200–201).

Critics who sort through the paradoxes of organizational identity presented in recruitment communication are indeed faced with Janus in the looking glass. While the task is complex, investigation of subtle paradoxes illuminates the means by which organizations build identification with audiences. Not only do the paradoxes warrant attention, but also the way an organization resolves those paradoxes warrants investigation to fully understand the persuasive process.

The paradoxes within recruitment videos can be explained first as an attempt to appeal to a multifaceted audience, constituted by multiple and diverse publics. If identity stems from those values cherished by significant others, then an appeal to a broadly construed audience manifests itself in some manner of diversity. For example, some job seekers may be attracted to the benefits associated with a large organization, while others may be attracted by benefits affiliated with a small organization. This does not imply necessarily that the organization is engaged in an attempt to offer a "false front." Rather, these paradoxes are a manifestation of a necessarily multifaceted phenomenon. An identity, Cheney (1985) notes, stems from a number of associations that "are sometimes concentric and sometimes in conflict" (p. 107). Like the two-faced Janus, an organization's identity need not be limited to one or the other of its faces, but can be both. It may present itself as small, in that is has certain qualities often associated with a small company, such as the ability to personally attend to the needs of individual employees, customers, and communities. In this way an organization may dissociate itself from the impersonal traits often affiliated with big companies, even as it also presents itself as a multinational conglomerate that has access to multiple resources, opportunities for advancement, and other qualities that recruits find desirable.

As the projected multifaceted organization invites entry to would-be employees, however, it reflects familiar values cherished by its audience and simultaneously guards its portals. Specifically, it highlights those values that it identifies as a part of itself. Thus, while the projected identity has much with which a recruit may identify, it carefully guards the invitation to enter the organization. The potential recruit must accept the admonition that "the key to success is manufacturing" or that gaining the technical expertise desired by the organization truly leads to personal growth. When recruits can see themselves in the mirror held up to the organization's Janus, a reciprocal process of identification is underway. Thiokol's presentation of "our people" as competent allows the recruit to project future employment with the firm as an indication that, in the role of Thiokol employee, that recruit is competent.

And, as the newcomer in the recruitment video expresses desire to contribute to Dow because "I'll be doing something that really matters," paradoxically the organization expresses an assertion that *Dow* really matters. In fact, the paradoxes in corporate recruitment videos let organizations do great things.

NOTES

1. The author wishes to thank Steven L. Vibbert, Ed Schiappa, and Bill Elwood for their helpful comments on earlier drafts of this essay.

2. Dow Chemical U.S.A. (n.d.), *Great things are happening at Dow* (videotape). Midland, MI: Dow University Relations and Recruiting.

3. See, for instance, Nelson and Heath (1984). Early researchers who examined the frequency and purpose of film/videotape usage by organizations include Brush and Brush (1981) and Dranow et al. (1980). Prior to video, film was used for training purposes and organizations often sponsored educational films intended for a "public" audience (Barnouw, 1975). A Pennsylvania State University program focused specifically on the educational usefulness of film (Hoban and van Ormer, 1950).

4. The twelve videotapes examined were Dow Chemical U.S.A. (n.d.), *Great things are happening at Dow,* Midland, MI: Dow University Relations and Recruiting; Morton Thiokol, Inc. (1990), *Challenging tomorrow,* Aerospace Group Visual Productions; Exxon Corporation (n.d.), *Five Exxon MBAs talk about their careers,* New York: Exxon Corporation Administrative Services Department; Sherwin Williams (1985), *Sherwin Williams recruitment video,* Cleveland, OH: Sherwin Williams; Illinois Department of Transportation (n.d.), *Bridges to your future,* produced through the State of Illinois Information Service; Eastern Chemicals Division of Eastman Kodak (n.d.), *Corporate recruitment video;* Mervyn's (n.d.), *My customer comes first,* first in a series, *Intro to Mervyn's,* Hayward, CA: Mervyn's; Kimberly Clark (1987), *Kimberly Clark today;* Goodyear (n.d.), *Get the Goodyear blimp behind you,* Akron, OH: Goodyear Audio Visual Center; Lord Corporation (n.d.), *The sky's the limit;* Pillsbury (n.d.), *Pillsbury recruitment video;* Northern Illinois Gas (NI Gas) (n.d.), *Recruitment video.*

5. *Webster's New Universal Unabridged Dictionary, Deluxe Second Edition,* J. L. McKechnie, ed. (1983). The entry for *paradox* includes (1) a statement contrary to popular belief; (2) a statement that seems contradictory, unbelievable, or absurd, but that may be true in fact; (3) a statement that is self-contradictory in fact and, hence, false.

6. The work of Cheney and colleagues is most notable in this regard. See Cheney, 1985; Cheney and Tompkins (1985); Cheney and Vibbert (1987); Goldzwig and Cheney (1984). Application of the analogy is also recognized by others. See especially Mackenzie (1978); du Preez (1980).

7. For this exploratory study, the recruitment videos were selected from a list of 240 such videos made available in the Purdue University Placement Center. At this stage, I make no claim as to their representativeness, but view this exploration as a necessary first step toward identification of testable hypotheses.

PART IV
Case Studies of Internal Relations

10

The Rhetoric of Indoctrination

A Critical Analysis of New Employee Orientation

Mitchell S. McKinney[1]

Examination of the extant rhetorical analysis of corporate discourse reveals that most such analysis focuses primarily on the organization's external public relations messages. Cheney and Vibbert (1987) refer to such rhetoric as "corporate public persuasion" and describe corporate rhetoricians as "the makers and shapers of such campaigns that 'make' and 'remake' the organization for their various publics" (p. 179). Recently, however, scholars have noted the "blurring of organizational boundaries," as increasing attention has been given to corporate discourse that is strategically crafted for both internal and external audiences. As Cheney and Dionisopoulos (1989), citing Paonessa (1983), observe, "Many of these messages flow together, in that, for example, employees who receive internal messages also go home to watch corporate messages to the external public on television (e.g., about safety); thus, the traditional distinction between corporate communications *inside* the organization and public relations *outside* the organization makes little sense" (p. 145).

In developing their internal public relations campaigns, organizations have utilized a variety of persuasive message channels designed to influence current as well as future employees. Traditional forms of internal corporate rhetoric include house organs, employee newsletters, and corporate reports. Within the past few years, however, organizations have developed the use of corporate video as a new communicative medium. Used to reach both internal and external publics, videotaped messages serve a variety of functions. With external audiences, videos serve to recruit new members, to market new products, and to build a desired public image for the corporation. Internal corporate rhetoric via video includes such strategic uses as the introduction of new products and technology, the announcement of organization policy and procedures, and promotional messages for worker safety and a variety of personnel related topics. Perhaps one of the most common uses of corporate video is the new employe "indoctrination" video. The indoctrination video serves as a strategic persuasive discourse in which management seeks to foster company identification among new employees and create a desired corporate reality.

This chapter seeks to expand our understanding of internal public relations efforts through a critical-rhetorical analysis of an organization's attempt to create a desired image or reality for its new members. Specifically, a corporate indoctrination video shown during a new-employee orientation program serves as the text for analysis. First, a brief explanation of the critical-rhetorical approach to organizational discourse is provided, and then this approach is illustrated with analysis of the indoctrination video.

A CRITICAL-RHETORICAL APPROACH TO ORGANIZATIONAL COMMUNICATION

The adoption of a rhetorical-based theory of organization has significant implications for organizational communication analysis. The task of the organizational rhetorician is to study the organization's discursive practices, identify the resultant knowledge structures of these practices, and uncover the meanings that are created from such structures, meanings that produce organizing action. In short, a rhetorical-based theory of organization calls for rhetorical/textual analysis as the appropriate methodology for understanding the organization. Deetz (1982) succinctly describes the organizational analyst as rhetorical critic and states the advantages of such an approach:

> If the object of study with an interpretive approach is texts and activities treated as texts, the goals of interpretive research are seen as those of textual analysis. Exegesis and explication are a central part of this analysis. But what of value is obtained by textual analysis? And what does the organizational researcher accomplish by doing this? I will present three goals which I believe to be substantially different from those accomplished in most current organizational

research. They are (1) richer understanding of naturally occurring events, (2) criticism of false consensus and the forces which sustain them, and (3) the expansion of the conceptual base from which organizational members think and work. (p. 137)

In adopting such an approach, however, the organizational rhetorician's task must be more than that of mere interpretation of organizational symbolism or of uncovering the shared meanings that drive organizational actions. Instead, an enhanced understanding of organizational activity can be achieved through a critical analysis of organizational rhetoric. Again, Deetz states the necessity of a critical-rhetorical approach: "Research should perform a critical function by demonstrating where false consensus exists and the means by which it is constructed. . . . Interpretive research, to be useful, must become critical. Critical-interpretive research has as a goal appropriately directed action as well as understanding" (p. 139).

Mumby (1993) has characterized interpretive organizational research as adopting either a "descriptive hermeneutic approach" or a "hermeneutic of suspicion" approach. Analysis of the current interpretive program of the organizational culture perspective reveals that a critical focus is lacking in much of this body of work. Most organizational culture research has adopted a descriptive hermeneutic approach to organizational symbolism, with a primary focus of this work describing the unique features of a particular organization and demonstrating how certain symbolic forms are used to reinforce an organization's culture. Very little of this research has adopted a stance of hermeneutic suspicion that goes beyond mere description in analyzing the symbolic creation of knowledge structures (and accompanying structures of power), as well as an examination of the ways in which certain cultural or rhetorical practices serve to advantage, and disadvantage, particular organizational participants. Cheney (1983) has also noted the increased need for critical analysis of corporate rhetoric in modern organizations due to the changing communicative relationship between management and employee:

In the past they relied on more direct, even forceful, means of influence (e.g., close supervision, purely monetary rewards, and assembly-line "determinism"). And, of course, such methods are still quite evident. But today we often find managers and administrators less obtrusively encouraging individual involvement, support and loyalty. In short, fostering identification is the "intent" of many corporate policies, for with it comes greater assurance that employees will decide with organizational interests uppermost in mind. (p. 158)

The new-employee indoctrination video provides a particularly appropriate text in which to apply a critical-rhetorical analysis. The indoctrination rhetoric serves as strategic persuasive discourse in which management seeks to foster company identification among new employees and create a desired corporate reality. A critical analysis of such texts can provide evidence of the organization's value system and corresponding power and knowledge structures.

The indoctrination rhetoric is first situated in the larger context of the organizational socialization process. The socialization of new employees represents an important communicative process worthy of analysis. Specifically, the socialization of new employees is viewed as a rhetorical situation in which strategic messages are used to promote employee/organization identification and also to encourage employee commitment to the organization. In short, the indoctrination of new employees is a key internal public relations event for the organization. This chapter next proceeds with a brief description of the socialization process, identifying the rhetorical demands of this important event.

The Socialization Process

Defined as "the process by which a person learns the values, norms and required behaviors which permit him/her to participate as a member of the organization" (Van Maanen, 1975, p. 67), the socialization period represents a crucial time for the organizational newcomer who must ascertain needed role-related and culture-specific knowledge to function successfully as a participant of the organization. Through a variety of interactions, newcomers must learn what behaviors they are expected to adopt in order to perform their prescribed role within the organization. Additionally, culture-specific knowledge, including key beliefs, values, and norms, is also needed if newcomers desire to fit in and be rewarded for appropriate action in their new environment. While a few communication scholars have offered general descriptions of the socialization process (Van Maanen, 1975; Jablin, 1987), surprisingly few studies have adopted a discourse-based approach in analyzing actual messages used during this period.

In a recent review of the organizational communication research published from 1979 through 1989, Wert-Gray and colleagues (1991) found that, of the major topics comprising the corpus of organizational communication literature, the amount of scholarship dealing with the socialization process ranked near the bottom; only ten articles appeared within the past decade. In one of only three studies to examine the actual discourse of organizational socialization, Pribble (1990) describes the socialization process as "a logical point for studying rhetoric in organizations." According to Pribble, the socialization process is characterized by "the exhortation of an audience to follow particular should and oughts" (p. 255); it is a complex rhetorical event during which the organization must develop messages to encourage a newcomer to engage in specified behaviors and adopt desired beliefs and attitudes. In addition, strategic messages during this period promote employee/organizational identification and also encourage employee commitment to the organization. Defined by these persuasive demands, clearly a rhetorical analysis is appropriate.

Jablin (1982; 1984; 1985; 1987), perhaps the preeminent communication scholar to write about organizational socialization, offers a developmental socialization model charting the organizational participant's entry, assimilation, and exit. While Jablin's model describes the communication involved from pre-entry vocational choice to organizational withdrawal, early assimilation activities are perhaps the most significant to the newcomer's integration into a specific organization's culture or reality. During the assimilation period, an employee experiences a two-step process: encounter and metamorphosis. The encounter period represents the crucial time in which the newcomer "learns the requirements of his or her role and what the organization and its members consider to be 'normal' patterns of behavior and thought" (1987, p. 695). Jablin describes three key sources of communication that facilitate this learning: organizational/management, supervisor, and work group/coworkers. Interaction with supervisors is primarily oral in nature and deals with such matters as specific job instructions and performance expectations.

Work group/coworker interaction is also a primary source of communication in the encounter phase of socialization. Again, this discourse is primarily oral in nature and deals with both task and social relevant organizational knowledge. Two of the existing discourse-based studies of the socialization process (Brown, 1985; Stohl, 1986) both analyze stories shared among coworkers that facilitate newcomer socialization.

Finally, organization/management communication is also a key source of information in the assimilation phase. This information is presented in both written and oral form, such as the employee handbook and new-employee orientation session, and deals with such topics as policies and benefits, company history, corporate philosophy, and organizational mission. While a few researchers have studied the written forms of organization/management communication, analyzing such texts as employee handbooks and policy statements (Wolfe and Baskin, 1985; Vaughn, 1988), almost no research exists on the orientation session for new employees. Perhaps the only exception to this dearth of scholarship is Pribble's (1990) analysis of the rhetorical strategies used to promote ethical values in a medical technology firm's new-employee orientation program. Jablin (1987) comments on this lack of research:

> Interestingly, few empirical studies have explored the nature of the oral orientation programs that organizations present, typically through their personnel departments, to newcomers. In fact, essentially all we know about these programs is that they are frequently available to newcomers. . . . Unfortunately, the nature of the content of these programs has yet to be examined, though prescriptive essays on this subject indicate that programs often focus on issues similar to those covered in employee handbooks. (p. 697)

Thus far, a newcomer's organizational encounter during the assimilation phase of the socialization process has been identified as a key internal public relations event for the organization. Unfortunately, however, very little is known of the actual rhetorical practices used in the orientation of new organizational participants. To further our understanding of such practices, the following analysis adopts as its text a new-employee indoctrination video shown during new-employee orientation at Midwest Pharmaceutical (a pseudonym for a Midwest-based national manufacturer and distributor of pharmaceutical products). First, the indoctrination video is described and then the chapter concludes with a critical analysis of the rhetorical strategies utilized.

Indoctrination at Midwest Pharmaceutical

The new-employee video for Midwest Pharmaceutical is a 35-minute introduction to the company that is shown to new associates during employee orientation. The video's narrators consist of the company's founder and chairman of the board, along with the Midwest Pharmaceutical executive team, consisting of the president and chief executive officer, the senior executive vice president and chief operating officer, and the executive vice president. The company's founder as well as all members of the executive team are white males. Providing a historical overview of the company, the film develops three dominant themes: growth of the company, product development, and the "spirit" of Midwest Pharmaceutical. Analysis of the video's language and visual images, however, suggests that this rhetoric far from develops strategic messages that foster identification and commitment among new employees.

The company's founder begins his welcome to new employees by sharing a rags-to-riches story of how he single-handedly built Midwest Pharmaceutical:

> Let me take you back in time when Midwest Pharmaceutical first started. One person, $5,000, no products, no customers, trying to compete against the giant pharmaceutical companies of this great country. Impossible? No! But tough? Yes! I was working as a medical representative for a small drug company in Smalltown, although my home and territory was in Midwest City. After six months I'd been successful enough they made me Midwest sales manager—no salary, straight commission, paying my own expenses. As sales manager, I made a small percentage of what my salesmen made and sold. The second year I made more money than the president and that was unfortunate. They reduced my commissions. I stayed another year. I built it back up. This time they reduced my territories. It did not seem fair to me, so I thought, "Let's start another company."

Growth of the Company

Following the founder's opening narrative, the next segment of the video chronicles the rapid growth of Midwest Pharmaceutical by charting the geographic movement of the company and its corresponding physical expansion. From the founder's basement operation, the company made four subsequent relocations. All of the former locations are highlighted in the video, complete with detailed explanations of the size and condition of each facility. The growth sequence finally ends as the founder, in a climatic musical crescendo with aerial camera shots, proudly boasts of his crowning achievement, the firm's present corporate headquarters, Midwest Pharmaceutical Park: "150 acres, high on a hill." In addition to the corporate office, the company has ten supporting facilities throughout Midwest City, and each of these facilities is also highlighted in the video along with the reporting of each plant's square-footage measurements.

Indeed, nearly halfway through their introduction to the company, new employees have heard from only one organizational member—the company founder—and have been introduced only to "his" buildings.

After the protracted architectural tour, the Midwest Pharmaceutical executive management team is introduced, and each team member, in turn, pays homage to the company fonder and comments on the phenomenal growth of the organization: "The growth from a one-man operation in 1950 to today has been remarkable," or "In the last few years Midwest Pharmaceutical has been growing very, very rapidly." Again, like their superior, the comments of each top executive are almost exclusively related to bricks and hardware: "At Midwest Pharmaceutical we have some of the finest manufacturing facilities in the country as well as the world," or:

> We constantly update this facility with the latest manufacturing equipment as well as computer-driven inventory systems. You name it, we have the very, very latest. In addition to Building C, we recently expanded our Toxilab manufacturing support in Orange County, where we moved that group into a brand new facility to support their expanded sales. The third site is in Texas, where it's involved in supporting our diagnostic division. All of these are the best, the finest in the pharmaceutical industry.

The founder's opening narrative, along with the praise he receives from his executive officers, creates for the organization an Horatio Alger–type hero who started with nothing and now proudly rules from high on a hill his vast pharmaceutical empire. Indeed, as the previous excerpt illustrates, employees are regarded simply as "groups" who are moved in order to occupy a "brand new facility." Furthermore, when the executive comments that "all of *these* are the best, the finest in the pharmaceutical industry," he is referring not to the current or new employees, who constitute the organization, but rather to the buildings and support equipment.

The apparent message from such discourse is that the most valued resources at Midwest Pharmaceutical are its buildings and support equipment. In addition to the verbal praise of these objects, visual evidence also supports this conclusion. For example, when showing scenes within the various buildings, employees are highlighted only in relationship to the service of a particular machine. In most instances, employees, who usually appear in masks and gloves, are shown feeding chemical materials into a machine or packaging products.

Product Development   Similar to the highlighting and praise of buildings and equipment, the second major section of the indoctrination video extols the variety of products developed by Midwest Phar-

maceutical. As a long list of drugs is announced, masked lab technicians work intently with the chemical compounds and anonymous
glove-clad hands carefully bottle the various drugs. Along with these
visual images, the founder and his executive team pay their verbal
respects to Midwest Pharmaceutical's wonder drugs: "We have the best
products." In fact, "We are the pioneers in developing new products."
Described throughout the video, the pharmaceuticals are described as
"unique products," "innovative compounds," and the "most sophisticated health care products." Again, as these wonder drugs are praised,
the accompanying visual shots consist of glove-clad hands displaying
the drugs.

   In both the growth and product development sections of the film, it
is obvious that the people of Midwest Pharmaceutical occupy a subservient position in the management's reality of growth (buildings/equip-
ment) and product development. As described, it is not the dedicated
workers that make Midwest Pharmaceutical memorable, but rather it
is the organization's hero and his wonderful buildings, marvelous
equipment, and innovative products that are worthy of praise. Throughout the founder's praise of *his* company, the hardworking individuals
who staff the buildings, skilled workers who operate the machines, and
great minds who develop the products are completely ignored.

Spirit of Midwest Pharmaceutical

   After nearly 30 minutes of buildings, equipment, and products, the
last few minutes of the film are devoted to an interesting description
of the Midwest Pharmaceutical "spirit" and "culture." According to the
company president, "Everyone who comes in contact with *Midwest
Pharmaceutical* recognizes a difference here: a unique corporate culture." The company founder adds, "One of the things that you will
notice around here is the Midwest Pharmaceutical spirit. It's somewhat
intangible, but you can feel it and you can actually see the results." In
turn, each of the remaining senior executives testifies to the "spirit" of
Midwest Pharmaceutical. Apparently, this spirit is so ethereal that not
one of the three executives can account for the spirit or the results it
inspires. According to one, "Trying to describe this Midwest Pharmaceutical spirit is a very, very elusive thing, because to me you have to
be here, you have to see it, you have to feel it. It sort of defies
description." Another executive continues this theme: "The Midwest
Pharmaceutical spirit is hard to define. It's something you feel." Fi-

nally, "The Midwest Pharmaceutical spirit is a very difficult thing to define. It's the type of thing you have to experience rather than talk about."

Finally, the founder ends his introduction of the company with a direct appeal to his new employees: "Let us work together as a team and not only keep Midwest Pharmaceutical the best, but set an example that those giant pharmaceutical companies will try to equal. I ask that each of you leave here with your head held high, with pride in your heart, and say to yourself, 'I work for the best company in the world. I'm a Midwest Pharmaceutical associate.'"

It is revealing that the last minutes of the video are in almost complete contrast to the preceding 30 minutes. With no real acknowledgment of the contributions of the employees, only a few words are offered at the conclusion of the film articulating the importance of the individual worker. This disparity suggests that management at Midwest Pharmaceutical has adopted the now fashionable management technique of articulating a desired "corporate culture." The popular form of these hollow cultures is to describe an efficiently operating work group brought together by some indescribable familial or spiritual bonding. While projecting a surface-level commitment to employees, the enacted value structure of Midwest Pharmaceutical appears to be one of commitment to physical growth and respect for technology and for the supremacy of product development.

DEVELOPING IDENTIFICATION AND
COMMITMENT AT MIDWEST PHARMACEUTICAL

To evaluate the effectiveness of this discourse, one first must consider the essential exigencies of this rhetorical situation. As previously discussed, the organization–new employee interaction presents a situation in which the corporate rhetor has a unique opportunity to foster a sense of organizational identification and commitment with this important internal audience. While few analyses of message-focused studies exist of the socialization/orientation situation, Cheney (1983) has developed a typology of organizational identification strategies used in corporate written discourse.

Cheney's treatment of organizational identification is based on Burke's view of rhetoric. For Burke (1969), the goal of rhetoric is "strategic identification [as] a means of inducing cooperation in others" (p. 22). In applying his view of identification to corporate/organizational communication, Burke notes that identification allows one to "think of himself [sic] as 'belonging' to some special body more or less clearly defined" (1973, p. 268). The individual "identifies himself with some corporate unit (church, guild, company, lodge, party, team college, city, nation, etc.)—and by profuse praise of this unit he praises himself. For he 'owns shares' in the corporate unit—and by 'rigging the market' for the value of the stock as a whole, he runs up the value of his personal holdings" (1937, pp. 144–145). Cheney and Tompkins (1987) define this identification as the "substance" of the organization/participant relationship and describe the result of such a relationship as a commitment or "binding to action" (p. 9).

From Burke's notions of identification, Cheney (1983) noted four primary rhetorical strategies used to foster organizational identification: the common ground technique, identification through antithesis, the assumed or transcendent "we," and use of unifying symbols. While these strategies were initially applied to in-house corporate publications, their general applicability to organizational rhetoric makes them particularly useful for the analysis of such discourse as new-employee indoctrination. The following application of Cheney's typology to the rhetoric used in the Midwest Pharmaceutical indoctrination video reveals an overall lack of strategic message use in fostering organization/employee identification and commitment.

Described as the most important and frequently used technique in written corporate discourse (Cheney, 1983, p. 151), the common ground technique seeks to develop a close association or bond between the employee and organization. This technique is enacted through such rhetorical strategies as the expression of concern for individuals, recognition of individual contributions to the organization, espousal of shared values, testimonials by employees, praise by outsiders, and advocacy of benefits and activities. These strategies are glaringly missing from Midwest Pharmaceutical's new-employee indoctrination video.

First, the dominant discursive and visual strategies used in this video do not express concern for the organizational participant. As stated, the primary focus of this film is on the company's outstanding facilities and unique products. Furthermore, throughout the entire 35-minute video, the only organizational participants featured are the founder and his executive management team. For the new participants, it would seem apparent that what is regarded as important in their new organization is the heroic founder, his vast pharmaceutical empire, and his executive tribunal.

A second method by which the organizational rhetor can attempt to promote common ground or a bond with the new participant is through recognition of individual contributions. Cheney (1983) reports that organizations use this technique to motivate future and existing employees by recognizing those members who have excelled or distinguished themselves through great achievement. Again, Midwest Pharmaceutical's message to new employees seems to be that the only member of this organization who has achieved, and thus deserves, recognition is their founder. Beginning with his rags-to-riches narrative and continued with the homage paid to him by his executive team, the company founder is portrayed as a heroic figure and the central force in the organization. Indeed, not only do other employees fail to receive recognition when they are portrayed in the video, but also the visual images of masked faces and glove-clad hands only reinforce the delegitimation of the workers as insignificant organizational participants. While Midwest Pharmaceutical has developed the "most innovative compounds" and "the most sophisticated health care products," nothing is said about the talented and creative individuals who were instrumental in developing these products.

The espousal of shared values is described as a case in which "the organization states explicitly that 'we' have the same interests as 'you'" (Cheney, 1983, p. 151). Examples of values frequently articulated by organizations include the importance of family, employee development and growth, and providing needed services to the community or society. Pribble's (1990) study illustrates a medical technology firm's skillful articulation of valuing family and providing products to help maintain human life. While the Midwest Pharmaceutical video describes the company's wonder drugs, its primary focus is on the actual process of development and marketing of these drugs, and not on the benefits to the patient or society. Apparently, Midwest Pharmaceuticals values process, product, and profits, the cornerstones of the founder's success story and of many new buildings. Certainly, given the products developed by this organization, it would seem appropriate to construct messages suggesting to employees that their creative efforts and dedicated work truly benefit society.

The advocacy of benefits and activities is yet another technique in which the organization may attempt to foster a bond with the employee. Management may emphasize employee development activities, training opportunities, or job benefits as a means of encouraging employee commitment. The primary benefit that Midwest Pharmaceutical offers employees is the privilege to staff the most modern facilities and to service the latest technology and equipment.

A final common ground technique is the offering of praise by outsiders and testimonies by employees. While no outsiders offered praise for Midwest Pharmaceutical, the heroic founder offered self-praise for his great achievements. In addition, members of the executive team offered testimonials praising the founder and his facilities and products. At no point, however, do the new employees hear praise or testimony from or about their fellow workers.

One rhetorical strategy that Midwest Pharmaceutical utilized was the attempt to promote identification through antithesis, or the act of uniting against a common enemy. In both his opening narrative as well as his concluding "charge" to the new employees, the company founder invoked a common enemy by pitting Midwest Pharmaceutical against the "giant pharmaceutical companies" of the world: "One person, $5,000, no products, no customers trying to compete against the giant pharmaceutical companies of this great country. . . . Let us work together as a team to not only keep Midwest Pharmaceutical the best, but set an example that those giant pharmaceutical companies will try to equal." The enemy that is posited by the founder—those "giant" companies—serves as a significant rhetorical feature of this text. Clearly, the founder values size and growth, especially in terms of the number of facilities and expanding product line, as a sign of prestige and power in the pharmaceutical field. Thus, an organizational reality is enacted in which greater size (translated by buildings and equipment) equals success. As illustrated in this video, the founder's dominant value of "building" a great and large company creates an identify formation or a system of meaning in which the role of the individual participant is ignored and devalued.

The assumed or transcendent "we" is an identification strategy in which a shared relationship is suggested by referring to all members of the organization as "we." Cheney (1983) describes this strategy as one that "allow[s] a corporation to present similarity or commonality among organizational members as a taken-for-granted assumption" (p. 154). In his opening narrative, rather than uniting with a transcendent "we," the company founder distances himself from the employees with the personal reference *I:* "I'd been successful enough they made me Midwest sales manager. . . . I made more money than the president. . . .

I built it back up." Furthermore, while members of the executive management team do use an inclusive "we," it is most often used to suggest actions taken by the corporate elite, rather than to promote commonality among all members of the organization: "We now have seven locations. . . . we constantly update these facilities. . . . we seek out major compounds on a worldwide basis."

Finally, the use of unifying symbols is a strategy in which the organization strategically uses a logo or symbolic representation to create a special sense of meaning and identification among employees. Pribble (1990) describes the use of this strategy by a medical technology organization: "Each new employee receives a medallion in which science and technology are represented by an electrical field raising a modern day Lazarus. Only BE employees receive the medallion which, when accepted, affirms their membership in this organizational community" (p. 262). Midwest Pharmaceutical attempts to unify through symbolism with its "unique corporate culture." As illustrated by a member of the executive team, the inability to clearly articulate this corporate spirit provides a less than convincing portrayal for the new member: "Trying to describe this Midwest Pharmaceutical spirit is a very, very illusive thing, because to me you have to be here. You have to see it. You have to feel it. It sort of defies description. I think it's a very, very wonderful thing and, to me, our number one challenge is keeping that spirit alive as we grow. There's absolutely no question in my mind we're going to be a billion dollar company sooner than a lot of people realize." Again, the dominant value that seems to define this unique spirit is success through growth. In an odd, discursive twist, the founder states that the spirit at Midwest Pharmaceutical is ultimately responsible for the company's growth success. New employees might be eager for cues to recognize that spirit so they also can participate in the company's success. Yet neither he nor the executives quoted in the video describe this elusive or illusory spirit.

CONCLUSION

Adopting Mumby's (1993) "hermeneutic of suspicion" stance, this interpretation attempts to illustrate the link between communication, power, and identity formation in the organization. As discourse designed to promote a sense of identification with its primary internal audience—its employees—the Midwest Pharmaceutical new-employee video fails to adequately fulfill the demands of the rhetorical situation. Rather than uniting the organization and the new employee, the rhetorical strategies utilized in this text could potentially serve to distance the new participant from the organization. By ignoring, and thus delegitimating, the role of the individual in the organization, a worker identity is created in which the member serves to fulfill the heroic founder's vision of a bigger and more successful company. This attitude may reflect the elusive corporate spirit that pervades Midwest Pharmaceutical: employees are human *resources,* only as valuable as the chemical resources that contribute to increased profits and new buildings. For the new participant, the indoctrination video serves as the organization's initial discursive attempt to establish a system of institutional meaning and dominance in which the role of the organizational participant is to fuel the growth of this pharmaceutical empire. Within the heroic founder's vision and power structure, the contributions of the individual worker are subservient to the more crucial goals of acquiring modern facilities, more sophisticated equipment, and innovative products.

As a key organizational narrative, this indoctrination discourse functions ideologically as it represents a dominant structure of meaning that privileges the founder's value of growth at the expense of the individual employee. Explicating the political function of narrative, Mumby (1987) writes, "Narratives not only evolve as a product of certain power structures, but also function ideologically to produce, maintain, and reproduce those power structures" (p. 113). In other words, employees that subscribe to the values that the video and, undoubtedly, other corporate texts articulate ultimately should view themselves as resources, not as valued individuals who constitute an organization and ensure its success.

The preceding critique of the Midwest Pharmaceutical indoctrination video exemplifies the type of internal public relations discourse that calls for a critical-rhetorical analysis. A critical examination of such discourse reveals dominant meaning systems that produce, maintain, and reproduce the organization's power structures. Such analysis is an attempt to answer Mumby's charge that "Very few studies to date have systematically examined specific communicative practices as they occur in organizational settings. This is a glaring omission in the sense that it is at the level of the everyday that relations of power are chronically reproduced" (1993, p. 22).

Methodologically, while analysis of a single text should not stand alone, one can apply an inter-textual approach with the examination of additional texts in identifying the dominant structures of meaning that guide organizational action.

In understanding corporate public relations activities, scholars must add to their study of the organization's external public messages analysis of the variety of strategic discourse developed by the organization for its internal members. Internal public relations campaigns utilize such diverse communicative mediums as the increasingly popular corporate video, house organs, employee newsletters, and corporate reports. As this chapter illustrates, a critical-rhetorical analysis presents itself as a most useful theoretical/methodological approach for understanding the discursive foundations of organizational life.

NOTE

1.   The author would like to thank Beverly Davenport Sypher for her helpful comments on earlier drafts of this chapter.

11

SANE/Freeze, Issue Status, and Rhetorical Diversification

Michael F. Smith

When the Berlin Wall fell in November 1989, it meant the beginning of the end of the Cold War between the United States and the Soviet Union and the need for massive military arsenals. Pundits wondered how the United States would spend the "peace dividend" that was expected from reduced military expenditures. Most agreed, however, that there would be significant changes in the environment in which the military-industrial complex would operate.

While the Pentagon and weapons producers adjusted to this new set of national priorities, there was another group that also had to adjust to the "new world order." SANE/Freeze, an activist organization that focused on nuclear weapons and disarmament issues, found that its primary issue had dropped from the national agenda. With the specter of nuclear war gone and arms control agreements signed, the media and most Americans turned their attention to other issues. This left SANE/Freeze to ponder the question: If you are a nuclear weapons activist group and nuclear weapons is not an issue, what do you do?

This was not merely an academic inquiry for SANE/Freeze, because the organization had lived through drops like this before. Founded in 1957 as the Committee for a Sane Nuclear Policy, SANE/Freeze had enjoyed both great success and great strife as an activist organization. After successfully pushing the United States and the Soviet Union to sign the Partial Nuclear Test Ban Treaty in 1963, SANE watched as the nuclear weapons issue all but dropped from the American agenda

(Boyer, 1984). After leading protests against the Vietnam War in the 1960s and early 1970s, SANE had to retrench after the war ended in 1973. In July 1977, SANE had an operating deficit of over $28,000 and only $702 in the bank (Katz, 1986). As the Intermediate Nuclear Forces Treaty was about to be signed in 1987, SANE's co-chair David Cortright (1987) warned of what he called the "dilemma of success": "We must . . . guard against the tendency for a dissipation of energy within the peace movement. When the superpowers' leaders meet and sign treaties, people naturally begin to feel that "things are being taken care of" and that their sacrifice and commitment are no longer necessary. All popular movements face this problem. . . . The best way to counteract it is to acknowledge victories and to offer a clear and compelling alternative vision for the future" (p. 10). Indeed, if SANE/Freeze wished to continue to operate as an organization, it needed to keep its issues salient to its members.

This challenge is not uncommon to activist organizations. While not a significant part of the public relations literature, activist groups face many of the same challenges as other organizations. Primary among these is the need to adapt to changes in the environment. This case study examines the means by which SANE/Freeze adapted to changes in the nuclear weapons issue. Specifically, I argue that SANE/Freeze utilized rhetorical issue management strategies to achieve what I call rhetorical diversification. Through its newsletter, SANE/Freeze was able to communicate to its members the status of the nuclear weapons issue and, ultimately, redefine both the organization and the goals it sought to achieve. In order to explore these notions, I first examine the relationship between issue management strategies and organizations and offer a method through which these strategies can be studied. Second, I examine how the status of the nuclear weapons issue changed between 1981 and 1991 and how SANE/Freeze adapted to those strategies. Finally, I offer some observations on how activist organizations can utilize rhetoric as a resource to manage issues with their members.

ISSUE STATUS AND ACTIVIST ORGANIZATIONS

Activist organizations are in the "business" of managing issues on the public agenda. These issues, which often compete with other issues for the public's attention, form the environment in which activist organizations operate. Here I first examine the rhetorical nature of issue management and then discuss why issues are important to an activist organization's survival.

Public relations and issue management scholarship has focused mainly on how corporate, for-profit organizations defend themselves from activist group attacks. However, sociological theorists argued nearly 50 years ago that public relations was one means of achieving social change. For example, Humphrey (1946) observed that public relations and social work were two fields that attempted to rectify social problems: "Originally utilized exclusively by business leaders as a systematic body of knowledge and technique, [public relations] has more recently been adapted to the needs of educational, social work, and ameliorative social pressure organizations" (p. 23).

Among the first to take a rhetorical approach to issue management were Crable and Vibbert. They suggested that an issue is "created when one or more human agents attaches significance to a situation or perceived 'problem.' These interested agents create or recreate arguments that they feel will be acceptable resolutions to questions about the status quo" (1985, p. 5). As people attach significance to issues, they define them in particular ways that limit their scope and terms of their resolution (Vibbert, 1987; Dionosopoulus and Crable, 1988).

Crable and Vibbert's definition of an issue suggests that problems do not become public issues until some human agent talks about them. Crable and Vibbert (1985) also suggest that issues pass through five status levels in their "life cycle" (p. 6). Vibbert (1987) claims that advocates of particular issues propel the issue through the life cycle through various rhetorical strategies. The goal in managing issues is to manage the issue's status through rhetoric. First, an issue gains *potential* status when agents form questions about a particular problem and build arguments to justify a particular answer to those questions. In the potential status, *definition* is the paramount rhetorical strategy, because advocates need to set the parameters of the issue and separate one issue from another. Second, an issue achieves *imminent* status when it gains an endorsement from other sources. At this level, a larger amount of the public begins to see linkages between an issue and their concerns. *Legitimacy* is the strategy that propels an issue through the imminent stage. Rhetors create messages aimed at making the issue important and worthy of the attention of a larger audience.

Third, the issue attains *current* status. At this level the issue becomes most noticeable by the public at large. The mass media tend to focus attention on the issue, and it not only becomes timely and newsworthy, but also a token of conversation for the public. As an issue becomes current, *polarization* becomes the dominant strategy. Opposing viewpoints, regardless of their number, tend to be reduced to two diametrically opposed options. The media, given their thirst for drama, become particularly important at this point. However, organizations themselves contribute to this dramatization by presenting their positions in terms that draw stark contrasts with their opponents.

Fourth, the issue reaches the *critical* level. At this point the issue is ready for decision. In the United States, the agent with the authority to answer public policy questions is the government. The strategy is to persuade decision makers to *identify* with one position or another. When an issue is resolved or fails to move successfully through the status levels, it becomes *dormant.* The issue is not dead, but merely asleep, ready to reach potential should someone once again attach significance to it.

The rhetorical strategies of issue management—definition, legitimation, polarization, and identification—seldom occur in isolation or in their pristine form. The nature of public policy debate is that, while government has the final authority to enact laws, citizens, corporations, and activist groups engage in public dialogue over issues. Each of these entities operates in an environment marked by the presence of others communicating about the same issues. Moreover, other issues are also passing through their life cycles. Thus, current or critical issues may push others into dormancy. Downs (1982) noted, for example, that issues are pushed toward dormancy as "new" issues "exert . . . a more novel and thus more powerful claim upon public attention" (p. 38). Thus, SANE/Freeze not only had to be sensitive to the issue management efforts of its opponents on the nuclear weapons issue, but also to the status of other issues on the public's agenda.

The interaction among various issues can affect the environment in which social movement organizations operate. This argument is based on the idea that there is seldom only one issue in development at any given time in a society. McCarthy and Zald (1977), for example, argue that there can be several social movements in development at any given time. Not every movement is at the same stage. Each movement is pushing its issue on the public agenda. The relative popularity of these issues may force the issues of other movements into dormancy. Activist organizations face the rhetorical challenge of maintaining the viability of both the organization and the movement. This is accomplished by maintaining the viability of the organization's issues to its members.

Attracting new members to organizations like SANE/Freeze and retaining those who already have joined is one of the ongoing struggles for activist groups. Scholars have used exchange theory (Salisbury, 1969; Wilson, 1973; Grunig, 1989) to explore the reasons why people join organizations. Exchange theory suggests that political interest groups marshall *incentives*—the benefits members attain through the group's activities—to recruit members (Olson, 1965).

Among the incentives for potential members are *purposive benefits*. These are primarily psychic benefits that arise from the pursuit of an ideological goal. For many activist organizations, purposive benefits are the most compelling incentives. A group's position on its primary issue not only advocates particular sorts of policy goals, but also embraces values that can be used to appeal to potential members and to retain current members. Ornstein and Elder (1978) label these benefits "symbolic" and argue that "many instrumental policy goals of groups may have primarily symbolic purposes" (pp. 29–30). To the extent that issues are a reflection of the issue organization's ideology, they are an important element in attracting new people to the organization. James and Rose-Ackerman (1986) note that nonprofit organizations' ideologies are vital to attracting and retaining members. However, Hrebenar and Scott (1982) caution that those organizations that rely primarily on purposive benefits are very unstable. They suggest that such organizations "must rely on the attractiveness of 'the cause' or 'the goal' in order to attract or maintain their membership" (p. 20). The way in which an organization communicates about its goals—its issues—is essential to membership attraction and retention. For SANE, its ability to establish and maintain the importance of nuclear weapons issues was important to its survival. I argue that SANE used the rhetorical nature of issues in order to redefine and reestablish the importance of its goals to its members.

Method: Issue Management Analysis

There were two major steps to exploring how SANE/Freeze adapted to the nuclear weapons issue. The first step was to trace the status of the nuclear weapons issue to assess how SANE's *issue environment* changed over time. I analyzed the issue's status using the Issue Development Graph (IDG) (Faulkner, 1985; Crable and Faulkner, 1988). The

IDG demonstrates how the status of an issue changes over time. The IDG allows the critic to trace the development of an issue as increasing attention is paid to it and as critical events drive the issue through its life cycle. I used the IDG to trace nuclear weapons issue as reported in *The New York Times, The Washington Post,* and *Time* magazine between 1981 and 1991. The status of the nuclear weapons was judged by two factors: (1) the number of stories that related to nuclear weapons, their development, or their deployment, and (2) the major themes that characterized the media's coverage of the issue. These themes corresponded to the changes in the number of stories and represented the major developments in the nuclear weapons issue to which SANE/Freeze adapted. I call these periods of development *eras.*

The second part of the study was an analysis of SANE's rhetorical responses to changes in its issue's status. I analyzed sixty-nine SANE (and, later, SANE/Freeze) newsletters published between 1981 and 1991. Though typically seen as a common public relations tool, newsletters are an important text through which to determine how organizations keep their issues salient to their members or potential members. For activist organizations, the newsletter can serve as both an information source and a rhetorical document. Newsom and Carrell (1991) posit that "sharing information with members is a principal way an organization sustains itself" (p. 380). In terms that suggest a rhetorical function for newsletters, Rayfield, Acharya, Pincus, and Silvis (1991) state that a newsletter "defines and explains the organization" (p. 282). Cheney and Vibbert (1987) argue that newsletters and other internal publications "serve to promote select values, foster select images, create select identities, and determine the status of select issues" (p. 181) to an organization's members.

The analytical focus of this study is rhetorical: what issue management strategies did SANE/Freeze use to manage changes in its issue's status? Various studies (Crable and Vibbert, 1983; Vibbert, 1987; Vibbert and Bostdorff, 1992) identify four primary argumentative strategies of definition, legitimation, polarization, and identification. Coombs (1990; 1992) developed a detailed typology of the various forms these strategies might assume. He maintains that the typology was designed "to explain the resources used in the issue management process and how these resources are used to manage issues" (1990, p. 4). These *resources* are linguistic and argumentative and are the resources upon which activist organizations draw for their survival. For each of the four issue management strategies, Coombs culled a variety of tactics from previous studies and theoretical articles. He identified the theoretical bases for each tactic and then provided a variety of forms the tactic might take.

I analyzed each of SANE/Freeze's newsletters using Coombs's (1990) typology. As Coombs notes, the myriad tactics he identified were not used universally—that is, not every tactic is used in every issue management case. The tactics may be brought to bear selectively upon each instance of issue management discourse. Thus, while I looked for examples of definition, legitimation, polarization, and identification in each of the articles analyzed, I resisted the temptation to let the schema act as a blinder to insights that a close reading of a text might offer. In fact, there were some important strategies that SANE used that did not fit neatly into Coombs's typology. Coombs's categories focused my analysis on issue management strategies, but there were exceptions to and extensions of these strategies. With this in mind, I now examine the nuclear weapons issue and how SANE adapted.

SANE/FREEZE AND THE NUCLEAR
WEAPONS ISSUE: 1981–1991

My analysis of the nuclear weapons issue's status revealed three general eras that developed between 1981 and 1991: (1) Reagan's Cold War and the People's Response: 1981-1984, (2) An Outbreak of Peace: 1985-1988, and (3) New Worlds: 1989-1992. Each era exhibits a change in the status of the nuclear weapons issue and, consequently, a change in SANE/Freeze's issue environment. In this section, I briefly trace the nuclear weapons issue's development in each of the three eras and explain how SANE/Freeze responded to these changes.

Reagan's Cold War and the People's Response: 1981–1984

During this first era, nuclear weapons were among the dominant news stories, propelled largely by President Ronald Reagan's military policies. Reagan's increases in defense spending, insistence on expensive and controversial weapons systems such as the MX and Pershing II missiles and the Strategic Defense Initiative, staunch anti-Soviet rhetoric, and international intervention to support anti-Communist movements all served to increase Cold War tensions and to drive the nuclear weapons issue to the top of the public's agenda. The public responded by protesting and rallying around the nuclear weapons freeze proposal, which called for the United States and the Soviet Union to "adopt a mutual freeze on the testing, production, and deployment of nuclear weapons and of missiles and new aircraft designed primarily to deliver nuclear weapons" (Forsberg, 1981, p. 1). Freeze ballot initiatives, mass rallies, and the birth of a coordinating organization, the Nuclear Weapons Freeze Campaign (NWFC), helped galvanize millions around the nuclear weapons issue.

The press coverage of the nuclear weapons issue peaked in 1983 and gradually dropped off thereafter. Nuclear weapons coverage in *The New York Times,* for example, nearly doubled between 1981 and 1982, from 567 stories to 1,045. The number plummeted to 865 in 1984, however. *The Washington Post* coverage exhibited a similar trend, with nuclear weapons articles jumping from 881 in 1981 to 1,229 in 1983, but fell to less than one-half that total in 1984—588. In *Time* magazine, the number of articles leapt from 19 to 46 between 1981 and 1982, rose to 60 in 1983, and dropped to 29 by 1984. These figures indicate that the nuclear weapons issue enjoyed a short but meteoric rise to the top of the media's agenda between 1981 and 1983, before falling off.

Between 1981 and 1984, SANE's membership nearly grew from from 29,000 to 75,000. This tremendous growth in both the organization and in the movement presented challenges to SANE. In order to address these challenges, SANE's newsletter writers utilized three predominant themes: (1) Us versus Reagan; (2) First among Equals; and (3) Resetting the Agenda. Each of these themes, in turn, used some of the rhetorical strategies of issue management to appeal to members.

Us versus Reagan   The first theme was SANE's attempt to react to the sweeping policy changes the Reagan administration began to pursue in 1981. To do this, SANE often defined its position in terms that contrasted sharply with the administration's.

Since Reagan's initiatives had received a great deal of press coverage, an advantage most presidents enjoy, SANE was able to reference Reagan's terms when arguing against his policies. SANE utilized the functional definitional strategy (Coombs, 1990). The *functional strategy* occurs when an issue manager defines (or redefines) the purpose of a term. According to Coombs, in order to use this strategy, a term must have a specific purpose in a particular context. Thus, for the administration, the increased military expenditures were justified because they were "defense" spending. But for SANE, increased military spending functioned to prepare the United States for war.

In criticizing the North Atlantic Treaty Organization's (NATO's) deployment of Pershing II missiles in Europe, SANE referred to the NATO leaders as "warlords" (Wilson, 1981). When the Pentagon announced plans to continue development of a neutron bomb, SANE accused Secretary of Defense Casper Weinberger of adopting "the . . . dangerous strategy of actually developing a nuclear warfighting capacity" (Baker, 1982). Efforts to develop a national civil defense plan were dismissed as efforts to prepare for war: "The frightening reality is that our government is conducting a many-pronged program to prepare the American people mentally for nuclear war" (Baker, 1982). And opposition to the MX missile, SANE's most prolonged anti-weapons campaign of the decade, was premised on the claim that the MX was "designed to knock out Soviet missiles in their silos as part of a first strike" ("MX alert," 1983). This first strike capability transformed the weapon's function from purely defensive to potentially offensive. Reagan's ethical justification for the weapons, then, was called into question.

The functional strategy presented SANE's position as being opposite to those of Reagan's. In order to achieve progress on its primary issue, nuclear weapons, SANE had to place itself in opposition to the recalcitrant Reagan policies. Because the issue was already in the news, this strategy helped polarize the positions of the administration and those opposed to it. However, because so many other organizations had joined the nuclear weapons disarmament crusade, SANE was faced with another challenge: how to distance itself from other arms control groups, but still remain part of the movement.

First among Equals   One indication of the nuclear weapons issue's tremendous popularity during this era was the number of organizations that joined the movement. With a plethora of organizations entering the anti-nuclear weapons movement, SANE used rhetoric to manage its identity. Cheney and Vibbert (1987) argue that a significant organizational challenge is "to develop a distinct identity while at the same time being recognized as part of the cultural 'crowd'" (p. 185). The task is to appear similar to, but separate from, other organizations. Cheney and Vibbert suggest that an organization adopts certain cultural values while pointing out what makes it special or unique.

SANE managed this challenge with its membership by suggesting that, although the organization acted in concert with other antinuclear organizations, it was a leader of these groups—not just part of the crowd. The terministic vehicle through which SANE claimed its legitimacy on nuclear weapons issues was the word "coalition." According to *The Random House College Dictionary,* a "'coalition' is a temporary alliance of *distinct* parties, persons, or states for *joint* action" (1982, p. 257, emphasis added). SANE joined with other organizations that shared its commitment to values. But SANE portrayed itself as a leading force behind these organization's efforts.

Perhaps the range of groups involved in the antinuclear weapons movement of this era and SANE's portrayal of its leading role in this movement is most clearly evident in this passage:

> Over 80 organizations, including the Episcopal Church, National Association of Social Workers, National Audubon Society, National Union of Hospital and Health Care Employees, United Food and Commercial Workers, and the YWCA of USA expressed their far-reaching opposition to the MX missile at a Capitol Hill press conference June 28th. The event, sponsored jointly by Common Cause and SANE, featured SANE, . . . Friends of the Earth, and Lawyers Alliance for Nuclear Arms Control. ("Pressure mounts," 1983)

The coalition that made up the antinuclear weapons movement was clearly defined here—religious and civic organizations, as well as labor unions, were united in their opposition to the MX missile. This seemed to indicate that the antinuclear movement was not just a bunch of radicals. And SANE led the parade.

Perhaps most vexing to members of the Nuclear Weapons Freeze Campaign, SANE grabbed some early credit for the freeze movement. The first time that SANE referred to the freeze in its newsletter the reference was framed by SANE's leadership on the issue: "New Jersey SANE, our oldest and largest group, continues to spearhead the campaign for a Nuclear Weapons Freeze in this state. With the help of many individuals and community organizations . . . [they] are now working to put a Freeze referendum on the ballot this fall" (Kraybill, 1982).

SANE also differentiated itself from other organizations by referring to its history of advocacy on nuclear weapons policy. By a fortuitous coincidence, SANE celebrated its 25th anniversary in 1982. Kraybill (1982) referred to SANE's "record of achievements over . . . two decades" (p. 1), which included the Limited Test Ban Treaty in 1963, the defeat of a proposed Anti-Ballistic Missile system in 1970 and the B-1 bomber in the late 1970s, and early protests against the Vietnam War. Coombs (1990) argues that one way by which an organization can achieve legitimacy is through a *tradition* of advocacy on a particular issue. Kraybill tied SANE's tradition to the present by suggesting that the Reagan administration's attempt to redefine the conditions of the ABM treaty and reintroduce the B-1 bomber would "nullify two of SANE's most significant political victories" (p. 2).

Resetting the Agenda   This theme was one that SANE adopted as the nuclear weapons issue began to fall off the public's agenda and as public policy victories proved more elusive than SANE's members had hoped. The huge popularity of the freeze was, as SANE's Chair David Cortright (1982-1983) noted, "largely symbolic." SANE had been unable to turn popularity into political force. There were few legislative victories during this period. In the House of Representatives, SANE issues were passed only 32 percent of the time between 1981 and 1984, according to voting records printed in *SANE World.* The Senate record was a dismal 15 percent. Even when SANE issues did pass, as in the House Freeze resolution, the wording had so compromised SANE positions that the organization's support was only lukewarm ("Will the real freeze," 1982). In the ultimate setback, Ronald Reagan was reelected in a 1984 landslide.

Stewart (1980) finds that one of the functions that social movement rhetoric must perform is to explain setbacks. In December 1983, David Cortright acknowledged, "These are difficult and challenging times for the nuclear freeze movement. Despite overwhelming public support for our goals, we have few victories to show for our efforts. The widespread public desire for halting the arms race has not yet been translated into political change" (p. 1). He urged SANE members to respond to the setbacks with "steadfastness of purpose." However, SANE was beginning to redefine just what the purpose of the organization was. The means by which this initial redefinition of purpose was accomplished was by slightly expanding the scope and reshuffling the order of issues addressed.

Coombs (1990) states that one way issue managers can define their issues is through the so-called *nonpersuasive tactic.* This strategy attempts to indicate what aspects of an issue are important. "Nonpersuasive" is a misnomer, since this tactic attempts to restructure the values associated with a term. It works particularly well when there are several specific sub-issues associated with a broader term. One means of communicating what an organization feels is important is through an agenda, a list of things to be accomplished. By including some things on the list at the exclusion of others or by placing some items higher on the agenda than others, issue managers emphasize what they feel is important. For SANE, the nuclear weapons freeze, the MX and Pershing missiles, Reagan's Strategic Defense Initiative, and the intervention in Central America were all aspects of the broader disarmament issue. As this era ended, however, the relative importance attached to the issues changed.

Since people join an activist organization because of the issues it advocates, it is logical to assume that they might leave the organization if those issues change. SANE's leaders might have heeded the results of a membership survey to determine the organization's agenda ("Poll results," 1983). The issues that members most wanted to see on the agenda, in rank order, were (1) the nuclear freeze, (2) military budget cuts, (3) removal of missiles in Europe, (4) the MX missile, (5) Central America, (6) economic conversion. Since SANE expanded its agenda greatly during the next era of issue development, membership wishes were to become a concern for the organization.

An Outbreak of Peace: 1985–1988

During this second era, the nuclear arms issue did not receive the popular attention it enjoyed during Reagan's Cold War, but was still on the national agenda. The most significant trend during this period was the gradual reduction in tension between the Soviet Union and the United States, characterized by progress in arms control talks, the emergence of Soviet leader Mikhail Gorbachev, and the signing of the INF agreement in 1987.

Media coverage of the nuclear weapons issue, after an upward spike in 1985, dropped steadily through 1988. Coverage in *The New York Times* dropped from 1,253 in 1985 to 609 in 1988. This trend was also reflected in *The Washington Post* and *Time.*

In order to deal with the drastically changing status of the nuclear weapons issue in this era, SANE utilized two interrelated themes: (1) Redefining the Movement, and (2) Utilizing Multiple Issues.

Redefining the Movement   From 1981 through 1985, *SANE World*'s masthead claimed that it was the "newsletter of action on disarmament and the peace race." This definition of purpose indicated that SANE would address both "disarmament" issues and "peace" issues. The ability to choose between these two terms meant that SANE could use varying levels of ambiguity in order to describe the kind of movement that SANE represented. This ambiguity allowed SANE to ally itself with various sectors of its "social movement industry" (McCarthy and Zald, 1977). As several authors have noted (DeBenedetti, 1980; Carter, 1992), the peace movement has traditionally represented several different goals, including protesting particular wars, general pacifism, and weapons reductions. Each goal is rooted in different ideologies and conceptions of just what "peace" means.

During the Outbreak of Peace era, SANE used the term "disarmament movement" when it addressed what had typically been nuclear weapons issues, such as specific weapons systems, nuclear arms proliferation, and nuclear weapons testing. For example, in 1985 SANE began a campaign to attain a Comprehensive Nuclear Test Ban (CTB). In announcing this effort, Glennon (1985) wrote, "SANE and several other arms control and disarmament groups are spearheading a new effort to halt nuclear tests as a strategy for implementing a freeze" (p. 1). Here, actually, are two initiatives—the CTB and the freeze—under the rubric "disarmament."

The use of the disarmament term was especially evident during the period when SANE merged with the NWFC to form SANE/Freeze in 1987. The NWFC was the archetypal "single-issue" organization that had risen to prominence on the popularity of the freeze initiative. NWFC leaders were reluctant to address other issues, even nuclear weapons systems, because they thought that doing so would dilute the power of the freeze proposal (Ferguson, 1988; Solo, 1988). When SANE merged with the NWFC, the newsletter announced that the organization was "one of the few disarmament groups that can mobilize large numbers of its own constituents" (Cortright and Cottom, 1987). SANE/Freeze's first action as a unified organization was to sponsor a Test Ban Caravan to lobby Congress for the CTB, a nuclear weapons issue in the narrow sense ("Test ban caravan," 1987). One of the difficult transitions for any two organizations that merge is to accommodate each other's traditional goals and activities. The NWFC was a doggedly determined, single-issue organization. The first efforts of the new SANE/Freeze organization probably appealed to the old NWFC membership.

However, SANE/Freeze also identified itself as a peace organization. Cortright and Cottom (1987), using a slightly mixed metaphor, wrote,

"We envisioned that the warp of an immense grassroots network and the woof of a strong national organization would create a fine peace and disarmament cloth—one that would be tight-woven and durable for the long haul" (p. 2). Under the rubric of "peace," SANE began to advocate a greater variety of issues.

SANE/Freeze's campaign to protest United States involvement in Central America was called a "Stand up for Peace in Central America" campaign ("SANE launches," 1987). Under this title, SANE began a series of actions designed to "activate U.S. citizens on behalf of peace in the region" (p. 7). Later, SANE/Freeze represented the peace movement to urge progress at the 1986 Geneva summit. On behalf of an "influential and unified U.S. peace movement," SANE/Freeze leaders met with Gorbachev prior to the summit (Cortright, 1986). Among the issues they raised with the Soviet leader were the nuclear test ban, initiatives to verify nuclear test ban compliance, concern about human rights for Soviet Jews, and Soviet positions regarding South Africa.

SANE also hosted a conference for its members entitled "Peaceworks," where a "multiracial, multiethnic, multioccupational crowd of attendees symbolized how broad the coalition for peace and disarmament has become" ("Peaceworks' lesson," 1986). According to SANE's communication director, "This is the realization of the New Left dream: a multiracial, multi-issue coalition—now grounded in political pragmatism" (p. 1).

As the Outbreak of Peace era continued into 1988, the number of issues that fell under the peace label grew while the number of disarmament issues shrank. Before the 1988 presidential election, SANE/Freeze reviewed the Reagan presidency and claimed, "Some of the greatest victories for peace and justice have been won during the nation's most conservative Cold War Presidency" ("Working for," 1988). Among these "peace" victories were, "The successful campaign to cap the MX program, the creation of a national holiday in honor of Dr. Martin Luther King, Jr., the imposition of economic sanctions (although limited) on the apartheid government of South Africa, and the defeat of the Bork nomination to the Supreme Court" (p. 1). In this interpretation of the decade, only one issue fell within the rubric of a narrowly defined disarmament issue. Calling itself a peace organization, then, allowed SANE/Freeze to address a greater variety of issues. It was this expansion in the number of issues that led to the next theme of this era.

Utilizing Multiple Issues   As the bottom fell out of the nuclear weapons issue, SANE/Freeze began to actively link its traditional issues, such as arms control and nuclear weapons, with new issues like the economy and the environment.

First, SANE/Freeze linked military issues with the economy. This tactic initially took the form of arguing that the United States should convert more of its economic resources to activities other than weapons production. For example, one activist in Iowa linked her city's economic problems with continued nuclear testing: "Every time our government explodes a nuclear weapon they blow up our entire city budget" (Shorr, 1987, p. 19). In his Senate testimony in support of the INF treaty, SANE/Freeze president William Sloane Coffin (1988) said, "In the world at large, it is increasingly apparent that geoeconomics is replacing geopolitics. We have only to look across the Pacific at 80 million Japanese who, since World War II, have not tested a bomb, bared a bayonet, nor landed paratroopers on some Third World island; yet they are the chief creditor nation of the world. We, on the other hand, with arsenals brimming, are now the chief debtor nation of the world" (p. 7). These themes were emphasized by other SANE/Freeze efforts. SANE organizer Ira Shorr (1988) wrote, "The peace movement of today recognizes the threads that connect the arms race to military intervention and economic justice" (p. 20). In 1988, SANE/Freeze linked the economy and its longtime efforts to ban nuclear weapons testing with the campaign called "Stop Testing, Start Investing in America" (Cottom, 1988). Taking note of some reforms in the Soviet Union's economy, *SANE World* writers wondered if there might be an "economic conversion race" that might be analogous to the arms race ("Seeds of," 1987).

The second issue SANE linked with peace was the environment. SANE's most sustained effort at linking the environment with peace began in 1986, when the organization began to address the problems of nuclear weapons production. The first major effort was a hearing entitled "Chernobyl: USA," which drew an analogy between the United States' weapons production plants and the ill-fated Soviet nuclear reactor. The speakers at the hearing claimed that "nuclear weapons production has been equivalent to a quiet Chernobyl, causing illness, death, and environmental destruction for 40 years" ("SANE convenes," 1986). Cortright and West (1986) claimed, "The nuclear weapons assembly line snakes its deadly way through the American landscape. Those who work on the assembly line—and those who have the misfortune of simply living near it—are at deadly risk" (p. 4). In the year following that hearing, federal investigators discovered problems at the Hanford plant in Washington state, the Savannah River plant in South Carolina, and the Fernald Plant in Ohio ("DOE confirms," 1987, p. 5).

The links between the economy and the environment were attempts to develop what have been called "multiple issues" (Tesh, 1984). Multiple issues are those that appear to fall under one label (e.g., peace), but are linked by their advocates to other political or moral ideologies. Thus, while SANE/Freeze advocates attached the "peace" or "disarmament" label to their advocacy efforts, they also added a variety of issues to the agenda by appealing to shared values.

It should be noted that SANE/Freeze did not attach itself to just any other issue. The environment and the economy seemed to meet two requirements. First, they were consonant with the organization's previous advocacy efforts. For example, SANE/Freeze had maintained throughout the early 1980s that there was a link between the nuclear weapons buildup and the economy. However, the activists focused their rhetoric on weapons, not the economy. Second, the environment and the economy were issues that were making their way to the top of the public's agenda by 1988.

One of SANE/Freeze's founders, Norman Cousins, endorsed the move to multiple issues. Cousins recalled that when SANE was founded in 1957 it had sought members from "various organizations, not just from the peace field, but from labor, civil liberties, and women's groups as well. SANE became a coalition of organizations with the express purpose of putting an end to nuclear testing" (West, 1987). This passage is significant because it helped legitimate SANE's efforts at developing multiple issues (Coombs; 1990, 1992). First, it notes how SANE had traditionally sought other groups with shared values to form coalitions around particular campaigns. This helped establish legitimacy through shared values. Second, it established a link between one of SANE's original issues, nuclear testing, and other issues, establishing legitimacy through tradition. If such a link had been made before, then it might be made again. Finally, the founder of SANE had legitimized these links with an endorsement.

Establishing the legitimacy of the multiple issues was important, since organizations run the risk of offending members when they tackle issues that do not seem consonant with members' goals. This was illustrated by member response to some of SANE's early initiatives against intervention in Central America. One member wrote, "I joined in order to help work for a sensible U.S. *nuclear* policy, as the name of the organization implies. . . . SANE is out of its element when it goes beyond nuclear concerns. Please inform me of the constitutional provision of SANE under which it enters policy disputes other than nuclear" (Allen, 1985). In her response, *SANE World*'s editor referred to SANE's tradition of working on multiple issues: "While SANE's main focus has, and will continue to be, nuclear disarmament, the organization has always worked on peace and military spending issues, as well" ("Editor's note," 1985). This exchange represents some of the perils that organizations face when they expand their agendas. However, if an organization's primary issue is falling from public view, moving onto other issues might be the only option for organizational survival.

New Worlds: 1989–1991

It is no understatement to say that this era was marked by a sea change in U.S.–Soviet relations and, consequently, public perception regarding the threat posed by nuclear weapons. As the Cold War ended, there was an accounting of its costs. This accounting revealed that the legacy of the Cold War included unsafe nuclear weapons production facilities. And, as the United States and the former Soviet Union turned their weapons from each other, they discovered that several other countries were eager to join the nuclear weapons club. The Gulf War heightened the world's awareness of arms proliferations.

But the nuclear weapons issue nearly dropped from the pages of *The New York Times, The Washington Post,* and *Time.* In *The New York Times,* the coverage dropped from 467 articles in 1989 to 365 in 1991. *The Washington Post* went from 386 to 281 between 1989 and 1991, while *Time*'s coverage slipped from 17 articles to 13.

During this period, SANE/Freeze utilized two major strategies: (1) merging the multiple issues, and (2) reshaping the coalition. These strategies not only helped SANE/Freeze consolidate the issues it had begun to address in the Outbreak of Peace era, but they attempted to reestablish SANE/Freeze as a legitimate activist organization.

Merging Multiple Issues The first strategy involved SANE/Freeze's attempt to merge the issues of peace, economics, and the environment. There were several ways the organization tried to do this.

First, SANE/Freeze once again redefined its purpose by adding the term "security" to its range of values (along with "peace" and "disarmament"). In 1989, the organization's official name was changed to SANE/Freeze: Campaign for Global Security (Schultz, 1989). SANE/Freeze officials made it clear that, in order to survive, multiple issues needed to be embraced. Coffin, for example, said, "Disarmament, a clean environment, a more just economy—these are the elements of a new pro-Earth vision that could reanimate the American peace and social justice movement" (Schultz, 1989, p. 9). Not only did Coffin's words link the issues of disarmament, the environment, and the economy, but he suggested that the movement—and, by implication, SANE/Freeze—needed to be "reanimated."

The second way that SANE/Freeze merged its issues was through the newsletters' editorial philosophy. While the stories still were about nuclear weapons–related issues, particularly production and testing, the emphasis was not on those issues, per se, but on their impact on the environment and the economy. For example, the lead paragraph on a story about nuclear weapons production facilities started with a direct reference to the environment: "With *Time*'s recent selection of 'the endangered planet Earth' for its year-end 'Man of the Year' issue, the popular newsmagazine underscored what the peace and environmental movements have warned for years—our planet is in peril" (Shaw, 1989, p. 5). Since the lead of any news story tells the reader what's important, it is apparent that SANE/Freeze wanted readers to view its traditional concern with nuclear weapons production (a "peace" issue) in the framework of the environmental issue.

SANE/Freeze News writers made similar, subtle links between weapons and the economy. For example, SANE/Freeze launched the "Peace Economy Campaign," which a lead paragraph touted as "a galvanizing force among peace, human service, labor and environmental groups for addressing unmet community needs" ("Peace economy campaign," 1989, p. 1). The linkage, where "peace" becomes an adverb for "economy," was an unobtrusive way of tying together two seemingly diverse issues. Once again, this sentence appeared near the beginning of the story, indicating that the economy was not just an afterthought to the "real" issues of disarmament, but was, in fact, central to SANE's advocacy.

As the decade ended, the merging of issues became even more pronounced. Feldman (1989) combined all three terms in the title of his article: "Global Security through Environmental Conversion." In an interesting combination of words, he merged the environment with (economic) conversion, all under the umbrella of global security, which was SANE/Freeze's new purpose. In the lead paragraph, Feldman argued for the links: "The environmental crisis, and growing public and media attention to its devastating impact, has created new opportunities for military budget reductions. A key obstacle to repairing past environmental damage has been the tremendous costs involved" (p. 7). Here Feldman recognized that the resurgence in the status of the environmental issue created opportunities for both economic reform and military issues advocates.

The merging of the triumvirate of security, economic, and environmental issues was further solidified at the 1990 SANE/Freeze national convention, when Coffin ("SANE/Freeze sets goals," 1990) said, "We also recognize that . . . disarmament, ecology and economic justice are inextricably linked, and that only by serving the first can sufficient funds be saved to serve the other two" (p. 1). He then announced that the organization's five-year programs "will focus on jobs and the environment" (p. 1).

The commitment to the environment and economic issues became such that it influenced SANE/Freeze's response to even the most obvious peace issues. The headline to the story that reported the organization's Gulf War protests said that SANE/Freeze was "Leading the Call for Peace in the Middle East and a Peace Economy at Home." Moreover, the lead paragraph not only spoke of the violence of the war, but also noted that "analysts called [the war] 'the most environmentally destructive conflict in the history of warfare'" ("Leading the call," 1991, p. 1). Thus, by merging its multiple issues, SANE/Freeze also shaped the way in which it responded to specific events that influenced those issues.

The merging of multiple issues during the New World era was subtle but significant. In the Outbreak of Peace era, SANE/Freeze used multiple issues to re-legitimize the nuclear weapons issue. The argument was that SANE/Freeze advocated nuclear weapons *and* the environment or nuclear weapons *and* the economy. In the New World era, the merging of multiple issues meant that SANE/Freeze could argue that peace *is* the environment *is* the economy *is* our security. Rather than separate links, the issues became one.

Reshaping the Coalition   SANE/Freeze still needs to gain legitimacy as an advocate on these issues. As with the nuclear weapons issue in the early 1980s, the economy and the environmental issues had attracted many advocacy groups to form their own "issue industries." In order for SANE/Freeze to gain legitimacy in these industries, especially since they did not enjoy a tradition with these issues, it united with other organizations to form coalitions.

SANE/Freeze joined environmental groups in a variety of actions. In 1990, for example, SANE/Freeze joined the Natural Resources Defense Council and 20 other organizations in a lawsuit against the Department of Energy, the agency that managed the United States' nuclear weapon production plants (Miller, 1990). "Thanks to the pressure mounted by SANE/Freeze and environmental and peace groups," SANE/Freeze convinced the Department of Energy to suspend plans for new nuclear weapons facilities ("SANE/Freeze contributes," 1989, p. 1). Also, in response to the environmental hazards that nuclear plants represented, SANE/Freeze was "working closely with environmental groups to keep weapons plants closed and clean up the environmental mess through its 'Keep Them Shut!' campaign headquartered at the Washington State SANE/Freeze chapter" ("How nuclear weapons," 1989, p. 6). It is interesting to note that, by operating the coalition from a SANE/Freeze location, the organization could once again claim that it was leading these like-minded groups—first among equals.

Ironically, SANE needed all the legitimacy it could get on the environmental issue after one embarrassing faux pas involving *SANE/Freeze News*. One of the issues was mailed wrapped in protective plastic shrink wrap. Environmentally sensitive members wrote letters to the editor. In fact, the "now-infamous plastic bag provoked a larger number of letters than any other issue in recent memory" ("Mailbag: 'Plastic . . . Ugh!'" 1989, p. 21). This perhaps serves as a warning to activist organizations and their newsletter editors to practice what they preach.

SANE/Freeze also joined economic issue coalitions. SANE/Freeze promoted its Peace Economy Campaign through a coalition called the Campaign for New Priorities, which was a "national coalition SANE helped found" (Shorr, 1991a). This particular effort involved nationally recognized groups that addressed both the economy and environmental issues: the "2 million member" National Education Association and the "6 million member" National Wildlife Foundation (Shorr, 1991a). Since SANE/Freeze's membership stood at approximately 150,000, the size of the other organizations in the coalition lent some legitimacy to the scope of the peace economy coalition. Once again,

SANE/Freeze was not just a part of the coalition advocating new budget priorities; it was "at the center of [this] national effort" (Shorr, 1991b). So, even as SANE/Freeze legitimated its forays into new issues by joining coalitions, it also tried to distinguish itself from the crowd by claiming leadership.

CONCLUSIONS: IMPLICATIONS OF SANE/FREEZE'S RHETORICAL DIVERSIFICATION

Between 1981 and 1991, the nuclear weapons issue went through several transformations to which SANE/Freeze responded. Although it is difficult to judge unequivocally how successful SANE/Freeze's efforts were, there were some indications of the organization's health. Financially, SANE/Freeze's budget dropped from $2.5 million to $1.6 million between 1990 and 1991 (Foundation for Public Affairs, 1992). Since just over half of the organization's income came from membership dues, this might be an indication that the organization was not particularly effective in its efforts to retain members. However, it seemed as if membership had stabilized by 1992 to around 150,000— nearly six times larger than the organization was in 1981.

This study illustrates a strategy I call *rhetorical diversification*. In economics and management, organizations expand into other industries or markets in order to broaden the range of resources coming into the system. If one enterprise is not doing well, the corporation diverts resources away from that operation. If things get really bad, the operation is suspended or sold. Rhetorical diversification occurs when an organization expands what it defines as its primary issue and begins to talk about other ones. The economic metaphor has been utilized by McCarthy and Zald (1977) to suggest that social movement organizations pursue "issue niches" with a larger social movement industry. By utilizing multiple issues, linked through common values, an organization can build issue niches that might help it survive downturns in the issue economy. As an example of what happens when an organization does not diversify, we need look no further than the Nuclear Weapons Freeze Campaign. This single-issue group merged with SANE in order to survive. SANE/Freeze had diversified to the point that even outsiders recognized its multi-issue nature. The editors of a children's book designed to raise money for several activist organizations described SANE/Freeze as "one of the nation's largest grassroots peace and justice organizations [whose programs] develop the inextricable link between peace, the environment, and economic justice for all" (Durell and Sachs, 1990).

Ultimately, the struggle for activist groups that protest against prevailing policies is to identify what it is they stand for. For an issue as broad as peace, the diversity of meanings available provide a rich rhetorical resource, which even SANE/Freeze might not have tapped fully. As William Sloane Coffin noted, "Peace has many meanings. It means bread to the hungry, a roof to the homeless, and to the unemployed, the knowledge that they will be able to provide for their children. King was right: 'Peace is not the absence of conflict but the presence of justice'" (1989, p. 22).

NOTE

The author wishes to thank the staff of the Swarthmore College Peace Collection for assistance in assembling the SANE/Freeze newsletters.

12

Issue Management During Corporate Mergers

A Case Study of AT&T and NCR

Kelly Fudge

According to *Business Week*, the AT&T/NCR merger registered at the top of all major business transactions in 1991 (Woolley, 1992). Indeed, merger activity on the whole has been on the rise as companies strive to position themselves in a global marketplace. Mergers have historically been treated by managers and researchers as solely a financial activity. Yet mergers involve people in organizations and not the organizations in any abstract sense. Because of this focus on financial matters, the human issues associated with mergers have been largely ignored. But a change in an organization means changing the people who create the organizational culture. Mergers are as much a communication process as a financial or management activity. They are emotional events that create an expectancy for change and stimulate organization cohesiveness, yet the acquiring management's overconfidence about the ease of integration and the speed of change can result in unplanned personnel changes and stressful events. Also, their degree of uncertainty and speed and scale of change distinguish them from any other organizational events (Cartwright and Cooper, 1992). How organizations manage issues and deal with crises are communication processes that determine the success of the venture. These communication processes begin long before the merger itself; they start with the takeover announcement and set the stage for communications to come. By analyzing the communication strategies and discourse during a major merger, such as AT&T and NCR, managers and communication researchers may more effectively develop contingency plans for mergers and acquisitions.

ISSUE MANAGEMENT AND MERGERS

Issue management concerns itself with the need to adjust organizations to public policy and the need to have public policy realistically reflect the requirements of organizations (Heath and Nelson, 1986). Public policy is any critical issue that may become involved in governmental regulation. In order to employ much of the issue management literature, mergers must be defined as a public policy. With the precedents of the antitrust acts and FCC regulations, this definition is easily imposed, yet the exact policies themselves are changing at a rapid rate. Therefore, organizations must engage in foresight, policy development, and advocacy to achieve this mutual adjustment with public policy. Foresight includes identifying, monitoring, analyzing, and prioritizing issues. Policy development requires the resolution of internal interests on public issues for a cohesive external advocacy, while advocacy incorporates all the communication efforts to reach targeted audiences and eventually accomplish the campaign goal.

These activities are further integrated into a four-stage interactive issue management model (Jones and Chase, 1979; Chase, 1984). The first stage, issue identification, includes understanding the public policy process, monitoring environmental changes, identifying specific objectives linked to corporate goals, and determining salience. Stage two, issue analysis, determines the origin of the issue, attempts to isolate influences, and locates media gatekeepers, opinion leaders, and any other friendly/unfriendly constituents. The issue change strategy stage is a decision-making stage in which the organization commits to an issue. In making this decision, risks are considered, as well as timing and direction of the change. Companies often select a style of change (reactive, adaptive, or proactive) in this stage. The final stage produces an issue action program. The communication campaigns developed lay the foundation for determining targeted publics, designing messages, selecting channels, and setting up controls (Heath and Nelson, 1986).

These issue management activities revolve around public opinion, but the communication specialist must be aware that no single dominant public opinion exists. Each of the corporation's publics possesses independent opinions and demands unique communication strategies. These key publics—employees, shareholders, customers, suppliers, and the community—need sufficient information about the corporation in order to understand corporate needs. Yet the disseminated information must be needed and desired by the public receiving it (Heath and Nelson, 1986). Short-term public scanning should be sensitive to what groups believe, how strong their beliefs are, and how willing they are to act on these beliefs. The types of topics discussed in issue campaigns do not lend themselves to the simplistic messages contained in most marketing campaigns; rather, they require longer, more complicated campaigns to gain attention and to create an impact. Still, issue managers engage in persuasive events, aiming to change public opinions. In most issue management situations, public opinion is unpredictable and the issues are intangible. So converting the unbeliever may be quite a difficult task and requires a clear understanding of communication goals, as well as the proactive development of contingency plans (Heath and Nelson, 1986).

Advocacy Advertising and Issue Management

Obtaining and disseminating accurate information in a timely fashion is one of the key responsibilities of issue management. An issue management strategy for information dissemination that has become increasingly popular in the last few years is advocacy advertising. According to the 1981 Association of National Advertisers' survey, advocacy advertising campaigns seek to satisfy one of three purposes (Heath and Nelson, 1986):

1. to inform or educate target publics on subjects important to a company's future;
2. to advocate specific actions on matter affecting the company, its industry, and business in general; and
3. to communicate corporate concerns and achievements on social and environmental issues.

When engaging in advocacy advertising, companies must be careful to associate the identity of the company with the issues position, to maintain consistent dialogue with the public, to respect the reader's intelligence, to interest readers by relating to their self-interests, and to test the effectiveness of the campaign (O'Toole, 1975). In preparing the communication campaign or issue action program, specific goals should be set that are sensitive to the needs of the public and the corporation. Then stakeholders—those people with a vested interest in the success of the company—must be identified and examined for their beliefs, the salience of their beliefs to issue management, and their interest in the issue (Heath and Nelson, 1986).

In addition to the targeted audiences for a campaign mentioned previously, media leaders substantially influence the issue agenda because they decide the content of the news. Not only do these people interject their own opinions, they are also affected by the values or policies of the organization for which they work (Littlejohn, 1983). Therefore, issue managers should be aware of the media's agenda-setting function and its impression on their communication campaign (see McCombs, 1977, for agenda-setting information). For instance, agenda-setting effects are more pronounced at the beginning of the issue cycle, while the effects are less pronounced as the issue matures. An issue tends to stay on the media agenda, however, as long as new information is released. Issue managers may provide information to the media in a timely manner to maintain the issue agenda and to help the media (and public) understand the corporation's view (Heath and Nelson, 1986).

In designing messages, rhetorical statements are often phrased as propositions of fact, value, or policy (Heath and Nelson, 1986). Fact propositions are characterized by objectivity and verifiability. Value propositions involve claims of right and wrong, and policy statements support corporate interests to provide the best products and services in harmony with public interest. Value statements establish common ground and increase identification, but policy statements that combine public self-interest with company interest are the most persuasive. Such policy statements or messages often reveal how the company values productivity, profitability, and progress. In general, messages should focus on how a company's products and activities link to current socioeconomic questions and to the company's effect on the individual. A message focused on economics rather than emotion tends to have a stronger impact (Bateman, 1975). By taking the facts, values, and policy approach, a campaign assessment may be conducted by estimating shifts in level of knowledge, relevant values, and behaviors. Furthermore, a media analysis may determine what messages are being transmitted and how the public responds to them.

The selection of specific communication channels should rely on three factors: the targeted audience, private editorial standards, and the extent to which regulation permits access. Typical channels include paid advertising, sponsored articles, editorials, CEO comments, sponsored public affairs programming, press releases, personal contact by key staff and management, newsletters, employee communication, and speeches (Heath and Nelson, 1986). Issue communication seeks to influence the direction of information reported in typical news stories. Because these issues require lengthy discussions, print media are suitable for advocacy messages. Newspapers allow for short-term response time, whereas magazines are good for demographic appeal. Also, editorial and financial sections are hospitable locations for issue discussions. Television usually has short-term agenda-setting effects, while newspapers' effects are longer lasting but slower rising (Littlejohn, 1983). Depending upon the goals of the campaign, these channel attributes may be insignificant. However, since news is a selective presentation of reality, issue managers should not expect equal coverage or balanced treatment of an issue. Most news is not new, but cyclical updates, so issue managers must carefully release and position advocacy messages (Heath and Nelson, 1986).

Crisis Communication and Mergers

When a crisis strikes, communication takes on new saliency in the corporation. Crisis response strategies must be designed to provide accurate information as quickly as possible to important publics. Employees, customers, and shareholders become apprehensive during turbulent times and desire a climate of trust with management. Audiences are particularly attentive during these times of crisis, and crisis offers special opportunities for communication with publics (Heath and Nelson, 1986). If communication strategies are in place, the issue manager's job becomes routine and possibilities for success increase dramatically. However, when communication strategies do not exist or are not adaptive, the issue manager resides in an ambiguous and precarious situation. Crisis communication strategies have been the topic of much research, and the type of crises frequently analyzed are product failures, safety problems, environmental concerns, and industrial accidents (see Center and Jackson, 1990). However, research on communicating during corporate takeovers is lacking. Given that there were 2,346 mergers between companies in the United States, totaling more than $60 billion, in 1982 and that in 1988 the number increased to 2,805 mergers involving foreign and domestic firms for an exchange of $346 billion (*Journal of Business Strategy,* 1989), this lack of research attention is surprising and somewhat disturbing for those interested in public relations.

Whether the organization is acquiring, defending, or engaging in a mutual merger, communication with key publics penetrates phases of a takeover—from initial announcement to the merging of corporate cultures. These corporate takeovers involve a great deal of risk on the part of both participants. The takeover victim loses its independence, resulting in employees losing their jobs, the community losing an economic source, and customers losing a supplier. The acquiring company may risk financial debt, loss of employees, loss of corporate image, and disruption of business operations during the transition. Communication during the takeover may function to sway public opinion one way or the other, to ease the transition process and the apprehension of all involved, to create a common corporate culture, to merge business strategies or missions, or to persuade shareholders to retain the independence of the company. By examining specific organization strategies, communication managers may better develop contingency plans for these corporate crises, and the existence of a well-developed contingency plan may just determine for whom the communication manager works.

Communicating to Internal Publics   Although mergers and acquisitions may increase competitiveness of an organization, "down-in-the-trenches" restructuring often reduces morale, productivity, and employee commitment (Lew, 1988). While the accountants bury themselves in the figures, the communication professionals must handle the tough human issues. Lew offers several tips for dealing with corporate turmoil:

1. Get involved early. A long-term problem demands long-term attention and sales.
2. Be prepared to juggle critical trade-offs. Shareholder interests must be balanced against employee interests.
3. Develop a human layoff strategy.
4. During tough times, top management should be more visible.
5. Be positive. Management should explain how all of this trouble will pay off.

6. Increase face-to-face communication between supervisors and staff. The listening component of programs should be increased through focus groups and surveys.
7. Set an agenda. Tell the public when phases will be completed.

Especially in times of change, employees must feel as if they have an impact and control of their futures.

Communicating to External Publics   Equally crucial, external communication must address shareholders, customers, the community, public officials, and the media. When dealing with the media, the organization should develop a fact sheet, including terms of agreement, number of shares involved, cost of the deal, management structure of both organizations, investment bankers involved, key historical facts, and assets of both institutions (Lew, 1988). Although the general attitude towards communication has been "don't tell anyone anything," communication is necessary for a company under attack. People need to know what is going on, why, and what it will mean to them.

For an organization under attack, communicating effectively to shareholders can determine its livelihood. Managing an organization for profitability and growth while satisfying the short-term goals of investors is a great dilemma for corporate managers. The maximization of shareholder value is a tactic frequently used by takeover proponents and is considered the first (and only) priority by many investors. Today, companies must learn as much about their shareholders and about the stock market as possible. Programs that contain profiles of each shareholder and detailed information on company stock activity allow companies to respond to rumors promptly and effectively. Also, these companies are less vulnerable to surprise takeovers if they are on top of the market and aware of lags in potential sale price. In the past, corporations fighting takeovers turned to technical tactics, such as charter amendments, fair-price formulas, and shareholder rights plans, but these tactics resulted in poor shareholder perceptions of the corporation (Wilcox et al., 1989). A good-guy, bad-guy view is readily accepted by the media, politicians, academics, the public, and shareholders.

Corporations who know their shareholders and understand the market may benefit from employing the proxy contest along with strong communication. For instance, the 1989 Honeywell proxy contest is notable for several reasons (Wilcox, 1989). First, it was the first time that private investors and public pension funds formed a group to solicit proxies. Second, the results were extraordinary, with shareholders demonstrating negative control over corporate decision making in five business days. Finally, the Honeywell case emphasized the importance of communicating to shareholder interest, concerns, and power.

Besides a proxy contest, organizations defend themselves through other defensive tactics. In the fall of 1988, Kroger fended off not one suitor but two—the Haft family and Kohlberg Kravis Roberts & Company. Today, Kroger remains a public company after undertaking a massive $5.5 billion corporate restructuring (Bernish, 1989). From the onset, Kroger's refusal to be for sale and discouragement of bidding were dismissed by analysts. Analysts speculated about which parts Kroger would have to sell to pay off their large debt. Other analysts commented on their weak stock performance over the past several years or on their conservative, overly bureaucratic management style. However, as it became clear that Kroger would not be taken over, public opinion shifted, and people viewed Kroger as an aggressive retailer with many advantages.

For two months during the takeover fight, Kroger developed and maintained an extensive communication program that consisted of letters to employees and shareholders explaining the restructuring plan, a press conference for the media (videotaped for internal distribution), and a presentation for financial analysts (Bernish, 1989). Kroger found that the best response under conditions of uncertainty was no response, contrary to what Lew advises above. Although cautious in approaching the media, they did not ignore the media completely. Kroger CEO Lyle Everingham indicated the importance of the press in his observation, "corporate takeover struggles are ultimately fought over money . . . but the battleground is the pages of your newspapers" (Bernish, p. 27). The battles are fought in the press because it is a legally safe way of learning the opponent's intentions without direct contact. Kroger reminded the media and other participants that their restructuring plan was an extension of strategies in place for years. However, most of the coverage indicated that Kroger was restructuring due to external pressures and that the plan would eventually be called off for the highest bidder.

As a result of this speculation, a new group arose—arbitragers. These high-rolling gamblers determine the ultimate value of the takeovers, leveraged buyouts, and restructurings by inputing capital to drive up the stock price, which in turn creates more interest and additional investment. Arbitragers have a strong need for information and seem to know more about what is happening than the companies themselves. Thus, they are often anonymous sources for news stories, although their objectivity is questionable. Everingham gives several suggestions for journalists and companies under attack (Bernish, 1989):

1. Business journalists ought to take a second look at their sources.
2. Business coverage of takeovers ought to include the long-term perspective as well as the headline-grabbing spots.
3. Corporations involved in takeovers need to do a better job communicating to their employees and other constituents.
4. Corporate spokespeople ought to have more leeway to provide background information and perspective.

Yet another defensive merger tactic is demonstrated by the Sterling Drug, Inc., case. In 1988, Sterling Drug, Inc., received a hostile bid from a Swiss firm, F. Hoffman-La Roche & Co. After weighing its options, Sterling chose to seek a "white knight." Sterling sought out Eastman Kodak, who agreed to buy them for $5.1 billion, making Kodak a major player in the pharmaceutical business. An interview with former Sterling CEO John Pietruski in the *Journal of Business Strategy* (1989) describes how his contingency plan helped rescue his company from a hostile acquirer.

After consulting investment bankers and lawyers, the board met to develop a communication plan. Sterling decided that communication with employees was critical, so every morning memos, written by Pietruski, were sent to employees, detailing the company actions on the previous day. If there were no actions, the memos attempted to ease employee concern, assure them that management was looking at all alternatives, and reinforce commitment to employees' interests as management carried out their fiduciary responsibility to the shareholders. These memos enabled morale to remain at a high level throughout the takeover. Also, as part of the defensive maneuvers, Sterling filed several court challenges against Roche. Roche's response was to raise the bid. Faced with being unable to develop a realistic alternative to Roche's generous offer, Sterling was forced to look for a white knight. Since Kodak had been previously identified as a viable possibility in the contingency plan, Sterling contacted them. This was a strategic transaction, versus a synergistic one, for Kodak, since they were not established in the pharmaceutical business. Strategic transactions are long term and not driven by short-term financial and cost reductions;

therefore, more people benefit in this type of transaction (*Journal of Business Strategy,* 1989).

Unfortunately, success stories of communication efforts can often only be called such after the fire is extinguished and the smoldering rubble cleared. Can communication during a takeover make or break a company? Is the press a battleground for hostile opponents? These two questions were posed for an in-depth study of corporate takeovers and, in particular, for an analysis of a recent hostile takeover by AT&T. The concepts of issue management, advocacy advertising, and crisis communication provide a solid foundation for this analysis.

METHOD

If Everingham is correct that the press is a battleground for corporate takeovers, then print media are appropriate for analysis of communication during mergers. Also, mergers are complicated issues that require lengthy discussion, attributes the print media can accommodate. Furthermore, companies often distribute press releases to various media in order to summarize their actions, to serve as sources for news stories, and to influence the reporting of favorable information. Therefore, public communication media were employed in this study to examine the merger activity between NCR and AT&T. Newspaper articles were collected from a daily national newspaper, *The Wall Street Journal,* and a daily local newspaper, *The Dayton Daily News,* and magazine articles were collected from *Computerworld* and *The Economist.* These sources allowed for the observation of several angles: national, local, trade, and financial. All articles printed in these sources between December 1990 and March 1991 were included in the sample. Articles that contained information about the merger, about either company's internal or external communication efforts, or about opinions of external persons (e.g., community members or financial analysts) were selected for analysis. Articles that contained redundant information were eliminated. Advertisements in the aforementioned sources were also included in the sample if they dealt with the merger, rather than new products or financial information.

The articles were analyzed using a time series strategy, comparing the series of events to the advocacy advertising model, issue management plan, and previously cited strategies. The articles were unitized by sentence and then analyzed for themes or statements that revealed a particular rhetorical strategy or stage of the issue management model.

An instrument was developed to include the Jones and Chase issue management stages of issue identification, issue analysis, issue change, and issue action. Strategies from the advocacy advertising campaign model were coded (e.g., associate the identity of the company with the issue position, maintain consistent dialogue with public, interest readers by relating to their self-interests, and respect the reader's intelligence). Finally, the suggestions of Lew (1988) and Wilcox (1989) on crisis communication to internal and external publics were taken into consideration and noted for absence or presence. The goal of the analysis was to assess the contingency plans of AT&T and NCR as communicated in print media.

RESULTS AND DISCUSSION: THE AT&T/NCR MERGER

Both AT&T and NCR adhered to certain stages of the Jones and Chase interactive model of issue management. On November 8, 1990, *The Wall Street Journal* published false rumors of merger negotiation talks between NCR CEO Chuck Exley and AT&T CEO Bob Allen. Although in error, this article initiated action by AT&T. Less than one month later, on December 3, AT&T, the largest telecommunications company in the United States, went public with its intention to acquire NCR, the U.S.'s fifth largest computer company. Although the "takeover" issue for NCR may have been identified when AT&T's offer went to press, the real issue to be managed emerged in the text of letters by Exley and Allen that were published with the initial announcement.

As an indication of the Jones and Chase issue identification stage, Exley framed the issue for management: "No ultimatum or demand will intimidate the board of directors of NCR into doing disservice to the company, its customers, shareholders, and employees" ("AT&T goes," 1990). Repeatedly, Exley referred to "the *best interests of the shareholders* and other stakeholders of NCR," the *unfairness* of the proposal to NCR's shareholders, the *commitment* of the board to protect NCR and its shareholders and other stockholders, and the board's responsibility to build value for its shareholders ("Exley," 1990). Also, the references to the "unsolicited proposal" and a "disruptive takeover battle" indicated how NCR management framed the merger and their role within it. For NCR, the issues of commitment to stakeholders, financial responsibility to shareholders, and warranted defensive acquisition tactics were identified underneath the umbrella of a "takeover," rather than a friendly merger.

On the other hand, Allen identified issues for the publics of his company in his December 2 reply letter; he emphasized AT&T's "dedication to the completion of this transaction" (Allen, 1990). He also focused on the extraordinary opportunity for NCR stockholders and AT&T's desire for NCR autonomy under their reign, which permit "uninterrupted relationships with NCR employees, customers, and suppliers." Most convincingly, Allen asserted what would continue to be his rhetorical claim for the rest of the courtship: "Combining NCR and AT&T will create a strong American company with technological, financial, and marketing strength to compete successfully in the global information market." Because Exley emphasized NCR stakeholders, Allen addressed many stakeholders' concerns in his reply. As a result, the stakeholders (or "public opinion") materialized as the primary focus of the issue campaign, followed closely by economic matters.

The issue analysis stage of their contingency plans was detected in the identification of friendly and unfriendly constituencies or pressure groups and the origins of the merger issue. Exley attributed AT&T's takeover interests to AT&T's failing computer business, which had lost almost $2 billion since 1984 ("Execs rebuff," 1990). Exley stated, "The proposal made to us is a kind of reverse acquisition, with NCR the surviving computer operation. . . . We simply will not place in jeopardy the important values we are creating at NCR in order to bail out AT&T's failed strategy" ("AT&T launches," 1990). Exley also pointed out that the history of mergers in the computer industry is full of disasters. AT&T, however, purported a more ambiguous and macroscopic origin. Increased competition around the globe and a need to "remain in the computer business because its customers in the 1990s will need to link people, organizations, and their information in a seamless . . . global computer network that is easy to use as the current telephone system" were the dominant motives communicated ("AT&T bets," 1990). Analysts speculated that AT&T was frustrated with "taking it on the chin" in its computer business and that the situation was debilitating for employee morale.

Additionally, each organization named pressure groups and constituents. For NCR, the stakeholders were of primary concern—employees, customers, suppliers, community members, and shareholders. NCR also sought support from local government officials, such as Tony Capizzi, city commissioner, and Tony Hall, the district's representative to the House of Representatives. Local media, *The Dayton Daily News* and various television stations were relied upon as the company's communication horns that would publish favorable NCR news stories and unfavorable AT&T information. Even the Communications Workers of America supported NCR, although AT&T employed 110,000 workers; however, AT&T had also cut an additional 100,000 workers since 1984 ("AT&T readies," 1990). Finally, the industry analysts emerged as a potential pressure group, since they are often opinion leaders for some investors and sources for news stories. AT&T selected the Chemical Bank of New York as the broker and Morgan Stanley and Company as the manager of the acquisition. Other important groups for AT&T included NCR shareholders, Maryland and Ohio court systems, industry analysts, the Dayton community, NCR employees, AT&T employees, the union, and the media.

During the issue change strategy stage, communication strategies for pressure groups were prioritized and the organizational approach set. NCR saw the need to communicate immediately to shareholders and employees, followed by the customers and the community. After the surprise attack, NCR attempted to adopt a proactive stance through internal and external communications, the filing of court cases and other defensive tactics, and the setting of a "fair value" price. AT&T lunged for the NCR stockholders, since they anticipated a proxy contest and wanted to use the contest to company advantage. Furthermore, the company addressed the Dayton community, NCR employees, and NCR customers in a national press release. Although proactive in staging the initial attack and disseminating the national press release, AT&T fell into a reactive or adaptive stance in later communication events, while NCR remained proactive. These stances will be elaborated in the breakdown of internal and external communication by both companies.

In the final but most important stage, the issue action program, communication strategies and campaigns were developed and implemented by the companies. These campaigns were similar to political campaigns in four ways. First, there was a well-defined offer after a bid (20 days) and a set time limit before the proxy meeting. Second, audiences had cyclical interests in the issue. Interest among groups increased and decreased over time, with the most attention paid to initial and final periods of the merger. Also, those with vested interest were more receptive to messages, but could also filter a larger majority of these messages. Third, considerable uncertainty affected campaign planning. Court cases and defensive tactics may have failed, and shareholders may have called a proxy meeting to achieve the short-term profits. Fourth, success in the takeover campaign was decisive in its outcome. There were clear winners and losers (Rice and Atkin, 1989).

In planning the issue action program, NCR and AT&T attempted to use these characteristics to their advantage. Because of the set time limit, AT&T probably felt comfortable with their reactive communication stance; they laid out the deal and now could sit back and wait for the proxy meeting. NCR, on the other hand, engaged in a frenzied communication effort, addressing many publics through targeted messages and various channels. They adopted a shotgun approach: aim many messages in one direction and hope one of them hits the bullseye. While NCR's approach worked well with the cyclical interests of the publics, AT&T's approach did not on its own. Yet, since NCR was keeping the issue on the public agenda, AT&T could afford to be reactive. From an analysis of the newspaper articles and messages reported in the articles, the following communication strategies for the publics emerged.

Communication to Internal Publics by NCR

Although discussion of communication to employees was sparse in the publications, readers could determine to some extent the level and amount of communication engaged in by NCR management. In a letter to employees on the day of the surprise attack, Exley warned, "We may face a lengthy takeover battle" ("AT&T launches," 1990). Exley recognized the importance of communicating to employees immediately with nondeceptive information. He did not try to minimize the threat or the challenge that lay ahead. By threatening to resign if AT&T succeeded and by insisting that he would not leave NCR hobbled in debt, Exley managed the image of commitment to the company, which may have alleviated some employee apprehension about corporate instability and change. Initial employee reaction to the AT&T proposal was various. While some were apprehensive and some indignant, other employees welcomed the change. One NCR systems analyst said, "I think it may be a good idea . . . for one AT&T doesn't have a computer division." Another systems analyst praised the idea. He saw the merger as producing a company with the clout to compete with IBM ("Reaction to takeover," 1990).

Much later in the battle, *The Dayton Daily News* reported unconfirmed rumors that Exley had scheduled time on a communication satellite to report to employees ("NCR may report," 1991). Employees would be notified of the time through an in-house newsletter. Also, the article reported that the Financial News Network had broadcasted NCR's plans to introduce a new employee stock ownership program (ESOP). Indeed, NCR did announce a $500 million employee stock program only to have it later defeated in a court case. NCR claimed to adopt the plan to "draw employees' and shareholders' interests together" ("NCR gives stock," 1991). It was a strong, proactive move towards company employees.

Whether it was initiated secretly by NCR or by members of the community, the strongest communication effort was the "Salute to the People of NCR" day, which brought 8,000 supporters to a local arena for a rally. Many attendees were dressed in corporate colors and wore buttons saying "Thank you NCR." Banners draped the balconies, and members of the Communications Workers of America Local 4322 wore t-shirts that said, "Hey AT&T—Reach Out and Touch Someone Else!" Employee sentiment filled the paper: "It's great to see acknowledged the relationship NCR and the community has had for a very long time," and "This is local stuff here. . . . Ya gotta buy the local stuff " ("8,000 rally," 1991). NCR's history and accomplishments also comprised an entire section of this special edition. NCR was rallying support from stockholders, politicians, and fellow business members through this event. This defensive tactic presented NCR as a long-standing community member that cares about its people and their morale and, moreover, reminded people that AT&T was not interested in protecting people. An added persuasive touch was the numerous "thank you" NCR advertisements from local businesses.

Employees were kept abreast of the situation over satellite when certain *Dayton Daily News* employees mistakenly printed and distributed signs that said, "Board recommends to shareholders SALE OF NCR TO AT&T" ("It was no big deal," 1991). In later articles after the defeat of the ESOP, an NCR spokesperson noted that "AT&T has a stock ownership plan for its employees. . . . Many NCR employees will wonder why AT&T would deny NCR employees a program that AT&T has provided to their own employees" ("AT&T asks court," 1991). Through these types of statements, NCR management attempted to create the "good-guy, bad-guy" scenario for the proposed merger. Still, many employees who were stockholders were looking at the AT&T merger with something other than loathing; they were watching their investments increase. "There are people walking around with calculators. . . . The talk I hear is 'how much are you going to make,'" one employee remarked. "This is money from heaven" ("AT&T bid smacks," 1991). Some employees consulted financial advisers and were torn between loyalty and financial gains. Exley perceived the majority of employees as being job focused. Some employees reported being excited about the merger of vast resources, others worried about AT&T selling off parts of NCR, and a few were indifferent to the event.

The final communication analyzed was an advertisement from NCR board of directors thanking all NCR stakeholders for their support over the previous four months. Employees were thanked for their "concentration, dedication, and commitment to excellence in products and services," allowing NCR to continue moving towards their "full potential as a global leader in enterprise-wide information systems and services" ("Thousands of thank yous," 1991).

NCR management set the goal of keeping a constant dialogue with their employees, and the analysis of print news demonstrated that they accomplished their goal. While its communication began as guarded and admonishing, the management maintained the image of commitment and attempted to increase employee morale and loyalty through positive feedback. Although in-house communications were not included in this analysis, the external channels of communication relayed employee opinion and many of the communication strategies employed. NCR wanted its publics to view them as concerned corporate citizens.

Communication to Internal Publics by AT&T

Little was reported in external publications regarding the communication strategies that AT&T undertook with the employees of its computer operation or concerning the opinions of this public. *The Wall Street Journal* reported late into the battle that AT&T was offering bonuses to workers remaining with the unit for up to six months following the merger. Many employees had begun to look for other jobs, and, although AT&T was offering incentives, the telecommunications giant was not guaranteeing jobs after the merger. In November, Robert Kavener, AT&T's data systems chief, was instructed to seek a merger with NCR or the unit would be cut loose ("AT&T offering incentives," 1991). AT&T's computer business and employees were to be subsumed by NCR if the merger was successful. This communication plan for AT&T employees from an organizational communication perspective was not textbook perfect. Instead, it reinforced the typical image of the "cold corporation" that has little regard for morale, corporate responsibility, and commitment to employees. AT&T appeared to consider maximizing the bottom line of utmost priority and supporting their employees of the leastmost. For NCR employees, the image should have been frightening. Perhaps the lack of AT&T employee opinion coverage in the news was a strategic move by AT&T. If the opinions were unfavorable, the discussion of these in national media may have damaged their position. Also, one could assume that AT&T engaged in few communication strategies with their employees since there was so little news about them.

Communication to External Publics by NCR

Since the primary and most progressive communication channel with external publics was advocacy advertising, this analysis focuses on that strategy more than on the public opinion exercised in the news. The most significant influence (and toughest public to persuade) in this battle was the shareholder; therefore, this group commanded the most concentrated communication efforts. Exley set the ultimate goal concerning shareholders in his first letter to Allen, when he vowed to work in the best interest of the shareholders. Just as he was able to identify that a primary concern of employees was job security, Exley effectively targeted the motives of many shareholders—short-term gain and profit. At this point, he was able to develop an advocacy advertising campaign aimed at persuading shareholders to hold onto their stock and have faith in the long-term progress of NCR.

The design of the messages clearly followed the advocacy advertising model presented in Heath and Nelson (1986). The company was associated with the ad through the use of large corporate logos. Public self-interest was addressed through fact, value, and policy statements. For instance, in one of the first such ads, Exley economically supported his objection to AT&T's $90 per share offer: "This $90 offer is only a 29% premium over the 1990 high of $72.25, the stock's highest price in 1990, prior to December. In addition, the $6 billion offer is $2 billion less than the company's total market capitalization just two years ago" ("An interview," 1991). The NCR CEO included value statements about the offer. NCR shareholders should receive the value they are helping to create; the "short termism bred by hostile takeovers like this one is a grotesque mutation of pure capitalism," he claimed. He strengthened these value statements by reiterating the NCR mission to build the company while building value for investors. Policy statements were combined with value statements for a rhetorically savvy message. "There is simply no value to our shareholders to tender into this offer. . . . AT&T will simply use these shares to help them achieve their real objective, buying NCR as cheaply as possible," he said. The advertisement emphasized three themes—productivity, profitability, and progress of the company—while stressing economics.

As the proxy date neared, the messages became more pointed and certain. A March 1 advertisement commented, "You are entitled to the full value of your NCR investment—value which we believe far exceeds AT&T's $90 offer" ("An important message," 1991). The rest of the ad informed shareholders of NCR intentions to outperform the AT&T offer, of their record of solid financial performance, of the true value of NCR stock, and of the outlook for that year and the next. Text addressed all three types of statements (fact, value, policy) and themes (productivity, profitability, progress) in the previous ad, but differed by repeating a desired action—the immediate return of the blue proxy cards.

Another advocacy advertising tactic involved attaching a "note" to what appeared to be a normal product advertisement. The note stated that products like the one advertised were one reason the company was confident it could deliver long-term value for investors and urged shareholders to defeat AT&T's effort to acquire NCR ("Free your organization," 1991). In a March 20 advertisement, NCR employed AT&T's own slogans. The headline stated, "You have an important choice to make about your NCR investment" ("You have," 1991). Again, the ad attempted to drive home the commitment of NCR to shareholders, the revolutionary products, the strong financial performance, the future of the company, and the gross inadequacy of AT&T's offer. What was the final appeal? Sign, date, and return the blue proxy cards.

The final advocacy advertisement was completely different in message content, as it was published after the proxy meeting of March 28. This ad began with "thousands of thank-yous" and went on to address all of the NCR stakeholders by group. Once again, the commitment to deliver full value through products was stated, but this time the board added "or through a transaction that delivers full value to NCR stakeholders" ("Thousands of thank yous," 1991).

So, through the end of its campaign, NCR promised productivity, profitability, progress, and commitment to shareholder interest. Statements were related to shareholder beliefs in terms of facts, values, and policies, producing a theoretically effective rhetorical instrument. Beyond advocacy advertising, NCR communicated with shareholders through letters, television, and news stories. Other external publics that received attention included customers, suppliers, analysts, and the Dayton community. Customers were assured continued service over the past four months through CEO comments on commitment to business operations and were addressed in the "thank-you" advertisement. AT&T industry analysts were addressed by Exley in a speech ("NCR to call meeting," 1991). Reports said that he was met "with a polite response" and many questions. Earlier in the battle, Exley had met with money managers who owned 1.9 million shares collectively to gain support ("NCR rebuffs AT&T," 1990). Although their fiduciary responsibility was with their clients, these managers acknowledged NCR as being sincere in its commitment. Lastly, communication with the community was facilitated through active use of the local media, the NCR appreciation day, and local government officials. The community was noted in the "thank-you" advertisement for its "outpourings of loyalty and affection" ("Thousands of thank yous," 1991). Out of all the communication strategies, the community plan may have been the most effective. With 8,000 people attending a rally and several others loathing an AT&T takeover, NCR had at least succeeded in creating a hostile environment for a hostile predator. In a letter to the editor, one disgruntled Daytonian even compared AT&T's unwanted takeover attempt with Saddam Hussein's takeover of Kuwait ("AT&T's actions," 1991).

Whether these advertisements were successful empirically can only be determined by the proxy results. In the final analysis, NCR lost the contest; the merger was imminent. Did its campaign fail? Shareholder opinion was mixed throughout the event, and when the underlying drive of many shareholders, especially investment firms, is considered, the lack of campaign success is understandable. These investment firms, some of which owned over 500,000 shares of NCR stock, are in the business for the quick profit, not the long-term success of organizations. Therefore, the tactics employed by NCR did not persuade these firms because they are by definition interested in what AT&T was offering. Changing the believer is often more difficult than changing corporate behavior (Heath and Nelson, 1986).

Communication to External Publics by AT&T

Again, AT&T engaged in little communication to external publics beyond its initial statement of intentions. In December announcements, AT&T addressed concerns of several external publics, including NCR employees, NCR customers, the Dayton community, and NCR shareholders. By emphasizing that NCR would remain autonomous under AT&T reign, AT&T snuffed many of the concerns of the NCR stakeholders. The Dayton community was relieved that AT&T would maintain the Dayton world headquarters and operations, suggesting no loss of jobs in the area. AT&T even stated that it would continue supporting the NCR philanthropies in Dayton, such as ArtsDayton and area universities ("Board letter," 1990). Some NCR employees were excited about the probable job security and future global information system promised by AT&T, and the customers consumed information concerning the continuation of NCR products and services. Customers were also influenced by the synergistic possibilities, due to the common use of UNIX system and AT&T's interest in open, cooperative computing ("AT&T bets," 1990). AT&T considered these publics less influential in the merger outcome and, therefore, did not communicate with these publics once the initial deal was outlined. On the contrary, AT&T emphasized the special opportunities the offer provided NCR shareholders.

Following the board's rejection of the $90 offer, Allen responded to Exley in a letter, "AT&T feels it has no choice but to go ahead tomorrow and commence its cash tender offer . . . to allow NCR shareholders to decide for themselves" ("AT&T launches," 1990). Because AT&T adopted a stock swap approach, many shareholders found the deal attractive, rather than a cash sale that required stockholders to pay capital gains tax ("AT&T/NCR," 1990). By January 17, AT&T reported receiving requests from 25 percent of shareowners to hold a proxy meeting. An AT&T spokesperson remarked, "Clearly, NCR stockholders are sending a message to the NCR board of directors that they support the deal and want NCR to negotiate a merger with AT&T" ("AT&T plays big cards," 1991). AT&T in its solicitation to shareholders stated that it wants to retain NCR management, but clarified intentions to seek a replacement to the thirteen-member NCR board of directors ("Produce list," 1991).

Many stockholders expressed the opinion that the companies were destined to merge; the question remained "at what price?" The March

5 edition of *The Dayton Daily News* reported that AT&T had made a definite move. The company sent out a letter and revised proxy cards to NCR shareholders. The letter renewed AT&T's appeal for ousting of NCR directors. In the cover letter, Allen said, "NCR management continues to attempt to entrench itself with additional maneuvers. . . . When you tender approximately two-thirds of NCR shares [to AT&T] you'd think they [NCR board] would listen, but they haven't. Were these actions taken with your interests in mind? Is the board thinking of your financial well-being? . . . We think not" ("AT&T sends," 1991).

After AT&T successfully blocked the ESOP adopted by NCR, a merger was only a matter of time for many shareholders. AT&T was predicted to win a majority of votes needed to replace four NCR directors at the proxy meeting and confidently issued a new bid of $100 per share if shareholders ousted all thirteen board members ("AT&T sends," 1991). Similar to NCR, AT&T attempted advocacy advertising to stockholders. The ads strongly resembled NCR's in type and format, perhaps strategically for attention purposes, and delayed company identification since AT&T was not portrayed as the "hero" by the media. The first ad began "make your voice heard" and then instructed NCR shareholders on how to tender their shares ("Make your voice heard," 1991). The advertisement directly addressed the public interest through factual financial information, value statements centering around choice, and policy statements urging shareholders to action. Although profitability was emphasized in this ad, the other themes of NCR's ads—productivity and progress—were omitted. AT&T was targeting the fundamental value of many shareholders—short-term profit.

The second advertisement asked who owned the company and asserted that NCR directors had forgotten for whom they worked ("Whose company is it," 1991). This advertisement co-occurred with the letter and proxy card mailing. Although the ad contained very few facts, it was laden with value statements in combination with policy claims. While the last ad stressed profitability, this ad only hinted at increased profits; rather, it concentrated on controlling the future of the company you own. Printed only three days prior to the proxy meeting, the last advertisement analyzed utilized the AT&T slogan "the right choice" ("What is the right choice?," 1991). This advertisement presented a table of gains under the AT&T offer and under NCR as a stand-alone company. The ad demonstrated the profitability, progress, and productivity associated with choosing AT&T by signing and sending the white proxy cards and motivated the action through the personal choice tactic.

CONCLUSIONS

Whether AT&T could attribute a win at the proxy meeting to a campaign success is questionable. Did AT&T manipulate the news stories and stakeholders' opinions well? Was the desire and belief system already present in the shareholders employed by AT&T to its advantage? Was AT&T's reactive advocacy advertising effective? Based upon its victory at the proxy contest, it would seem so. AT&T effectively defeated NCR, and the merger was underway. Although theoretically AT&T's campaign was rather weak, it produced results. How can this inconsistency be explained? In the initial stages of the campaign, many industry analysts were vying for the merger. One analyst, as quoted in *The Wall Street Journal,* said, "Take the money and run," and another investor advised, "Don't stonewall, negotiate out a transaction for everyone's benefit" ("AT&T launches," 1990). These analysts may have influenced shareholders' decisions to tender their shares to AT&T. No one wanted to miss out on the deal of the year.

However, a better explanation lies within the structure of owning shares. Many NCR shares were owned by investment firms, and arbitragers may have gotten involved. These two groups have no interest in organizational longevity or commitment; rather, they operate on making the dollar the quickest way possible, which in this case was to capitalize on AT&T's offer. The shareholders were undoubtedly the most important group to target in this event. AT&T had a much easier persuasion task because the belief system was already in place. It simply had to reinforce the belief and to avoid making any major mistakes. However, NCR was faced with the task of changing many opinions and of reassuring some wavering ones. Although NCR put forth a well-developed campaign, it could not undermine the goals of many shareholders. The issue of money overcame any others, and the proxy contest tactic did not lend itself to strong counter-rhetoric. Therefore, in this case, the communication strategies during the merger did not make or break the company. Pietruski, CEO of Sterling Drug, Inc., asserted that, until legislation is passed, more and more deals resulting from investment bankers acting as deal makers and not sound business advisers will occur. Quick profits over the success of the corporation does not create a healthy marketplace. Some legislation is needed to level the playing field (*Journal of Business Strategy*, 1989).

What would have happened had NCR chosen a route other than the proxy contest? Could NCR have chosen to restructure as Kroger did? Many analysts said no; Exley simply did not have the available cash flow, and he was adamant about not wounding his company. Could NCR have utilized Sterling's strategy and searched for a white knight? At first, analysts thought a knight was not available—not many companies can compete with AT&T's offer. Although a little late, *The Dayton Daily News* business editor offered his advice in a retrospective March 31 edition. NCR could have "married a Swiss, Britain, or German company. . . . NCR could have linked up with ABB, the Swiss maker of electrical distribution and power generation equipment." Or, "because the dollar is weak against the mark," a German company may have been an option ("Chuck Exley," 1991). Such is the benefit of hindsight. What could have been done does not matter for the computer maker and the telecommunication giant. AT&T merged with NCR, and NCR held its position long enough to acquire a generous price for its stock.

The next challenge facing the companies is the merging of their diverse cultures and the avoiding of a corporate identity crisis. This problem creates a whole new need for communication strategies if the new company hopes to maintain a strong position in the industry. Thus, specific messages must be designed to effectively communicate to public self-interest. These messages must then be sent through appropriate communication channels and, finally, evaluated for effectiveness through an analysis of public opinion. As Portugal and Halloran (1986) state, "Corporate identity is prospective and progressive—it looks ahead and seeks to guide the corporation as well as its evaluators, to serve as a catalyst for internal consensus and initiative, and to reflect a genuine concern for the interests and issues regarded as important by specific audiences."

Issue management is an integral part of daily business operations and must be treated as such by organizations. The development of contingency plans and the continuous monitoring of environments will allow organizations to become proficient in issue management. With this background and commitment, hostile raiders may be defeated and the defending team victorious.

EPILOGUE

Many events have occurred within the new company since March 1991, the ending point of this chapter's analysis, and some of them are contrary to AT&T's promises. Below are ten key occurrences.

First, Exley claimed that everyone who had a stake in the success of the new enterprise should help welcome AT&T to NCR headquarters. Robert Allen announced that any job cuts from consolidation will come from AT&T's ranks. Lee Hoevel, NCR's vice president for technology and development, said he would promote "techie bonding" between his people and those at Bell Laboratories (Coy, 1991a). A transition team was employed to set goals and to define a mission. One writer stated that the success of the merger depended on whether AT&T would continue to let NCR manage things (Barker, 1991).

Second, AT&T announced a converged product line strategy based on NCR's System 3000 family. AT&T Computer Systems' Extended Industry Standard Architecture machines were discontinued. The merged organization's stated goal was to establish leadership in open systems integration (Arnaut, 1991).

Third, AT&T sought new talent from outside the company. Chairman Robert Allen chose Jerre L. Stead to head the business communications unit and Alex J. Mandl as chief financial officer (Coy, 1991a).

Fourth, Exley retired as chairman on February 18, 1992, when the merger was legally completed. He was replaced by Gilbert Williamson, former NCR president. Exley stated that a number of AT&T networking software and networking hardware products would be released for the NCR sales organization. NCR was gradually converting customers for AT&T's workstation line to its line. The impact of the merger on the two firms was perceived positively (Booker, 1991). In September 1992, one year after their companies merged, Robert Allen and Gilbert Williamson held a press conference at which they reported that the merger is working. Williamson called it a smooth transition; NCR adhered to its basic business plans and has operated a profitable computer business (Hammer, 1992).

Fifth, NCR service representatives—who took over service and support for the Information Systems Network when AT&T purchased the company—were criticized by users for being unfamiliar with the product, delivering the wrong parts, and concluding service and repair work before the job is finished (Duffy, 1992).

Sixth, NCR CEO Gilbert Williamson stepped aside and was replaced by Stead. Stead pointed to a new AT&T desktop videoconferencing system, introduced in late March 1993, as an example of the kind of AT&T-NCR cross-pollination he will accelerate (Whiting, 1993). Stead, credited with the success at AT&T's business products division, said that NCR must focus more intensely on customer needs. Stead also wanted to streamline decision making by empowering teams of workers from different departments so that they can circumvent the usual hierarchies (Fink, 1993).

Seventh, the NCR acquisition reversed AT&T's previous computer-related losses and added profitability, giving AT&T a significant international presence by leveraging the 60 percent of NCR's revenue that is generated outside the United States. NCR also provided real-world marketing and product strategies for AT&T Bell Laboratories' technology (Coursey, 1993).

Eighth, NCR landed an unprecedented $32-million branch automation and ATM deal with New York's Chemical Banking Corporation (Iacobuzio, 1993).

Ninth, in October 1993, NCR began selling a line of PCs under the AT&T brand name. This was the first line of products introduced by the companies since the merger (Dixon, 1993).

Tenth, in January 1994, NCR Corp. was officially renamed AT&T Global Information Solutions to reflect efforts to merge its communications and computing expertise. The new name replaced the NCR brand name on most products, except for equipment that had historically been associated with the vendor—automated teller machines and retail point-of-sale systems (Hoffman, 1994a). Despite NCR's efforts to focus, users had mixed feelings about its performance to date and its strategic direction. Users expressed some skepticism about how the company's restructuring efforts will affect support (Hoffman, 1994b).

Three years after the merger, there is still no consensus on whether the merger was a success. Yet most of the above changes are positive for the company and suggest a successful merger of corporate cultures. A new name has been selected that may result in an increase in organizational cohesiveness; a new CEO, who has little history with either company, reigns, which may provide a fresh perspective and minimize any animosity that resulted from the merger process. The downside includes personnel loss and some quality reductions in service.

Mergers and acquisitions involve a human factor that may be handled most effectively through communication plans and sensitivity to public self-interests. The AT&T/NCR merger provides an interesting case study for issue management and crisis communication and should be considered by managers facing or launching an attack. Another useful source is Cartwright and Cooper's (1992) six-point inventory for future merger success:

1. Make an informed choice of merger partner that takes into account culture as well as finance.
2. Engage in effective people planning before the merger event.
3. Recognize the importance of people and their concerns, and take actions that address these.
4. Get to know the acquired organization or other merger partner and the way it operates, including at the grass roots level.
5. Establish effective communication networks and opportunities for employee participation.
6. Remain in touch with employees and monitor the success of the integration process.

PART V
Case Studies of Local Situations

13

Communication in Ballot Issue Campaigns

A Rhetorical Analysis of the
1991 Cincinnati Public Schools Levy Campaign

Jeffrey P. Joiner and Kathleen M. German

In the fall of 1991, the Cincinnati Public School System faced a tremendous fiscal challenge. A series of tax levies in previous years failed and the school system faced serious financial cuts. In another effort to acquire operating funds, the school board placed a $9.83 million levy on the ballot.[1] According to a poll conducted by *The Cincinnati Post,* while almost 80 percent of Cincinnati voters would agree to accept higher taxes if they thought it would help children get a better education, "only about 43 percent of voters say they back the district's 9.83-mill levy on the November ballot" ("Vote yes," 1991). This poll, conducted just three weeks before election day, summarizes the challenge faced by the 1991 levy campaign managers. Public opinion had eroded to the point where citizens had little faith in the future of the Cincinnati Public School System and were unwilling to vote for a school tax levy. Al Tuchfarber, a political scientist at the University of Cincinnati, gave the school board a 5 percent chance of passing the levy. In spite of these overwhelming odds, the levy passed ("Vote yes," 1991). The victory was "nothing short of a miracle," according to Chuck Schultze, president of Cincinnatians Active to Support Education, or CASE (personal interview, March 2, 1992).

The purpose of this chapter is to investigate the pivotal elements in the public relations campaign which preceded this remarkable reversal of public opinion. We begin with the examination of the unique features of ballot issue campaigns and then proceed to a discussion of the 1991 Cincinnati School levy campaign.

BALLOT ISSUE CAMPAIGNS: AN EXPANDING FORCE IN AMERICAN POLITICS

In recent years, ballot issue campaigns have increased dramatically, both in number and importance.[2] In 1980, 185 ballot proposals appeared in 18 states. By 1988, 238 statewide ballot issue proposals were voted on in 41 states, along with thousands of local ballot proposals (Carlin and Carlin, 1989; "Referendum's rising importance," 1980). This dramatic increase in the use of direct legislation from 1980 demonstrates the rising importance of ballot issues in American politics ("Referendum's rising importance," 1980).

Ranging from traditional issues, such as bonds and taxes, to volatile social questions, such as smoking, gay rights, nuclear power plants, and official state languages, direct voter participation promises to alter the nature of traditional governance. According to Prentice and Carlin (1987), "With the growing use of initiative and referendum by both state and local governments . . . citizens are playing a more direct role in shaping public policy" (p. 1). Some have argued that this type of grass roots campaign represents the future of political persuasion in the United States (Carlin and Carlin, 1989; Hall, 1983). As the importance of ballot issue campaigns increases across the country, so too does the relevance of studying these campaigns.

However, most rhetorical critics have concentrated on single-candidate, national campaigns—usually, presidential ones.[3] This limits our understanding of the political process, focusing attention on the largest, seemingly most important campaigns. While the study of presidential campaigns is certainly both valid and enlightening, it ignores other types of campaigns.

In addition, rhetorical theories that are designed to appraise political candidate campaigns are of limited utility for the analysis of ballot issue campaigns because fundamental differences exist between them.[4] Ranney (1981) identified three unique characteristics of ballot issue campaigns that are essential in understanding their communication dimensions: first, political parties are usually much less active and prominent in referendum campaigns. This removes party labels that for most voters in candidate elections are the most powerful indicators of which contestants merit support; second, the special nature and requirements of the mass communications media, particularly television, make it more difficult to portray the pros and cons of propositions than candidates' records and personalities; and third, the absence of party labels in referenda deprives them of much of the structure and continuity that usually characterize candidate elections (this, in turn, makes it more difficult to inform and activate voters in referendum campaigns).

This chapter explains how the Cincinnati school levy campaign successfully adapted to these three obstacles in ballot issue campaigns. We will examine each barrier in turn and determine how the campaign surmounted it.

CINCINNATI AND SCHOOL LEVY CAMPAIGNS: BACKGROUND AND ANALYSIS

Throughout the first half of this century, the school district received overwhelming support from the people of Cincinnati and the levy campaign organizers had to do little but put up a few signs announcing that a tax levy would be on the ballot. Since the first organized tax levy was presented to Cincinnati voters in 1915, there has been a tax levy on the ballot approximately every other year.[5] Of the forty-six attempted levies between 1915 and 1990, thirty-three carried and thirteen failed, a 71.7 percent success rate (Leslie and Siefferman, 1991).

However, during the mid-1960s public support for school levies changed. Between 1966 and 1979, Cincinnati Public Schools lost ten of fourteen levy attempts, including six in a row from 1972 to 1979 (Leslie and Siefferman, 1991). This left the school district in dire straits. During that decade, inflation and the cost of living rose considerably, and the school district suffered an additional setback as the purchasing power of the dollar declined.

The Cincinnati Public Schools' 1990 tax levy campaign, "Vote FOR Kids," again failed to pass. In spite of the high voter turnout, the levy lost by over 16,000 votes (57 percent to 43 percent) in what most citizens perceived to be a landslide defeat (Rhodes, 1991). Contributing to the levy failure were nationwide anti-tax sentiment, a drop in Cincinnati students' achievement scores, widely reported problems with discipline, organized opposition, fairly negative media attention, and general public irritation with the quality of education (Leslie and Siefferman, 1991, p. 1). Much of the blame for these problems fell on superintendent Lee Etta Powell.

Following the 1990 levy defeat, dramatic changes were made that were reflected in the 1991 ballot initiative. Those changes adapted to the unique rhetorical nature of the ballot issue campaign and accounted for the overwhelming success of the 1991 tax levy campaign (see Bitzer, 1968, pp. 10–11).

The 1991 Campaign: Organization

A primary limitation in ballot issue campaigns is that they often function without political party identification. Lacking the clear political party affiliations and organizational structure present in candidate campaigns, ballot issue campaigns are often loosely connected and sometimes chaotic. Three changes between 1990 and 1991 provided the essential leadership structure needed for a successful campaign. These included hiring public relations professionals to conduct the campaign, featuring new school superintendent J. Michael Brandt as spokesperson for the levy, and developing proactive responses to reluctant voters.

Public Relations Professionals Consultants hired to assess the 1990 levy defeat suggested that, while it was "important to retain all of the aspects of 'grassroots' campaigning . . . campaign strategy and the ability to quickly respond to crisis must be improved" (Leslie and Siefferman, 1991, p. 18). This recommendation resulted in the hiring of Brewster Rhodes, a professional campaign manager. The practical strategic leadership that Rhodes provided was crucial to the success of the levy. For the first time, one person coordinated long-term planning and daily operations. This allowed campaigners to spend the first five months of 1991 in damage repair and consensus building and the second five months in active campaigning.

While the campaign was run by public relations professionals, J. Michael Brandt, the new superintendent of Cincinnati schools, assumed visible leadership. Not only did voters see and hear Brandt on television and radio, but his picture and signature were featured on campaign literature. Because much voter dissatisfaction stemmed from disapproval of former superintendent Powell, the campaign associated the new superintendent with reform. An editorial in *The Cincinnati Post* expresses this sentiment: "Indeed, the selection of Brandt as superintendent—who ascended to the district's top post directly from the trenches of a high school rather than through the insulated administrative bureaucracy—is a sign that business as usual will no longer do" ("Vote yes," 1991). Even though her name was never mentioned, Powell became the scapegoat for the school district, while Brandt became its savior.

Brandt took an additional leadership step, announcing the elimination of 142 jobs in the district's downtown office. The district would save $16 million during the next two years because of the restructuring (Reeves, 1992). The announcement was well-received by the citizens of Cincinnati. Krista Ramsey (1992) of *The Cincinnati Enquirer* stated, "Brandt gave Cincinnatians a cause for hope. . . . It will be a system that serves. Not a bloated flow-chart of administrators, but one that, finally, serves children" (p. B1). By streamlining administration, Brandt signaled leadership that served voter interests.

J. Michael Brandt   While the replacement of Powell with Brandt was a visible gesture, Brandt also played a key role in this election because he was depicted as a candidate. Much of the campaign literature and media coverage focused on Brandt as a catalyst for change, a symbol of reform.

One critical message reaching many of the voters in Cincinnati was a thirty-second television commercial starring Superintendent Brandt.[6] While this commercial certainly had other functions such as educating voters on the changes that were taking place, it spotlighted the changes in leadership.

A secondary type of leadership utilized by the campaign was the endorsements by prominent individuals.[7] The levy had the personal support of Governor George Voinovich and Archbishop Daniel E. Pilarczyk. But the individual who brought the most attention to the school levy campaign was the Rev. Jesse Jackson. One day before the election, Jackson spoke in Cincinnati, urging passage of the school levy. Jackson stated, "This levy is about productivity, it's about world competition, it's about putting America back to work, it's about an alternative to welfare and despair, it's about dignity and self-respect, it's about a better Cincinnati, it's about a better Ohio, it's about a better America" (J. Jackson, videotape, November 4, 1991).

Jackson bolstered the levy with his personal credibility. Another benefit of Jackson's endorsement was increased media coverage. Jackson's appearance was featured on every major television and radio station in the Cincinnati area, bringing further attention to the levy campaign.

Proactive Leadership   Campaign managers took action even before the school levy campaign began, with proactive steps to enhance
the image of the Cincinnati school system (Schultze, personal
interview, March 2, 1992). The mayor's Soapbox on Education, the
Buenger Report, and the new school policies all helped create a
positive environment.

The development of a positive image was reinforced by the mayor's
"Soapbox on Education." Thirty different sessions were held all over
the school district. These soapbox meetings gave citizens the chance
to air their complaints about the school system. Over 2,000 people
attended sessions and, for the first time in many years, the people of
Cincinnati felt that they had some impact on school policy.

On September 5, the "Cincinnati Business Committee Task Force on
Public Schools: Report & Recommendations," commonly known as the
Buenger Report, was published. This study, conducted by members of
the local business community, evaluated the operation of the city's
public schools and recommended improvements. The Buenger Report
"slammed hard at the administration, but also paved a way for things
to change" (Schultze, personal interview, March 2, 1992). Campaign
organizers presented the Buenger Report findings as the light at the end
of a tunnel. This provided the voters with an image of the school system
as a progressive, improving organization.

Bolstered by the recommendations of the Buenger Commission
Report, the school board began to pass tighter scholastic policies,
including "no-pass, no-play" sports policy, rigid new discipline guidelines, and stronger attendance standards. This was orchestrated with an
emphasis on informing the public about positive changes. For example,
a press conference was held to announce the implementation of the new
discipline policy. Later in the campaign, voters were reminded of the
new discipline policy when the school board announced 5,000 suspen-
sions in the first quarter of the school year. In addition, a new attendance policy mandated parental contact for every unauthorized
absence and allowed the superintendent to recommend suspension of
driver's licenses of chronic truants and court citations for parents of
habitually truant students (*1991 levy fact book*). The school board also
announced a crackdown on "social promotion"—the practice of passing students even when they should be held back—and the implementation of tougher graduation requirements (Leslie, personal interview,
December 20, 1991). To further promote the new image, improved

achievement scores were revealed—10.8 percent in mathematics, 9.3 percent in language, and 5.2 percent in reading (*1991 levy fact book*).

Step Two: Activation

Many initiative and referenda campaigns fit the category of *minimal-information elections*. That is, in an issue campaign voters typically will be presented with less information than in a candidate race. Minimal-information elections tend to produce "little ego-involvement, interest, and turnout" (Carlin and Carlin, 1989, p. 231). Minimal information results from characteristics of ballot issue campaigns, including limited funds, special restrictions on election promotions, and highly complex issues that are often difficult to communicate in effective electronic messages.

In a study of minimal-information campaigns, Fleitas (1971) reached two conclusions that have implications for ballot issue campaigns: voters who possess little information "are apt to formulate a decision on almost any information that comes their way," and voters with peripheral interest represent the majority in minimal-information campaigns (p. 434). In ballot issue campaigns, voters often have little ego-involvement and thus spend little time considering the issue. In order to develop Cincinnati voter involvement, three strategies were employed: voter registration, extensive use of personal endorsements, and recruitment of a large volunteer corps.

Voter Registration   One of the most effective strategies for fighting opposition to the school levy came in the form of voter registration. In the summer of 1991, a Cincinnati Public School survey found that 70 percent of district parents were not registered to vote. It rapidly became apparent that a large portion of potential YES voters were not voting at all. The campaign reacted to this information by mounting a comprehensive registration drive. Levy campaign volunteers made 85,000 phone calls to parents in the district. Before the end of the campaign, over 600 teachers had been made deputy registrars, and 6,000 new voters had been registered (J. Leslie, personal interview, December 20, 1991). This was a major success for the campaign because 85 to 90 percent of newly registered voters potentially would vote yes (Campbell, 1989).

According to campaign manager Brewster Rhodes (1991), "The turnout of 53.3% was the highest in an 'off' year election in at least a decade and was nearly as high as the 1990 gubernatorial election" (p. 1). In 1990, the voter turnout was 56.4 percent; in 1989, 45.4 percent; in 1987, 45.7 percent. The increase in 1991 was probably due to newly registered voters.

Other evidence of the success of the voter registration drive is seen in the high correlation between the number of additional voters in each ward in 1991 and the number of additional votes for the levy. For example, in the College Hill neighborhood, there was an increase of 1,036 new voters in 1991. In that same neighborhood, there were 1,048 more votes for the levy compared to 1990. Overall, support was up in each of the twenty-nine city districts (Rhodes, 1991).

Endorsements   The primary way in which this campaign attempted to gain the trust of the voters was through endorsements. According to Hamilton and Cohen (1974), "Endorsements by organizations and prominent individuals should be trumpeted. Voting is influenced tremendously by affiliations and reference groups; it is more of a social than an individual act" (p. 107). Four sources of endorsements were utilized: (1) organizations, (2) prominent individuals, (3) teachers and principals, and (4) ordinary citizens. Not only did campaign organizers seek out endorsements, but unsolicited endorsements rolled in almost every day (Leslie, personal interview, December 20, 1991). These endorsements were featured in campaign literature.

The 1991 levy campaign received endorsements from literally hundreds of different organizations, representing every major group and organization in Cincinnati—Cincinnati Bar Association, Black Taxpayers Association, Cincinnati City Council, the Republican Party, the Democratic Party, NAACP, League of Women Voters, Cincinnati Housewives League, Baptist Ministers Conference, and the Cincinnati Youth Collaborative (Schultze, personal interview, March 2, 1992).

The 1991 campaign initially tapped the business community when CASE asked the Cincinnati Business Committee to form the Buenger Commission. The net result was to cement a powerful alliance with Cincinnati businesses. With the implementation of the Buenger Report reforms, the school district further developed rapport with community businesses.

Finally, ordinary citizens provided peer endorsements. For example, residents of Pleasant Ridge received "Here's what your Pleasant Ridge neighbors are saying about Issue 7," a mailing featuring statements of five to seven neighborhood residents. Presumably, the targeted voters could identify with the people quoted in the flyers because of their common geographic location. Citizens were also asked to endorse the campaign by signing petitions. The sole purpose of the petitions was to encourage positive behavior in voters. Hopefully, going to the polls and voting would spring from the relatively simple act of signing a petition.

Broad levy support throughout the district was also demonstrated in the "human billboard." On Monday, November 4, late afternoon drivers saw an estimated 10,000 levy supporters lining sidewalks and holding pro-levy signs near 85 Cincinnati Public School buildings. According to Jene Galvin, billboard organizer and chair of the Cincinnati Federation of Teachers' Political Action Committee, "We are looking for a dramatic demonstration of the bandwagon phenomenon that we're feeling in the closing moments of the campaign" (CASE News Release, November 1, 1991).

Volunteers Another indicator of levy support was the dramatic increase in volunteers. While the 1990 campaign recruited 300 volunteers, the 1991 campaign had 3,000 volunteers at its disposal (Leslie, personal interview, December 20, 1991). The volunteer pool formed a tangible voter base. Initially, large rallies provided volunteer-voters with new information. Later, information was supplemented in a weekly flyer published by CASE and circulated to every campaign volunteer. This flyer was the primary way in which the campaign organizers communicated with the 3,000 volunteers. These flyers served to update and to motivate volunteers.

Many Cincinnati educators were also featured in the campaign. Teachers and principals provided personal endorsements. For example, Paula Hanley, a science teacher from Western Hills High School stated, "The message is clear. Without the passage of this levy it is our children who will suffer" (Brandt, 1991, p. 4). The Cincinnati Federation of Teachers also published a flyer entitled "Why Teachers Support Issue 7" that was mailed to Cincinnati residents. From it, voters learned that 97 percent of Cincinnati teachers supported the new discipline policies. Campaigners also attempted to gain the support of the voters by mailing 20,000 handwritten postcards from Cincinnati School students to voters.

Step Three: Issue Development

The final and perhaps most fundamental difference between issue and candidate campaigns is that ballot issue campaigns necessitate discussion of "the issues." However, issue development is not easily conducted through the mass media typically employed in candidate races. This is due, in part, to the constraints under which the broadcast media must operate. Swanson (1977) claims that "drama is the key to campaign reporting because of the need for network news to reduce an entire day's activities into a few minutes while simultaneously providing entertainment to ensure ratings" (p. 241). Many issue campaigns lack what Swanson calls "melodramatic imperative" (p. 241). The result is that highly complex issues, like school finance elections, are not easily captured by the typical image creation strategies inherent in candidate media campaigns.

In order to combat this problem, the campaign developed three predominating strategies: targeting specific audiences, reducing complex issues to tangible, personal examples, and, finally, exploiting specific language strategies to enhance their messages.

Audience Targeting   As already noted, voters were targeted geographically by neighborhoods. The campaign also targeted certain groups. In particular, a strong appeal was directed at Catholic voters, since those with children in private or parochial schools have traditionally not supported tax increases for public education. Catholic parents were sent two special mailings. The first, "7 Reasons Why Parents Who Send Their Children to Private or Parochial Schools Should Support Issue 7," included a copy of Archbishop Pilarczyk's letter of endorsement. The second mailing was a letter from Brandt. It attempted to gain voter trust by recognizing the special interests of parents who preferred parochial schools.

Simplified Issues   Political scientists have noted that tax issues are particularly difficult to pass because people are inclined to vote NO unless they are given compelling reasons to do otherwise (Carlin and Carlin, 1989; Ranney, 1981). In such cases, education of voters is a key element in the campaign. The challenge for campaigners is to overcome voter reluctance by convincing them that benefits of the tax increase outweigh the personal costs (Carlin and Carlin, 1989).

According to Banach (1986), "Facts and logic, by themselves, rarely sell anything. If your campaign literature is a series of statistics and pie charts, you're headed for trouble. These materials have to be translated into language people can understand . . . and most people don't understand multi-million dollar school budgets" (p. 18). Most of the educational messages were personalized direct mailings. The campaign organizers attempted to reach each potential voter with at least five different mailings (Leslie, personal interview, December 20, 1991). To enhance voter understanding of complex issues, each mailing had a distinct purpose and focused on simplified issues. For example, *The 1991 Levy Fact Book* provided answers to common questions. Like other campaign messages, *The Fact Book* explained the reforms taking place in the public schools. For example, the first question asked was "What is the new superintendent/school district doing about some of the issues that face this urban school district?" The answer outlined the new discipline policy, educating voters with specific details. Thus, reform was associated with the new discipline policy. This question also reminded voters that Brandt was new, as the campaign attempted to break from past administrative failures. In essence, the campaign argued that new leadership voided old criticisms. Portions of *The Fact Book* were periodically inserted into *The Cincinnati Enquirer, Cincinnati Herald, The Cincinnati Post,* and *Catholic Telegraph,* broadening voter exposure to the campaign, reinforcing previous messages, and chipping away at opposition to the tax levy.

Besides natural resistance to tax increases, the levy campaign faced organized opposition from Citizens for Educational Diversity (CED). CED advocated parental choice, claiming that defeat of the levy would force the school board to issue vouchers, allowing parents to select which school their children would attend. CED favored vouchers.

This argument was neutralized through the direct use of fear appeals. The campaign messages insisted that defeat would not lead to a voucher system, but, in fact, would bankrupt the system. A vote for the tax levy became a vote to keep Cincinnati schools out of bankruptcy and free from state control.

Language Strategies   Association of "reform" with the school levy functioned to simplify complex campaign issues. Reform encompassed everything from streamlined administration to stricter classroom discipline, implying change in a positive direction. This single word permeated campaign messages and summarized what voters wanted to hear.

Another strategy included comparing the Cincinnati school district to surrounding districts. Such comparisons were sprinkled throughout the campaign, depicting Cincinnati as a school district on the cutting edge of public education. For example, in "A Message from the Superintendent," Brandt (1991) told voters, "The Board just mandated graduation requirements that are the toughest of any big city school district in Ohio. Now our standards exceed those of Mariemont, Oak Hills, Princeton, Sycamore, and Wyoming. We are serious about good education" (p. 2). By comparing Cincinnati to affluent, highly respected area schools, Brandt attempted to elevate respect for his school system.

The 1991 Levy Campaign: Conclusions and Implications

In most school districts throughout this country, the days are gone when a few yard signs and an editorial or two will result in the passage of a school tax levy. According to *Budget/Finance Campaigns* (1977), "Now it takes an all-out effort by a great many educators, parents, civic groups, and interested citizens, welded into a highly functional campaign organization, to be successful at the polls with a school finance election" (p. 7). To meet these demands, advocates must employ rhetorical strategies adapted to the unique nature of ballot issue campaigns. The 1991 Cincinnati tax levy campaign was successful largely because it adapted to the unique demands of ballot issue campaigns. First, it provided proactive leadership through public relations professionals and Brandt. Second, it activated voters through registration, endorsements, and volunteers. Finally, the complex issues of the campaign were simplified, audiences targeted, and language strategies employed.

In this process, the essential functions of communication present in successful issue campaigns were satisfied: (1) education, (2) trust development, (3) promotion of a positive image, and (4) neutralization of the opposition (Carlin and Carlin, 1989).

This campaign educated voters by emphasizing specific steps taken in school reform. Proactive leadership earned community trust. A positive image was created by implementing sweeping changes in administration and school policies. Neutralization of the opposition was accomplished by recruiting key people into the campaign and establishing direct responses to opposition arguments.

Implications   Thousands of school districts across the nation put tax proposals on the ballot each year. The challenges of these campaigns provide the communication scholar with intriguing questions about the nature of ballot issue campaigns. Further understanding of school finance campaigns not only adds to general knowledge of political communication, but may provide guidelines for successful future campaigns. A persuasive strategy that proves to be effective in Cincinnati may engage voters in Columbus or Buffalo or Portland because ballot issue campaigns share common characteristics.

All indications are that such direct participation in the local democratic process will continue to dominate political campaigns. The funding of our schools is one of the most fundamental tax issues. According to Estes (1974), "Our public schools are the last significant outpost of local control, ranking with town meetings found in small New England communities. Citizens participate directly and indirectly in school governance; they vote on levy and bond issues and in board elections; they speak out at board meetings; and they can run for the board with a limited budget and little red tape" (p. 15). In the present period of financial retrenchment, such fundamental tax issues become points of community controversy.

Further impetus for the study of issue campaigns is obvious when we survey past research on political events. Communication scholars have analyzed candidate races, especially at the national level, but have neglected ballot issue campaigns. The increased frequency and importance of issue ballots at state and local levels warrant serious study from a communication perspective.

Future Implications   Ballot issue campaigns someday may be used on a national level. According to Hall (1983), "Though direct legislation has traditionally been the purview of the states, the likelihood of a national referendum has been given some lip-service. Nuclear energy, ERA, and gun control have all been mentioned prominently as possible national referendum possibilities" (p. 6). In 1978, Senator Charles Grassley of Iowa advocated a national referendum system because "it further extends the principles of our system of checks and balances" ("Grassley suggests," 1978, p. 1).

More recently, 1992 presidential candidate H. Ross Perot expressed similar interest in a national referendum system that would allow American citizens to directly vote on raising taxes or going to war. While the Perot plan was attacked for being extra-constitutional (Will, 1992), the fact that such referenda systems continue to be discussed lends credibility to the argument that it is important to understand ballot issue campaigns. Whether or not national referenda are implemented, the financing of local education through tax levies is a current reality, and such tax issues promise to remain controversial for years to come.

NOTES

1. In Ohio, property tax levies are initiated by boards of education and voted upon by the electors in the school district. Under Ohio law, there are two types of tax levies available that provide additional operating revenue to meet current expenses: current operating levies and emergency levies (Whitman and Pittner, 1987). The 1991 Cincinnati Public Schools levy was a current operating levy.

2. The *American Dictionary of Campaigns and Elections* (Young, 1987) describes ballot propositions as, "Issues that are placed on the ballot to be voted on at the same time that a scheduled primary or general election is held. Ballot propositions are usually in the form of a question upon which voters are able to vote yes or no. Ballot propositions are widely used in the United States. In a typical general election, about 4 out of 5 states will decide statewide ballot issues."

3. Johnson (1990) divided 600 recent books and articles among the following five categories: (1) general study of political communication, (2) approaches to analyzing political communication, (3) forms of strategies, (4) the role of the media, and (5) women and politics.

4. Hall (1983) noted that a vast majority of literature on persuasive political campaigns has focused on one of three areas: (1) the explanation of campaign results with a principal focus on candidates, thus making it candidate-issue oriented, (2) impacts of media on election results, or (3) the examination of sociological, psychological, and political correlates of human behavior.

5. In those early days, the levy campaigns were organized and run by the Cincinnati Business Committee (CBC) (Chuck Schultze, personal interview, March 2, 1992). This committee included business people from several companies in Cincinnati. Ohio law prohibits a board of education from using school funds to "support or oppose the passage of a school levy or bond issue or to compensate any school district employee for time spent on any activity intended to influence the outcome of a school levy or bond issue election" (Ohio Revised Code, section 3517.01).

6. Although it was given the most attention, the television commercial was not the only broadcast message in the campaign. The Cincinnati Federation of Teachers funded a radio spot, with the goal of reaching weekday commuters. The radio commercial carried the same audio message.

7. The use of endorsements to win an election is a strategy suggested in most school finance campaign resources (Goldstein, 1984; Banach, 1986; Nusbaum, 1987; Kromer, 1988; and Funk, 1990). Nusbaum noted, "The creation of a winning attitude through the association of positive people in the campaign is of utmost importance" (1987, p. 8).

14

Public Relations and the Ethics of the Moment

The Anatomy of a Local Ballot Issue Campaign

William N. Elwood

There is no morality in the propaganda game; therefore, it serves no purpose to render a moral judgment on propaganda.

—*Jacques Ellul*

Propaganda *is* reprehensible.

—*Stanley Cunningham*

Almost every public relations book deals with ethics. The subject usually appears as an appendix or an afterthought, as a final chapter, section, or panel discussion. Perhaps as a response to the reputation of 1980s as the decade of greed, ethics has become a leading concern for institutions and for the field of public relations. According to Bovet, a 1992 Conference Board survey found that about 40 percent of the companies surveyed had instituted ethics training programs for both top and middle managers. Preston Townley, president of The Conference Board, argues, "Public relations professionals play a 'critical' role in communicating a company's commitment to ethics to employees and other publics" (in Bovet, 1993, p. 25). Yet the chair of the public relations committee for the Public Relations Society of America (PRSA) posits that the negative connotations associated with the practice of public relations "relate to perceptions about our ethical standards" (p. 24). This is hardly surprising, as particular ethical public relations lapses have been broadcast across the nation and the world. Richard Nixon's infamous recorded decision to "PR over" the Watergate burglary did little to obfuscate the incident or to advance the profession's reputation. In the early 1980s, one PRSA president resigned over allegations regarding unethical conduct. And some people still boycott Exxon gasoline stations because they perceive that the company failed to perform ethically in the *Valdez* incident, the environmental cleaning of Prince William Sound, and Exxon's public relations rhetoric regarding the situation.

This chapter differs from other efforts to process public relations and ethics. It is not the book's final chapter; more importantly, it argues to abandon the imposition of preexisting ethical standards on public relations and to recognize that the practice of public relations is a vehicle for constructing contemporary ethics in our daily lives.

Theorist Ron Pearson (1989b) states, "Public relations practice is situated at precisely the point where competing interests collide." It is "the site of moral tension . . . at the boundary between client interests and public or audience interests" (p. 67). Currently, this moral tension is the site of an ongoing debate regarding public relations and ethics. For example, Pearson argues that public relations ethics should be based on Habermas's idea of communication symmetry (1970; see German, this volume, for a discussion of Habermas's ideas). A similar idea is that public relations practice should be two-way communication, a dialogue with equal input from powerful corporate citizens and individual human citizens (e.g., Elwood, 1994; Johannesen, 1981; Pearson, 1989a). The two terms, or perspectives, that endure in the discussion of communication ethics are *teleological* and *deontological*. Teleological can be explained by the adage "the end justifies the means"; in other words, the moral quality of any communicative activity should be judged by the ethical merit of its ultimate goals. In contrast, a deontological orientation is based on the premise that acts in and of themselves are either right or wrong; the consequences of acts are immaterial to their ethical assessment.

The incongruous situation is that public relations and communication scholars argue in terms long used in the discussion of ethics within a newly emerged discipline that studies human behavior that is significantly influenced and informed by twentieth-century technology. This chapter avoids the terms *teleological* and *deontological* because they are inappropriate in discussing ethics and public relations within our late twentieth-century situation.

MacIntyre (1984) maintains that we possess only "the fragments of a conceptual scheme, parts of which now lack those contexts to which their significance derived. We possess indeed simulacra of morality, we continue to use many key expressions. But we have, very largely, if not entirely, lost our comprehension, both theoretical and practical, of morality" (p. 2). In other words, we have inherited a variety of moral resources from a long line of heterogeneous cultures and needlessly discuss current ethics with leftover terminology (p. 10). The "appearances of morality persist even though the integral substance of morality has to a large degree been fragmented and then in part destroyed" (p. 5).

Since the advent of the telegraph, the electronic mass media have altered the content, structure, and experience of discourse. Postman (1985) notes that each medium of communication organizes our thought processes and influences "the way we define and regulate our ideas of truth" (p. 18). McLuhan states that the media are the message (1964, pp. 23-25; see also 1960, pp. 125-135; McLuhan and Fiore, 1967); most scholars concur that each medium dictates what does and does not constitute information. This disparate, fragmented communicative experience has fostered the perception that most citizens are unable to understand issues and hence are unable to do anything about them. The rhetoric of public relations practice is unique because it is often communication in which one rhetor officially is not human. Individual employees may craft discourse and spokespeople may voice discourse, but such discourse is removed from its humanness by dint of its corporate authorship and because it is mass mediated, and thus distanced from members of publics. Given this disjointed communicative experience in which rhetoric and thought are fragmented from one another and from the contexts that inspired or informed them, it may be inappropriate to impose an ethical code created in the distant past upon a postmodern, postindustrial age.

Instead, I argue that public relations rhetoric constructs an *ethics of the moment,* criteria by which to judge the rightness or wrongness of an issue and its potential resolutions, all of which the rhetoric articulates. In short, each situation is discrete from others. Ethics is created for and by each situation, even in conversations regarding ethics. For example, the American debate regarding the legality of abortion includes two disparate and equally valid ethical stances. Those who believe that abortion should be illegal argue from the position that a zygote is a human being; thus, to terminate such a pregnancy is to kill that human being, an act that violates both divine and man-made law. In contrast, people who believe that abortion access should remain legal argue this point from a number of positions. First is the democratic tenet that all human beings are endowed with individual rights.

Second, Americans extend that belief as the freedom of choice, the right to choose the course of one's life. In this case, such a choice includes a woman's right to choose what happens to and inside her body. This choice includes the ability to bring a pregnancy to term and bear a child or to terminate that pregnancy during the period when doctors and a female patient believe an embryo is not a self-sustaining human being. According to MacIntyre (1984), "Every one of the arguments is logically valid or can be easily expanded so as to be made so; the conclusions follow from the premises. But . . . it is precisely because there is in our society no established way of deciding between these claims that moral argument appears to be necessarily interminable" (p. 8). Public relations rhetoric eliminates such interminable ambiguity by limiting choices and delineating the "right" action to take during the ethics of the moment such rhetoric creates.

In this chapter, I first discuss the contemporary discussion on ethics. Second, I explain my idea of the ethics of the moment. Third is a discussion of the situation regarding a local issue referendum campaign. Fourth, I present a case study analysis of the campaign. Fifth, and finally, I close with a discussion and observations.

THE ETHICS OF RHETORIC AND THE RHETORIC OF ETHICS IN PUBLIC RELATIONS

An odd phenomenon in our ongoing discussion of ethics is that we argue as if ethics is an objective "thing" that, if we only could verbalize, would provide a code that would allow us to conduct ethical or moral rhetoric. Ironically, this assumption ignores the fact that we argue for or against ethical codes and present ethical codes through rhetoric. As philosopher Henry Johnstone (1981) maintains, "Ethical problems about programs and policies [are] in fact rhetorical problems. If I am worried about the rightness of a course of action I do not first determine the rightness and then argue for taking the action; for the rightness resides in the argument itself, in the way the argument enhances or impedes the capacity of the audience to make up their own minds. I believe deliberation about acts does in fact take place at this single level, and cannot be broken down into ethical deliberation and rhetorical deliberation" (pp. 312–313). Although I cite Johnstone to situate my discussion, he himself is deontologically oriented. In his words, "The rightness or wrongness of an act does not reside in its consequences. The act is right or wrong in itself" (p. 306). In contrast, a teleological approach to ethics is rooted in the belief that "The moral quality or value of actions, persons, or traits of character is dependent on the comparative nonmoral value of what they bring or try to bring about" (Frankena, 1973, p. 14). Because ethics and rhetoric are inextricably intertwined and a discussion of ethics and public relations in a public relations context by necessity involves corporate rhetors, the notion of power, or rhetorical access, is involved. Briefly stated, individual citizens and institutions have equal opportunities, but not necessarily equal resources, to influence public policy. For example, I hardly have as large a media budget as the American Medical Association to influence the national discussion regarding health care reform. Likewise, Crable and Vibbert in this volume demonstrate the influence that a global oil company can have even when it purchases space in Sunday newspaper rotogravures to appear unpersuasive. Clearly there is an imbalance of public relations power when it comes to accessing the mass media.

The history of the public relations field is also the theory of ethical choices. During an interview with Bill Moyers (1989) on the history of public relations, Bernays commented that he conceived of his definition of public relations in relation to Jefferson's idea of democracy as government by consent of the governed. To alter the process of government, one must obtain the consent of the governed. According to Bernays (1952), "The engineering of consent is the very essence of the democratic process, the freedom to persuade and suggest. . . . Theoretically and practically the consent should be based on the complete understanding of those whom the engineering attempts to win over." Bernays admits that "demagogues" can engineer consent "for antidemocratic purposes as successfully as those who employ them for socially desirable ends" (pp. 160-161). Pearson argues that organizations that eliminate the existence of dialogue abridge the democratic process (1989b, p. 127; see also Day, 1961, and Holden, 1988). Bernays exhorts those who engineer consent to practice public relations "for socially desirable ends" and to "be constantly aware of the possibilities of subversion" (1952, p. 161). In short, Bernays suggests that unethical PR practices include *not* acting in the public interest and misleading or lying to constituents. Although Bernays did not describe his campaign in this way, he engineered public consent for women smoking cigarettes in public, a behavior that previously was unconscionable. Asked by a tobacco executive to increase sales, Bernays asked a group of debutantes to walk in New York City's annual Easter Parade while "holding torches of freedom." This moment, during which women of high social standing promenaded on Fifth Avenue with their cigarettes and their gentlemen escorts, promoted a new social standard that permitted women to smoke in public. Photographs of this 1920s media event appeared in newspapers; opinions and actions changed accordingly, and a new penchant for cigarette smoking became entrenched in American ethics (for Bernays's account of this promotion, see Moyers, 1989).

In his seminal work on *Power,* Coleman (1974) acknowledges "the marginality of natural persons to corporate actors" (p. 35). He states, "The power held by corporate bodies (whether business corporations, trade unions, governmental bodies or still another form) is in the hands of no person, but resides in the corporate person itself" (p. 37). According to Mumby (1988), "Power is exercised . . . when one group is able to frame the interests (needs, concerns, world view) of other groups in terms of its own interests" (p. 3). Briefly stated, power is terminological control; to control the terms about a particular issue is to influence the way people think about those issues and the ethical choices involved with them. Cheney and McMillan (1990) expound on the practice of analyzing organizational rhetoric and write, "The ubiquity and power of institutional discourse function to decenter (and thus minimize) the individual self, the acting subject or agent" (p. 97). Coleman acknowledges this power concentrated among institutions and likens this concentration of public relations power to the concentration of democratic political power. He posits that a democracy is based on the idea that citizens have natural rights and cede direct control over those rights. Thus, one has no "voice in the [daily] use of his rights by government officials," save for the elections in which one can choose alternate individuals to whom we cede the same rights (1974, p. 42). In a similar way, "The individual person has given up to corporate actors not ultimate and absolute control over his rights, but effective and immediate control over those rights" (p. 42). Coleman accedes that the increased concentration of power among institutions and thus the marginalization of individuals "brings about a widespread subjective feeling of powerlessness," but that citizens can regain a sense of control by reducing "the scope of one's horizons"—horizons initially broadened by the electronic mass media—and concentrating "one's interest in and attention to those events that are very near at hand" (pp. 37, 53). This particular case study and the chapter that preceded it are examples of citizens reasserting interest and action on local issues that are within their purview.

In chapter 2 of this book, Brummett encourages us to eschew the indictments of public relations rhetorical practices, to acknowledge that individual and corporate citizens attempt to establish hegemony through rhetoric, and to examine just how that happens. In summary, there is no equal access to Congress nor to a thirty-second commercial during the Super Bowl nor to a full-page ad in *Time* magazine. We cannot argue ourselves into such a situation, nor can we argue for a teleological or deontological public relations ethics that institutions and practitioners will practice universally. We can, however, acknowledge our current state of affairs *and* acknowledge the range of reasoning powers among the citizenry; we can critique rhetorical public relations efforts in this fashion. Ellul provides such a perspective.

Ellul (1981) argues against imposing a traditional ethical approach to the practice of public relations. He refers to public relations rhetoric and its dissemination through media as "propaganda." In fact, he posits that there is a basic "incompatibility between ethics and propaganda" (p. 171). Ellul acknowledges that ethical codes are a symbolic construction: "All ethics is necessarily an ethics of encounter. One doesn't have a moral behavior alone. And it is the exchange of words which allows me to construct myself on the moral level, while at the same time my words allow others to believe. Together, we choose an orientation" (p. 174; see also Berger and Luckmann, 1966). In contrast to the discursive construction of a moral self, "Propaganda creates a morality, an ethic, a certain type of wished-for behavior. It furnishes man with a criterion for good and evil" (pp. 162-163). Much like religion, Ellul argues, propaganda "leaves no latitude of choice nor any field undetermined" (p. 163). Public relations constructs issues, resolutions, right, and wrong.

The difference between the discursive construction of the moral self and the ethics that propaganda provides is that public relations rhetoric is broadcast through mass media. It loses the qualities of direct exchange and encounter. When one views a commercial on television, reads a newspaper report, or opens a direct mailing, one is confronted not only with an issue, but also with the right and wrong tactics for resolving that issue (see Crable and Vibbert, 1985). There is little or no possibility for an "exchange of words." Instead, the issue and the ethics of the moment are rhetorically delineated. Although this perspective acknowledges the hegemony of institutions to dominate mass-mediated discourse regarding issues, it does not discount the ability of human beings to think about the competing perspectives in the public arena and to make their own decisions.

Cunningham's scathing critique of propaganda includes this statement: "There is no denying that propagandists *choose* their words and images, and that propagandees, in turn, are epistemically responsible for what they choose to believe" (1992, p. 244). In short, corporate rhetors strategically respond to public relations situations, and individual members of publics judge the facticity and usefulness of such rhetoric. As in the critical stage of issue management (Crable and Vibbert, 1985), the public relations situation and the rhetoric present themselves simultaneously to citizens who, to borrow from *Philip Morris Magazine,* have the freedom to choose from competing discourses within the propaganda of an issue. They also may reject all viewpoints and choose another for themselves. The issue of growth management in Sarasota County, Florida, is one of those situations.

THE PUBLIC RELATIONS SITUATION: SO MANY PEOPLE IN SO LITTLE TIME

Over the past two decades, many Americans created a population explosion when they emigrated from the Midwest and Northeast to the Sunbelt, an area that includes Florida, Georgia, Texas, and California. These Sunbelt states have achieved greater national political significance as their populations have increased. Once the U.S. Census Bureau completes its count of American citizens each decade, state legislators alter House of Representatives district lines in accordance with population shifts; Sunbelt states have received additional districts as a result of the 1990 census.

The growth that warranted increased political significance in national politics and the evolution of Atlanta, Houston, Miami, and Tampa into metropolitan areas also created problems. Municipal and county governments were ill-equipped to provide infrastructure for the new inhabitants that poured into new land developments. For example, many Atlanta regional water distribution systems cannot meet their customers' demands; other area systems simply have self-destructed through overuse. According to Atlanta journalist Fox McCarthy (1990), "The real problem [for the Sunbelt] is a steadily increasing demand, a demand fueled by population growth" (p. G1).

The *Sarasota Herald-Tribune* predicted, "The 1990s may go down as the Catch-Up decade as residents pay for the rampant growth of the past 20 years." The same news story listed many of the "issues expected to top the agenda of the final decade of the twentieth century," including "insufficient supplies of drinking water, the need for new and wider roads to handle urban sprawl, polluted streams and bays" (Zaloudek, 1990a, p. 16A). Florida legislators have taken an active role to ameliorate the stress on infrastructure and services. The Florida legislature passed the Local Government Comprehensive Planning and Land Development Regulation Acts in 1985 and 1986 that mandated each Florida county government to create a growth management plan. The title of the Sarasota County plan is *Apoxsee*, a Seminole word that means "tomorrow." State laws require each county plan to permit land development only when area governments can provide services, including water, sewers, and roads adequate to handle the projected number of new inhabitants. This provision of the plan is called *concurrency* (*Apoxsee*, 1989, p. 1). Although the state of Florida requires concurrency and growth plans, not all Floridians are pleased with the results of growth management policies. Some believe that the growth management restrictions have not gone far enough, and some believe that the extant regulations are too restrictive. Not surprisingly, two perspectives were typically voiced by individual citizens and land developers. Even in Tallahassee, the state capital and Leon County seat, land developers criticized the local growth management plan as too restrictive, while county commissioner Gayle Nelson responded that the plan " 'doesn't give the security [against overdevelopment] the people want' " (Fineout, 1990, p. 4A).

Sarasota County commissioners feebly attempted to resolve growth-related problems. First, they convinced the electorate to float a bond issue to purchase land for a future water supply, only to find after the purchase that much of that water required treatment for radioactivity. After treatment, an increased radioactive effluent would require disposal in the Gulf of Mexico. The two coastal cities most convenient for disposal sites refused to grant such permission and vowed to fight the county government if it attempted to gain disposal sites for the toxic water through eminent domain. Despite such conditions, the commissioners resolved to make this site the main source for drinking water in Sarasota County (Sams, 1990a, p. 5B).

Second, the commissioners later purchased property adjacent to the planned water reservoir for a landfill. A common saying dictates that one should not place waste products where one consumes. Regardless, the commissioners contracted for an expensive study that eventually confirmed such folk wisdom: underground seepage from an adjacent landfill could taint the water supply irreversibly. Despite this finding and the County Planning Board's unanimous opposition to the proposed site, the commissioners remained committed to both sites (Fitzgerald, 1990, p. 1A).

Third, the state fined one commissioner for improper conduct regarding a proposed road. County commissioners authorized construction of a new road that, when constructed, will run through a large tract of the commissioner's land, increasing its potential for development and thus its value. Meanwhile, the commissioners failed to improve overburdened county roads that the Florida Department of Transportation had given its lowest possible rating (Sams, 1990b, p. 22A). Sarasota County government may have enacted its comprehensive plan in 1989, but its commissioners demonstrated incompetence and possible corruption toward implementing it.

Concurrently, developers lobbied for reprieves from the local government's regulatory powers mandated by the state (Matrullo, 1990, p. 11), while a Florida Atlantic University study determined that the majority of Sarasota County residents wanted stronger land-use regulations and were even willing to pay higher taxes to improve the environmental qualities of Sarasota Bay and other natural environs (Roat, 1990, p. 1). In short, growth management is not a monolithic issue, but a multifactored issue construct related to population growth. These factors coalesced as a group of organized, individual citizens proposed zoning variance reform and a two-year, private enterprise building moratorium as the panacea for Sarasota County's growing pains.

County residents perceived their area's expanding population as a serious threat to the environment and to their lifestyles (Roat, 1990, p. 1). A two-year moratorium on all construction except for public works and private remodeling is a serious, even drastic, resolution to the growth management issue. However, the moratorium (in fact, part of a proposed addendum to the county government charter) was the only alternative resolution to *Apoxsee* presented during the time preceding the election. The proposed county charter amendment would ban new development for two years and would require a unanimous vote by county commissioners on proposals to increase land zoning densities already outlined in *Apoxsee*. The citizens who proposed the resolution organized themselves as GEO, an acronym for Growth-restraint and Environmental Organization. They gathered a sufficient number of registered voters' signatures to place their proposed resolution on the September ballot.

THEMES IN THE CONSTRUCTION OF THE ETHICS OF GROWTH MANAGEMENT: AN ANALYSIS

In this growth management case, GEO advanced familiar, local problems of road gridlock, water rationing, and polluted waterways to promote voting for the charter amendment. GEO also minimized the economic predicaments that a two-year building moratorium potentially could create. GEO initiated public discussion of the issue and advocated its resolution by claiming, "It's high time to remove control of the County's destiny from another branch of that suspect band of bankers, builders, and bureaucrats" (*GEO Journal*, 1990, p. 2).

Going to Hell in a Handcart:
Recounting Growth-Related Problems

Not surprisingly, GEO referred to its adversarial relationship with big business when it claimed, "For too long, the system in Sarasota County has been dominated . . . by the developers and the land speculators and others who favor a pro-growth, quick-buck, big tax, damn-the-environment future for Sarasota County that would short change all of us, our children, and our grandchildren" ("Because you care," n.d., p. 4). According to GEO, big business and the governmental system that it controlled had endangered the common people and their progeny. Sarasotans who lived with a rationed water supply, a bay polluted by raw sewage, traffic jams on inadequate roads, and an ever-increasing number of housing developments and strip malls, without the implementation of concurrency guaranteed in *Apoxsee*, were well aware of their peril. Thus, GEO's rhetoric did not need to discuss the unpleasant realities associated with rapid development; instead, its rhetoric described the cause of citizens' dire straits, the evil axis of developers and confederate politicos. Left unstopped, these villains would "short change" everything and everyone in Sarasota County to make a profit and move on. In GEO's opinion, if the people did not assert themselves through the charter amendment, they surely would inherit a developer-created and more desperate environmental quagmire that citizens would have to resolve at costs higher than if they enacted zoning reform and a temporary building moratorium.

GEO members crafted and proposed a county charter amendment to forestall this threat. The organization's rhetoric defined a vote in favor of the amendment as grass roots political action that would reclaim populist control from "that suspect band of bankers, builders, and bureaucrats" (*GEO Journal*, 1990, p. 2). In all its campaign literature, GEO listed its board of directors, mostly private citizens and community activists including Jack Conway, the former president of Common Cause. GEO members also offered me access to the organization's membership list, leaving little doubt that "GEO is a grassroots organization that listens to what local residents want for their neighborhoods, their county, and their environment" ("Because you care," n.d., p. 1).

GEO's advocacy rhetoric maintained a causal tone throughout its campaign; ostensibly *Apoxsee*, the county's comprehensive plan, was worthless because county officials were in big business' back pocket. While the GEO rhetoric evoked fears of a business-government-banking conspiracy reminiscent of the Grange movement, GEO also assured Sarasotans that they still had a chance to assert their control to tame the rascals and to save their surroundings. However, the rhetoric glossed over potential economic effects that a two-year building moratorium could have. To essentially ignore the economic effects of a construction moratorium proved to be an unfortunate rhetorical choice for GEO.

It's the Economy, Stupid: Giving Growth Management an Individual Bottom Line

Citizens for Responsible Solutions (CRS) presented an opposite version of what would happen if the electorate voted for GEO's policy resolution: "Thousands of jobs would be lost. Unemployment will increase. Schools and public services will be cut as a result of a smaller tax base. Nearly everyone in Sarasota County will suffer as a result of this moratorium" ("An open letter," 1990). In other words, the community that already had enough growth-related troubles would be hell-bent for disaster if citizens affirmed the proposed growth management plan. CRS essentially said resolutions to growth-related problems could be found in the existing county growth management plan and concentrated on economic aspects of the discussion.

In 1990, approximately 10,000 county residents worked in construction to meet the population explosion. Obviously, such a moratorium would place their jobs in jeopardy. To ease the concerns of this group, GEO had little to say except, "Enough building permits will likely have been put into the pipeline . . . to provide plenty of jobs during the first year of the moratorium. A renaissance of renovation projects will help pick up some of the slack in the second year" ("GEO questions and answers," 1990, p. 1). While the prospect of renovation-related jobs may have quieted some fears, CRS responded to this definition and rhetorically constructed a desperate financial picture of moratorium effects. Through repeated rhetorical efforts, CRS also reduced the county charter amendment that included zoning variance reform to "the GEO moratorium," which concentrated public attention on negative effects for construction and the local economy.

The organization also relied upon specialty items to refine its rhetorical campaign for specific audiences. In addition to the direct mail pieces, billboards, and taxi and bus signs that the organization had leased, CRS enlisted construction company vehicles, construction workers, and the workers' personal cars to propagandize for the campaign. CRS sponsored t-shirts and bumper stickers that construction firms gave to their employees to place, respectively, on their bodies and automobiles. These items were emblazoned with the CRS logo and slogan, "Save my job! Vote NO! on the moratorium." The use of the first-person pronoun on these items helped to promulgate the idea to readers that construction workers and their families were CRS members and that the individuals who wore the t-shirts and displayed the stickers on their cars were the authors of the anti-moratorium messages.

Moreover, CRS intelligently targeted an active and predominantly affluent public—senior citizens. Retirees constituted one-third of county residents; many favored the charter amendment. They also harbored memories of the Great Depression. In an outstanding example of targeting a message to a public, the organization approved a sign (Burja, 1990) that asked viewers, "Remember the Great Depression?" This headline appeared over a photo of a pathetic urchin who looked like he had stepped out of *The Grapes of Wrath*. Beneath the photo, the rhetoric continued, "It affected *everyone! No one* wants a Depression in Sarasota. Vote 'NO' on the Moratorium." For the target public, this argument is pragmatically elegant. Certainly a case of reduction to the absurd, it plays to memories of impoverished childhoods that inspired members of this public to work hard, to save money, and to pay off the mortgage as soon as possible so that one's family would never end up on the street. Such factors and a postwar economy of abundance facilitated the creation of the most wealthy and politically active public in the United States today. Changing the minds of senior citizens was crucial to defeat the proposed charter amendment.

CRS made an important rhetorical choice not to place its name on this poster that appeared in businesses and professional offices frequented by members of this public. In fact, no rhetoric regarding an author's identity appeared on the poster. The only evident author is the pathetic, pictured child, whose presence personifies desperate childhood memories that could remind senior citizens that a contemporary Great Depression could leave them penniless, homeless, and without enough time or energy to rebuild their lives. If senior citizens could identify with that impoverished child-author, the accompanying fears could obliterate rational perceptions of their current, comfortable states of existence. The poster's rhetoric evokes the prospect of a poor and desperate old age and might convince retirees to vote against the charter amendment, even though many originally had signed the petition to place the amendment on the ballot. CRS's public relations rhetoric was ubiquitous and targeted effectively to different Sarasota County publics.

If It Ain't Broke, Don't Fix It: Give *Apoxsee* a Chance

Just as GEO had little to say on the economic effects of a building moratorium, CRS advocated no new resolutions to the problems that constituted the growth management issue. In fact, the only resolution CRS ever proposed to deal with the growth management issue was "the county comprehensive plan, known as APOXSEE, [that] can strictly control growth without hurting people and raising taxes" ("Straight talk," 1990). CRS's rhetoric proclaimed that "the right solution for Sarasota County," indeed, "the best way to protect Sarasota's future," was "the comprehensive planning process" under which county government had inadequately operated (*CRS News*, 1990, p. 3). CRS never mentioned that "the comprehensive planning process" dictated by *Apoxsee* had done little or nothing to stave off the problems associated with growth management over the previous nine years. Regardless, CRS stated that *Apoxsee,* the plan that county officials had followed, had facilitated a few viable resolutions that made "better sense than the extreme and poorly drafted GEO proposal" (*CRS News,* 1990 p. 3). CRS ventured as far as to claim that GEO's position "prevents solutions" and "creates problems instead of solving them" ("Straight talk," 1990, p. 2).

Name Dropping: Using Credible Sources
to Establish Ethos

One of the first tenets that every speech teacher and student learns is that, to establish credibility in an area in which one lacks expertise, cite recognized authorities. The simple point is that one may not have ethos in a particular subject, but recognizes those who do. By citing those sources, rhetors link the credibility of respected figures to themselves. For example, CRS mailed "Straight Talk on the GEO Moratorium" to every registered voter in Sarasota County. According to CRS, the conspiracy in Sarasota was not big business, but GEO itself, "a small group of extreme 'no-growth' advocates . . . running a slate of candidates for county political office." CRS hinted at a GEO conspiracy, stating, "The GEO moratorium was drafted in secret by a small group of 'no growth' extremists" ("Straight talk," 1990, p. 1). In addition, CRS rhetoric posited that the moratorium would result in "a deep recession, thousands of jobs lost and serious revenue shortfalls for county government that will require property tax increases and cuts in county services." As proof, the organization cited "an independent study conducted by Wharton Econometric Forecasting Associates (WEFA)," a prestigious economic forecasting concern. According to CRS, this "independent study" predicted that "Our taxes will increase over 30 percent" and that there would be "8,000 construction jobs lost, total employment falls by 12,000 jobs, total personal income declines 10 percent. . . . The GEO moratorium would transfer 'net worth' from the middle class to the rich." CRS cited WEFA as the forecaster of this economic gloom. Such a citation certainly added credibility to its claims; however, the citation also omitted the fact that CRS itself had commissioned the study. This omission is hardly surprising; public knowledge of such authorship and sponsorship would contour the predictions as biased and counteract the CRS rhetoric that claimed the moratorium was "the wrong solution" for average working people and that citizens should "vote no!"

CRS listed its directors, all prominent businesspeople, in some of its literature. However, it defined itself as "a broadly based citizens' coalition. . . . CRS members come from all walks of life in Sarasota

County" ("Citizens for Responsible Solutions," n.d.). The corporate author never defined itself as a political action committee sponsored by major corporations that conduct business in Sarasota County, nor did local news stories reveal CRS's primary sponsorship. Instead, CRS listed the names of prominent people under the heading, "These community leaders urge you to VOTE NO on the GEO Moratorium." This list included a Roman Catholic brother who founded a nonprofit senior citizens center, the superintendent of schools, the president of the public hospital, presidents of the local chambers of commerce, and a state senator and representative, among others. These individuals had high credibility and may have endorsed CRS's position against the county charter amendment, but they certainly did not constitute the authors, or "citizens," of CRS. However, such names did provide CRS's position with credibility and perhaps an illusory premise of authorship that characterized CRS's recommendation as the right thing to do. In fact, news stories acquiesced in CRS's portrayal of its opposition and typically defined CRS as "the anti-moratorium political action committee" (Loverude and Sams, 1990, p. 1A).

ETHICS OF THE MOMENT: THE CONSTRUCTION OF RIGHT AND WRONG THROUGH PUBLIC RELATIONS

Two ethical codes emerged through the rhetoric in this local ballot issue campaign. First, rapid, poorly managed growth had spoiled the environment and had made life less convenient and perhaps dangerous for current residents. To continue such actions would continue to diminish the natural surroundings and, more importantly, bequeath a besmirched world to the next generation who would likely become bankrupt as they attempted to atone for the sins of their fathers. Following this ethical code, the only "right" decision would be to vote for the proposed county charter amendment. The second code reversed the order of concerns. It placed the proposed charter amendment in the forefront and claimed that it would bring immediate economic ruin to local governments and to citizens of all economic and age groups. Thus, to vote for the amendment was to be responsible for an unemployed work force, impoverished elderly, and governmental agencies that would be ill-equipped to provide regular services, let alone services for the newly disenfranchised. Consistent with MacIntyre's observations on Western society, each argument "is logically valid or can be easily expanded so as to be made so; the conclusions follow from the premises" (1984, p. 8). In this case, voters could not resolve the competing claims regarding growth management, each of which emanated from disparate perspectives. The first ethical code asked people to think in the abstract, about people who had yet to move to Sarasota and about the future. The second code evoked thoughts about the economic present and an imminent, desperate economic future. Not surprisingly, people voted with their pocketbooks when this ethics of the moment provided these two rhetorically constructed, ethical choices. However, their commitment to environmental restoration and preservation and to resolving growth-related problems appeared undiminished.

Seventy-five percent of the voters elected to defeat the charter amendment (Loverude and Sams, 1990, p. 1A), yet 60 percent of eligible voters were willing to "limit economic growth to deal with problems like growth, water supplies, traffic and pollution"[1] (Rufty, 1990, pp. 1A, 22A) only two months after the election and after CRS ceased its public relations activities. CRS's campaign rhetoric simply may have revealed flaws in GEO's rhetorical and ethical reasoning. However, CRS had a distinct advantage in this campaign. GEO had a $7,000 treasury raised primarily through individual supporters; with that money it rented office space, bought postage stamps, and had its public relations rhetoric created by amateurs. Its opposition—*corporate* citizens including Federated Stores, Inc., Sears, Roebuck & Company, major grocery chains, and the State Board of Realtors—helped to create a war chest of at least $300,000. Furthermore, Barnett Bank, the largest bank in Florida, provided the organization with office space and supplies, a secretarial staff, computers, and a phone system. The bank also paid the CRS chairman's salary so that CRS funds could be spent exclusively on advertisements, direct mailings, and specialty items. Moreover, the National Association of Homebuilders provided CRS with two professional communication consultants to craft its rhetoric (McLeroy, 1990, *passim*). CRS never included this information when it defined itself as an institution constituted only of concerned individuals. Such a definition encouraged citizens to perceive the two organizations as equals in membership and resources. Had CRS presented its list of key sponsors, that information certainly would have provided citizens with a perspective to resolve the competing claims, a perspective on authorship that would have contextualized the two authors as big business versus individual citizens. Instead, the ethics of the moment proffered a choice between economic ruin for one's self and fellow citizens or a distant, greener future; the rhetoric did not frame the issue of growth as an ethics of authorship, but as an issue of economic welfare.

GEO's members were able to obtain at least 20 percent of the electorate to sign a petition to place the county charter amendment on the ballot. Despite the charter amendment's defeat, 49 percent of the Sarasota electorate polled at election time defined growth as the most important problem the community faced; 60 percent stated that *Apoxsee,* the plan that CRS said was "the best solution" for growth management, was incapable of resolving problems related to growth management in Sarasota County[2] (Judd, 1990b, p. 1A). No public opinion poll was performed when the growth management issue emerged during the summer of 1990. However, a poll executed two months after the election found that 60 percent of residents were willing "to limit economic growth to deal with problems like inadequate water supplies, traffic congestion, and pollution" (Rufty, 1990, p. 1A). Two months after the election, a majority of eligible voters favored a policy resolution that they had rejected.

Despite the lack of a pretest, the existing public opinion polls and my analysis lead to the conclusion that people look to public relations campaign rhetoric—in fact, all mass-mediated rhetoric—for the "right" thing to do. GEO initiated the growth management issue; the rhetorical-ethical perspective that motivated over 20 percent of registered voters in Sarasota County to sign a petition that placed the charter amendment on the ballot became less palatable when CRS entered the scene and portrayed those same concerns as a prescription for economic ruin. If GEO had been able to offer a second ethics of the moment, an ethics of authorship that featured local, grass roots citizenry versus big-business, big-city corporations, it might have been able to reduce the impact of CRS's economic perspective.

More recently, a 1994 survey commissioned by the Sarasota County Commission found, "Most people think that Sarasota County is growing too quickly, and they believe county government is encouraging that growth" (Foster, 1994, p. 1B). This same year, a coalition of community organizations including GEO introduced a petition to place an amendment in the November election that would require the Sarasota "City Commission to obtain the consent of City voters at a general election before adopting any amendment to the Land Use Element of the Comprehensive plan which would increase the intensity (average daily traffic count) or density (number of residential dwelling units per acre) to which any land in the City may be rezoned" (*Who do you trust?*, 1994). Not only does this resurgence of interest in the growth management issue demonstrate the efficacy of rhetoric to construct an ethics that reverses public opinion, but also it illustrates Crable and Vibbert's (1985) principle that issues are never solved but are *re*solved; they become dormant only to emerge in the future. One component to the revived growth management issue that may receive more attention is the idea of authorship. A news article that recounts "allegations of bullying, harassment, and downright dirty trickery" by pro-development forces describes the situation:

> On one side stands We the People, a partnership of GEO, the Growth-restraint and Environmental Organization, and CONA, the Council of Neighborhood Associations. The group wants on the ballot a proposal that neighborhood rezoning must be decided by Sarasota city voters, NOT by bureaucrats and politicians. On the other side, spoiling for a fight, stands Citizens for Responsible Planning [CREP], bankrolled by the Florida Home Builders and the Sarasota Board of Realtors to the tune of $25,000. In a previous incarnation as Citizens for Responsible Solutions, CREP in 1990 played a strong role in defeating GEO's proposed building moratorium. (Stone, 1994)

Such news coverage and CREP members' harassment of voters in polling places (Stone, 1994) may result in a growth management-issue resolution that displeases "that suspect band of bankers, builders, and bureaucrats" (*GEO Journal,* 1990, p. 2).

The Influence of the Ethics of the Moment: Increased Democratic Participation

Coleman (1974) states that citizens can change their sense of reduced spheres of influence. To regain a sense of control, he advises the citizen "to withdraw, to reduce the scope of one's horizons . . . to limit one's interest in and attention to those events that are very near at hand" (p. 53). In other words, citizens should recognize that all politics is local and, to quote bumpersticker philosophy, think globally and act locally. The growth management issue campaign prompted such political action in Sarasota County. Many residents increased their political involvement. Supervisor of elections Joanne Koester attributed the charter amendment campaign for the addition of "more than 20,000 people to the voting roles" (Zaloudek, 1990b, p. 8A) as well as a record 57 percent of registered voters who turned out for the primary election

(Loverude and Sams, 1990, p. 1A). This initial participation may lead to increased democratic participation through election attendance and through new candidates for local government offices. In addition, all incumbent county commissioners lost their bids for reelection; three new commissioners took office. Although this result could be related to the general discontent among the American electorate during 1990 (Gibbs, 1990), it also could be linked to the GEO campaign that illuminated discrepancies and improprieties in commissioners' policy decisions. Regardless, the ethics of the moment constructed through the competing public relations campaigns stimulated increased interest and participation in local government. Similarly, MacIntyre (1984) writes,

> What matters at this point is the construction of local forms of community within which civility and the intellectual and moral life can be sustained through the new d?rk ages which are already upon us. . . . The barbarians are not waiting beyond the frontiers; they have already been governing us for some time. And it is our lack of consciousness of this that constitutes part of our predicament. (p. 263)

The barbarians that govern us are the mass media that provide us with more information that we would ever want to know. Postman (1988) argues that the mass media have helped to construct a new idea of intelligence, that values "knowing *of* lots of things, not knowing *about* them" (1988, p. 14). He also posits that television is a "'meta-medium,' an instrument that not only directs our knowledge of the world, but our knowledge of *ways of knowing* as well" (pp. 78–79). Our contemporary barbarism, then, is not necessarily individuals, but our lack of acknowledgment that the mass media have shaped our contemporary rhetorical and ethical practices. The way to civilize the barbarians is, as Coleman recommends, to focus again on the local level and to reestablish community ties.

The growth management issue in Sarasota County illuminates three ideas. First, the inventions of the twentieth century have changed the human American experience significantly. It is only recently that we have begun to acknowledge the influences of those inventions on our lives and how our experiences are changed. Second, after a generation of preoccupation with presidential elections and avoidance of civic government, citizens are refocusing on the policy process in their hometowns. Third, public relations rhetoric creates an ethics of the moment by which individuals make decisions regarding an issue.

Individual citizens are rediscovering that all politics are local and that growth management issues never die, they just re-emerge.

NOTES

1. Survey conducted by the University of South Florida, December 7–10, 1990, for The New York Times Group regional newspapers. Margin of error, 4 percent.

2. Survey conducted by the University of South Florida, August 17–18, 1990, for the *Sarasota Herald-Tribune*. Margin of error, 4 percent.

PART VI
Future Directions

15

Critical Theory in Public Relations Inquiry

Future Directions for Analysis
in a Public Relations Context

Kathleen M. German

The practice of contemporary rhetorical criticism reflects its grounding in social formations (Ehninger, 1968); critical theory extends this orientation. In spite of the density of original writings and the complexity of fundamental concepts, critical theory increasingly informs investigation into communication as a social activity, adding to our understanding of cultural phenomena. The aim of the critical theory is to comprehend the formations of social culture by examining communication.

To the extent that public relations contributes to social formations through communicated messages, it can be explored with the critical theory perspective. We may come to terms with the rhetoric of organizations by adapting the critical theory model of public dialogue. It raises challenging questions of authorship, intent, audience, and responsibility. Most important, in an age of unequal access to channels of mediated public communication, it also addresses the problem of individuals engaging organizations in public debate. This essay first establishes the basic tenets of critical theory, then applies it to some of the case studies presented in this book, and, finally, offers suggestions for future investigation.

WHAT IS CRITICAL THEORY?

In brief, critical theory stimulates reflection on human society in order to discover how people should live. Its aim is to liberate thought and action by assisting members of society to expose and surmount the forms of individual, social, and political domination that constrain them (Burleson and Kline, 1979). The means to liberating thought is examining speech acts to determine how domination occurs.

Jurgen Habermas (1974), a key figure in the development of critical theory, identifies the public sphere as the arena where individuals come together to examine the affairs of the community. In the sense of an old-fashioned marketplace or public forum, we gather to engage in public dialogue. Directing attention to this dialogue may help us understand not only what is happening, but also who we are in relationship to those events. This close examination of our communication combats "one dimensional consciousness," or the acceptance of the existing social order as defining the limits of our rationality.

Distortions in the public dialogue prompted by unequal distributions of power, information, or access to organizational voices skew the dialogue and strengthen domination. It is not surprising that Habermas (1974) identifies public relations as one of the factors contributing to the false consciousness of modern society. Along with mass media, advertising, and corporate control of culture, public relations has tilted the balance of power dramatically, displacing rational individuals as the major sociopolitical force (Best and Kellner, 1991). Critical theory's ambition is to expose these distortions, or false consciousness, thereby ending the domination of the corporate voice in the public sphere. Scrutiny of the public dialogue, including public relations messages, is central to critical theory.

Does Critical Theory Fit Public Relations?

To maintain its social, economic, or political image, an organization must address ideas and issues to a public. That public is normally defined in response to the interests of the organization. That is, organizations solicit their publics for communication. In this sense, such messages can never be neutral but must depend on relationships cultivated by the organization. This relationship function of public relations messages has been widely recognized. Typical of others, Cutlip, Center, and Broom (1985) summarize the function of public relations as a relationship: "Public relations is the management function that identifies, establishes, and maintains mutually beneficial relationships between an organization and the various publics on whom its success and failure depends" (p. 4). While some may argue with the judgment that such relationships are mutually beneficial, the focus on the establishment of relationships is central. Such definitions focusing on relationships are echoed by many public relations specialists (see, e.g., Baskin and Aronoff, 1988; Grunig and Hunt, 1984; Newsom, Scott, and Turk, 1993; Seitel, 1992; Simon, 1984). So, to the extent that public relations depends on relationships developed through messages, it is open to the judgments of critical theory.

What Are the Tenets of Critical Theory?

Habermas's ultimate goal is to construct a theoretical perspective that takes into consideration the communication processes that lead to social consensus on values. For him, social values are the cement of society; we must be cognizant of how public communication contributes to the erection and maintenance of these values. Habermas's ultimate ambition is to bring about cognitive evolution resulting in major improvement in the human condition (Wuthnow, Hunter, Bergesen, and Kurzeil, 1984). While some doubt the practicality of this goal, the process offers a framework for examining the social value structure built through public dialogue (Crespi, 1987; Huspek, 1991; Pasewark, 1986).

To examine social values we must raise them to the level of consciousness. Only then is it possible to subject these implicit agreements to critique. Naturally, Habermas is keenly interested in the process of communication because, for him, communication gives explicit, behavioral content to these implicit understandings. Adapting the works of Wittgenstein, Searle, and Austin, Habermas highlights the speech acts that constitute communication.

In particular, speech acts offer clues about subjective meanings. They convey messages about the patterns of culture based on fundamental values that organize thought and social interaction (Habermas, 1979). The values by which we select how to live, how to design our cities, how to govern ourselves, and even how to interact are all embedded in our speech acts. If we understand the implicit assumptions that frame our communication about such social priorities, then we can make more informed choices. The unexamined society lets implicit assumptions, rooted largely in prevailing social values, dictate the choice of social priorities. Aware of the web of values surrounding us, we can progress toward a higher stage of cultural evolution. This is done by raising the values located in messages to the status of observable objects, which then become the focus of reflection and criticism. In many ways, this process is fundamentally that of rhetorical criticism.

Before we can investigate how Habermas proposes to critique culture, we should understand the central role of communication in the process of culture building (Habermas, 1994). Communication legitimizes social norms, conveys facts about the world, and renders human interaction possible. It is both the creator of culture and the evidence of its creation. As such, communication contributes to value building because it is infused with the assumptions of such values. By analyzing the generalized or universal properties built into communication, the critic comes to understand the meanings generated among individuals. The critic's goal is to discover more effective ways to communicate about collective concerns. The results contribute to the capacity of individuals to engage in self-reflection and effective communication (Best and Kellner, 1991; Held, 1980; McKerrow, 1989).

Habermas distinguishes between two fundamental uses of language in communication. The *rational-purposive* function of language is instrumental (much like Aristotle's notion of "techne"). It is used to manipulate and transform the environment (Habermas, 1979). The physical world, including other people, is treated as a means to an end. Rational-purposive speech behavior is primarily concerned with organizing people's relations with the material world in an instrumental way.

Briefly stated, such communication is designed to get people to do things. In Habermas's view, this function of communication is distorted. Its source is the pervasive influence of science and technology; the communication in these two realms is systematically ruled by rational-purposive language (Habermas, 1970). Science and technology invade every aspect of modern society, promoting economic growth through the manipulation of physical and social environments while paying no attention to self-conscious reflection about social values.

Since science and technology have become the dominant institutions, they have increasingly subverted traditional social institutions such as family and religion, infecting them with rational-purposive thinking. In this process, our attitudes toward science and technology have changed as well; science and technology have become part of the external world of nature, a world over which humans have no control. Science and technology are no longer the products of human ingenuity or decision making. This change renders objective and uncontrollable something that should be subject to collective decision making. In sum, science and technology rule human thought rather than the reverse. Communication in the public sphere then partakes of rational-purposive speech behavior, mimicking the worlds of science and technology. To the extent that it does, humans are rendered powerless; family and religious values are replaced by those of the rational-purposive domain. We are victimized by our technology. It acts upon us, rather than us acting within it.

The superior function of language Habermas labels *communicative action* (similar to Aristotle's use of "praxis"). This phrase suggests a web of intersubjective relationships among people that makes possible both individuality and mutual dependence. Human interaction creates reciprocal expectations and establishes a framework that allows us to live as members of collective social institutions. It is on this basis that social values ought to be derived and internalized.

In its relationship to the material world, communicative action is involved with the distribution of production. However, it differs from rational-purposive uses of language because communicative action takes into account collective goals. This assumes that individuals are able to truthfully and sincerely express their intentions to others. It also assumes that communication accurately expresses the consensus that exists among people concerning the norms of communication. Systematically distorted communication is for Habermas and other critical theorists the same as false consciousness was for Marx. It prevents the resolution of major social crises.

In order to assess the functioning of language, the critical theorist must reconstruct the prevailing understandings that are shared among individuals but are taken for granted by those individuals. This requires knowledge of the rules by which meaning is constructed within situations (Benjamin, 1976). Habermas and others concede that it is probably impossible to construct universal laws for every communication situation. However, finite categories can be generated based on shared characteristics among situations.

Because communication is central in constructing culture, critical theory examines communication to discover the rules by which we create meaning. Habermas narrows the focus on communication to a specific vocabulary winnowed from speech-act theory. By pointing to specific speech acts and their implied values, he hopes to raise the level of consciousness from rational-purposive action to communicative action.

Speech-act theory recognizes structure or sets of communication rules that reveal universal patterns; these patterns are largely implicit. World views, self-concepts, patterns of moral reasoning, norms of legality, and patterns of legitimation form primary structures or sets of rules. Such speech acts express content and situate that content within a particular relational context that allows for all participants to elicit meaning. Habermas (1976) adapts the distinction between propositional (illocutionary or relationship) speech acts to suggest what is occurring in utterances. To further refine the performative dimension of the speech act, he delineates additional relationship functions, including the relationship of speaker to hearer, the relationship of speaker to medium of the utterance, and the relationship between the speaker's utterance and internal subjectivity. These relationship functions will be illustrated in the next section by putting the case studies in this volume within the framework of critical theory.

To summarize, all public communication is derived from the basic model of dialogue that not only establishes information (its locutionary or propositional function) but also who we are in relationship to that information (its illocutionary or performative function). For the critical theorist, entry into public communication imposes demands on participants; they must consider the propositional as well as the performative function of their messages. In addition to these responsibilities, spokespersons for organizations, including public relations practitioners, have an impact beyond making a profit; they create culture. As a result, public relations does not just contribute messages and products to the public dialogue, but it also creates relationships that hold consequences for the evolution of society. We can investigate those relationships by asking about the legitimation created by public relations messages, the relationship of the receivers to the organization, the power of all participants to enter equally into the dialogue, and even the relationship of the spokesperson to the organization.

WHAT APPLICATIONS OF CRITICAL THEORY CAN BE MADE?

Habermas charges public relations messages with contributing to the distortion of society. In order to discover how public relations messages have encouraged this distortion, we must direct our attention beyond the content of the messages to the relationships established between the communicator and the public to the performative functions of the message. We can begin with the cases offered in this volume, examining each of them through the lens of critical theory. This perspective may expose the false consciousness and may offer some common features for future investigations. In particular, we will focus on the relationship of the organization to its public, the distribution of power, the use of rational-purposive thinking and the values endorsed in the organization's message.

Richard E. Crable and Steven L. Vibbert feature Mobil Oil's epideictic advocacy aimed at Sunday newspaper readers in a format designed to empower them rather than "the power brokers of public policy." Mobil Oil is portrayed as the victim, vicariously identifying with the lives of its readers. The corporation associates itself with values, such as truth, fair play, free enterprise, and the American dream: "The messages are short, casual, almost offhand, and yet they merge with the American value system." As Crable and Vibbert suggest, the Sunday newspaper format may mask the true purpose of the messages, which is to allow the building of premises for future arguments.

Crable and Vibbert also observe that six major issues are treated, but with no consistent pattern. The propositional content of the messages is not as revealing as the performative content where readers are invited to participate through contests, features, and shared values. The relationships established through the performative content are fused by the social values of family life, Sunday leisure, and the American dream. What Crable and Vibbert label the alliance between Mobil and its readers is a message developed at the performative level. The implications of the relationship are profound. The responsibility for advocacy on behalf of Mobil Oil is shifted to its readers. At the performative level, Mobil Oil becomes part of their constellation of values as they form a partnership, instilling loyalty that can be tapped in the future. Thus, "the seeming collage of offhand and breezy items" is up to something completely different at the performative level. Critical theory would point to the performative message as the central one.

Beyond this, a further revelation is that Mobil Oil's communication is instrumental; it is designed to get people to do things. The rational-purposive nature of its public statements does not contribute to the evolution of communication. Instead, it further entrenches the stranglehold of technological thinking. Through its communication, Mobil Oil affected public perception and fortified the voice of big oil.

Another way to conceptualize the reliance on rational-purposive thinking is to consider the basic inconsistency of the message. Mobil Oil becomes the voice of big oil, yet also presents itself as the voice of the meek. In addition, Mobil misstates its case. The end result cannot be communicative action, because as Habermas (1994) notes, "In situations of concealed strategic action, at least one of the parties behaves with an orientation to success, but leaves others to believe that all the presuppositions of communicative actions are satisfied" (p. 216). The long-term cultural implication of this deception is to reinforce rational-purposive communication.

Keith Michael Hearit investigates instances where corporations act in ways that are incongruent with social values and subsequently attempt to reestablish their social legitimacy through apologia (Allen and Caillouet, 1994). Like Crable and Vibbert, Hearit suggests that corporations use rhetoric rooted in values that resonate for targeted publics. He identifies the common values and dissociation tactics in the apologia messages, testing whether corporate apologia conform to the characteristics of individual apologia. Perhaps another way to appraise this inquiry is to investigate the corporate voice disguised as the voice of an individual. It is apparent that the corporation offers social legitimacy at both the propositional and performative levels. Hearit finds corporate messages addressing the issues of competency, the ability to function effectively in the economic arena, or the propositional dimension of the message. The corporation also establishes a relationship with the community by speaking as an individual defending its actions. Thus, the corporation creates a performative dimension of communication.

The messages are framed within the values of honesty, responsibility, and self-control. These assume that corporations, like individuals, are subject to similar standards of honesty, responsibility, and self-control. Upon reflection, the comparison is untenable. The corporate messages imply that the relationship of the corporation to the public good is the same as any individual's responsibility would be, no more—in spite of the huge differences in power and impact, to say nothing of the fact that corporations are not human.

Another inherent contradiction occurs in these apologia messages. While the corporation seeks social legitimacy, it does not need it. In fact, as Hearit claims, there is no real connection between organizational decline and undermined social legitimacy. This basic contradiction discloses that the public communication is occurring within an unequal power base—corporations have power and simply seek recognition of it from their publics.

Critical theory provides the framework for asking why the corporation is personified in moments of crisis. Corporations shift their images from impersonal giants of technology to those of individual citizens under duress. Perhaps the standards for accountability change as the corporate voice becomes that of an individual. If the corporation fails in its attempts to regain social legitimacy, it may suffer only public antipathy on an interpersonal level rather than on political or economic sanctions. Some scholars have suggested that corporations exploit the strategies employed by individuals by posing as individuals on a consistent basis (Toth and Heath, 1992). How does this voice of the corporation-as-person affect the nature of the public dialogue? Answering these questions about the performative dimensions of communication may reveal more fully the extent to which corporate rhetoric legitimizes the capitalistic economic system. Hearit suggests that corporate apologia differ from individual apologia in the areas of competence and rhetorical resources. Perhaps this is a clear admission of the hidden value of capitalism at work in public relations messages.

Jamie Press Lacey and John T. Llewellyn observe media's role in defining the Alar controversy, suggesting that media are powerful speakers whose voices are often hidden behind "the facts." The mediated voice tells us what facts are and who we are in relation to those facts. Like corporations, media contribute enormously to the maintenance of social values and therefore demand our critical attention (Heck, 1980; White, 1987).

The appearance of facticity in mediated messages hints at the rational-purposive language of science and technology. Even more central is the contradiction between science as the protector of public health and the media message that casts the public into the role of protector. Clearly, this message is rooted in the American value system, stressing the individual's triumph over government bureaucracy. However, the public is merely the facilitator of the action; science remains the true source of the message. This contradiction points to the false consciousness reinforced by the message.

Lacey and Llewellyn illuminate the centrality of definitions of "risk" in the Alar controversy. They identify the roles of characters in the risk controversy—victims, perpetrators, protectors—and trace these roles to the language of the messages. It seems as though, veiled in the language of facticity, the messages contain potent performative dimensions, especially when fear of "the world" is induced through expressive language. The fundamental deception is that we assume we are operating rationally when we are not. Further investigation might reveal that the narrative structure snares the receiver in role-associated actions or, as Habermas (1994) puts it, in "a normative bond that obliges him to act in a certain way" (p. 204). One might also ask how the narrative structure resonates against the fabric of social values spinning out an ideology.

Jeffrey L. Courtright studies a series of advertisements featuring the Church of Scientology. These advertisements pit L. Ron Hubbard against the "Merchants of Chaos." As Courtright suggests, the struggle can be seen as an epic story of good versus evil if one accepts Hubbard as the epic hero. The epic frame also creates a relationship to the reader on the performative level as readers participate in the narrative.

The performative level of the messages works if the reader accepts the implicit relationship. That is, the reader must recognize the worth of Hubbard as the hero. Once this assumption is accepted, then the testimonials from members of the Church of Scientology gain meaning. However, their meaning revolves around the hero. They participate, not as part of the heroic persona, but as observers of the epic tale. While the message encourages them to think that as humans they have unlimited potential, the message also implies that they are subordinate to Hubbard. Their worth, in reality, is derivative of his heroism. While they can share in the glory of the hero, they are not heroic themselves. Thus, the freedom promised by Scientology is realized only through discipleship, an inherent contradiction that is revealed at the relationship level of the message.

Patricia Paystrup looks at the controversy over plastics recycling in which a loose coalition of grass roots groups oppose businesses. A key element in this public relations campaign is the role of definition. Is plastic a natural resource? Or, is it an environmental threat? Each definition has implications for how one should be involved in the controversy; each exerts definitional hegemony over the issues arising in the controversy (Dionisopoulos and Crable, 1988). And, each definition implies a relationship between the individual and the world, bringing with it responsibilities and obligations. In this light, the propositional level of definitions determines the performative level of relationships.

In another mutation, the redefinition of plastic as a natural resource aligns economic and environmental concerns, two previously contradictory ideas. The critical theorist might suggest that this realignment disguises rational-purposive communication, allowing technological thinking to dominate. In addition, the public relations messages reinforce the values of the technological-scientific world (e.g., plastic lumber is better than wood).

Another issue developed by Paystrup is the reactive versus adaptive responses of corporations to public opposition. What does the approach tell us about the social construction of values and about the relationship of the corporation to the medium? The reactive messages dispute facts of solid waste disposal. The adaptive messages, however, reclassify plastics as recyclables, aligning them with natural products; they merge the technological and the natural worlds. This new identity for plastics also alters the relationship between audience and object. It changes the fundamental issues by placing the responsibility for the landfill crisis on the consumer rather than the producer. The question moves from "Should corporations produce plastic packaging?" to "Will you recycle it?" Such messages are aimed at getting people to recycle while completely ignoring any questions about changing packaging. In this case, the values of the scientific and technological world have prevailed over other values.

Mitchell S. McKinney establishes a critical theory perspective arguing for a critical-rhetorical approach to locate false consensus and its mode of construction. He examines the orientation process by which new employees at Midwest Pharmaceutical learn the values and norms of the organizational culture. In this case, the public relations messages are aimed at an internal public, seeking to fit newcomers into their new environment. Several features of the videotaped public relations message stand out. The company founder and company facilities dominate the videotape. The result is that the new employee is distanced from the company; technology is valued over people. The critical theorist would suggest that the performatic dimension of the message reveals these relationships. The new employees roles are defined for them in the verbal message emphasizing the products and the visual messages of gloved workers' hands. These messages contribute to rational-purposive thinking, which reinforces the reign of technology. The value structure revealed in the videotape is clearly technological; the facilities dominate the technicians.

Critical theorists would probably view this rational-purposive language as a weakness of the message just as McKinney does. However, their reasons are different. McKinney evaluates the videotape as failed communication because it does not establish identification with new employees. But, the message reveals a clear relationship of the new employee to the organization; in this respect, the message works well. The problem is that it works through rational-purposive language. It reinforces values that subordinate people to products and humanity to technology. An interesting contradiction in the message highlights the problem. Midwest Pharmaceutical pits itself as an underdog against giant pharmaceutical companies, yet Midwest values greater size and growth in its own facilities and product lines. It argues both sides of the same value. On one hand, Midwest is the little company calling for fair play. On the other, Midwest values its own size.

Jeffrey P. Joiner and Kathleen M. German investigate the 1991 Cincinnati Public School levy campaign in order to discover what contributed to its success. The unique features of ballot issue campaigns are explained and applied to the 1991 levy. The components of organization, activation, and issue development are isolated. In each case, the inherent problems of ballot issue campaigns are discussed and the strategies used to surmount them are identified. The focus remains at the propositional level of the messages.

The performative level of the messages may offer additional insight. It appears that the extent to which voters recognized their relationship to the problems of the school district determined their commitment to the ballot levy. This is particularly obvious in two areas. As school superintendent, J. Michael Brandt ran more like a candidate than as a spokesperson for the campaign. He opposed the former school superintendent as though she were an opponent, and Brandt spoke like a candidate in televised advertisements.

In addition, there were voters who held no stake in the public schools, such as the parents of parochial school children and childless voters. The messages still held appeal for these people. The relationship implied by the messages was that somehow these people also had a stake in the quality of the school district. Specific audience targeting and selective language strategies encouraged such relationships and, in turn, cultivated votes. The underlying value in the entire campaign, especially evident in the endorsements by the coalition of local businesses, was the utility of schools as an extension of the economic structure.

William N. Elwood's rhetorical study of political action poses ethical questions surrounding the 1990 primary election in Sarasota County, Florida. The conflict centers on county development and establishes a dialogue in which opponents seem evenly matched. Elwood argues that the dialogue is skewed because the identity of one participant is concealed. In other words, the author's identity constitutes a false relationship with the receiver and that relationship influences the receiver's perception of the message. To the extent that corporate powers unite but adopt a "just like you" or grass roots identity, they are distorting the dialogue with a hypothetical identity. For example, use of the first person pronoun and pictures of pathetic children on posters in the corporate messages reinforce this personal identity and misdirected the receivers. Florida voters are encouraged to view the communication as occurring between equal participants. In reality, they are eavesdropping on a conversation between an illusory identity established for high corporate sponsorship and an underfunded grass roots organization. The balance of power appears equal but it is not; business interests dominate this public debate.

It appears that corporations are protecting their interests by adopting the values and voice of the public. In this case, technological communication poses as communicative action. This deception brings the critic back to the questions about corporate voice raised by Hearit. Although the circumstances are somewhat different, the corporate coalition is using the identity of an individual. It represents itself as human and asks for evaluation of its position on the same terms used for evaluating human actions.

For the most part, these case studies focus on the propositional content of public relations messages. Critical theory offers an expanded perspective that isolates the assumptions about relationships created by the messages. Even though brief, this review found several common themes in these public relations messages. They align the corporation with the public through redefinition, disguise unequal power distribution, reinforce rational-purposive thinking, and play on values that are contradictory within the same message. Ultimately, the critical theorist must question whether the conditions for dialogue exist in these communication situations.

What Are Further Applications of Critical Theory?

Public relations practitioners are in the business of producing relationships with publics through the manipulation of symbols. They seek to locate the individual receiver within a managed frame of reference. In other words, public relations has an architectonic function; it helps shape how various publics see their worlds (Cheney and Dionisopoulos, 1989; McKeon, 1971). Critical theory offers a way to explore this function of messages elevating assumptions for critique. In addition to the applications already made, we can explore the role of truth, the individual, and power in public discourse.

Some current scholarship on public relations examines the tension created as public relations practitioners are caught between the demands of their conflicting roles (Acharya, 1985; Cheney, 1992; Ettema and Glasser, 1987; Grunig, 1989b; Pearson, 1989b; Ryan, 1987). Often, the underlying problem is that public messages circumvent the "cooperative readiness to arrive at an understanding" (Burleson and Kline, 1979, p. 421). Communicative action that depends on the open exchange of arguments wherein the satisfactory conclusion is decided by the prevalence of the better argument is supplanted by coercion or misrepresentation. One test for communicative action is to determine the extent a message promotes the participation of the public or contributes to the ability of the public to offer independent arguments. If the message promotes the construction of the free exchange of arguments or the conditions of rationally motivated consensus on which the freedom to examine arguments lies, then it contains the fundamental opportunity for truth. If the message functions to constrict audience participation, then it lacks truth, since it exploits unexamined social values such as those of science and technbology. As Rorty (1982) has proposed, the ultimate test of truth in discourse resides in how a message works for or on a particular audience.

Another basic concern is the role of the individual in public communication. The individual seems to have become an extension of the corporation as public relations messages subsume heterogeneous listeners into targeted "publics." Individuals assume a common identity through their relationship to the message. The problem in this collective identity is that it subsumes and thereby devalues the individual by emphasizing the group. This shift of emphasis places responsibility on corporations and groups. Individual accountability for choice is lost because the individual is no longer part of the relationship. To improve the quality of the public dialogue, the individual must be returned to a position of accountability.

In addition, as the critics of culture have noted, whenever one public is defined, others are excluded (Hallin, 1987). Targeting publics privileges some relationships and not others (Wander and Jenkins, 1972; Wander, 1984). Thus, the way the relationship is defined and shaped is as important as the information or arguments advanced in the message. In the framework of critical theory, the performative content must be explored to discover its effect on the propositional content of the message. What is not said about the relationship can be as important as what is said. What is not said may reveal what is assumed, who holds power, and which social values are endorsed.

The ultimate question posed by critical theory addresses the balance of power in public dialogue. When corporations engage in public communication, it is monologue. The resources available to corporations, as demonstrated in many of the essays in this volume, far outweigh those available to individuals, even if they join together to express alternate viewpoints. Critical theorists envision an evolution in public communication that restores the balance of power and assures mutual respect as the key to relationships among audiences. Through critical theory, we redress the imbalances that prevent the free public exchange of ideas. At the very least, as a first step, critical theory recognizes the imbalance and attempts to rectify it.

We expect, perhaps naively, our spokespersons to work in our best interests when they seek power over us. McGee and Martin (1983) argue from the example of public servants, such as government officials, that this is an inherently contradictory idea. In a similar fashion, it makes little sense that public relations practitioners who have a similarly dual role will always adhere to the higher standard of reinforcing social values that are in the best interests of the public. It may even be unrealistic to assume that public relations practitioners know what is in the public interest. The responsibility for discovering what is best for all of us depends on everyone contributing to the public dialogue.

Ultimately, public relations is based on a will to power. Public relations messages reflect the interests of the dominant powers, which in our society are entrenched political and financial interests. The goal of public relations is most often the protection of that power base, and to that end it may take the form of image manipulation, crisis management, political influence, or financial gain. Whatever the means, the goal remains relatively constant. Public relations messages are grounded in the economic values of the corporation. Critical theory recognizes the existence of powerful motivations that support the vested interests of capitalism. They are revealed most decisively in crisis situations when competing viewpoints demand responses (Wander, 1981). We can use the critical theory perspective to expose the values of the corporation by examining the message relationships it attempts to create. When such performative content is uncovered, individuals are in a better position to formulate their responses. In the long term, as critics, we are responsible for an evolution in the nature of the public dialogue; we must participate in our own emancipation.

CONCLUSIONS

Habermas's critical theory establishes a comprehensive framework for the study of communication processes and phenomena. It evaluates the politically constraining and dominating ideologies of our culture by weighing the truth of the rhetor's claims. Initially, critical theory discovers the elements of discourse and their role in inhibiting or allowing freedom of argument among speakers. Understanding the forms of knowledge produced through public debate or discourse helps us to clarify our duties, responsibilities, and obligations in public communication. It also demonstrates that the validity of argument is a function of the quality of the argumentative transaction or the relationship between speech acts and the form of social interaction in which people engage.

Critical theory offers a way to examine the unconscious dimensions of messages. One such dimension is how the communication encourages the audience to see itself (Black, 1970; Ong, 1975). In order to discover the role created for the audience in the message, critical theory encourages us to look to the discourse for clues about who is speaking, what roles are implied for the listener, and what values are assumed. Public relations messages tell us not only who is talking and what has happened, but who we are in relationship to these things. The critic is encouraged to look beyond the propositional content to the performative dimensions of the message.

With critical theory, you may have noticed a return to the Greek ideal where understanding the rhetorical creation of relationships is vital to the education and well-being of all responsible citizens. This ideal has significant implications for all forms of public advocacy, including the practice of public relations. Critical theory calls for a paradigm shift beginning with the way we engage each other in public debate. It has raised intense debate among postmodern critics over issues such as evolutionary ideal, the nature of culture, the values of modernity, and the rationality of human experience. The intensity of the debate itself may partially reassure critical theorists that we are evolving toward a more ideal speech situation that includes a myriad of voices.

References

AApology. (1991, January 8). *The New York Times,* p. A5.

Acharya, L. (1985). Public relations environments. *Journalism Quarterly, 62,* 577–584.

Adams, H., ed. (1971). *Critical theory since Plato.* New York: Harcourt, Brace, Jovanovich.

Aldington, R., and Ames, D. (1974). *New Larousse encyclopedia of mythology, Ninth impression.* New York: Hamlyn Publishing Group Ltd.

Alexander, L. D., and Matthews, W. F. (1984). The ten commandments of corporate social responsibility. *Business and Society Review, 50,* 62–66.

Alinsky, S. D. (1971). *Rules for radicals: A practical primer for realistic radicals.* New York: Random House.

Allen: "Reached an impasse." (1990, December 3). *The Dayton Daily News,* p. 10A.

Allen, M. W., and Caillouet, R. H. (1994). Legitimation endeavors: Impression management strategies used by an organization in crisis. *Communication Monographs, 61,* 44–62.

Allen, P. (1989a, February 27). *NRDC releases report showing children at risk from pesticides.* Available from National Resources Defense Council (NRDC), 1350 New York Ave., Washington, DC 20005.

Allen, P. (1989b, February 27). *NRDC will sue E.P.A. for failure to protect children.* Available from NRDC, 1350 New York Ave., Washington, DC 20005.

Allen, P. (1989c, March 7). *NRDC launches a national campaign to protect children against pesticides in food.* Available from NRDC, 1350 New York Ave., Washington, DC 20005.

Allen, R. N. (1985, January/February). From our members [letter to the editor]. *SANE World, 24,* 2.

Alvesson, M. (1990). Organization: From substance to image? *Organization Studies, 11,* 373–394.

American Airlines says pilots are staging sickout. (1990, December 26). *The Wall Street Journal*, p. A3.

American Plastics Council. (1992a). How to save the planet and the picnic at the same time. Print advertisement.

American Plastics Council. (1992b). Some benefits of plastic last for only half a second. Print advertisement.

American Plastics Council. (1992c). Your new carpeting may already be in your refrigerator. Print advertisement.

Amoco. (1989a). Do we really want to return to those good, old-fashioned days before plastics? Print advertisement.

Amoco. (1989b). Let's dig a little deeper into the notion that much of our garbage is made up of plastics. Print advertisement.

Amoco. (1989c). We'd like to uncover a hidden natural resource. Print advertisement.

Amoco. (1990). We'd like to recycle the thinking that plastics can't be recycled. Print advertisement.

An open letter to the citizens of Sarasota County. (1990, August 15, September 1). Full-page advertisement placed in *Sarasota Herald-Tribune*.

Ansoff, I. (1980). Strategic issue management. *Strategic Management Journal, 1,* 131–148.

Apoxsee: The revised and updated Sarasota County comprehensive plan. (1990). Sarasota, FL: Sarasota County Planning Department.

Apple growers asserted. (1989, May 16). *The Wall Street Journal*, p. A1.

Aristotle. (1953). *The ethics of Aristotle: The Nicomachean ethics translated* (J. A. K. Thomson, trans.). Middlesex, UK: Penguin Books Ltd.

Aristotle. (1991). *On rhetoric: A theory of civic discourse* (G. A. Kennedy, trans.). New York: Oxford University Press.

Arnaut, G. (1991, July). NCR, AT&T computer systems announce converged product line. *ComputerData*, pp. 1, 13.

Arnett, R. C. (1992). *Dialogic education: Conversations about ideas and between persons.* Carbondale, IL: Southern Illinois University Press.

AT&T actions mirror Saddam's [letter to the editor]. (1991, March 8). *The Dayton Daily News*, p. 7A.

AT&T asks court to rule NCR stock plan invalid. (1991, March 6). *The Dayton Daily News*, p. 1A.

AT&T bets computer business on NCR takeover. (1990, December 10). *Computerworld*, p. 1.

AT&T bid smacks windfall for many NCR stockholders. (1991, March 10). *The Dayton Daily News*, p. 1A.

AT&T goes after NCR. (1990, December 3). *The Dayton Daily News*, p. 1A.

AT&T launches $6.12 billion cash offer for NCR after rejection of its stock bid. (1990, December 3). *The Wall Street Journal*, p. 3A.

AT&T offering incentives to staff at computer unit. (1990, March 1). *The Wall Street Journal*, p. 3B.

AT&T plays big cards against NCR. (1991, January 17). *The Dayton Daily News*, p. 1B.

AT&T readies hostile NCR bid. (1990, December 4). *The Wall Street Journal*, p. 2A.

AT&T sends new NCR proxies to shareholders. (1991, March 5). *The Dayton Daily News*, p. 1A.

AT&T/NCR make their stands. (1990, December 17). *Computerworld,* p. 6.

Baker, B. (1982, February). The great escape: Civil Defense in the 80s. *SANE/World, 21,* pp. 1–2.

Balutis, A. P. (1976). Congress, the president, and the press. *Journalism Quarterly, 53,* 509–515.

Banach, W. J. (1986, Summer). Here's to the winners. *Tennessee School Boards Journal,* 18–23.

Barker, P. (1991, May 23). Buyout could carve up AT&T Canada. *Computing Canada,* pp. 1, 6.

Barnouw, E. (1985). *Tube of plenty: The evolution of American television.* New York: Oxford University Press.

Baskin, O. W., and Aronoff, C. E. (1992). *Public relations: The profession and the practice* (2nd ed.). Dubuque, IA: Wm. C. Brown Publishers.

Bateman, D. N. (1975). Corporate communications of advocacy: Practical perspectives and procedures. *Journal of Business Communication, 13,* 3–11.

Because you care. (n.d.). GEO promotional brochure.

Behar, R. (1986, October 27). The prophet and profits of Scientology. *Forbes,* p. 314.

Behar, R. (1991, May 6). The thriving cult of greed and power. *Time,* pp. 50–57.

Beniger, J. R., and Westney, D. E. (1981). Japanese and U.S. media: Graphics as a reflection of newspapers' social roles. *Journal of Communication, 31,* 14–27.

Benjamin, J. (1976). Performatives as a rhetorical construct. *Philosophy and Rhetoric, 9,* 84–95.

Bennett, W. L. (1975). Political scenarios and the nature of politics. *Philosophy and Rhetoric, 8,* 23–42.

Benoit, W. L., and Brinson, S. L. (1994). AT&T: Apologies are not enough. *Communication Quarterly, 42,* 75-88.

Benson, J. A. (1988). Crisis revisited: An analysis of strategies used by Tylenol in the second tampering episode. *Central States Speech Journal, 39,* 49–66.

Berg, D. M. (1972). Rhetoric, reality, and mass media. *Quarterly Journal of Speech, 58,* 255–263.

Berger, P. L., and Luckmann, T. (1966). *The social construction of reality: A treatise in the sociology of knowledge.* New York: Anchor Books.

Bernays, E. L. (1923). *Crystallizing public opinion.* New York: Boni and Liveright.

Bernays, E. L. (1928). *Propaganda.* New York: Horace Liveright, Inc.

Bernays, E. L. (1952). *Public relations.* Norman, OK: University of Oklahoma Press.

Bernays, E. L. (1965). *Biography of an idea: Memoirs of public relations counsel Edward L. Bernays.* New York: Simon and Schuster.

Bernish, P. (1989, July/August). Fighting a takeover battle in the press. *Across the Board,* pp. 25–28.

Berry, J. M. (1984). *The interest group society.* Boston: Little, Brown.

Best, S., and Kellner, D. (1991). *Postmodern theory.* New York: Guilford Press.

Bitzer, L. (1968). The rhetorical situation. *Philosophy & Rhetoric, 1,* 1–15.

Bivins, T. (1991). *Handbook for public relations writing* (2nd ed.). Lincolnwood, IL: NTC Business Books.

Black, E. (1970). The second persona. *Quarterly Journal of Speech, 56,* 109–119.

Blankenship, J., and Sweeney, B. (1980). The "energy" of form. *Central States Speech Journal, 31,* 172–183.

Blum, A. (1990, October 17). Colleges must eliminate tobacco stocks from their portfolios. *The Chronicle of Higher Education*, p. A56.

Blum, A. (1991, March 28). The Marlboro Grand Prix: Circumvention of the television ban on tobacco advertising. *The New England Journal of Medicine*, p. 913.

Blumberg, L., and Gottlieb, R. (1989). *War on waste.* Washington, DC: Island Press.

Blumer, H. (1979). Symbolic interaction. In L. Budd and B. Rubin, eds., *Interdisciplinary approaches to human communication.* Rochelle Park, NJ: Harden.

Board letter to Bob. (1990, December 7). *The Dayton Daily News*, p. 8A.

Bolles, R. N. (1987). *What color is your parachute? A practical manual for job hunters and career changers.* Berkeley, CA: Ten Speed Press.

Bolles, R. N. (1994). *The 1994 what color is your parachute.* Berkeley, CA: Ten Speed Press.

Booker, E. (1991, September 30). Retiring Exley sees NCR/AT&T synergy. *Computerworld*, p. 6.

Botan, C., and Hazelton, V., eds. (1989). *Public relations theory.* Hillsdale, NJ: Lawrence Erlbaum Associates.

Bovet, S. F. (1993, November). The burning question of ethics: The profession fights for better business practices. *Public Relations Journal*, 24–29.

Bowen, D. E., Ledford, G. E., Jr., and Nathan, B. R. (1991). Hiring for the organization, not the job. *Academy of Management Executive, 5*(4), 35–51.

Boyer, P. (1984, March). From activism to apathy: The American people and nuclear weapons, 1963–1980. *Journal of American History, 70,* 821–844.

Brandt, J. M. (1986). *The Ohio school finance handbook.* Westerville, OH: Ohio School Boards Association.

Brandt, J. M. (1991). *A message from J. Michael Brandt.* A publication of Cincinnatians Active to Support Education.

Broom, G. M., Lauzen, M. M., and Tucker, K. (1991). Dividing the public relations and marketing conceptual domain and operational turf. *Public Relations Review, 17,* 219–226.

Brown, M. H. (1985). That reminds me of a story: Speech action in organizational socialization. *Western Journal of Speech Communication, 49,* 27–42.

Brown, W. R., and Crable, R. E. (1973). Industry, mass magazines, and the ecology issue. *Quarterly Journal of Speech, 59,* 259–272.

Brummett, B. (1976). Some implications of "process" or "intersubjectivity": Postmodern rhetoric. *Philosophy and Rhetoric, 9,* 21–49.

Brummett, B. (1979). A pentadic analysis of ideologies in two gay rights controversies. *Central States Speech Journal, 30,* 250–261.

Brummett, B. (1994). *Rhetoric in popular culture.* New York: St. Martin's Press.

Brush, D. P., and Brush, J. M. (1977). *Private television communications: An awakening giant.* Boston: Herman Publishing, Inc.

Brush, D. P., and Brush, J. M. (1981). *Private television communications: Into the eighties.* New Jersey: International Television Association.

Bryant, D. C. (1953). Rhetoric: Its function and its scope. *Quarterly Journal of Speech, 39,* 401–424.

Buckley, J. T. (1991, May 31). From the hip: Scientologists' ad feud causes rumble (editorial). *USA Today*, p. 13A.

Budget/finance campaigns. (1977). Arlington, VA: National School Public Relations Association.

Buenger, C. L., Chair. (1991). *The Cincinnati business committee task force on public schools: Report & Bulletin,* pp. 1–12.

Burgoon, M. (1989). Instruction about communication: On divorcing Dame Speech. *Communication Education, 38,* 303–308.

Burja, W. (1990, July 18). Personal interview with creator of Moratorium/Great Depression moratorium poster.

Burke, K. (1937). *Attitudes toward history.* New York: The New Republic.

Burke, K. (1942). The study of symbolic action. *Chimera, 1,* 7–16.

Burke, K. (1966). *Language as symbolic action.* Berkeley, CA: University of California Press.

Burke, K. (1968). *Counter-statement.* Berkeley, CA: University of California Press. (Original work published in 1931.)

Burke, K. (1969). *A rhetoric of motives.* Berkeley, CA: University of California Press.

Burke, K. (1973a). *The philosophy of literary form.* Berkeley, CA.: University of California Press. (Original work published in 1941.)

Burke, K. (1973b). The rhetorical situation. In L. Thayer, ed., *Communication: Ethical and moral issues* (pp. 263–275). London: Gordon and Breach.

Burke, K. (1974). *A grammar of motives.* Berkeley, CA: University of California Press.

Burke, K. (1984a). *Attitudes toward history* (3rd ed.). Berkeley, CA: University of California Press.

Burke, K. (1984b). *Permanence and change* (3rd ed.). Berkeley, CA: University of California Press.

Burks, D. M. (1970). Persuasion, self-persuasion, and rhetorical discourse. *Philosophy and Rhetoric, 3,* 109–119.

Burleson, B., and Kline, S. (1979). Habermas' theory of communication: A critical explication. *Quarterly Journal of Speech, 65,* 412–428.

Burns, J. (1992, June 22). New name can sharpen a hospital's image—or diffuse checkered past. *Modern Healthcare,* pp. 76–78.

Butler, S. D. (1972). The apologia, 1971 genre. *Southern Speech Communication Journal, 36,* 281–289.

Butler, D., and Ranney, A. (1978). *Referendums: A comparative study of practice and theory.* Washington, DC: American Institute for Public Policy Research.

Buxton, B. M. (1989, June). Apple prices depressed following apple scare. *Agricultural Outlook,* pp. 16–18.

Caldwell, L. (1989). International environmental politics: America's response to global imperatives. In M. J. Vig and M. E. Kraft, eds., *Environmental policy in the 1990s* (pp. 301–325). Washington, DC: CQ Press.

Callari, J. (1989, September). How did plastics become the target? *Plastics World,* pp. 12–18.

Campbell, G. (1989). *Win at the polls: A finance campaign planner.* Arlington, VA: National School Public Relations Association.

Campbell, K. K. (1982). *The rhetorical act.* Belmont, CA: Wadsworth Publishing Company.

Campbell, K. K., and Jamieson, K. H. (1976). Form and genre in rhetorical criticism: An introduction. In K. K. Campbell and K. H. Jamieson, eds., *Form and genre: Shaping rhetorical action* (pp. 9–32). Falls Church, VA: Speech Communication Association.

Campbell, R. (1991). *60 Minutes and the news*. Urbana: University of Illinois Press.

Carbone, A. (1992, March). Industry and the environment: Making business part of the solution. *USA Today*, pp. 32–34.

Carlin, D. P., and Carlin, J. (1989). A typology of communication functions in ballot issue campaigns. *Political Communication and Persuasion, 6,* 229–248.

Carter, A. (1992). *Peace movements: International protest and world politics since 1945*. London: Longman.

Cartwright, S., and Cooper, C. L. (1992). *Mergers and acquisitions: The human factor*. Oxford: Butterworth-Heinemann.

CASE news release. (1991, November 1).

Castro, J. (1990, June 25). One Big Mac, hold the box! *Time*, p. 44.

Caywood, C., and Ewing, R. (1991). Integrated marketing communications: A new master's degree concept. *Public Relations Review, 17,* 237–244.

CBS News. (1989, February 26). A is for apple. *60 Minutes, 21*(23), 10–14.

Celis, W. (1992, 20 August). Businesslike with business's help, Cincinnati schools shake off crisis. *The New York Times*, p. A14.

Center, A. H., and Jackson, P. (1990). *Public relations practices: Managerial case studies and problems* (4th ed.). Englewood Cliffs, NJ: Prentice Hall.

Chajet, C., and Shachtman, T. (1991). *Image by design: From corporate vision to business reality*. Reading, MA: Addison-Wesley.

Charles, J., Shore, T., and Todd, K. (1979). *The New York Times* coverage of Equatorial and Lower Africa. *Journal of Communication, 29,* 148–155.

Chase, W. H. (n.d.). Issue management conference—A special report. *Corporate Public Issues and Their Management, 7,* 1–2.

Chase, W.H. (1984). *Issues management: Origins of the future*. Stamford, CT: Issues Action Publishing.

Chatman, J. A. (1989). Improving interactional organization research: A model of person-organization fit. *Academy of Management Review, 14,* 333–349.

Cheney, G. (1983). The rhetoric of identification and the study of organizational communication. *Quarterly Journal of Speech, 69,* 143–158.

Cheney, G. (1985). *Speaking of who "we" are: The development of the U.S. Catholic Bishops pastoral letter: The Challenge of Peace as a case study in identity, organization, and rhetoric*. Unpublished Doctoral Dissertation. Purdue University, West Lafayette, IN.

Cheney, G. (1991). *Rhetoric in an organizational society: Managing multiple identities*. Columbia, SC: University of South Carolina Press.

Cheney, G. (1992). The corporate person (re)presents itself. In E. L. Toth and R. L. Heath, eds., *Rhetorical and critical approaches to public relations* (pp. 165–183). Hillsdale, NJ: Lawrence Erlbaum Associates.

Cheney, G., and Dionisopoulos, G. N. (1989). Public relations? No, relations with publics: A rhetorical-organizational approach to contemporary corporate communications. In C. H. Botan and V. Hazleton, Jr., eds., *Public relations theory* (pp. 135-157). Hillsdale, NJ: Lawrence Erlbaum Associates.

Cheney, G., and McMillan, J. J. (1990). Organizational rhetoric and the practice of criticism. *Journal of Applied Communication Research, 18,* 93–114.

Cheney, G., and Tompkins, P. K. (1985). Communication and unobtrusive control in contemporary organizations. In R. McPhee and P. Tompkins, eds., *Organiza-*

tional Communication: Traditional themes and new directions (pp. 179–210). Beverly Hills: Sage Publications.

Cheney, G., and Tompkins, P. K. (1987). Coming to terms with organizational identification and commitment. *Central States Speech Journal, 38*, 1–15.

Cheney, G., and Vibbert, S. L. (1987). Corporate discourse: Public relations and issue management. In F. M. Jablin, L. L. Putnam, K. H. Roberts, and L. W. Porter, eds., *Handbook of organizational communication* (pp. 165–194). Beverly Hills: Sage Publications.

Chuck Exley should have checked with me. (1991, March 31). *The Dayton Daily News*, p. 1F.

Church of Scientology International (1991a, May 28). What magazine gets it wrong in 1991? (advertisement). *USA Today*, p. 11A.

Church of Scientology International (1991aa, July 19). What is greatness? (advertisement). *USA Today*, p. 5A.

Church of Scientology International (1991b, June 14). The story that *TIME* couldn't tell. *USA Today* (advertising supplement).

Church of Scientology International (1991bb, July 22). I am a Scientologist (advertisement). *USA Today*, p. 7A.

Church of Scientology International (1991c, June 17). The true story of Scientology (advertisement). *USA Today*, p. 5A.

Church of Scientology International (1991cc, July 23). I am a Scientologist (advertisement). *USA Today*, p. 4A.

Church of Scientology International (1991d, June 18). The vital statistics of Scientology (advertisement). *USA Today*, p. 10A.

Church of Scientology International (1991dd, July 24). I am a Scientologist (advertisement). *USA Today*, p. 7A.

Church of Scientology International (1991e, June 19). The creed of the Church of Scientology (advertisement). *USA Today*, p. 5A.

Church of Scientology International (1991ee, July 25). I am a Scientologist (advertisement). *USA Today*, p. 5A.

Church of Scientology International (1991f, June 20). The aims of Scientology (advertisement). *USA Today*, p. 8A.

Church of Scientology International (1991ff, July 26). I am a Scientologist (advertisement). *USA Today*, p. 7A.

Church of Scientology International (1991g, June 21). My philosophy: L. Ron Hubbard (advertisement). *USA Today*, p. 7A.

Church of Scientology International (1991gg, July 29). I am a Scientologist (advertisement). *USA Today*, p. 5A.

Church of Scientology International (1991h, June 24). L. Ron Hubbard developed the technology to handle the reactive mind (advertisement). *USA Today*, p. 9A.

Church of Scientology International (1991hh, July 30). I am a Scientologist (advertisement). *USA Today*, p. 4A.

Church of Scientology International (1991i, June 25). L. Ron Hubbard developed the technology to handle life (advertisement). *USA Today*, p. 6A.

Church of Scientology International (1991ii, July 31). I am a Scientologist (advertisement). *USA Today*, p. 7A.

Church of Scientology International (1991j, June 26). L. Ron Hubbard developed the technology to handle work (advertisement). *USA Today*, p. 11A.

Church of Scientology International (1991jj, August 1). I am a Scientologist (advertisement). *USA Today,* p. 7A.

Church of Scientology International (1991k, June 27). L. Ron Hubbard developed the technology to handle illiteracy (advertisement). *USA Today,* p. 8A.

Church of Scientology International (1991kk, August 1). The Church of Scientology: Our message to you (advertisement). *USA Today,* pp. 6A–7A.

Church of Scientology International (1991l, June 28). L. Ron Hubbard developed the technology to handle drugs (advertisement). *USA Today,* p. 12A.

Church of Scientology International (1991m, June 28). L. Ron Hubbard: The man and his works. *USA Today* (advertising supplement).

Church of Scientology International (1991n, July 1). We believe human rights are worth fighting for (advertisement). *USA Today,* p. 4A.

Church of Scientology International (1991o, July 2). We believe religious freedom is worth fighting for (advertisement). *USA Today,* p. 5A.

Church of Scientology International (1991p, July 3). We believe a fair tax is worth fighting for (advertisement). *USA Today,* p. 8A.

Church of Scientology International (1991q, July 5). We believe honest government is worth fighting for (advertisement). *USA Today,* p. 6A.

Church of Scientology International (1991r, July 8). The a-r-c triangle (advertisement). *USA Today,* p. 4A.

Church of Scientology International (1991s, July 9). How to live with children (advertisement). *USA Today,* p. 7A.

Church of Scientology International (1991t, July 10). The dynamics of existence (advertisement). *USA Today,* p. 9A.

Church of Scientology International (1991u, July 11). Is it possible to be happy? (advertisement). *USA Today,* p. 5A.

Church of Scientology International (1991v, July 12). The tone scale (advertisement). *USA Today,* p. 7A.

Church of Scientology International (1991w, July 15). How to detect the antisocial personality (advertisement). *USA Today,* p. 8A.

Church of Scientology International (1991x, July 16). The third party law (advertisement). *USA Today,* p. 7A.

Church of Scientology International (1991y, July 17). The race against man's savage instincts (advertisement). *USA Today,* p. 5A.

Church of Scientology International (1991z, July 18). Honest people have rights too (advertisement). *USA Today,* p. 9A.

Cicero. (1942). *De oratore* (E. W. Sutton and H. Rackham, trans.). Cambridge, MA: Harvard University Press.

Cigler, A. J., and Loomis, B. A., eds. (1991). *Interest group politics* (3rd ed.). Washington, D.C.: Congressional Quarterly.

Citizens for Responsible Solutions (CRS). (n.d.). Fact sheet.

Clark, D. L. (1957). *Rhetoric in Greco-Roman education.* New York: Columbia University Press.

Cobb, R. (1990, September 6). Style marketing. *Marketing,* pp. 29–30.

Coffin, W. S. (1988, Summer). Testimony on the INF Treaty before Senate Foreign Relations Committee. *SANE World/Freeze Focus, 27,* 7.

Coffin, W. S. (1989, Winter/Spring). [Review of *Parting the Waters*]. *SANE World/Freeze Focus, 28,* 22.

Coleman, J. S. (1974). *Power and the structure of society.* New York: W. W. Norton and Company.

Colford, S. W. (1989, November 13). Congress eyes PM's "rights." *Advertising Age,* p. 1.

Colford, S. W. (1991a, February 25). Polystyrene ad fights bad image. *Advertising Age,* p. 16.

Colford, S. W. (1991b, November 11). Tobacco companies hit by FTC. *Advertising Age,* p. 58.

Communication. (1981). Special issue on ethics in communication. *6*(2).

Companies combat solid waste. (1989, September 18). *Modern Plastics,* p. 30.

Condit, C. M., and Selzer, J. A. (1985). The rhetoric of objectivity in the newspaper coverage of a murder trial. *Critical Studies in Mass Communication, 2,* 197–216.

Condit, C. M. (1990). The birth of understanding: Chaste science and the Harlot of the Arts. *Communication Monographs, 57,* 323–327.

Conley, T. (1986). The linnaean blues: Thoughts on the genre approach. In H. W. Simons and A. A. Aghazarian, eds., *Form, genre, and the study of political discourse* (pp. 59-78). Columbia, SC: University of South Carolina Press.

Conroy, P. (1989, November 10). Fired up over Philip Morris. *The Washington Post,* p. D1.

Coombs, W. T. (1990). *A theoretical extension of issue status management: An extension of the four argumentative strategies.* Unpublished dissertation, Purdue University, West Lafayette, IN.

Coombs, W. T. (1992). The failure of the Task Force on Food Assistance: A case study of the role of legitimacy in issue management. *Journal of Public Relations Research, 4,* 101–122.

The corporate image: PR to the rescue. (1979, January 22). *Business Week,* p. 50.

Cortright, D. (1983, December). *Where do we go from here? Next steps for the peace movement. SANE World,* p. 1.

Cortright, D. (1986, January/February). SANE at the summit: Report from Geneva. *SANE World, 25,* 1–2.

Cortright, D. (1987). The peace movement, INF, and beyond. *SANE World/Freeze Focus, 26,* 8–10.

Cortright, D., and Cottom, C. (1987, Autumn). The fruits of merger. *SANE World/Freeze Focus, 26,* 2.

Cortright, D., and West, R. (1986, July/August). The nuclear weapons production chain: America's assembly line of death. *SANE World, 25,* 4–5.

Corydon, B., and Hubbard, L. R., Jr. (1987). *L. Ron Hubbard: Messiah or madman?* Secaucus, NJ: Lyle Stuart.

Cottom, C. (1988, Summer). CTB report: Stop testing, start investing. *SANE World/Freeze Focus, 27,* 5.

Coursey, D. (1993, March 8). AT&T moves to the front. *Computerworld,* pp. 35–36.

Courtright, J. L. (1992, November). *The Church of Scientology and the legal environment of moral issues management.* A paper presented at the 78th annual convention of the Speech Communication Association, Chicago, IL.

Cowan, E. (1975a, October 22). Judge asks halt to Exxon suit. *The New York Times,* p. 65.

Cowan, E. (1975b, October 24). F.T.C. rejects bid to drop oil case. *The New York Times,* p. 65.

Cowan, E. (1981, February 3). F.T.C. staff eases view in oil case. *The New York Times,* p. D1.

Coy, P. (1991a, September 2). AT&T reaches out and taps some new talent. *Business Week,* p. 80.

Coy, P. (1991b, May 20). Can 'techie bonding' overcome bad blood? *Business Week,* p. 39.

Crable, R. E. (1976). *Argumentation as communication.* Columbus, OH: Charles E. Merrill Publishing Company.

Crable, R. E. (1977). Ike: Identification, argument, and paradoxical appeal. *Quarterly Journal of Speech, 63,* 188–195.

Crable, R. E. (1986). The organizational "system" of rhetoric: The influence of megatrends into the twenty-first century. In L. W. Hugenberg, ed., *Rhetorical studies honoring James L. Golden* (pp. 57–68). Dubuque, IA: Kendall/Hunt.

Crable, R. E. (1990). "Organizational rhetoric" as the fourth great system: Theoretical, critical, and pragmatic implications. *Journal of Applied Communication Research, 18,* 115–128.

Crable, R. E., and Faulkner, M. M. (1988). The issue development graph: A tool for research and analysis. *Central States Speech Journal, 39,* 110–120.

Crable, R. E., and Vibbert, S. L. (1983). Mobil's epideictic advocacy: "Observations" of Prometheus-bound. *Communication Monographs, 50,* 380–394.

Crable, R. E., and Vibbert, S. L. (1985). Managing issues and influencing public policy. *Public Relations Review, 11,* 3–16.

Crable, R. E., and Vibbert, S. L. (1986). *Public relations as communication management.* Edina, MN: Bellwether Press.

Crespi, F. (1987). Social action and the ambivalence of communication: A critique of Habermas' theory. *European Journal of Communication, 2,* 415–425.

Croft, M. (1989, August). Beyond the corporate logo. *Accountancy,* pp. 65–66.

Crowther, K., and Wilson, E. (1990). How to research companies. In *CPC Annual. 34th Four-Year College edition I* (pp. 20–24). Bethlehem, PA: College Placement Council.

CRS News. (1990, Summer). Direct mail newsletter-brochure.

CSWS. (1989). The urgent need to recycle. Print advertisement.

Culbertson, H. M., Jeffers, D. W., Stone, D. B., and Terrell, M. (1993). *Social, political, and economic contexts in public relations: Theory and cases.* Hillsdale, NJ: Lawrence Erlbaum Associates.

Cunningham, S. B. (1992). Sorting out the ethics of propaganda. *Communication Studies, 43,* 233–245.

Cutlip, S., Center, A., and Broom, G. (1985). *Effective public relations.* Englewood Cliffs, NJ: Prentice-Hall.

Dalton, M. (1993, July). Planning for failure. *Global Trade and Transportation,* p. 23.

Davids, M. (1988). Labor shortage woes. *Public Relations Journal, 44,* 24–29.

Day, D. G. (1961). The ethics of democratic debate. *Central States Speech Journal, 17,* 5–14.

Dayton throws a party for its corporate uncle. (1991, February 28). *The Dayton Daily News*, p. 3.

DeBenedetti, C. (1980). *The peace reform in American history*. Bloomington, IN: Indiana University Press.

Deetz, S. A. (1981). Critical interpretive research in organizational communication. *Western Journal of Speech Communication, 44*, 131–149.

Deetz, S. A. (1992). *Democracy in an age of corporate colonization: Development in communication and the politics of everyday life*. New York: State University of New York Press.

Dionisopoulos, G. (1986). Corporate advocacy advertising as political communication. In L. L. Kaid, D. Nimmo, and K. R. Sanders, eds., *New perspectives on political advertising* (pp. 82-106). Carbondale, IL: Southern Illinois University Press.

Dionisopoulos, G., and Crable, R. E. (1988). Definitional hegemony as a public relations strategy: The rhetoric of nuclear power after Three Mile Island. *Central States Speech Journal, 39*, 134-145.

Dionisopoulos, G., and Vibbert, S. L. (1983, November). *Re-fining generic parameters: The case for organizational apologia*. Paper presented at the meeting of the Speech Communication Association, Washington, DC.

Dionisopoulos, G. and Vibbert, S. L. (1988). CBS vs. Mobil Oil: Charges of creative bookkeeping in 1979. In H. R. Ryan, ed., *Oratorical encounters* (pp. 241-251). New York: Greenwood Press.

Dixon, M. M. (1993, November). AT&T brand name PCs from NCR. *Dealerscope Merchandising*, p. 100.

Dixon, R. D., Lowery, R. C., Levy, D. E., and Ferraro, K. F. (1991). Self-interest and public opinion toward smoking policies: A replication and extension. *Public Opinion Quarterly, 55*, 241-254.

DOE confirms weapons plants are unsafe. (1987, Summer). *SANE World, 26*, 5–6.

Donohue, G. A., Tichenor, P. J., and Olien, C. N. (1972). Gatekeeping: Mass media systems and information control. In F. G. Kline and P. J. Tichenor, eds., *Current perspectives in mass communication research* (Vol. I) (pp. 41–69). Beverly Hills: Sage Publications.

Douglas, M. (1985). *Risk acceptability according to the social sciences*. New York: Russell Sage Foundation.

Dow ads boost recycling. (1990, January 15). *Advertising Age*, p. 15.

Dow calls for media blitz to stem anti-plastics tide. (1990, March). *Modern Plastics*, pp. 10–12.

Dow Chemical U.S.A. (n.d.). *Great things are happening at Dow* (videotape). Midland, MI: Dow University Relations and Recruiting.

Dow Plastics. (1990). You're looking at 64 milk bottles and 2 shampoo containers. Print and television advertisements.

Dowling, J., and Pfeffer, J. (1975). Organizational legitimacy: Social values and organizational behavior. *Pacific Sociological Review, 18*, 122-136.

Downs, A. (1972). Up and down with ecology: The "issue attention cycle." *Public Interest, 1*, 31–40.

Dranow, P., Moore, L., and Hickey, A. (1980). *Video in the 80s*. New York: Knowledge Industry Publications, Inc.

Du Preez, P. (1980). *The politics of identity*. New York: St. Martin's Press.

Duffy, J. (1992, June 1). Service woes continue to plague AT&T ISN users. *Network World,* pp. 33, 36.

Dunn, W. S. (1986). *Public relations: A contemporary approach.* Homewood, IL: Irwin.

DuPont. (1990). We've got to stop treating our garbage like garbage. Print advertisement.

Durrell, A., and Sachs, M., eds. (1990). *The big book for peace.* New York: Dutton Children's Books.

Dusky, L. (1990, January). How to find the companies where women succeed. *Working Woman,* pp. 81–88.

Dutton, J. E., and Dukerich, J. M. (1991). Keeping an eye on the mirror: Image and identity in organizational adaptation. *Academy of Management Journal, 34,* 517–554.

Dutton, J. E., and Duncan, R. B. (1987). The creation of momentum for change through the process of strategic issue diagnosis. *Strategic Management Journal, 8,* 279–295.

Earthworks Group. (1989). *50 simple things you can do to save the earth.* Berkeley, CA: Earth Works Press.

Edelman, M. (1988). *Constructing the political spectacle.* Chicago: University of Chicago Press.

Editor's note. (1985, January/February). From our members. *SANE World, 24,* p. 2.

Education on solid waste is goal of new campaign. (1991, June). *Modern Plastics,* pp. 42-44.

Ehninger, D. E. (1968). On systems of rhetoric. *Philosophy and Rhetoric, 1,* 131–144.

8,000 rally to show their support for NCR. (1991, February 28). *The Dayton Daily News,* p. 3A.

Ellis, D. (1982). The shame of speech communication. *Spectra, 18,* 1–2.

Ellul, J. (1981). The ethics of propaganda: Propaganda, innocence, and amorality. *Communication, 6,* 159–175.

Elwood, W. N. (1989). Call for Philip Morris: Redeeming smokers through the drama of protest rhetoric. *The Florida Communication Journal, 17,* 23–28.

Elwood, W. N. (1994). *Rhetoric in the war on drugs: The triumphs and tragedies of public relations.* Westport, CT: Praeger Publishers.

EPA moving to phase out sales of Alar-treated food. (1989, September 5). *The Wall Street Journal,* p. C9.

Estes, N. (1974). *Marshalling community leadership to support the public schools.* Bloomington, IN: Phi Delta Kappa.

Ettema, J., and Glasser, T. (1987). Public accountability or public relations? Newspaper ombudsmen define their role. *Journalism Quarterly, 64,* 3–12.

Even captains get the flu. (1991, January). *Time,* p. 45.

Execs rebuff $6 billion offer. (1990, December 3). *The Dayton Daily News,* p. 1A.

Exley: "Not in best interests." (1990, December 3). *The Dayton Daily News,* 10A.

Farnham, A. (1992, July 13). Mike Miles snuffs smokers' mag. *Time,* p. 14.

Farrell, T. B., and Goodnight, G. T. (1981). Accidental rhetoric: The root metaphors of Three Mile Island. *Communication Monographs, 48,* 271–300.

Faulkner, M. M. (1985). *Deadly force and issue management: A case study of police, the public, and public policy at the national level and in three major American cities.* Unpublished master's thesis, Purdue University, West Lafayette, IN.

Feldman, J. (1989, Fall/Winter). Global security through environmental conversion. *SANE/Freeze News, 28,* p. 7.

Fenton, D. (1989, October). How a PR firm executed the Alar scare [letter to the editor]. *The Wall Street Journal,* p. A22.

Ferguson, B. (1988, April). Different agendas, styles shape SANE/Freeze. *Bulletin of Atomic Scientists, 44,* 26–30.

Fina. (1990). How to recycle . . . into. . . . Print advertisement.

Fineout, G. (1990, July 10). Last debate on growth plan fierce. *Tallahassee Democrat,* pp. 1A, 4A.

Fink, R. (1993, June 8). The dance instructor. *Financial World,* pp. 26–27.

Fisher, W. R. (1984). Narration as a human communication paradigm: The case of public moral argument. *Communication Monographs, 51,* 1–22.

Fisher, W. R. (1989). Clarifying the narrative paradigm. *Communication Monographs, 56,* 55–58.

Fitzgerald, B. (1990, July 27). Planners vote no on Walton Tract. *Sarasota Herald-Tribune,* pp. 1A, 10A.

Fleitas, D. W. (1971). Bandwagon and underdog effects in minimal-information elections. *American Political Science Review, 65,* 434.

Ford, J. L. C. (1969). *Magazines for millions: The story of specialized publications.* Carbondale, IL: Southern Illinois University Press.

Forsberg, R. (1981). *Call to halt the nuclear arms race.* Philadelphia: American Friends Service Committee.

Foss, S. K. (1984). Retooling an image: Chrysler Corporation's rhetoric of redemption. *Western Journal of Speech Communication, 48,* 75–91.

Foss, S. K., Foss, K. A., and Trapp, R. (1985). *Contemporary perspectives on rhetoric.* Prospect Heights, IL: Waveland Press.

Foster, H. (1994, May 4). Survey takers criticize growth: The participants in a County Commission poll said the county is growing too quickly. *Sarasota Herald-Tribune,* pp. 1B, 4B.

Foundation for Public Affairs. (1992). *Public interest profiles, 1992–1993.* Washington, DC: Congressional Quarterly.

Fox, J. F. (1982a). Communicating on public issues: A changing role for the CEO. *Public Relations Quarterly, 27,* 19–26.

Fox, J. F. (1982b). The politicizing of the chief executive. *Public Relations Journal, 38,* 20-24.

Frankena, W. K. (1973). *Ethics* (2nd ed.). Englewood Cliffs, NJ: Prentice-Hall.

Franzoni, L. (1991, October). Playing the name game. *Bank Marketing,* pp. 20–23.

Free your organization from the limitations of conventional systems. (1991, March 14). *The Wall Street Journal,* p. 1.

Freedman, A. M., and Cohen, L. P. (1993, February 11). Smoke and mirrors: How cigarette makers keep health question "open" year after year. *The Wall Street Journal,* p. A1.

Friedman, S. M., Villamil, K., Suriano, R., and Egolf, B. (1991, August). *Alar and apples: News coverage of a major risk issue.* Paper presented at the annual meeting of the Association for Education in Journalism and Mass Communication, Boston, MA.

Fruit frights. (1989, March 17). *The Wall Street Journal,* p. A16.

Fruit growers pull commercials to protest report by CBS on Alar. (1989, May 7). *The New York Times*, p. I36.

Frye, N. (1957). *Anatomy of criticism: Four essays.* Princeton, NJ: Princeton University Press.

Funk, D. L. (1990). *Victory at the polls: A strategic plan for successful school finance election.* Oregon School Study Council.

Galberson, W. (1993, July 5). Seattle Times places a ban on tobacco advertisements. *The New York Times*, p. 1.

Galbraith, J. K. (1983). *The anatomy of power.* Boston: Houghton Mifflin.

Gallup, G., Jr., and Newport, F. (1990, July). Many Americans favor restrictions on smoking in public places. *The Gallup Poll Monthly*, pp. 19–25.

Gamson, W. A. (1975). *The strategy of social protest.* Homewood: Dorsey Press.

Gardner, J. (1992, November 9). Plastics seek $18M image boost. *Advertising Age*, p. 12.

Garfield, B. (1992, December 23). Plastics industry molds wrong approach in ads. *Advertising Age*, p. 18.

Gayley, C. M., ed. (1894). *Classic myths in English literature* (3rd ed.). Boston: Ginn and Company.

GE Plastics. (1990). Life after death: A recycling strategy to stop burying technology alive. Print advertisement.

GEO Journal. (1990, July). Organizational newsletter.

GEO questions and answers. (1990). Position paper.

Gerth, J. (1981, January 1). SEC's future focus in doubt. *The New York Times*, p. D7.

Giacalone, R. A., and Payne, S. L. (1987). Are business leaders staging a morality play? *Business and Society Review, 62*, 24.

Gibbs, N. (1990, November 19). Keep the bums in. *Time*, pp. 32–34, 39–42.

Glaberson, W. (1993, July 5). Seattle Times places a ban on tobacco advertisements. *The New York Times*, p. 1.

Gladwell, M. (1990, February 24). Virginia Slims tournament is backed by "blood money," Sullivan charges. *The Washington Post*, p. A3.

Glennon, E. (1985, February). Unfinished business: SANE tackles nuclear testing. *SANE World, 24*, 1–2.

Goethals, G. T. (1990). *The electronic golden calf: Images, religion, and the making of meaning.* Boston: Cowley Press.

Goffman, E. (1970). *Stigma: Notes on the management of spoiled identity.* Englewood Cliffs, NJ: Prentice-Hall/Penguin. (Original work published 1963.)

Gold, E. R. (1978). Political apologia: The ritual of self-defense. *Communication Monographs, 45*, 306–316.

Golden, J. L., Berquist, G. F., and Coleman, W. E. (1983). *The rhetoric of Western thought* (3rd ed.). Dubuque, IA: Kendall/Hunt Publishing Company.

Goldman, E. F. (1948). *Two-way street: The emergence of the public relations counsel.* Boston: Bellman Publishing Company.

Goldstein, W. (1984). *Selling school budgets in hard times.* Bloomington, IN: Phi Delta Kappa.

Goldzwig, S., and Cheney, G. (1984). The U.S. Catholic bishops on nuclear arms: Corporate advocacy, role redefinition, and rhetorical adaptation. *Central States Speech Journal, 35*, 8–23.

Graber, D. A. (1976). *Verbal behavior and politics.* Chicago: University of Illinois Press.

Grassley suggests a nationwide initiative be developed. (1978, July 2). *Waterloo Courier,* p. 1.

Gray, J. G., Jr. (1986). *Managing the corporate image: The key to public trust.* Westport, CT: Quorum.

Green, M. (1990). Luring kids to light up. *Business and Society Review, 73,* 22–26.

Green, P., and Gerkin, A. E. (1989). Self-interest and public opinion toward smoking restrictions and cigarette taxes. *Public Opinion Quarterly, 53,* 1–16.

Greening of plastics pervasive theme at NPE. (1991, August). *Modern Plastics,* p. 36.

Gregory, J. R. (1991). *Marketing corporate image: The company as your number one product.* Lincolnwood, IL: NTC Business Books.

Grunig, J. E. (1989a). Sierra Club study shows who become activists, *Public Relations Review, 15,* 3–24.

Grunig, J. E. (1989b). Symmetrical presuppositions as a framework for public relations theory. In C. H. Botan and V. Hazelton, eds., *Public relations theory* (pp. 17–44). Hillsdale, NJ: Lawrence Erlbaum Associates.

Grunig, J. E. (1993). Image and substance: From symbolic to behavioral relationships. *Public Relations Review, 19,* 121–140.

Grunig, J., and Hunt, T. (1984). *Managing public relations.* New York: Holt, Rinehart and Winston.

Gutin, J. (1992, March). Plastics-a-go-go. *Mother Jones,* p. 3.

Gwin, L. (1990). *Speak no evil: The promotional heritage of nuclear risk communication.* New York: Praeger Publishers.

Habermas, J. (1970a). Systematically distorted communication. *Inquiry, 13,* 49–55.

Habermas, J. (1970b). Towards a theory of communication competence. *Inquiry, 13,* 360–375.

Habermas, J. (1974). The public sphere: An encyclopedia article. *New German Critique, 3,* 49–55.

Habermas, J. (1976). Some distinctions in universal pragmatics: A working paper. *Theory and Society, 3,* 155–159.

Habermas, J. (1979). *Communication and the evolution of society.* Boston: Beacon.

Habermas, J. (1994). Intermediate reflections: Social action, purposive activity, and communication. In T. Enos and S. Brown, eds., *Professing the new rhetorics* (pp. 204–220). Englewood Cliffs, NJ: Prentice-Hall.

Hainsworth, B. E. (1990). The distribution of advantages and disadvantages. *Public Relations Review, 16,* 33–39.

Hall, J. (1983, November). *Direct legislation campaigns and parapolitical organizations: A case for communication analysis.* Paper presented at the annual meeting of the Speech Communication Association, Boston, MA.

Hallin, D. (1987). The American news media: A critical theory perspective. *Mass communication review yearbook 6.* Beverly Hills: Sage Publications.

Hamilton, E. (1942). *Mythology* (2nd ed.). Boston: Little, Brown.

Hamilton, H. D., and Cohen, S. H. (1974). *Policy making by plebiscite: School referenda.* Lexington, MA: Lexington Books.

Hammer, D. (1992, October, 15). AT&T & computer marriage starts at Bell Labs interface. *Telephone Engineering & Management,* p. 19.

Hanson, D. (1991, April 8). Plastics industry maps major recycling plan. *Chemical and Engineering News*, pp. 25–26.

Harrell, J., Ware, B. L., and Linkugel, W. A. (1975). Failure of apology in American politics: Nixon on Watergate. *Speech Monographs, 42*, 245–261.

Hart, R. P. (1990). *Modern rhetorical criticism.* Glenview, IL: Scott, Foresman/Little, Brown.

Hathaway, J. S. (1990). The Alar controversy: How an outraged public banned a carcinogenic chemical. *Journal of Pesticide Reform, 10*, 4–6.

Hazlett, T. W. (1982). *TV coverage of the oil crisis: How well was the public served? Volume III: An economist's perspective.* Washington, DC: The Media Institute.

Hearit, K. M. (1992). *Organizations, apologia, and crises of social legitimacy.* Unpublished doctoral dissertation, Purdue University, West Lafayette, IN.

Heath, R. L. (1992). The wrangle in the marketplace: A rhetorical perspective of public relations. In E. L. Toth and R. L. Heath, eds., *Rhetorical and critical approaches to public relations* (pp. 17–36). Hillsdale, NJ: Lawrence Erlbaum Associates, Publishers.

Heath, R. L., and Nelson, R. A. (1986). *Issues management: Corporate public policymaking in an information society.* Newbury Park, CA: Sage Publications.

Heck, M. C. (1980). The ideological dimension of media messages. In S. Hall, ed., *Culture, media, language* (pp. 120–156). London: Hutchinson.

Heibert, R. E., Ungurait, D. F., and Bohn, T. W. (1991). *Mass media VI: An introduction to modern communication.* New York: Longman.

Heier, A. (1989a, May 14). *EPA proposes to cancel the pesticide daminozide (Alar).* Available from United States Environmental Protection Agency, Office of Public Affairs, Washington, DC, 20460.

Heier, A. (1989b, June 2). *Daminozide (Alar) sales halted, stocks recalled.* Available from United States Environmental Protection Agency, Office of Public Affairs, Washington, DC, 20460.

Held, D. (1980). *Introduction to critical theory: Horkheimer to Habermas.* Berkeley, CA: University of California Press.

Hendrix, J. A. (1992). *Public relations cases* (2nd ed.). Belmont, CA: Wadsworth Publishing Company.

Hershey, R. D. (1981, January 29). President abolishes price controls on US-produced oil. *The New York Times*, p. A1.

Hinsberg, P. (1990, August 20). "Times" to Scientology: Don't quote us. *ADWEEK Western Advertising News*, p. 52.

Hoban, C. F., and van Ormer, E. B. (1950, December). *The literature of cinema: Instructional film research 1918–1950.* Report prepared for the Pennsylvania State College Instructional Film Research Program.

Hoffman, T. (1994a, March 14). NCR sites wary of AT&T strategy. *Computerworld*, pp. 1, 8.

Hoffman, T. (1994a, January 31). NCR loses name, gains AT&T moniker. *Computerworld*, p. 4.

Holden, B. (1988). *Understanding liberal democracy.* Oxford, UK: Philip Allan.

Holland, L. V. (1955). Kenneth Burke's dramatistic approach to speech criticism. *Quarterly Journal of Speech, 41*, 352–358.

Holsti, O. R. (1969). *Content analysis for the social sciences and humanities.* Reading, MA: Addison-Wesley Publishing Company.

Hoover, J. D. (1989). Big boys don't cry: The values constraint in apologia. *Southern Communication Journal, 54,* 235–252.

How nuclear weapons production brings peace and environmental activists together: The closing of Rocky Flats demonstrates the power of the combined efforts of both movements. (1989, Fall/Winter). *SANE/Freeze News, 28,* p. 6.

Hrebenar, R. J., and Scott, R. K. (1982). *Interest group politics in America.* Englewood Cliffs, NJ: Prentice Hall.

Hume, S. (1991, January 29). McDonald's: Case study. *Advertising Age,* p. 32.

Humphrey, H. H., III. (1990, August). Let's keep "green" clean! *Progressive Grocer,* pp. 130-131.

Humphrey, N. D. (1946). Social problems. In A. M. Lee, ed., *New outline principles of sociology* (pp. 1–45). New York: Barnes and Noble.

Huntsman Chemical. (1990). Think of them as your new home . . . think recycle. Print advertisement.

Huspek, M. (1991). Taking aim on Habermas's critical theory: On the road toward a critical hermeneutics. *Communication Monographs, 58,* 225–233.

Iacobuzio, T. (1993, August). Behind the scenes at Chemical: An NCR contract, and much drama. *Bank Systems & Technology,* pp. 21-22.

Images. (1991, September). A publication of the Cincinnati Public Schools.

An important message to NCR shareholders. (1991, March 1). *The Wall Street Journal,* p. 9A.

Industry fights back: The debate over advocacy advertising. (1978, January 21). *Saturday Review,* p. 20.

Industry group remaps stand on solid waste. (1992, July). *Modern Plastics,* p. 35.

Industry leaders call for a dose of realism in recycling programs. (1991, June). *Modern Plastics,* pp. 44-46.

An interview about AT&T's hostile offer to NCR with Chuck Exley, chairman and chief executive officer of NCR Corporation. (1991, January 11). *The Dayton Daily News,* p. 2A.

It was no big deal, despite what "Daily News" boxes said. (1991, February 27). *The Dayton Daily News,* p. 1B.

Iyengar, S. (1991). *Is anyone responsible: How television frames political issues.* Chicago: University of Chicago Press.

Jablin, F. M. (1982). Organizational communication: An assimilation approach. In M. E. Roloff and C. R. Berger, eds., *Social cognition and communication* (pp. 255–286). Newbury Park, CA: Sage Publications.

Jablin, F. M. (1984). Assimilating new members into organizations. In R. N. Bostrom, ed., *Comunication yearbook 8* (pp. 526–626). Newbury Park, CA: Sage Publications.

Jablin, F. M. (1985). An exploratory study of vocational organizational communication socialization. *Southern Speech Communication Journal, 50,* 261–282.

Jablin, F. M. (1987). Organizational entry, assimilation, and exit. In F. M. Jablin, L. L. Putnam, K. H. Roberts, and L. W. Porter, eds., *Handbook of organizational communication* (pp. 679–740). Beverly Hills: Sage Publications.

James, E., and Rose-Ackerman, S. (1986). *The non-profit enterprise in market economies.* New York: Harwood Academic.

Janofksy, M. (1993a, June 5). Spinning the data on cigarette taxes. *The New York Times,* p. 37.

Janofsky, M. (1993b, June 29). E.P.A. finding: Tobacco's loss? Evidence for industry lawsuit appears somewhat shaky. *The New York Times,* p. 29.

Javna, J. (1991, May 29). Recycling plastics a tricky issue. (Lafayette, IN) *Journal and Courier,* p. C-9.

Johannesen, R. L. (1981). *Ethics in human communication.* Prospect Heights, IL: Waveland Press.

Johnson, A. (1990). Trends in political communication: A selective review of research in the 1980's. In D. Nimmo and D. Swanson, eds., *New directions in political communication* (pp. 329–362). Beverly Hills: Sage Publications.

Johnston, W. B., and A. H. Packer. (1987). *Workforce 2000: Work and workers for the 21st century.* Indianapolis: Hudson Institute.

Johnstone, H. W., Jr. (1981). Towards an ethics of rhetoric. *Communication, 6,* 305–314.

Jones, B. L., and Chase, W. H. (1979). Managing public issues. *Public Relations Review, 5,* 3-23.

Journal of Business Strategy. (1989, September/October). Antidote for a hostile offer. pp. 4–8.

Judd, A. (1990a, July 29). Floridians' eyes on Sarasota. *Sarasota Herald-Tribune,* pp. 1A, 17A.

Judd, A. (1990b, August 25). Moratorium poll: 72% no. *Sarasota Herald-Tribune,* pp. 1A, 11A.

Katz, M. S. (1986). *Ban the bomb: A history of SANE, the Committee for a Sane Nuclear Policy, 1957–1985.* New York: Greenwood Press.

Killer apples. (1989, March 9). *The Wall Street Journal,* p. A16.

King, R. L. (1985). Transforming scandal into tragedy: A rhetoric of political apology. *Quarterly Journal of Speech, 71,* 289–301.

Kraybill, C. (1982, March). Looking towards the next 25 years: New chapters in SANE's history. *SANE World, 21,* 1–2.

Kromer, W. F. (1988, June). The election is over, what's next? *Michigan School Board Journal,* p. 1.

Kruse, N. W. (1977). Motivational factors in non-denial apologia. *Central States Speech Journal, 28,* 13–23.

Kruse, N. W. (1981). Apologia in team sport. *Quarterly Journal of Speech, 67,* 270–283.

La Rue, S. (1993, April 23). Plastics get activists' stamp of disapproval. *San Diego Union Tribune,* p. B1.

Landler, M., and Carey, J. (1993, February 15). Philip Morris' top lobbyist could use a new Rolodex. *Business Week,* p. 62.

Langer, S. K. (1957). *Philosophy in a new key: A study in the symbolism of reason, rite, and art.* Cambridge, MA: Harvard University Press. (Original work published 1942.)

Lawler, Ballard. (1990, April). *A research report to the Michigan Department of Agriculture: Michigan consumer food safety study.* Available from Dr. Charles Atkin, Michigan State University.

Lawren, B. (1990, October–November). Plastic Rapt. *National Wildlife,* pp. 11–19.

Leading the call for peace in the Middle East and a peace economy at home. (1991, Spring). *SANE/Freeze News, 30*, 1–2.

Leaversuch, R. D. (1990, December). Will McDonald's switch have a ripple effect? *Modern Plastics,* pp. 42–45.

Lee, G. (1991, September 9). Tobacco lobby lights a preemptive strike: Efforts target local anti-smoking laws. *The Washington Post,* p. A13.

Leslie, J. (1991, December 20). Personal interview with authors Joiner and German.

Leslie, J., and Siefferman, J. (1991, November). 1990 levy campaign report. In *1991 school levy result summary.* Prepared by the Cincinnati Public Schools.

Levin, D. P. (1988a, June 3). Consumer group asks recall of Suzuki Samurai as unsafe. *The New York Times,* pp. A1, D4.

Levin, D. P. (1988b, June 10). Test charge draws fire from Suzuki. *The New York Times,* pp. D1, D14.

Levin, G. (1990, November 14). Consumer turning green: JWT survey. *Advertising Age,* p. 13.

Levin, M. (1988). The tobacco industry's strange bedfellows. *Business and Society Review, 65,* 11–17.

Levine, J. (1991, December 9). Self-made press lords. *Forbes,* p. 302.

Levitt, L. (1985). Public relations as a source of power. *Public Relations Review, 11,* 3–9.

Levy, T. H. (1985). *Organizational rhetoric: Multinational corporations' legitimation in Brazil, France, and the United States.* Unpublished doctoral dissertation, University of Maryland, College Park, MD.

Lew, H. L. (1988, July/August). Communicating in turbulent times: How communicators can calm the troubled waters of business change. *Communication World,* pp. 46–48.

Lindquist, V. R. (1990). *The Northwestern Lindquist-Endicott report 1990* (44th annual report). Evanston, IL: Northwestern University.

Lindquist, V. R., and Endicott, F. S. (1986). *Trends in the employment of college and university graduates in business and industry* (40th annual report). Evanston, IL: Northwestern University.

Ling, D. A. (1972). A pentadic analysis of Senator Edward Kennedy's address to the people of Massachusetts, July 25, 1969. *Central States Speech Journal, 21,* 81–86.

Linkugel, W. A., and Razak, N. (1969). Sam Houston's speech of self-defense in the House of Representatives. *Southern Speech Journal, 43,* 263–275.

Littlejohn, S. W. (1983). *Theories of human communication.* Belmont, CA: Wadsworth.

Llewellyn, J. (1990). *The rhetoric of corporate citizenship.* Unpublished doctoral dissertation, University of Texas, Austin, TX.

Loverude, D., and Sams, J. (1990, September 5). Moratorium and GEO beaten; Chiles and Martinez win big. *Sarasota Herald-Tribune,* pp. 1A, 10A.

Lowery, R. C., Levy, D. E., and Ferraro, K. F. (1991). Self-interest and public opinion toward smoking policies: A replication and extension. *Public Opinion Quarterly, 55,* 241–254.

MacIntyre, A. (1984). *After virtue: A study in moral theory* (2nd ed.). Notre Dame, IN: University of Notre Dame Press.

Mackenzie, W. J. (1978). *Political identity.* New York: St. Martin's Press.

Mahdenberg, H. J. (1975, August 25). Mobil opposes decontrol of oil, urges phaseout of price curbs. *The New York Times,* p. A1.

Mailbag: "Plastic . . . ugh!" (1989, Winter/Spring). *SANE World/Freeze Focus, 28,* 21.

Make your voice heard. (1991, February 27). *The Dayton Daily News,* p. 3B.

Marken, G. A. (1990, Spring). Corporate image—we all have one, but few work to protect and project it. *Public Relations Quarterly,* pp. 21–23.

Marshall, E. (1991, October 4). A bite out of the market. *Science, 254,* 21.

Masterton, J. (1991, February 1). Mixed signals for sponsored magazines. *Folio: The Magazine for Magazine Management,* p. 29.

Matrullo, T. (1990, July 30). Tether on growth. *Sarasota Herald-Tribune Business Monday,* pp. 11–12.

McAllister, B. (1990, August 9). Philip Morris's hometown lobbyists. *The Washington Post,* p. A10.

McCall, G. J., and Simmons, J. L. (1978). *Identities and interactions* (revised ed.). New York: The Free Press.

McCarthy, F. (1990, July 1). Breaking bad water habits. *The Atlanta Journal and Constitution,* pp. G1, G4.

McCarthy, J. D., and Zald, M. N. (1977). Resource mobilzation and social movements: A partial theory. *American Journal of Sociology, 82,* 486–502.

McCombs, M. (1977). Agenda setting function of the mass media. *Public Relations Review, 3,* 89–95.

McDonald, P., and Gandz, J. (1992). Getting value from shared values. *Organizational Dynamics, 20*(3), 64–77.

McGee, M., and Martin, M. (1983). Public knowledge and ideological argumentation. *Communication Monographs, 50,* 47–65.

McKeon, R. (1971). The uses of rhetoric in a technological age: Architectonic productive arts. In L. F. Bitzer and E. Black, eds., *The prospect of rhetoric: Report of the National Development Project* (pp. 44–63). Englewood Cliffs, NJ: Prentice-Hall.

McKeon, R. (1987). *Rhetoric: Essays in invention and discovery.* Woodbridge, CT: Ox Bow Press.

McKerrow, R. E. (1989). Critical rhetoric: Theory and praxis. *Communication Monographs, 56,* 91–111.

McLeroy, D. (1990, July 18). Personal interview with the chairman of Citizens for Responsible Solutions.

McLuhan, M. (1960). The effect of the printed book on language in the 16th century. In E. Carpenter and M. McLuhan, eds., *Exporlations in communication* (pp. 125–135). Boston: Beacon Press.

McLuhan, M. (1964). *Understanding media: The extension of man.* New York: Signet.

McLuhan, M., and Fiore, Q. (1967). *The medium is the massage: An inventory of effects.* New York: Bantam Books.

McMillan, J. (1987). In search of the organizational persona: A rationale for studying organizations rhetorically. In L. Thayer, ed., *Communications—organizations* (Vol. 2, pp. 21–45). Norwood, NJ: Ablex.

Means, K., and McClung, J. (1991, March 27). *New survey shows public confidence restored after Alar.* Available from Center for Produce Quality, P.O. Box 1417–C35, Alexandria, VA, 22313.

Meier, B. (1990, November 6). For this pounding, Volvo had help. *The New York Times,* pp. D1, D17.

Meyrowitz, J. (1985). *No sense of place: The impact of electronic media on social behavior.* New York: Oxford University Press.

Miller, J. (1990, Spring). Activists compel DOE to prepare impact statements. *SANE/Freeze News, 29,* p. 3.

Miller, K. (1992). Smoking up a storm: Public relations and advertising in the construction of the cigarette problem, 1953–1954. *Journalism Monographs, 136,* 1–35.

Miller, R. (1988). *Bare-faced messiah: The true story of L. Ron Hubbard.* New York: Henry Holt. (Original work published 1987.)

Mintz, M. (1992, May 6). Marketing tobacco to children. *The Nation,* p. 577.

Mitroff, I. I. (1984). *Stakeholders of the mind.* San Francisco: Jossey-Bass.

Moe, T. M. (1980). *The organization of interests.* Chicago: University of Chicago.

Moore, J. A. (1989, March 7). *Preliminary assessment of "Intolerable risk: Pesticides in our children's food."* A report by the Natural Resources Defense Council. Available from United States Environmental Protection Agency, Office of Public Affairs, Washington, DC, 20460.

Moore, R. L. (1994). *Selling God: American religion in the marketplace of culture.* New York: Oxford University Press.

Moyers, B. D. (1989). *The public mind: Image and reality in America, illusions of news* (video cassette). Alexandria, VA: PBS Video.

Mumby, D. K. (1987). The political function of narrative in organizations. *Communication Monographs, 54,* 113–127.

Mumby, D. K. (1988). *Communication and power in organizations: Discourse, ideology, and domination.* Norwood, NJ: Ablex.

Mumby, D. K. (1993). Critical organizational communication studies: The next 10 years. *Communication Monographs, 60,* 18–25.

Murphy, J. J. (1974). *Rhetoric in the Middle Ages.* Berkeley: University of California Press.

Murphy, P., and Dee, J. (1991, May). *Dupont and Greenpeace: The dynamics of conflict between corporations and activist groups.* Paper presented at the annual meeting of the International Communication Association, Chicago, IL.

MX alert. (1983, May). *SANE World,* p. 1.

Napoles, V. (1988). *Corporate identity design.* New York: Van Nostrand Reinhold.

NCR gives stock to employees to thwart AT&T. (1991, February 22). *The Dayton Daily News,* p. 1A.

NCR may report to employees via satellite today. (1991, February 21). *The Dayton Daily News,* p. 1A.

NCR rebuffs AT&T; faces proxy battle. (1990, December 17). *The Wall Street Journal,* p. 2B.

NCR to call meeting. (1991, January 22). *The Dayton Daily News,* p. 1A.

Nelson, R. A., and Heath, R. L. (1984). Corporate public relations and new media technology. *Public Relations Review, 10,* 27–37.

Newsom, D., and Carrell, B. (1991). *Public relations writing: Form and style* (3rd ed.). Belmont: Wadsworth Publishing.

Newsom, D., Scott, A., and Turk, J. V. (1989). *This is PR: The realities of public relations* (4th ed.). Belmont, CA: Wadsworth Publishing Company.

Newsom, D, Scott, A., and Turk, J. V. (1993). *This is PR: The realities of public relations* (5th ed.). Belmont, CA: Wadsworth Publishing Company.

Nichols, M. H. (1952). Kenneth Burke and the "new rhetoric." *Quarterly Journal of Speech, 38,* 133–144.

Niebauer, W. (1989). *The publicity process* (3rd ed.). Ames, IA: Iowa State University Press.

1991 levy fact book. (1991). Prepared by the Cincinnati Public Schools.

Noonan, P. (1990). *What I saw at the revolution: A political life in the Reagan era.* New York: Random House.

Not out of the picture yet. (1989, November 13). *Time,* p. 84.

Nothstine, W. L., Blair, C., and Copeland, G. A., eds. (1994). *Critical questions: Invention, creativity, and the criticism of discourse and media.* New York: St. Martin's Press.

Nusbaum, T. G. (1987). *The use of internal and external marketing to turn critics into fans.* Paper presented to the National School Boards Association convention, San Francisco, CA.

N.Y. to ban tobacco ads on transit vehicles. (1992, June 29). *Advertising Age,* p. 8.

Observations. (1976–1980). Mobil Oil Corporation's series of advocacy advertisements published in *Family Weekly* (FW), the *Atlanta Journal and Constitution Magazine* (AJCM), and *Atlanta Weekly* (AW).

O'Dwyer, J. (1991, July 17). *Jack O'Dwyer's Newsletter,* p. 8.

The Ohio school finance handbook. Westerville, OH: Ohio School Boards Association, p. 11.

Olins, W. (1978). *The corporate personality: An inquiry into the nature of corporate identity.* New York: Mayflower.

Olins, W. (1990). *Corporate identity: Making business strategy visible through design.* Cambridge, MA: Harvard Business School Press. (Original work published in 1989.)

Olson, K. M. (1989). The controversy over President Reagan's visit to Bitburg: Strategies of definition and redefinition. *Quarterly Journal of Speech, 75,* 129–151.

Olson, M. (1965). *The logic of collective action.* Cambridge, MA: Harvard University Press.

Ong, W. (1975). The writer's audience is always a fiction. *PMLA, 90,* 9–21.

An open letter to the citizens of Sarasota County. (1990, August 15, September 1). Full-page advertisement placed in *Sarasota Herald-Tribune.*

Opposition to plastics packaging on the rise. (1988, May). *Pulp and Paper,* pp. 31–33.

Oravec, C. (1976). "Observation" in Artistotle's theory of epideictic. *Philosophy and Rhetoric, 9,* 162–173.

Ornstein, N. J., and Elder, S. (1978). *Interest groups, lobbying, and policymaking.* Washington, DC: Congressional Quarterly Press.

Orr, E. J. (1978). How shall we say: "Reality is socially constructed through communication"? *Central States Speech Journal, 29,* 263–274.

O'Toole, J. E. (1975). Advocacy advertising shows the flag. *Public Relations Journal, 31,* 14–16.

Paonessa, K. A. (1983). *Corporate advocacy and organizational member identification: A case study of General Motors.* Unpublished master's thesis, Purdue University, West Lafayette, IN.

Pasewark, K. (1986). Communicative irrationality and political discourse in Jurgen Habermas: A theological experiment. *Communication Yearbook, 9,* 741–755.

Peace economy campaign helps communities reclaim millions lost during Reagan military build-up. (1989, Summer). *SANE/Freeze News, 28,* 1.

Peaceworks' lesson: Peace can win. (1986, May/June). *SANE World, 25,* 1.

Pearson, R. (1987). Public relations writing methods by objectives. *Public Relations Review, 13,* 14–26.

Pearson, R. (1989a). Business ethics as communication ethics: Public relations practice and the idea of dialogue. In C. H. Botan and V. Hazelton, eds., *Public relations theory* (pp. 111–131). Hillsdale, NJ: Lawrence Erlbaum Associates.

Pearson, R. (1989b). Beyond ethical relativism in public relations: Coorientation, rules, and the idea of communication symmetry. In J. E. Grunig and L. A. Grunig, eds., *Public relations research annual, Volume 1* (pp. 67–86). Hillsdale, NJ: Lawrence Erlbaum Associates.

Perelman, C. (1979). *The new rhetoric and the humanities: Essays on rhetoric and its applications.* Dordrecht, The Netherlands: D. Reidel Publishing Company.

Perelman, C. (1982). *The realm of rhetoric.* Notre Dame, IN: University of Notre Dame Press.

Perelman, C., and Olbrechts-Tyteca, M. (1969). *The new rhetoric: A treatise on argumentation* (J. Wilkinson and P. Weaver, trans.). Notre Dame, IN: University of Notre Dame Press.

Pesticides termed high cancer risk for children. (1989, February 25). *The New York Times,* p. 130.

Philip Morris Companies, Inc. (1991). News release.

Philip Morris Magazine, advertising rate card 6.

Philip Morris Magazine (1985–1991 inclusive).

Pinsent, J. (1969). *Myths and legends of ancient Greece.* London: Hamlyn Publishing.

Plastic goes green. (1990, August). *Scientific American,* p. 101.

Plato. (1956). *Phaedrus* (W. C. Helmbold and W. G. Rabinowitz, trans.). Indianapolis: Liberal Arts Press.

Plato. (1960). *Gorgias* (W. Hamilton, trans.). Harmondsworth, UK: Penguin.

Poll results. (1983, February). *SANE World, 23,* 2.

Pollay, R. W. (1990). Propaganda, puffing, and the public interest. *Public Relations Review, 16,* 39–54.

Pomice, E., Black, R., Collins, S., and Newman, R. (1992, January). Is your job safe? *U.S. News and World Report,* pp. 42–48.

Portugal, J., and Halloran, K. D. (1986, April). Avoiding a corporate identity crisis. *Management Review,* pp. 43–45.

Post, J. E. (1978). *Corporate behavior and social change.* Reston, VA: Reston Publishing Company.

Postman, N. (1985). *Amusing ourselves to death: Public discourse in the age of show business.* New York: Viking.

Powerful new group will take over from CSWS. (1991, December). *Modern Plastics,* pp. 36–38.

Prentice, D. B., and Carlin, J. (1987, November 6). *The stages and functions of communication in ballot issue campaigns: A case study of the Kansas campaign for liquor by the drink.* A paper presented to the National School Boards of America convention, San Francisco, CA.

Pressure mounts against the MX. (1983, July/August). *SANE World, 22,* p. 3.

Pribble, P. T. (1990). Making an ethical commitment: A rhetorical case study of organizational socialization. *Communication Quarterly, 38,* 255–267.

Price, V. (1992). *Public opinion.* Newbury Park, CA: Sage Publications.

Procter and Gamble. (1990). *Lemon Cascade LiquiGel* (automatic dishwashing detergent). Cincinnati: U.S. Patent 4,714,562.

Produce list, federal judge order NCR. (1991, January 30). *The Dayton Daily News,* p. 1B.

Progress report on the windfall (editorial). (1981, February 7). *The Washington Post,* p. A20.

Protess, D. L., Cook, F. L., Doppelt, J. C., Ettema, J. S., Gordon, M. T., Leff, D. R., and Miller, P. (1991). *The journalism of outrage: Investigative reporting and agenda building in America.* New York: Guilford Press.

"PS." (1990, April). Earth Day insert for *Modern Plastics.*

Ramsey, K. (1992, May 14). Brandt knows he must serve the students. *The Cincinnati Enquirer,* p. 1B.

The Random House college dictionary (L. Urdang, ed.). (1982). New York: Random House.

Ranney, A. (1981). *The referendum device.* Washington, DC: American Enterprise Institute for Public Policy.

Rayfield, R. E., Acharya, L., Pincus, J. D., and Silvis, D. E. (1991). *Public relations writing: Strategies and skills.* Dubuque, IA: Brown.

Reaction to takeover proposal mixed. (1990, December 3). *The Dayton Daily News,* p. 12A.

Recession brings shift in environmental focus. (1992, February). *Modern Plastics,* p. 42.

Recycling firms attacking solid waste problem. (1989, July). *Plastics World,* p. 10.

Reeves, L. D. (1992, May 14). Brandt announces cut in staff. *The Cincinnati Enquirer,* p. 1A.

Referendum's rising importance. (1980, November 17). *Time,* p. 73.

Reinhold, M. (1972). *Past and present: The continuity of classical myths.* Toronto: A. M. Hakkert.

Reisch, M. (1992, June 22). Dow sets big plastics recycling program. *Chemical & Engineering News,* p. 16.

Resin companies' new tactic in solid waste: consumer ads. (1989, November). *Modern Plastics,* pp. 11–12.

Resin price drop fails to slow green initiatives. (1991, October). *Modern Plastics,* p. 38.

Resin suppliers organize for solid waste battles. (1988, July). *Modern Plastics,* p. 14.

Rhodes, B. (1991). Cincinnati, OH: *1991 school levy result summary.*

Rice, R. E., and Atkin, C. K. (1989). *Public communication campaigns* (2nd ed.). Newbury Park, CA: Sage Publications.

Riley, S. G., ed. (1992). *Corporate magazines of the United States.* Westport, CT: Greenwood Press.

Roat, P. (1990, July 22). People want shoreline preservation along bay. *Sarasota Times*, pp. 1, 15.

Rorty, R. (1982). *Consequences of pragmatism*. Minneapolis: University of Minnesota Press.

Rosenfield, L. W. (1968). A case study in speech criticism: The Nixon-Truman analog. *Speech Monographs, 35*, 435–450.

Rosetti, L. (1988). The rhetoric of Zeno's paradoxes. *Philosophy and Rhetoric, 21*, 145–152.

Rosewicz, B. (1989a, February 27). Group maintains rules on pesticides endanger children. *The Wall Street Journal*, p. B3.

Rosewicz, B. (1989b, March 10). Pesticide risk from apples: Who's right? *The Wall Street Journal*, pp. B1, B3.

Ross, I. (1976, September). Public relations isn't kid-glove stuff at Mobil. *Fortune*, pp. 197–202.

Rowan, K. R. (1990, June). *Building a rhetoric of risk communication: Strategies for communicating about uncertain hazards and dangers*. Paper presented at the annual meeting of the International Communication Association, Dublin, Ireland.

Rufty, B. (1990, December 16). Residents choose environment over growth. *Sarasota Herald-Tribune*, pp. 1A, 22A.

Russell, T., and Verrill, G. (1986). *Otto Kleppner's advertising procedure* (9th ed.). Englewood Cliffs, NJ: Prentice-Hall.

Ryan, H. R. (1982). Kategoria and apologia: On their rhetorical criticism as a speech set. *Quarterly Journal of Speech, 68*, 254–261.

Ryan, H. R. (1984). Baldwin vs. Edward VIII: A case study in kategoria and apologia. *Southern Speech Communication Journal, 49*, 125–134.

Ryan, H. R., ed. (1988). *Oratorical encounters*. New York: Greenwood Press.

Ryan, M. (1987). Organizational constraints on corporate public relations practitioners. *Journalism Quarterly, 64*, 473–481.

Salisbury, R. S. (1969). An exchange theory of interest groups. *Midwest Journal of Political Science, 13*, 1–32.

Samra, R. J. (1993). The image of the physician: A rhetorical perspective. *Public Relations Review, 19*, 341–348.

Sams, J. (1990a, July 25). Landfill far from certain. *Sarasota Herald-Tribune*, pp. 1B, 5B.

Sams, J. (1990b, October 3). All 3 incumbents get the ax: Sarasota commissioners ousted. *Sarasota Herald-Tribune*, pp. 1A, 22A.

Samuels, B. E., Begay, M. E., Hazan, A. R., and Glantz, S. A. (1992). Philip Morris's failed experiment in Pittsburgh. *Journal of Health Politics, Policy, and Law, 17*, 329–351.

Sandman, P. M. (1987). Risk communication: Facing public outrage. *EPA Journal, 13*, 21–22.

SANE convenes national hearing on nuclear weapons production. (1986, July/August). *SANE World, 25*, 1.

SANE launches new citizens' campaign: Stand up for peace in Central America. (1987, January). *SANE World, 24*, 7.

SANE/Freeze contributes to initial victory against nuclear weapons. (1989, Summer). *SANE/Freeze News, 28,* 4.

SANE/Freeze sets goals for new decade. (1990, Spring). *Sane/Freeze News,* p. 1.

Schauer, I. (1990, August). Innovative techniques lure quality workers to NASA. *Personnel Journal,* pp. 100–108.

Schiappa, E. (1985). Dissociation in the arguments of rhetorical theory. *Journal of the American Forensic Association, 22,* 72–82.

Schlegel, F., and DeQuincy, T. (1974). *The Princton encyclopedia of poetry and poetics.* Princeton, NJ: Princeton University Press.

School tied to tobacco now scorns smoking it. (1991, May 19). *The New York Times,* p. B8.

Schultz, S. (1989, Winter/Spring). 1988 National congress charts SANE/Freeze's future. *SANE World/Freeze Focus, 28,* 8–9.

Schultze, C. (1992, March 2). Personal interview with authors Joiner and German.

Second life for styrofoam. (1989, May 5). *Time,* p. 84.

The secrets of success. (1991, October). *Inside PR,* pp. 14–19.

Seeds of an economic conversion race? (1987, Summer). *SANE World, 26,* p. 8.

Seeger, M. W. (1986). The Challenger tragedy and the search for legitimacy. *Central States Speech Journal, 37,* 147–157.

Seitel, F. P. (1987). *The practice of public relations* (3rd ed.). New York: John Wiley and Sons.

Seitel, F. P. (1992). *The practice of public relations* (5th ed.). New York: Macmillan Publishing Company.

Shabecoff, P. (1989a, March 17). 3 U.S. agencies, to allay public's fears, declare apples safe. *The New York Times,* p. A16.

Shabecoff, P. (1989b, May 16). Apple industry says it will end use of chemical. *The New York Times,* p. A1.

Shaw, K. (1989, Winter/Spring). The nuclear threat at home: For thousands of families, the American dream has become a nightmare. *SANE World/Freeze Focus, 28,* pp. 5–7, 21.

Shearer, H. (1991, September 8). Man bites town: The burning question: Did the founding fathers really intend to guarantee our right to smoke? *Los Angeles Times Magazine,* p. 6.

Shorr, I. (1987, Autumn). SANE/Freeze makes CTB top issue in Iowa. *SANE World/Freeze Focus,* p. 19.

Shorr, I. (1988, Summer). Bringing home the cost of the arms race. *SANE World/Freeze Focus, 27,* p. 20.

Shorr, I. (1991a, Summer). Time for a peace economy. *SANE/Freeze News, 30,* pp. 3, 5.

Shorr, I. (1991b, Winter). Peace economy campaign heats up. *SANE/Freeze News, 30,* p. 1.

Siegel, D. (1989, January). No news isn't good news: Effective media relations. *NASSP,* p. 8.

Silas, C. J. (1990, January). The environment: Playing to win. *Public Relations Journal,* p. 10.

Simon, R. (1984). *Public relations: Concepts and practices* (3rd ed.). New York: John Wiley and Sons.

Simon, R., and Wylie, F. W. (1994). *Cases in public relations management*. Lincoln-wood, IL: NTC Business Books.

Smith, C. (1992, July 13). The player: Rising-star media consultant Mandy Grunwald comes out swinging for Clinton. *New York*, pp. 50–55.

Smith, K. (1990). *Alar: One year later—a media analysis of a hypothetical health risk* (special report). New York: American Council on Science and Health.

Smock, D. (1991, April). Waste is a hot market right now. *Plastics World*, p. 11.

Smoking under fire in Virginia: HHS targeting 17 states. (1991, October 5). *Roanoke Times and World News*, p. A1.

Sobol, M. G., Farrelly, G. E., and Taper, J. S. (1992). *Shaping the corporate image: An analytical guide for executive decision makers*. New York: Quorum.

Solo, P. (1988). *From protest to policy: Beyond the freeze to common security*. Cambridge, MA: Ballinger.

Solomon, C. (1990, December 28). American Air wins temporary order barring its pilots from sickouts. *The Wall Street Journal*, p. A3.

SPI creates an image program for industry. (1989, May). *Modern Plastics*, pp. 24–25.

Sproule, J. M. (1988). The new managerial rhetoric and the old criticism. *Quarterly Journal of Speech, 74*, 468–486.

Steps to ban Alar announced. (1989, May 14). *The New York Times*, p. I24.

Sternberg, K. (1990, November 14). McDonald's polystyrene pullout draws mixed reviews. *Chemical Week*, p. 22.

Stewart, C. J. (1980). A functional approach to the rhetoric of social movements. *Central States Speech Journal, 31*, pp. 298–305.

Stewart, C. J. (1988, April). *The rhetoric of legitimation*. Paper presented at the annual meeting of the Southern Speech Communication Association, Memphis, TN.

Stewart, C. J., Smith, C. A., and Denton, R. E. (1984). *Persuasion and social movements*. Prospect Heights, IL: Waveland Press.

Stipp, D. (1992, September 21). Lag in plastics recycling sparks heated debate. *The Wall Street Journal*, p. B1.

Stohl, C. (1986). The role of memorable messages in the process of organizational socialization. *Communication Quarterly, 34*, 231–249.

Stone, D. (1994, September 21). Harum-scarum at the polls. *The Weekly*, p. 12.

Straight talk on the GEO moratorium. (1990, August). CRS brochure mailed to all Sarasota County registered voters who were not CRS members.

Stuller, J. (1990, January-February). The politics of packaging. *Across the Board*, pp. 41–50.

Suplee, C. (1990, December 12). Industry opens drive to curb cigarette smoking by minors, effort decried as hypocritical public-relations move. *The Washington Post*, p. A3.

Suzuki. (1988a, June 9). Suzuki charges bias in Consumer Reports testing. Brea, CA: American Suzuki Corporation Automotive Division.

Suzuki. (1988b, June 9). Remarks by Doug Mazza, vice president and general manager, American Suzuki Corporation Automotive Division. Brea, CA: American Suzuki Corporation Automotive Division.

Swanson, D. L. (1977). And that's the way it was? Television covers the 1976 presidential campaign. *Quarterly Journal of Speech, 63*, 239–248.

Target is big enough to bring critical mass in computers and shares strategic goals. (1990, December 4). *The Wall Street Journal*, p. 1A.

Tesh, S. (1984). In support of "single-issue" politics. *Political Science Quarterly, 99,* 27–44.

Test ban caravan pressures Congress to end nuclear testing. (1987, Autumn). *SANE World/Freeze Focus, 26,* 4.

Thayer, A. (1991, December 2). Group to tackle public concerns over plastics. *Chemical & Engineering News,* p. 16.

Thompson, D. B. (1981). Issue management: New key to corporate survival. *Industry Week, 23,* 77-80.

Thousands of thank yous. . . . (1991, April 5). *The Dayton Daily News,* p. 13B.

Tilsner, J. (1993, July 5). Secondhand smoke's second hearing? *Business Week,* p. 40.

Tobacco issues: Part 2, Hearings before the Subcommittee on Transportation and Hazardous Materials of the Committee on Energy and Commerce, US House of Representatives, 101 Congress. (1990). Washington, DC: U.S. Government Printing Office, pp. 2–3.

Tobacco's toll: 1 death in 4. (1992, April 10). *Roanoke Times and World News,* p. A6.

Toensmeier, P. (1990, April). Smothering in plastics. *Modern Plastics,* pp. 41–45.

Tompkins, P. K. (1987). Translating organizational theory: Symbolism over substance. In F. M. Jablin, L. L. Putnam, K. H. Roberts, and L. W. Porter, eds., *Handbook of organizational communication* (pp. 70–96). Beverly Hills: Sage Publications.

Toth, E. L., and Heath, R. L., eds. (1992). *Rhetorical and critical approaches to public relations.* Hillsdale, NJ: Lawrence Erlbaum Associates.

Toth, E., and Trujillo, N. (1987). Reinventing corporate communications. *Public Relations Review, 13,* 42–53.

Toulmin, S. (1969). *The uses of argument* (2nd ed.). Cambridge, UK: Cambridge University Press.

Treadwell, D. F., and Harrison, T. M. (1994). Conceptualizing and assessing organizational image: Model images, commitment, and communication. *Communication Monographs, 61,* 63–85.

Trinidad, D. (1991, December 31). Adrienne Rich charts a difficult world: The acclaimed poet talks of art, anger and activism. *The Advocate,* pp. 82–84.

Tucker, K., Derelian, D., and Rouner, D. (1994). *Public relations writing: An issue-driven behavioral approach* (2nd ed.). Englewood Cliffs, NJ: Prentice Hall.

Valentine, P. W. (1991, September 12). Billboard foes put up a fight. *The Washington Post,* p. C6.

Van Mannen, J. (1975). Breaking in: Socialization to work. In R. Dubin, ed., *Handbook of work, organization and society* (pp. 67–120). Chicago: Rand McNally.

Van Voorst, B. (1993, October 18). Recycling: Stalled at curbside. *Time,* pp. 78–80.

Vatz, R. E. (1973). The myth of the rhetorical situation. *Philosophy and Rhetoric, 6,* 154–161.

Vaughn, M. A. (1988). Interpretive research in organizational communication and the rhetorical critic. *Communication Reports, 1/2,* 68–75.

Vibbert, S. L. (1984). *Epideictic advocacy: Value premises and corporate image building.* Paper presented at the annual meeting of the Speech Communication Association, Chicago, IL.

Vibbert, S. L. (1987). *Corporate discourse and issue management.* Paper presented at the meeting of the International Communication Association, Montreal, Canada.

Vibbert, S. L. (1992, October). *Responding to "more moral" issue management*. A paper presented at the 78th annual convention of the Speech Communication Association, Chicago, IL.

Vibbert, S. L., and Bostdorff, D. M. (1992). Issue management in the "lawsuit crisis." In C. Conrad, ed. *The ethical nexus: Values, communication, and organizational decisions* (pp. 103–120). New York: Ablex Publishing.

Vico, G. (1968). *The new science of Giambattista Vico* (T. Bergin and M. Fisch, intro. and trans.). Ithaca, NY: Cornell University Press.

Vico, G. (1990). On the study methods of our time (E. Gianturco, ed. and trans.). In P. Bizzell and B. Herzberg, eds., *The rhetorical tradition: Readings from classical times to the present* (pp. 711–727). Boston: Bedford Books of St. Martin's Press.

Volvo. (1990, November 6). *USA Today*, p. 2B.

Vote yes on Issue 7. (1991, October 11). *The Cincinnati Post*, p. 10A.

Wallis, R. (1975). Societal reaction to Scientology: A study in the sociology of deviant religion. In R. Wallis, ed., *Sectarianism: Analyses of religious and non-religious sects* (pp. 86–116). New York: John Wiley and Sons.

Wallis, R. (1977). *The road to total freedom: A sociological analysis of Scientology.* New York: Columbia University Press.

Wander, P. (1981). Cultural criticism. In D. Nimmo and K. Sanders, eds., *Handbook of political communication* (pp. 497–528). Beverly Hills: Sage Publications.

Wander, P. (1984). The third persona. *Central States Speech Journal, 35,* 197–216.

Wander, P., and Jenkins, S. (1972). Rhetoric, society, and the critical response. *Quarterly Journal of Speech, 58,* 441–450.

Ware, B. L., and Linkugel, W. A. (1973). They spoke in defense of themselves: On the generic criticism of apologia. *Quarterly Journal of Speech, 59,* 273-283.

Weatherly, M. (1971). Propaganda and the rhetoric of the American Revolution. *Southern States Communication Journal, 36,* 352–363.

Weaver, R. M. (1953). *The ethics of rhetoric.* South Bend, IN: Gateway Editions Ltd.

Weaver, R. M. (1970). Language is sermonic. In R. L. Johannesen, R. Strickland, and R. T. Eubanks, eds., *Language is sermonic: Richard M. Weaver on the nature of rhetoric* (pp. 201–225). Baton Rouge, LA: Louisiana State University Press.

Weber, M. (1978). *Economy and society: An outline of an interpretive sociology, vol. I* (G. Roth and C. Wittich, eds.). Berkeley, CA: University of California Press.

Webster's New Collegiate Dictionary. (1981). Springfield, MA: Merriam-Webster.

Weiss, A. (1989, July). The value system. *Personnel Administrator, 34,* 2.

Wert-Gray, S., Center, C., Brashers, D., and Meyers, R. (1991). Research topics and methodological concerns in organizational communication: A decade in review. *Communication Studies, 42,* 141–154.

West, R. (1987, Summer). Norman Cousins: Emissary for peace. *SANE World/Freeze Focus, 26,* 12–14.

What is the right choice? (1991, March 25). *The Wall Street Journal*, p. 9A.

What made Mobil a decontrol maverick? (1979, May 21). *Business Week*, pp. 32–33.

What's the future of plastics recycling? (1992, February). *Packaging*, pp. 57–58.

White, M. (1987). Ideological analysis and television. In R. Allen, ed., *Channels of discourse* (pp. 134–171). Chapel Hill, NC: University of North Carolina Press.

Whiting, R. (1993, May). NCR/AT&T: One era ends . . . another begins. *Electronic Business*, pp. 34-40.

Whitman, R. L., and Pittner, N. A. (1990). *Planning, promoting, and passing school tax issues.* Westerville, OH: Ohio School Boards Association.

Who do you trust? (1994, September 4). A We the People charter amendment petition/newspaper insert. *Sarasota Herald-Tribune.*

Whose company is it anyway? (1991, March 5). *The Wall Street Journal,* p. 13A.

Wight, D. T. (1990). Metaphysics through paradox. *Philosophy and Rhetoric, 23,* 63–68.

Wilcox, D. L., Ault, P. H., and Agee, W. K. (1989). *Public relations: Strategies and tactics* (2nd ed.). New York: Harper and Row.

Wilkins, L., and Patterson, P. (1987). Risk analysis and the construction of news. *Journal of Communication, 37,* 80–91.

Will, G. F. (1990, February 25). Tobacco's targets. *The Washington Post,* p. B7.

Will, G. F. (1992, June 29). The veep and the blatherskite. *Newsweek,* p. 72.

Will the real freeze resolution please stand up? (1982, May). *SANE World, 21,* 4.

Wilson, G. (1990). *Interest groups.* Cambridge, UK: Basil Blackwell.

Wilson, J. Q. (1973). *Political organizations.* New York: Basic Books.

Wilson, M. (1981, June). Nuclear holocaust haunts Europe. *SANE World, 20,* 1–3.

Wiseman, P., and Cox, J. (1990, May 25). Protest heats up against tobacco firms. *USA Today,* p. 1B.

Wolf, N., and Feldman, E. (1991). *Plastics: America's packaging dilemma.* Washington, DC: Island Press.

Wolfe, M. N., and Baskin, O. W. (1985). *The communication of corporate culture in employee indoctrination literature: An empirical analysis using content analysis.* Paper presented at the annual meeting of the Academy of Management, San Diego, CA.

Wood, A. (1990, May 2). Plastics: Can more be made of less? *Chemical Week,* pp. 36–38.

Wood, J. T., and Pearce, W. B. (1980). Sexists, racists, and other classes of classifiers: Form and function of ". . . ist" accusations. *Quarterly Journal of Speech, 66,* 239–250.

Woolley, S. (1992). The top 100 deals. *Business Week,* pp. 65-72.

Work, C. P. (1990, March 5). Where there's smoke: A firestorm over a new cigarette highlights two rival marketing strategies. *U.S. News and World Report,* pp. 57–58.

Working for a just peace in 1988. (1988, Spring). *SANE/FREEZE Action Alert,* p. 2.

Wuthnow, R., Hunter, J. D., Bergesem, A., and Kurzeil, E. (1984). *Cultural analysis: The work of Peter L. Berger, Mary Douglas, Michel Foucault, and Jurgen Habermas.* London: Routledge and Kegan Paul.

You have an important choice to make about your NCR investment. (1991, March 20). *The Wall Street Journal,* p. 23A.

Young, F. E., Moore, J., and Bode, J. (1989, March 16). *Joint statement by: Dr. Frank E. Young, Commissioner, Food and Drug Administration; Dr. John Moore, Acting Deputy Administrator, Environmental Protection Agency; and John Bode, Assistant Secretary for Food and Consumer Services, United States Department of Agriculture.* Available from USDA News Division, Room 404-A, Washington, DC, 20250.

Young, M. L. (1987). *The American dictionary of campaigns and elections.* New York: Hamilton.

Zaloudek, M. (1990a, January 21). In Sarasota County, it's time to play catch-up. *Sarasota Herald-Tribune*, p. 16A.

Zaloudek, M. (1990b, August 7). Issue plumps voting roles. *Sarasota Herald-Tribune*, pp. 1A, 8A.

Zarefsky, D. (1980). Lyndon Johnson redefines "equal opportunity": The beginnings of affirmative action. *Central States Speech Journal, 31*, 85–94.

Zarefsky, D. (1986). *President Johnson's War on Poverty: Rhetoric and history*. Tuscaloosa: University of Alabama Press.

Zarefsky, D., Miller-Tutzauer, C., and Tutzauer, F. E. (1984). Reagan's safety net for the truly needy: The rhetorical uses of definition. *Central States Speech Journal, 35*, 115–127.

Index

advocacy advertisements; examples of, 5; target audience of, 30; as rhetorical activity, 87; manage issues and reshape images, 88–89; satisfies three purposes; 215; in issue management; 215–17

Alar (daminozide), date controversy began, 47; "60 Minutes" report, 47; as a public relations case study, 50; news coverage about, 52–53; analysis of news coverage, 58–63

American Airlines, 119, 120, 124–26

apologia; defined, 117

Aristotle, 9, 6, 160, 282, 283; definition of rhetoric, 5; as public relations forbear who synthesizes rhetoric, public relations, and politics, 5

AT&T; merger with NCR, 22, 213–38

ballot issue campaigns, 242–43; Cincinnati school levy, 243–52; Sarasota, FL, growth moratorium, 264–70

Bernays, Edward L., 4, 12, 48, 137, 259, 260

Bitzer, Lloyd F., 10, 11, 87, 108, 109

Bostdorff, Denise M., 11, 143, 196

Botan, Carl H., 12

Broom, Glen M., 69, 280

Brummett, Barry, 7, 12, 153, 261

Burgoon, Michael, 15, 16, 19

Burke, Kenneth, 9, 38, 56, 70, 72, 77, 78, 80, 82, 83–84, 87, 97-98, 99, 101, 118, 121, 130, 161, 162, 184–86

Campbell, Karlyn Kohrs, 12, 118, 119, 129

Carrell, Bob, 3, 12, 196

Center, Allen H., 69, 280

Chase, W. Howard, 8, 78, 89, 135, 214, 223

Cheney, George, 11, 28, 69, 70, 72, 81, 119, 129, 157, 158, 160, 161, 162, 171, 175, 177, 184–87, 196, 199, 292

Church of Scientology International; image campaign of, 70–73, analyzed, 74–78

cluster-agon analysis, 70–73

communication; as speech acts, 281; constructs values and culture, 281–84. See also rhetoric

Conley, Thomas M., 118

Consumer Reports, 117, 119, 120, 122–24

Coombs, W. Timothy, 196–97, 198, 201, 206

corporate social responsibility: four commandments of, 57

Crable, Richard E., 8, 12, 27, 49, 70, 78, 79, 90, 119, 130, 135, 140, 143, 156, 193, 195, 196, 259, 273, 285, 288

crisis/risk communication; as question for study, 50; definition in Alar case, 53; advocacy advertising as response

About the Editor and Contributors

BARRY BRUMMETT is professor of communication at the University of Wisconsin-Milwaukee. He has published several articles and books, including *Contemporary Apocalyptic Rhetoric* (Praeger, 1991).

RICHARD E. CRABLE is professor and chair of the California State University Department of Communciation Studies in Sacramento.

JEFFREY L. COURTRIGHT is assistant professor of communication at the Miami University, Oxford, Ohio, teaching courses in public relations, organizational communication, and rhetoric. His work has appeared in *Public Relations Review*, and he also has contributed a chapter to the forthcoming book, *Warranting Assent: Case Studies in Argument Evaluation* (Edward Schiappa, Ed.).

WILLIAM N. ELWOOD is a principal investigator for a National Institute on Drug Abuse international research project, the Cooperative Agreement for AIDS Community-Based Outreach/Intervention Research Program. He also is president of the Aidos Institute, a nonprofit organization dedicated to research on drug abuse-related issues. Elwood's publications concentrate on rhetoric and drug policy and on concerns involving chronic, out-of-treatment injection drug and crack users. His book, *Rhetoric in the War on Drugs: The Triumphs and Tragedies of Public Relations*, is a 1994 Praeger publication.

KELLY FUDGE is a doctoral student in the Department of Speech Communication at the University of Texas at Austin.

KATHLEEN M. GERMAN is a professor at Miami University, Oxford, Ohio. She has written many articles and book chapters, has been the editor of *The Ohio Speech Journal,* and is co-author of a widely used public speaking textbook.

KEITH MICHAEL HEARIT is an assistant professor of external organizational communication at Northern Illinois University. His research interests include the areas of corporate apologia, corporate social legitimacy, and the rhetoric of technology. He previously has published in *Public Relations Review.*

RACHEL L. HOLLOWAY is assistant professor in the Department of Communication Studies at Virginia Polytechnic Institute and State University. She teaches in the areas of public relations and issue management. She is the author of *In the Matter of J. Robert Oppenheimer: Character, Rhetoric, and Politics* (Praeger) and chapters in *The 1992 Presidential Campaign: A Communication Perspective* (Praeger) and *Eisenhower's War of Words: Rhetoric and Leadership* (Michigan State University Press.)

JEFFREY P. JOINER has been on faculty in the Department of Communication at Miami University since 1992 and is currently the Assistant Director of Forensics.

JAMIE PRESS LACEY currently serves as communications manager for the American Association of Motor Vehicle Administrators (AAMVA), a nonprofit, educational organization based in Arlington, Virginia. She holds a bachelor's degree in communication studies from the University of North Carolina at Greensboro and a master's in speech communication from Wake Forest University.

JOHN T. LLEWELLYN teaches rhetorical criticism and organizational communication at Wake Forest University, where he is also Director of Graduate Studies.

MITCHELL S. McKINNEY is a doctoral candidate in communication studies at the University of Kansas. He is co-editor of *The 1992 Presidential Debates in Focus* (Praeger, 1994). He served as a White House Summer Fellow, and his research has appeared in the *International Jornal of Personal Construct Psychology.*

PATRICIA PAYSTRUP is an assistant professor of communication at Brigham Young University. Her research interests focus on how issue management and other advocacy strategies and techniques are used by competing interests in the battles over drafting and implementing environmental public policies.

THERESA A. RUSSELL-LORETZ is an assistant professor in the Department of Communication and Theatre at Millersville University in Millersville, Pennsylvania, where she teaches communciation and public relations courses.

MICHAEL F. SMITH teaches public relations, organizational communication, and other communication courses in the Communication Department at La Salle University.

STEVEN L. VIBBERT is professor of journalism at Butler University in Indianapolis.

ISBN 0-275-94971-0

90000>

EAN

9 780275 949716

HARDCOVER BAR CODE